AVANIMIUT

# AVANIMIUT

## A History of Inuit Independence in Northern Labrador

Carol Brice-Bennett

Revised by Lena Onalik and Andrea Procter

MEMORIAL UNIVERSITY PRESS

**Library and Archives Canada Cataloguing in Publication**

Title: Avanimiut : a history of Inuit independence in northern Labrador / Carol Brice-Bennett ; revised by Lena Onalik and Andrea Procter.

Other titles: History of Inuit independence in northern Labrador

Names: Brice-Bennett, Carol, 1949-2018 author. | Onalik, Lena, editor. | Procter, Andrea H., 1974- editor.

Series: Social and economic studies (St. John's, N.L.) ; no. 93.

Description: Series statement: Social and economic studies ; 93 | Revision and expansion of The Northlanders, commissioned by the Labrador Inuit Association (1996). | Includes bibliographical references and index.

Identifiers: Canadiana (print) 2023050566X | Canadiana (ebook) 20230505724 | ISBN 9781990445149 (softcover) | ISBN 9781990445156 (EPUB) | ISBN 9781990445163 (PDF)

Subjects: LCSH: Inuit—Newfoundland and Labrador—Labrador—History. | LCSH: Inuit—Newfoundland and Labrador—Labrador—Social life and customs. | LCSH: Inuit—Newfoundland and Labrador—Labrador—Politics and government. | LCSH: Inuit—Newfoundland and Labrador—Labrador—Social conditions.

Classification: LCC E99.E7 B75 2023 | DDC 971.8/20049712—dc23

Front cover photograph: Carrying firewood, Hebron, 1956 (Joan and Ross King photo, Them Days Archive)

Back cover photograph: Saglek Bay (Maria Merkuratsuk)

Copy editing: Richard Tallman

Cover design, page design, and typesetting: Alison Carr

Published by Memorial University Press
Memorial University of Newfoundland
PO Box 4200
St. John's, NL A1C 5S7
www.memorialuniversitypress.ca

Printed in Canada 29 28 27 26 25 24 23 1 2 3 4 5 6 7 8

Funded by the Government of Canada
Financé par le gouvernement du Canada
Canada

## CONTENTS

# MAPS, TABLES, FIGURES, AND ABBREVIATIONS

## Maps



## Tables

## Figures

## Abbreviations

| | |
|---|---|
| BC | Bethlehem, USA Collection, Moravian Archives |
| GRHBC | Journal of the HBC post at George River, HBC Archives |
| HBC | Hudson's Bay Company |
| HC | Herrnhut, Germany Collection, Moravian Archives |
| HCB | Hebron Church Book |
| HSC | Hebron Supplementary Catalogue |
| KCB | Killinek Church Book |
| NAC | National Archives of Canada, Ottawa |
| NHBC | Journal of the HBC post at Nachvak, HBC Archives |
| PA | *Periodical Accounts* of the Moravian Mission |
| PANL | Provincial Archives of Newfoundland and Labrador, St. John's |
| PBHBC | Journal of the HBC post at Port Burwell, HBC Archives |
| RCB | Ramah Church Book |
| SFG | Society for the Furtherance of the Gospel |

## BACKGROUND RESEARCH

**Background research for the original 1996 report was done by:**

Dr. James Hiller
Dr. Hans Rollmann
Regula Schule
Dr. Marianne Stopp
Edward Tompkins
Dr. James Tuck

## A NOTE ON THE USE OF HISTORICAL NAMES AND LANGUAGE

Many place names and personal Inuit names used in this book have changed over time. Depending on the context, we use both historical and Inuktitut names to clarify the archival materials. The English names of Hudson's Bay Company (HBC) trading posts can differ from the Inuktitut place name, such as the George River HBC post at Kangiqsualujjuaq. Missionaries, traders, and government officials often spelled Inuktitut words as they heard them, so we have included the contemporary spelling in square brackets. Some Inuktitut place names also reflect regional spellings, such as Killinek (Nunatsiavut) and Killiniq (Nunavik/Nunavut).

Some historical documents cited in this book also use offensive terms to describe Inuit. In certain cases, we have decided to use the original language to reflect historical attitudes and context.

"I don't need this [Christianity]. I have done nothing wrong. I want to stay with the one who has taken care of me all my life and fed me. I don't want to leave him. . . . I don't need a God or saviour, for if someone among us needs anything, then I'll heal him and make him alive and the Torngaks help me. I can do everything, and if you don't want to come to us and build a store, then it's no use."

*Semigak to Moravian missionaries, 1902 (Annual Report from Rama, 1902, Bethlehem USA Collection, Moravian Archives (BC): 57871)*

# PREFACE

*Lena Onalik and Andrea Procter*

**Lena:** When I was growing up in Makkovik, my family struggled, but I didn't quite understand the circumstances that led to why our family was the way it was. I grew up with love and affection, but in a home that was broken by trauma and alcohol. My grandparents had been relocated to Makkovik from the Nutâk/Okkak Bay area in 1956–57. They had both moved there from Hebron, and their parents had moved from further north before that. My grandparents told me about their homeland before moving to Makkovik, about their lives on the land, in the north. They spoke about their homes with such pride and happiness. I recognize now that they were also speaking with heartache and longing.

In Makkovik, my grandparents were not able to continue the life on the land that they knew in the north. People who were relocated from Okkak Bay and Hebron were segregated from the community and forced to live in the Nutâmiut or Hebronimiut sections of town. They were considered outsiders. My grandparents could not continue with their traditional activities. Hunting and fishing berths were taken up by the local people who felt that the newcomers were encroaching upon their land. My grandpa was a dog team racer. He adored his dogs and always broke down into tears when he reminisced about the past.

Alcohol played a huge role in their coping mechanisms, creating a difficult childhood for my mother and her sister. When I was growing up,

I lived with my mom, her sister, my grandparents, and first cousins. I often sat with my grandma and learned to clean sealskins, to sew, to prepare wild food, to throat-sing, and to understand the Inuktitut language, but my grandparents wanted me to be accepted in the community, so they primarily spoke English to me and Inuktitut to each other. I became a passive speaker: I could understand my language, but I did not have the confidence to speak it. My father's ancestors were settlers from Europe, so my identity is dual. My family thought they were doing the right thing by ensuring I could speak English in the world of settler people.

I grew up feeling as though I did not truly belong in Makkovik. I felt rootless and had low self-worth. On one hand, I came from a rich and vibrant culture, but on the other, I felt distant and ashamed of my roots. When I got to visit where my grandparents came from, I then realized the incredible loss they must have felt when they were forced to leave the place that provided them with everything they needed to survive, both physically and spiritually. Despite what they endured, they taught me about forgiveness and acceptance.

The first time I travelled to northern Labrador, my first impression was how vast and majestic it is. The mountains rise jaggedly to the sky; the landscape is barren of trees north of Napâttuk Bay. The beautiful river valleys

**Boys carrying mail (l-r): Anton Nochasak, John Andersen, Jerry Tuglavina, Hebron, 1950s (Hettasch family collection, Them Days Archive)**

roar with life. You can see that the land could be considered harsh, but then we came to a safe harbour where the seas were calm and the wind was still, and I realized this is a perfect place to set up a tent or build a sodhouse. Looking closer at my surroundings, I could see the remains of former habitation. I was not the only one who had been here. We were here before.

For the first time in my life, I felt a sense of returning home. I felt like I belonged. My great-grandma, my atitsiak Lena, was born in Ramah, and I always felt a sense of connection to her by being able to visit the place of her birth. Through this book, I learned that Ramah was where she was born and only lived for a short time. Nachvak was her family's home and where I have always felt drawn. My great-grandma Lena was part of the Tuglavina family of Nachvak.

Northern Labrador is the homeland of my people. Before Inuit were forced out of northern Labrador, my ancestors were born there. They lived, loved, lost, and survived there for generations. The Avanimiut held on to the traditional way of life as long as they could, resisting the move to mission stations and conversion to Christianity the longest. In northern Labrador, we see the remains of their sod houses and tent rings still visible in every hospitable harbour, cove, and inlet, a way of life that is remembered by our people to this day. The harsh yet beautiful landscape provided food and shelter for our ancestors, and continues to, through their descendants. We were here before, and we come here still.

**Andrea**: The first version of this book was written in 1996 by Carol Brice-Bennett as a confidential report for the Labrador Inuit Association, amid fierce political disputes over Inuit title and use of northern Labrador. She titled the report *The Northlanders*, after the Moravian missionaries' name for the northern Inuit. Once the dust had settled on the land claims negotiations and the creation of the self-governing region of Nunatsiavut was imminent, Brice-Bennett had hoped to publish it. The manuscript was, and continues to be, the only comprehensive historical account of Labrador Inuit life north of Hebron.

The Northlanders – or Avanimiut, as they are known in Inuktitut – were Inuit who maintained traditional lifeways, autonomy, and spiritual beliefs in northernmost Labrador. Between the 1770s and the 1940s, the Moravian Mission, the Hudson's Bay Company, and the Anglican Church made numerous attempts at incorporating them into their Christian and commercial trading domains, but Avanimiut often preferred their independence and kept at a distance. As a result, the Moravian missionaries did not document all aspects of their lives in meticulous detail, as they had done with Inuit who had joined their congregations farther south. Instead, Mission and trading records remark only fleetingly on the presence and activities of the proud and self-sufficient families who continued to live traditional Inuit lives, away from colonial intruders. The lives of Avanimiut were therefore relatively unknown to Kallunât (non-Inuit, people of European descent) and governments. This manuscript compiled, for the first time, all colonial accounts about these Inuit families who continued to live in their ancestral territories on the tip of the peninsula, providing a glimpse into their lives, families, and relationships.

For descendants of Avanimiut families and for anyone interested in the region's history, this compilation is a unique and valuable source of information. Recognizing this, Brice-Bennett and the Labrador Inuit Association/Nunatsiavut Government started working in the early 2000s to get this manuscript published. Unfortunately, the ambition was not realized, and Carol Brice-Bennett passed away in 2018. But officials in the Nunatsiavut Government continued to push for publication. A research partnership with Memorial University called *Tradition and Transition among the Labrador Inuit* proved to be the ideal mechanism to make this happen, and Lena Onalik and I agreed to revise the report into a book.

Many things have changed in northern Labrador since *The Northlanders* was written in 1996. The Nunatsiavut Government was established in 2005 after the Labrador Inuit Association's land claim was settled, and Inuit in the region once again have self-government. The Torngat Mountains National Park Reserve was created in the same year in the heart of the Avanimiut homeland, along with a co-operative park management board consisting of Inuit members from both Nunatsiavut and Nunavik.

But it is not only the political situation that has changed. Indigenous and non-Indigenous academics, historians, and anthropologists have also transformed the ways in which we approach Indigenous and colonial history. Scholars are increasingly sensitive about the inherent biases and erasures within colonial narratives of Indigenous history and recognize the need for Indigenous voices to tell their own history. Lena Onalik and I therefore modified the original *Northlanders* manuscript by incorporating historical Inuit writing and interviews into the text, as Inuit voices had been almost completely omitted. While maintaining the integrity of Brice-Bennett's original work, we added a more nuanced lens in considering the historical documentation of the Moravian Mission and the Hudson's Bay Company. Although the missionaries described their published reports in the *Periodical Accounts of the Moravian Missions* as "a series of plain, unvarnished statements," their writings were inherently influenced by their European perspectives and strategic manoeuvring within both Labrador and Mission politics.[1] The depth and wealth of the Moravian literature are alluring to historians, but the missionaries' documents must be treated critically. Likewise, the Hudson's Bay Company documents were written by men with their own interests and assumptions, and they need to be understood in this light. Lena and I also updated the book with recent literature and research and wrote new sections on the 1950s evictions and their consequences.

We also renamed the book. Avanimiut is the name that Inuit use to describe the northern families; Northlanders was the missionaries' term. While "Avanimiut" once had derogatory connotations, Lena and other members of younger generations of northern Inuit families are reclaiming the name as a source of pride. *Avanimiut: A History of Inuit Independence in Northern Labrador* illustrates this rich and dignified history and honours the strength of generations of Avanimiut families.

**Lena:** This book is so important to me and to others because it is a validation of us, of our connection to the north. For so many generations, our people have been displaced by relocation and feeling like we don't belong. But this book proves that we are descendants of the northland; we are truly Avanimiut. Through this book, we learn that the choices our ancestors made before us were not easy and were not fully of their own volition. Our ancestors were the last in the region to convert to Christianity and adapt to the life that relied heavily on the mission outposts. The choices our ancestors made were hard. Despite what they went through, our ancestors survived, and passed on their resilience to the next generations.

It took decades of becoming accustomed to and reliant on European goods before our ancestors left the north, but when the Mission and stores shut down in Hebron and Nutâk they were forced to move south. Now the history of Avanimiut is remembered with the pain and trauma that came with relocation. We must look beyond that and remember our amazing history of survival and resilience in the north.

My hope is that this book will help people to acknowledge the great sacrifices that their ancestors went through to get us to where we are today. Our history is of a people who not only survived but thrived. We should look upon our ancestors with pride. Too often we are seeing the Indigenous story told through a colonial lens. I believe it is important for us to have a voice in the story, so the story about us is told by us.

**William Tuglavina, Hebron, 1950s (Hettasch family collection, Them Days Archive)**

ACKNOWLEDGEMENTS

Thank you to the following people and organizations for your help in creating, supporting, and publishing this book:

Edna Asivak
Jamie Brake
Alison Carr
Aimee Chaulk
Michelle Davies
Michaela Doucette
Randy Drover
James Hiller
Susan Kaplan
Sophie Keelan
Simon Kohlmeister
Johannes Lampe
Rutie Lampe
Jodie Lane
Tim McNeill
Nigel Markham
Memorial University
Maria Merkuratsuk
Noah Nochasak
Nunatsiavut Government
Susan Onalik
Tim Onyszchuk
Isabella Pain
Fiona Polack
Peter Ramsden
Lisa Rankin
Hans Rollmann
Jamie Skidmore
Janet Skinner
Richard Tallman
Them Days Archive
Tradition & Transition among the Labrador Inuit Research Partnership
Mark Turner
Patty Way
Belinda Webb

James Âsivak Sr. at about 15 in Hebron (courtesy of Edna Asivak)

# INTRODUCTION

The name "Northlanders" was first used by European missionaries of the protestant Moravian Church in the late eighteenth century to describe Inuit living in the far northern region of the Labrador seaboard. This territory has an arctic environment, rugged and barren of trees, yet abounding with wildlife, especially in coastal waters. To the south, a more temperate climate, forests in sheltered valleys, and presence of both arctic and sub-arctic species created easier conditions for missionaries at the first three Moravian stations established for Inuit in northern Labrador in the eleven years from 1771 to 1782.[1]

"Northlanders" or "Avanimiut" was not just a directional reference for the Inuit population inhabiting this region. As this book will show, the term also identified a society of people who maintained their ancestral spiritual beliefs and cultural practices, and strongly resisted adopting Christianity during most of the nineteenth century. Their aversion to the Church diminished only with the death of senior family leaders, epidemic diseases that killed husbands, wives, and children or progressively weakened survivors, and poverty from game shortages as well as diminishing market values for natural resources like fur, seals, and fish. Avanimiut families gradually decided to join the Moravian congregation at Hebron, founded in 1830–31. At the mission station, they became devoted churchgoers until 1959, when they were exiled from the region after the Moravian Church closed its mission station and removed the resident minister. The Church's action forced the Newfoundland government to relocate the Inuit population to other southerly communities.[2]

Hebron exiles became known once again by a name reflecting their northern origin, but this time a version in their own language: other Inuit called them Avanimiut (or "people from the north"), often as an insult. The term implied intruders who were not born in the community and did not belong to it; therefore, their presence was unwelcome. Northern Inuit were noticeably different from southern Inuit: they spoke a distinct dialect, had darker complexions, were closely tied to their own kinship groups, and had not adopted many aspects of Euro-Canadian culture. Having been able to take only their portable belongings from Hebron, they had relatively few material possessions so were seen as poor and placed at the bottom of the social hierarchy in the coastal communities.[3]

Over the following decades, relocation reduced the once proud and confident Avanimiut to dispossessed outcasts, living at the edge both physically and socially of the Labrador communities.[4] Elderly Inuit remembered their northern ancestry and the knowledge of places, wildlife patterns, and cultural sites that were central to their identity. But their descendants grew up in southern communities and most of them did not associate with the Northland in the same way as their grandparents. For Labrador Inuit today, the Northland is a cultural and wildlife-rich region that they visit only seasonally, yet which reaffirms their integrity as an Indigenous people.

The research for this study was initially undertaken for a project sponsored by the Labrador Inuit Association (LIA), beginning in September 1994, to investigate Inuit occupancy and land use along the remote northern coast of Labrador. Responding to the assertion of a land claim to this area by the Makivik Corporation of Nunavik (northern Quebec), the LIA sought comprehensive information to construct the historical record of northern Inuit traditional rights. The Makivik claim was submitted to the Canadian government in 1987.[5] It contended that Inuit inhabiting the entire northeastern peninsula shared a common cultural ancestry and age-old social and economic relations. This territory was historically known as the Labrador Peninsula but when political divisions were created in the early twentieth century, Ungava Bay and the northwestern peninsula, affiliated with the Canadian province of Quebec, were distinguished from the Labrador coast, which was allied with the Colony (later Dominion) of Newfoundland. The Makivik document alleged that kinship, trade, and overlapping land-use patterns traditionally formed the basis for homogeneity among Inuit throughout the region. Contact with Europeans over the past three centuries and subsequent affiliations with religious and trade agencies separated Inuit into the Labrador and Quebec districts.[6] A ruling in 1927 on the location of a geographical boundary between the two northern territories, made by the Privy Council in London, further isolated the Inuit populations. Quebec government authorities have never accepted this decision, but the boundary was maintained after Newfoundland and Labrador became the tenth province of Canada in 1949.[7]

Land and resource rights of Inuit in northern Quebec were recognized in 1975 under a settlement of Indigenous claims to promote the development of hydroelectric projects through the James Bay and Northern Quebec Agreement, which established the Inuit territory called Nunavik.[8] A provision for resolving the interests in overlapping areas of land use by third parties, notably Labrador Inuit, was ignored. Nevertheless, the claim of Nunavik Inuit, represented by the Makivik Corporation, to land and offshore rights overlapping in remote northern Labrador was accepted as the basis for negotiation in 1993 by the federal government. The history and land occupation patterns of Inuit inhabiting the northern Labrador coast were not fully taken into consideration.

Despite this inattention to northern Labrador Inuit, an extraordinary wealth of historical records exists concerning their kinship groups, location, seasonal wildlife harvesting activities, trade, and social relations. All this was first documented, from the late eighteenth century onwards, by missionaries of the Moravian Church, an evangelical society based in Saxony, Germany.[9] Moravian missionaries had established communities in Greenland, Africa, Tibet, and the early American states

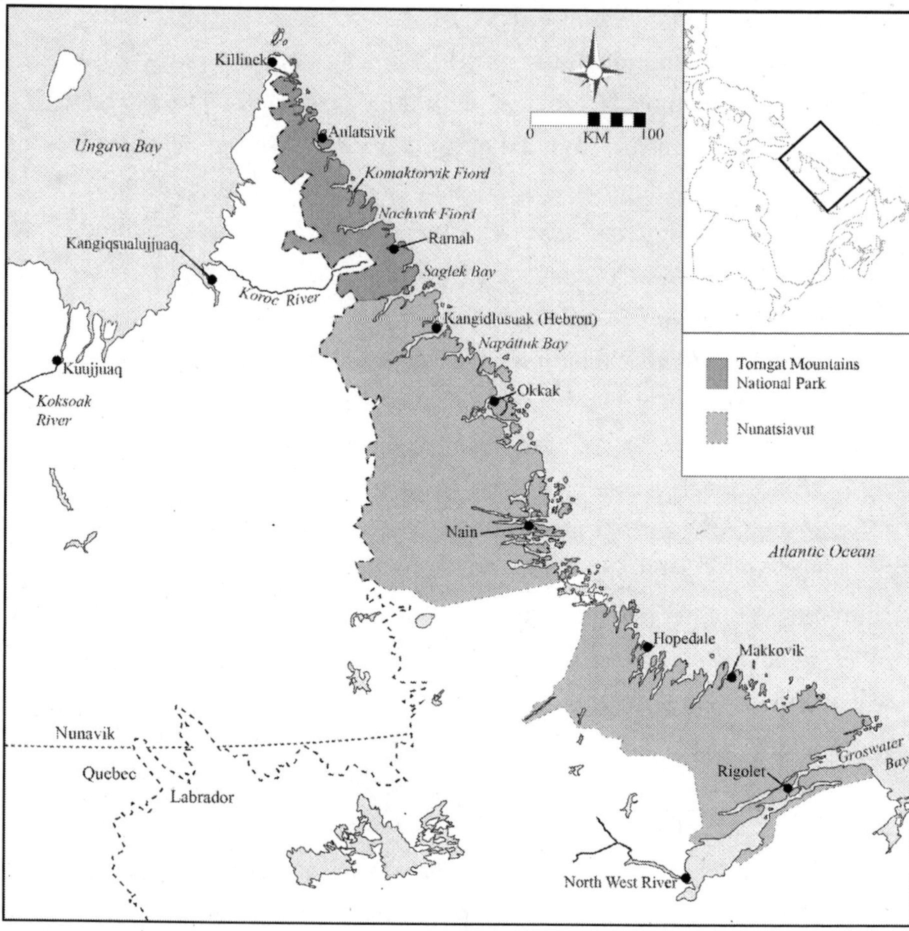


**MAP 1.** **Northern Labrador and Ungava Bay**

by the mid-eighteenth century when they began to look to Labrador. They tried to establish a mission station for Labrador Inuit in 1752 but abandoned the endeavour when Inuit killed seven members of the expedition.[10] In 1771, Moravian missionaries successfully built a station at Nain, followed by six more stations opened by the early twentieth century, which spanned the coast from Makkovik in the south to Killinek at the tip of the Atlantic seaboard. Only the three southernmost communities remain, located at Nain, Hopedale, and Makkovik.

Until the late decades of the nineteenth century, most Moravian

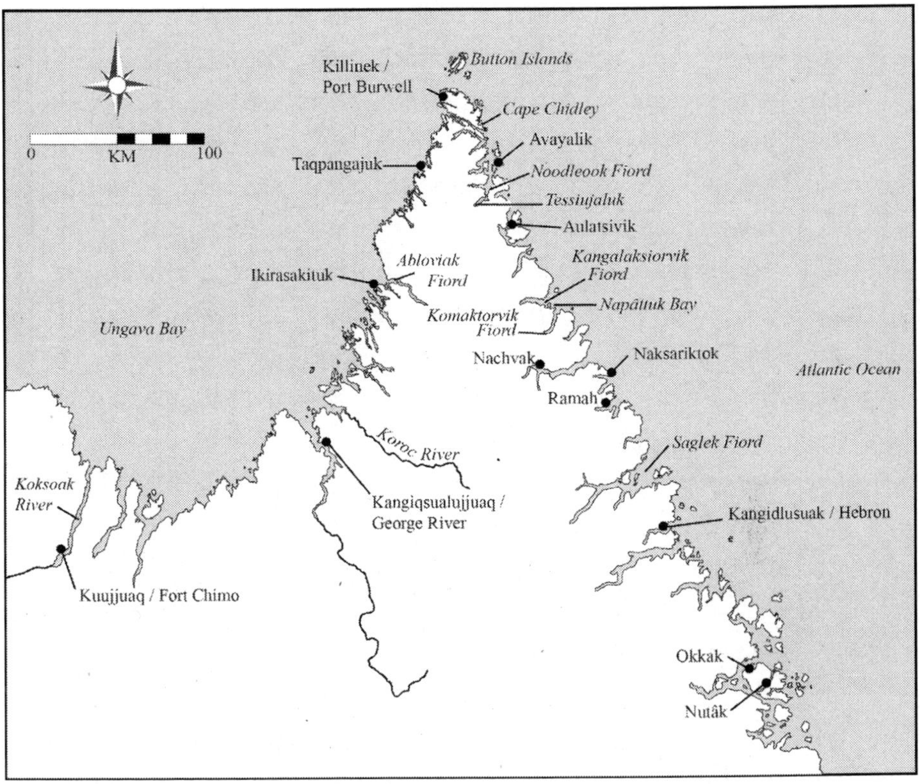


**MAP 2.** **The Quebec–Labrador Peninsula**

missionaries originated from Germany; consequently, the earliest records were written in their native language. Some documents were translated into English for publication in a quarterly journal, the *Periodical Accounts*, distributed to Moravian congregations and supporters in Britain and Ireland. Missionaries posted to northern Labrador, whether of German or English origin, had to learn to speak the Inuit language, Inuktitut, as their first task in developing a relationship with the Indigenous people. The Moravians introduced the Roman alphabet for transcribing Biblical texts and religious tracts into Inuktitut, and taught Inuit to read and write in their own language.[11]

Learning to read and write was a vital aspect of conversion to Christianity for Labrador Inuit.[12] Religious tracts and eventually the entire New Testament printed in Inuktitut allowed people to develop a richer understanding of Christian principles. By 1830, most of the congregation members at Moravian stations were literate, which made them distinct from Inuit adhering to their traditional spiritual beliefs and lifestyle.[13] New words for Christian religious concepts and other notions foreign to Inuit, like calculating time, were introduced in Inuktitut, usually based on modified German terms. Missionaries also developed a spelling system for Inuktitut that was influenced by the expression of sounds in German. These linguistic aspects ultimately gave Labrador Inuktitut a unique character compared to dialects spoken in other Inuit regions.[14]

The Moravians took great interest in this distinct population of Inuit from distant northern areas and sought to convince them to adopt Christianity and trade at the mission stations. The first Europeans to explore the northeastern coast of Ungava Bay were two Moravian missionaries who were guided by Inuit in 1811 on an expedition that reached the area of present-day Kuujjuaq in northern Quebec.[15] This book consequently treats the Northlands as a broader region than simply the northern Labrador coast, although its main objective is to trace the history of the Inuit population in Labrador.

Moravian archival collections revealed a considerable amount of information for this book about Inuit encampments and activities on the remote northern Labrador coast. They also provided details on the geography of arctic regions extending to the northwest, in Ungava Bay and along the shores of Hudson Strait, and on early trade relations linking Inuit groups throughout the area. Documents and maps dating to the late eighteenth and early nineteenth centuries, assessed for the first time through this research, contribute significant new knowledge about the entire fringe of the Labrador–Quebec Peninsula. These documents were made by Moravian missionaries directly from interviews with resident Inuit.

A team of specialists examined material in several archival collections for the original research for this study. A variety of original records and printed accounts provided details on family groups, the distribution of encampments, population movements, and the influence of European churches, trade agencies, and government departments in altering Inuit residence and economic activities during the nineteenth and twentieth centuries. Reports published in English in the *Periodical Accounts* between 1790 and 1960 are a primary reference on activities at Moravian mission stations operating on the Labrador coast. These articles contain annual reviews of each community, extracts from station diaries and correspondence by missionaries, and accounts of expeditions conducted in Labrador or of observations made by visiting Moravian officials.

The researchers studied original eighteenth- and nineteenth-century documents in Moravian archival collections held at Herrnhut (Germany), Bethlehem (Pennsylvania, USA), and London (England). This material included journals of expeditions, maps, community reports, and correspondence with European officials, most of which were written in German. Demographic details compiled from congregation registers, called Church Books (Kirchenbücher), which were kept at each Moravian community and recorded adult baptismal candidates, child baptisms, marriages, and deaths were crucial to the research. The team examined registers from four northern communities: Okkak (1776–1918), Hebron (1831–1959), Ramah (1871–1907), and Killinek (1904–1924). Carol Brice-Bennett assessed the documents in English, Dr. Hans Rollmann translated and examined the records in German from Moravian archival collections, and Regula Schule translated and analyzed notations in church registers.

A variety of other historical records contained additional information on the resident population, economic conditions, and local land-use activities, including journals kept by factors at trade posts operated by the Hudson's Bay Company (HBC), documents relating to the 1927 boundary decision, and federal government files concerning the re-establishment of a community at Port Burwell after 1960. Dr. Marianne Stopp examined microfiched copies of HBC journals from Nachvak, Port Burwell, and George River; Dr. James Hiller assessed evidence from the boundary dispute, and particularly the status of Killinek; and Edward

Tompkins reviewed files on federal initiatives at Port Burwell in the National Archives of Canada in Ottawa. The initial report submitted to the LIA also included an appendix, prepared by Dr. James Tuck, that outlined archaeological evidence on the prehistory of Inuit populations occupying the remote Labrador and Ungava Bay regions. This summary has not been included here to focus attention on the historical period.

Carol Brice-Bennett wrote the original *Northlanders* study for the LIA in 1996 and it was held as a confidential document pending negotiations to resolve Indigenous land rights issues in northern Labrador. Since 2000, the LIA and Brice-Bennett had hoped to publish this manuscript to enable Labrador Inuit and the public to better understand the range of circumstances and events that make the Avanimiut a vital component of the history and society of northern Labrador. As the Preface describes, Andrea Procter and Lena Onalik later modified the manuscript and incorporated additional material to create its current form.

## Book Outline

Chapter 1 of this book outlines the earliest interactions between Inuit and Europeans in Labrador and describes the extensive Inuit trading networks throughout the region. After the Moravian Mission established its first station and trading post at Nain in 1771, the missionaries made the first of many efforts to contact, document, and convert Inuit in the North. The Moravian records provide the earliest descriptions of northern Inuit settlements, family life, trading activities, travel routes, hunting and fishing practices, and reactions to Christian evangelism. When Inuit agreed to guide two missionaries, Kohlmeister and Kmoch, around the peninsula and into Ungava Bay in 1811, the Moravians' trip report ignited interest in the region from other trading companies as well. The Hudson's Bay Company, as Chapter 2 describes, used the information to expand into Ungava Bay with a post at Fort Chimo at Kuujjuaq in 1830, while the Moravian Mission established a new station for northern Inuit at Hebron. When the HBC closed its posts in Ungava Bay in 1842, Ungava Inuit travelled to northern Labrador to trade at Moravian posts, as Chapter 3 outlines. Always anxious to reach and document information about unconverted Inuit, the missionaries recorded the names and kinship relations of Inuit from Ungava Bay, as well as those of the fiercely independent Inuit at Saglek and elsewhere on the peninsula. The second half of the nineteenth century saw intense competition for Inuit trade between the Moravian Mission and the Hudson's Bay Company. Chapter 4 describes HBC efforts to frustrate Moravian attempts to expand into Ungava Bay, as the Company re-established its posts at George River [Kangiqsualujjuaq] and Fort Chimo [Kuujjuaq]. The Hudson's Bay Company also outmanoeuvred the Mission in northern Labrador by building new posts at Saglek in 1867 and Nachvak in 1868. In response, the Moravians established a mission station at Ramah in 1871. The Inuit evangelists Daniel and Gottlob also volunteered their efforts to convert northern Inuit to Christianity by living with them at Nachvak and Ungava Bay.

**(l-r): Jerry Nochasak and Renatus Townley, Hebron, 1950s (Hettasch family collection, Them Days Archive)**

Chapter 5 draws on records from the Moravian Mission and Hudson's Bay Company archives to create a detailed description of the unconverted Inuit who lived north of Hebron in the winter of 1868. The chapter offers the first comprehensive depiction of families' lives by identifying people's names, kinship relationships, travels, and leadership roles of Inuit who lived at Nulattatok/Sorviluk, Nachvak, Tessiujaluk/Aulatsivik, and Killinek. Chapter 6 continues with a more general exploration of both traditional Inuit life at Nachvak and Moravian Inuit life at Ramah between 1870 and 1900. During this time, competition between the Moravian Mission and the HBC over Inuit customers continued through difficult years of scarce game, low prices, and much hardship. Although the HBC post at Saglek closed in 1876, the number of Inuit in the Ramah congregation did not grow significantly, and the Moravian Mission continued to strategize how and where to reach the remaining unconverted Avanimiut. Chapter 7 describes the missionary work of the Anglican Church in Ungava Bay and the Moravian missionaries' reaction to their new rival in the region. When an Anglican minister established himself at Port Burwell on Killinek Island in 1899, the Moravians felt he was encroaching on their territory. Shortly after the Anglicans left in 1904, the Mission opened its northernmost and final station at Killinek.

Chapter 8 provides a detailed description of Inuit living between Ramah and Killinek between 1904 and 1908. Like Chapter 5, this chapter draws on Moravian and HBC records to create an in-depth depiction of the Inuit families who lived at Aulatsivik, Killinek, Komaktorvik, and Nachvak before the deadly 1904 influenza epidemic. It then describes their movements in the years following, when many families who had suffered losses moved to live with other relatives or to join Moravian congregations. Chapter 8 also describes the ongoing trade competition between the HBC post at Nachvak and the Moravian Mission post at Ramah and describes Inuit from Ungava Bay who traded at Nachvak. After the 1904 epidemic, however, both Nachvak and Ramah closed, partly due to the reduced number of Inuit in the area.

The Moravians continued in their efforts to convert northern Inuit at their new mission station at Killinek from 1904 to 1924. Chapter 9 examines the brief life of this station and the Inuit families who visited it, from the early days of lucrative sealing to more difficult days of game shortages, increased regulations and unclear jurisdictions of the Newfoundland and Canadian governments, competition from the HBC after 1916, and other mounting problems. Although the 1918 Spanish flu epidemic that decimated Okkak and Hebron did not reach Killinek, a scarcity

**Palmer River near Nachvak fiord (courtesy of Noah Nochasak)**

of game, high costs for imported goods and building materials, and the Moravian Mission's financial troubles eventually led to many Inuit moving south and the closure of the mission station in 1924.

Two years later, the Moravian Mission sold its trading rights to the HBC, ending its 150-year trading operation in northern Labrador. Chapter 10 describes the changes to Inuit life in Labrador precipitated by the HBC's trading policies through the 1930s and 1940s. With limited trade, credit, and relief payments, Inuit families suffered severely when markets for fish and seal dropped or wildlife populations plummeted. During this period, the last unbaptized northern Inuit joined the Hebron congregation. The Hudson's Bay Company post at Killinek/Port Burwell closed in 1938, and most of the remaining Inuit moved to either Kangiqsualujjuaq or Hebron. The HBC withdrew from northern Labrador altogether in 1942, transferring trade to the Newfoundland government. Difficult times and harsh HBC trading policies in Ungava Bay forced some

Inuit families to resist the traders' strict rules by finding trading alternatives in Labrador; some eventually moved to Hebron from Killinek, Nachvak, and Kangiqsualujjuaq.

Chapter 11 examines the final eviction of Inuit from northern Labrador. Without consulting the people of Nutâk and Hebron, the provincial government, the Moravian Mission, and the International Grenfell Association conspired to relocate northern Inuit to southern communities in 1956 and 1959. At the same time, the federal government worked to move Inuit from Quebec north to Killinek, where it was developing a commercial char fishery. Although Killinek was itself eventually closed in 1978, the Labrador Inuit were not informed of the federal government's plans in 1959, preventing them from having the option to move north to Killinek instead of south to Makkovik, Hopedale, or Nain. The evictions caused immense social and cultural harm to the independent and self-sufficient northern Inuit, who were forced into poverty, segregation, despondency, and despair. The homeland of the Avanimiut, now emptied of its people, became a national park in 2008. It survives as an important symbol of Inuit culture and pride in Labrador.

CHAPTER ONE

# Inuit and the Moravian Mission in Northern Labrador and Ungava Bay, 1771–1814

## Inuit Trade Networks in Labrador

Indigenous peoples have lived in Labrador for approximately 8,000 years, when the first Maritime Archaic peoples settled the region. Pre-Dorset peoples arrived about 4,000 BP, followed by the Groswater and Dorset people.[1] The ancestors of today's Inuit originated in Alaska and spread quickly throughout the Canadian Arctic and Greenland.[2] Some archaeologists argue that Inuit traded with Norse colonies in Greenland for iron and were searching for other sources of European goods when they migrated to other areas, including Labrador.[3] The earliest Inuit sites in Labrador are tentatively dated between 1200 AD and 1400 AD, as they made their way south along the Labrador coast.[4] Expanding into central and southern Labrador, they likely disrupted Innu families' seasonal use of marine resources. Innu were forced to live further inland as Inuit established themselves on the coastline.[5]

Inuit hunted large marine mammals such as whales, walrus, and seals. The sea was the main source of their sustenance, and the northern Labrador coast provided a rich marine environment. The landscape is dominated by deep fiords carving inland into majestic mountain ranges. While the northernmost tip consists of low rolling bedrock, the Torngat

Mountains, Kaumajat Mountains, and Kiglapait Mountains tower over the coastline between North Aulatsivik Island and just north of Nain. The cooling Labrador current flows south, bringing icebergs, pack ice, and frigid water to the entire coast. Trees grow as far north as Okkak Bay on the Labrador coast and Kangiqsualujjuaq on the Quebec side; beyond this treeline the land is mostly tundra, except in Napâttuk and in sheltered river valleys, where small forests grow.[6] Inuit families built snow houses (illuvigait) or sod houses (illusuat) for the winter, and lived in tents during warmer seasons. They travelled seasonally on water by umiat (large seal-skin boats; umiak, sing.) or Kajait (Kajak, sing.), and used dog teams to pull Kamutet (sleds; Kamutik, sing.) on ice and snow. Hunters focused mainly on the ocean and the sina (the edge of the land-fast sea ice), where they harpooned whales, walrus, and seals from Kajait, but they also ventured inland to hunt caribou and to fish in the rivers. Hunting large marine mammals and caribou required a large-scale cooperative effort, and Inuit society was based on sharing both labour and the harvest.[7]

As early as the sixteenth century, Inuit in Labrador traded with Europeans who arrived in the region to harvest whales, seals, and codfish. Starting in the early 1500s, Spanish Basque whalers travelled to the Strait of Belle Isle, at the southern extreme of the Labrador Peninsula, to fish the rich waters during the summer and fall seasons.[8] They were followed by French, American, and British fishermen in the seventeenth and eighteenth centuries. In return for iron and other goods such as wooden boats, fishing tackle, and clothing, Inuit provided baleen to the newcomers, as well as whale and seal oil, fur pelts, feathers and down, and walrus ivory. These European goods, particularly ironware, were highly valued by Inuit because they were more durable than commodities in the traditional Indigenous material culture.[9] Hostile attacks were common although some amicable trade exchanges did occur. Violence on both sides led to numerous murders, rapes, and the capture of Inuit slaves.[10] In the absence of peaceful trading interactions, Inuit sometimes obtained European goods either by raiding and plundering the fishing stations or by scavenging them after the fishermen departed for the season.[11]

During the first half of the eighteenth century, recurrent Inuit attacks on French cod fishing and sealing posts led to the creation of an informal boundary at Cape Charles north of Chateau Bay. The region to the north of this point was known as the "Esquimaux coast." While French merchants generally avoided the area, one entrepreneur named Louis Fornel succeeded in having peaceful exchange relations with Inuit and explored the coast in the summer of 1743.[12] Fornel gave gifts and traded for baleen with people he encountered on the way to the "Baye des Esquimaux" (Groswater Bay), the site of a year-round Inuit settlement.[13] Fornel did not know where Inuit obtained the baleen they used for trade and was uncertain whether they hunted whales themselves or found carcasses stranded on the coast.[14] After surveying the southern coast, Fornel opened a trade post in Hamilton Inlet near North West River. His post subsequently became the focus for regular and intensified economic exchanges with Inuit during the following decades. More peaceful trade relations also developed with other French merchants who opened additional fishing stations between Groswater Bay and the Strait of Belle Isle.

With the proliferation of trade, a new social order emerged in Inuit society as leaders assumed the role of intermediaries, or "middlemen," in a long-distance exchange network that circulated European goods northward and Inuit products southward along the Labrador coast.[15] These Inuit entrepreneurs had given up hunting whales in preference to accumulating baleen from whaling camps and supplying local inhabitants with foreign articles. The traders took most of the baleen to sell at Hamilton Inlet, where they would stay for the winter. Through shrewd trading and high profit margins, the Inuit middlemen gained extraordinary wealth that enhanced their prestige and authority in Inuit society.[16]

## The Moravian Mission Arrives

This economic regime was disrupted after 1763 when colonial jurisdiction over Labrador was ceded to Great Britain. A Governor of the Colony of Newfoundland now administered the territory, and he was determined to expand the British fishery and trade in Labrador while excluding the French.[17] With French merchants no longer allowed to trade along the coast, Inuit access to imported goods was severely reduced and trade relations were difficult to establish with the English and American agents who assumed control of the Labrador fisheries. Encounters were often hostile, and British authorities became concerned that Inuit threatened their control of the region and the expansion of fishery operations.[18]

Jens Haven, a Moravian missionary, proposed a plan for initiating peaceful relations with Inuit to the Governor of Newfoundland in 1764.[19] Haven had lived as a missionary in Greenland and had learned to speak Inuktitut. He believed that the Inuit population in northern Labrador was related to Greenland Inuit, and he wanted to create a mission aimed at converting them to Christianity. Inspired by Moravian missionary Johann Christian Erhardt's failed attempt in 1752 to establish a mission station in Labrador, when Erhardt and six of his crew were killed by Inuit near present-day Makkovik, Haven was driven to try again.[20] This time, the Moravians were better equipped to communicate with Inuit and to appreciate their economic situation. During a visit to southern Labrador, he recognized that obtaining European goods had become a necessity for Inuit and he felt that the absence of a regular trade system compelled people to attack and steal articles from fishing stations. Haven proposed that the Moravians operate a trade store as part of their mission on the north coast, thereby encouraging Inuit to live in the north and allowing the British to develop the southern coastal fisheries.[21] This attempt to contain Inuit in northern Labrador bolstered British interests in the south, and the Moravian missionaries soon had strong backing from British authorities.[22]

In 1765, Haven and three other Moravians travelled to Labrador to find a potential site for a mission station. The Governor of Newfoundland, Hugh Palliser, used the missionaries as Inuktitut interpreters to reach a peace and friendship treaty with Inuit in Chateau Bay, southern Labrador.[23] Although Inuit initially suggested Kikkertet (the Spotted Islands/Black Tickle area) as a prime Inuit settlement and therefore a good location for a mission station, the British government later encouraged the Moravians to establish a station farther north to be further away from British fishery interests.[24] The British government awarded the Moravian Brethren (sometimes known as Unitas Fratrum) the first of four land grants to establish mission communities on the northern Labrador coast in 1769.[25] On the advice of the Inuit leader Mikak, a woman who had been abducted and taken to England, where she had met Jens Haven, the Moravians selected a site near a major Inuit summer meeting-place and erected a base at Nain in 1771.[26] Moravian missionaries thus became the first permanent European residents in the region and proceeded to exert their influence on the entire economic, religious, and social order of Inuit culture.[27] The most immediate changes occurred due to their barter store at Nain, which undermined the dependence of Inuit on middlemen traders and provided people with a convenient and year-round supply of practical European articles.[28]

The Moravian involvement in commercial transactions served other purposes, aside from eliminating the necessity of trade networks with Inuit in southern Labrador. Their store attracted Inuit visitors to Nain and gave missionaries an opportunity to discuss Christian beliefs while people bartered for goods, thereby introducing the notion of conversion. In all their dealings with Inuit, the Moravians maintained a strict standard of exchange and formal contractual relations, aimed at impressing on Inuit the importance of Protestant values related to work, honesty, frugality, and thrift. They also initially sold a limited selection of European goods in an attempt to preserve Inuit material culture and self-sufficiency. Finally, and fundamentally to the Moravians, profits from the barter trade were used to cover the expenses of the mission.[29]

## The Northern Inuit Trade Network

The station at Nain gave the Moravians a foothold in the region, but they soon realized they had chosen a poor site for a winter settlement. They also recognized that their hope for a permanently settled Inuit congregation conflicted with the need for mobility in the Inuit land-based economy.[30] The missionaries started searching for better places to establish new settlements and explored the coast to the north and south of Nain. During the summer of 1773, Jens Haven led a northern expedition as far as Nachvak, initially guided by Kigluana, "son of the famous Seguliak."[31] Haven prepared two reports on the venture, which detailed the extent and organization of the Inuit trade network on the peninsula.[32]

The group landed at five sites along the northern Labrador coast, where Haven questioned Inuit about their activities and recorded information about inhabited settlements in the region extending westward to Ungava Bay, Hudson Strait, and Hudson Bay. Two of his main informants were an Inuk from Ungava Bay, who piloted their vessel from Saglek to Nachvak and had travelled extensively in Ungava Bay and along the Hudson Strait, and an elderly woman at Saglek who was also from Ungava Bay.[33] As the Moravians learned, a sizable Inuit population was involved in trade and social relations throughout the territory. According to Haven:

> From Nachvak to the North to Hudsons-Straight there are still 10 dwelling places, most of which are more populated than those to the south [and] whose inhabitants may be – according to my thinking – 1,660. Thus the number of the inhabitants of the coast of Labrador from 55 degrees to above 60 degrees would be ca. 3,000.[34]

This estimate implies that about 1,340 Inuit lived south of Nachvak and that the Inuit population in the northern region beyond Nachvak was higher.

Table 1 outlines Haven's record of Inuit settlement place names and number of winter sod houses (illusuat) or snow houses (illuvigait) at each location in the north. His estimate of the total population was based on an average of 20 people inhabiting a winter house and 10 people occupying an illuvigait.[35] Killinek was the only place north of Nachvak where illusuat were built. According to Haven's account, all the sites in Ungava Bay from Kangivak to Aiviktok consisted only of illuvigait.[36] He did not record any population estimate for the three most remote locations –

Nuvongok, Igloarsuk, and Ittibime – which his informants had not visited, although he evidently estimated 510 people at these sites in arriving at the total of 1,660 inhabitants.

Haven's description of the entire territory encompassed by the Labrador Sea, Hudson Strait, and Hudson Bay as "the coast of Labrador" is consistent with the view of Europeans at the time. Known as "the Labrador," the region also extended south to include the Lower North Shore of the Gulf of St. Lawrence, incorporating the extent of the sea ice. Very little was then known of the geography of the peninsula or of the interior of Ungava Bay. Since the seventeenth century, explorers travelling in the Arctic had avoided Ungava Bay because of the dangerous sailing conditions caused by abundant drift ice, shallow waters, and high tides.[37] Among other details, Haven's report revealed that the place name "Ungava" referred not only to a region but also to a settlement location including the two communities of Ungavak and Kok.[38]

Inuit throughout this region connected with each other through trade and social interactions. Haven described the trade network operating in the Labrador Peninsula as being "artigeingerichtet,"[39] meaning well organized in the sense of a coherently functioning enterprise. The systematic manner by which Inuit redistributed ironware and local products throughout the territory undoubtedly exceeded the missionary's prior conception of the extent of Indigenous trade on the eastern Labrador coast. The Inuit communication system also made them remarkably aware of the activities of both Inuit and Europeans in Hudson Strait and Hudson Bay.

Trade visits were the primary means by which Inuit in different communities would have exchanged information about significant events, but they also shared information when they met while hunting caribou in the interior. Inuit told Haven that southeast of Kangivak, a very wide bay and estuary of George River (Kangiqsualujjuaq) in Ungava Bay, a narrow and long river almost joined Nachvak Bay "so that the Nagvak and Kangiva people encounter each other often when hunting for reindeer [caribou]."[40] Similar meetings occurred in the interior to the

**TABLE 1. Distribution of the Inuit Population on the Northern Labrador and Ungava Coasts, 1772–73**

| Place | Estimated population |
|---|---|
| Agvitok [Hopedale area] | 270 |
| Nunainguk [Nain area] | 250 |
| Kivallik [Okkak Bay] | 160 |
| Napâttuk | 120 |
| Kangidlusuak [Hebron] | 120 |
| Saglek | 100 |
| Sorviluk | 40 |
| Nulattatok [Ramah Bay] | 30 |
| Nachvak | 80 |
| Komaktorvik | 30 |
| Killinek | 100 |
| Kangivak | 150 |
| Tasiujak | 200 |
| Aupaluk | 200 |
| Ungavak | 200 |
| Tuak | 100 |
| Aiviktok | 300 |
| Nuvongok<br>Igloarsuk<br>Ittibime | (510) |

Note: Of the Inuit communities from Nachvak south to 55 degrees latitude, Haven's estimate of 1,340 Inuit inhabitants in eight locations was inaccurate according to Taylor (1974: 13–15), who compared Haven's account to a report by Lieutenant Roger Curtis of the British Navy. Curtis also surveyed the coast north of Nain in 1773 but only travelled as far as Okkak Bay. His informants identified an additional three settlements not noted by Haven, between Saglek and Killinek (at Sorviluit [Sorviluk], Nullatartok [Nulattatok], and Komaktorvik), with a population of about 100 Inuit. Other adjustments made by Taylor result in a total estimate of 1,460 Inuit on the Atlantic coast of Labrador with the inclusion of Killinek; these figures are presented in Table 1.
Sources: Haven (1773b); Taylor (1974: 15).

**Saglek Bay (courtesy of Maria Merkuratsuk)**

south involving hunters originating from places between Kangidlusuak (Hebron) and Nain,[41] as well as between Inuit from western Ungava Bay and Hudson Bay in the vicinity of the Leaf River.[42] Such encounters were undoubtedly common between adjacent communities along the entire coast of the peninsula and contributed to the spread of information.

Haven learned that two sites on the northern Labrador coast, Napâttuk and Nachvak, were whaling and trading centres. Inuit from Nuneingoak (Nain), Agvitok (Hopedale area), and more southerly coastal areas usually travelled to Napâttuk in autumn or winter, either to hunt whales or to trade for whalebone (baleen) or oil with the permanent inhabitants. As its name indicates, Napâttuk is the only place north of Okkak where trees are found, and Inuit from Kangidlusuak (Hebron) and north travelled to the bay to cut wood for tools, Kajait, boats, and houses.[43] These visits had led to intermarriage and a resident population that was a "mix from all parts," according to Haven.[44] In contrast, Nachvak was a trade centre that attracted "more northern Eskimaux" who often stayed all winter to obtain ironware before they returned home.[45] Haven commented that baleen "was here [held] in no esteem" and that Nachvak Inuit paid dearly for ironware "as it came through two or three hands to them."[46] He witnessed a transaction in which Kigluana charged local Inuit over twice "the usual price" for European goods "without scruple."[47]

Baleen was not accorded any value at Nachvak for two reasons: first, Inuit were able to obtain all the resources they needed for trade from hunting at Nachvak and Saglek, and second, the distance travelled by some northern Inuit to trade at Nachvak made it "impossible to bring the whalefins so far in exchange."[48] There were five settlements between Nachvak and a site on the coast of Hudson Strait called Aiviktok, which was renowned for whale hunting and had the largest Inuit population in the region.[49]

The Inuit traders who provided Napâttuk inhabitants with ironware were also the main source of supply for Nachvak Inuit, but exchanges were not conducted in Nachvak itself. A buffer was maintained between the two groups by having goods exchanged at Saglek. Haven reported:

> One can divide the nation living on the East Coast into two parts: for the ones coming from the South seldom go farther than Kangertlorsoak [Kangidlusuak]; and the ones coming from the North seldom come farther down than Nachvak. Saglek, lying between the two, is frequented by sled in the winter by both.[50]

Haven learned that every community produced particular goods for exchange that supported the traditional subsistence economy: "In one place they make kettles of soft stone [soapstone] to sell, in yet another they build boats, in another they have walrus teeth [tusks], and farther on another one [has] whalebones and fins."[51] Wooden utensils and dogs were also barter items.[52] Reciprocal visits and exchange occurred among eight communities beyond Nachvak, stretching from Killinek at the tip of the Labrador Peninsula to Ungava Bay and Hudson Strait. Occasional contact also occurred with two other communities that Haven's informants described but had not visited personally. The approximate location of Inuit settlements in this region is shown on Map 3.

One of these two places was called Igloarsuk, which was located "at the northern corner of the land and had many inhabitants," and the other

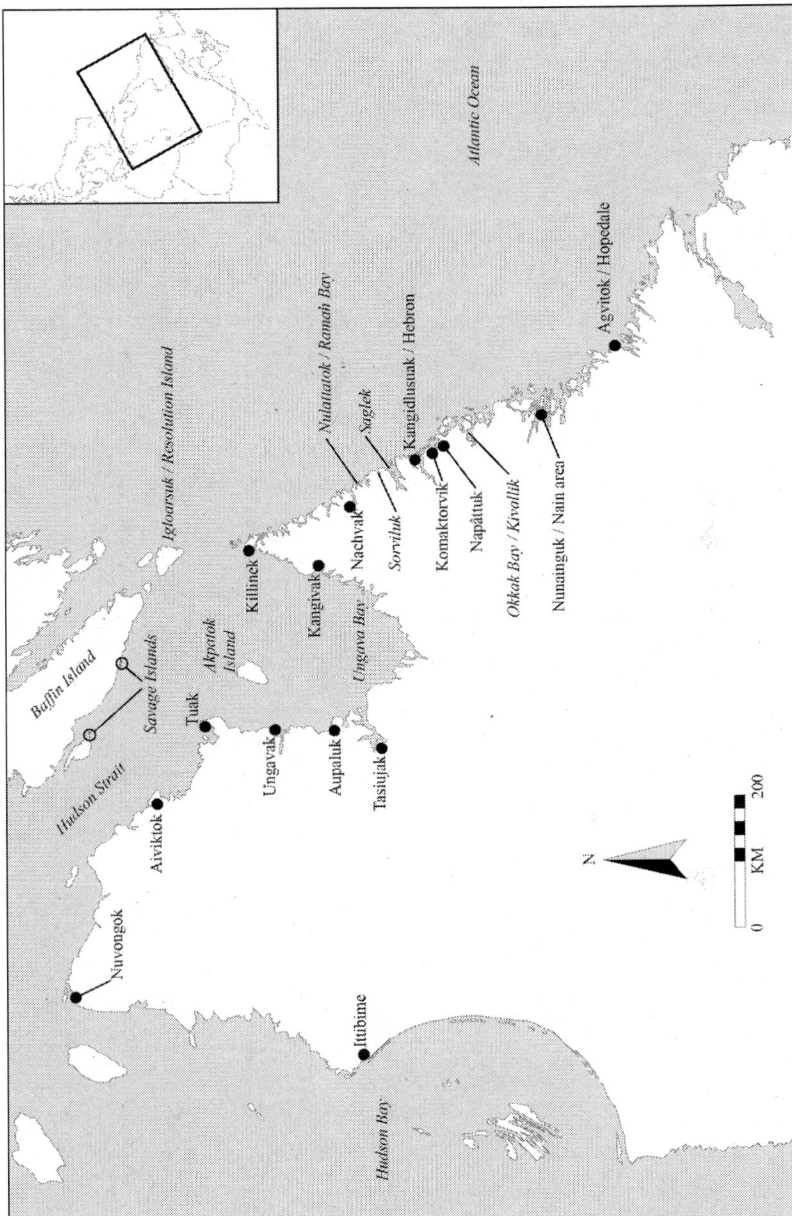


**MAP 3.** **Approximate location of historic Inuit settlements in northernmost Labrador, Ungava Bay, and Hudson Strait in the late eighteenth century**

place was Ittibime, which was "the last dwelling place of Inuit on the Labrador coast" where "Inuit end and soon after the Land-Indians [Algonquian] begin."[53] Inuit at Igloarsuk were known to trade annually with passing ships and reported that "Europeans had houses toward the west and the land Indians were their good friends."[54] Ittibime Inuit were said to have lacked boats (possibly meaning large umiat) but had Kajait and Kamutet, which allowed them to retreat quickly when Algonquian (Cree or Innu) approached; more Inuit were reported living on islands to the north of Ittibime.[55] These comments suggest that Ittibime referred to the southeastern coast of Hudson Bay (near Inukjuak)[56] and Igloarsuk was situated in Hudson Strait, in the vicinity of the Upper and Middle Savage Islands off the southern coast of Baffin Island.

Haven learned that Igloarsuk Inuit visited Ungava Bay and exchanged "cutlery" (Schneidzeug), meaning wrought iron tools, which they obtained from European ships in exchange for boats, Kajait, and soapstone lamps and kettles.[57] Although they would have used baleen in trade with the Europeans, the Igloarsuk Inuit did not seek an additional supply of the material from Ungava Inuit. Haven's informants emphasized that baleen was not an exchange commodity, stating "They don't know in the bay [Ungava] that the Europeans want to have whalebone and that they pay something for it."[58] Thus Haven understood that the Hudson's Bay Company, whose vessels sailed annually through Hudson Strait bringing supplies to posts operating in Hudson Bay, did not conduct much trade with Inuit. The major restraint to developing trade relations was, he believed, an inability to communicate:

> I thus conclude that the Hudsons Bay Company cannot talk with people or make them at least understand that they would buy more whalebone. I believe even less that they can inquire of them whether more of their people live nearby and invite them to places such as these.[59]

Haven's observation, however, was not entirely correct. Research published by Barr (1994) indicates that after about 1738, HBC officials specifically instructed captains of their ships to seek opportunities to conduct trade with Inuit during voyages through Hudson Strait, and gave them a 25 per cent commission on the net produce as an incentive. The vessels usually took a route close to the north shore of the strait, following a strong current and ice-free conditions, and commonly met groups of Inuit in the vicinity of the Middle and Upper Savage Islands where they engaged in trade. The HBC ships brought wrought iron tools such as knives, hatchets, hand saws, files, and chisels as well as pieces of old iron barrel hoops to trade. In return, Inuit traded baleen, pelts, walrus and narwhal tusks, seal oil, and whale oil.[60]

Trade encounters between Hudson Strait Inuit and HBC ships were limited to the short ice-free summer period but occurred regularly throughout the eighteenth century and continued well into the nineteenth century. Although a vast quantity of trade goods was brought from England for barter, the number of Inuit participating in trade at the Savage Islands was comparatively small, usually not exceeding 80 or 90 people. Barr concluded that Inuit could not have utilized all the goods themselves; instead, they likely acted as middlemen in reselling items through intergroup contacts that probably extended "throughout Baffin Island and much of the Central Arctic, as well as south to Ungava."[61]

The Savage Islands were the main point of entry for European manufactured goods in Hudson Strait. As Haven suggested, Inuit may not have fully understood the degree to which HBC agents were interested in bartering for baleen and other products since the two groups could not communicate in a common language. However, they certainly appreciated the opportunity to capitalize on their unique contact with Europeans. The Inuit of the area held a monopoly on the redistribution of ironware and other items, such as ornamental objects, through barter with different Inuit populations. In so doing, they were similar to southern Labrador Inuit traders, who had easy access to manufactured goods due to their interactions with European dealers and profited from the resale of articles to Inuit at Napâttuk and Nachvak. Hudson Strait Inuit were also like Nachvak Inuit in relying on their own production of baleen to satisfy their trade needs and not seeking additional supplies from other Indigenous groups.

Inuit from Igloarsuk who brought ironware for barter in Ungava Bay, as Haven described, were middleman traders, possibly from the Savage Islands, although other locations for Igloarsuk were suggested in later Moravian reports. These trade encounters depended entirely upon the initiative of the Igloarsuk people, according to Haven's informants, who stated that Ungava Inuit did not reciprocate by travelling to Igloarsuk.[62] Since Ungava Inuit could also obtain ironware from Nachvak, they may have preferred the shorter travel distance and perhaps gained better value from bartering on the northern Labrador coast. This initiative was also one-sided because no reference is made to travel by Nachvak Inuit to the Ungava region for trade or other purposes. Middlemen evidently played a key role in redistributing both European goods and Inuit products from different communities in the regional exchange network.

Nachvak Inuit demonstrated a shrewdness in trade dealings that led Haven to comment that "when they came to Traffick, they knew very well what they were about, what they should buy, & what to buy first."[63] When he asked if people had any walrus tusk, a piece the size of a hen's egg was brought to him and a knife was asked for it; he reluctantly accepted the deal, complaining the "knife was worth more in England than such a piece of Bone."[64] In making purchases, Inuit gave priority to clothing and tools for men, then selected knives and thimbles for women, and if they had any resources left, they finally bought ornaments and beads worn by women. Their "sensible unaffected behaviour" and bartering proficiency amazed the Moravian party,[65] despite the obvious experience that Nachvak Inuit had in trade relations with other Inuit.

Nachvak Inuit appear to have had limited contact with Europeans. Only one of the women in about 80 inhabitants was known to have seen a European; the woman was born at Agvitok and had moved north when she was very young.[66] Whether any of the males in the population had ever seen a European is not clear in the account. Men tended to travel more extensively than women and they may have intentionally excluded women from trade ventures to avoid possible sexual violence or abduction by Europeans.

Haven was impressed by the high standard of living among Nachvak and northern Inuit. He noted they had better household goods and tents than southern Inuit, although ironware was very scarce. "One sees [a] collection of wooden bowls, water buckets made of whalebone, large and small lamps of soft stone and kettles," he wrote.[67] Some of these items derived from inter-group trade that promoted the distribution of local resources and commodities, as well as linked communities to the north and west of Nachvak.

## New Moravian Stations: Okkak (1776) and Hopedale (1782)

Jens Haven's survey alerted Moravian missionaries to the large population of Inuit who lived north of Nachvak. Their perspective on "the coast of Labrador" now extended considerably farther westward to encompass the entire peninsula, from Labrador to Hudson Bay. Moravian officials began devising ways to contact northern Inuit, to advance Christianity as well as their own trade interests.

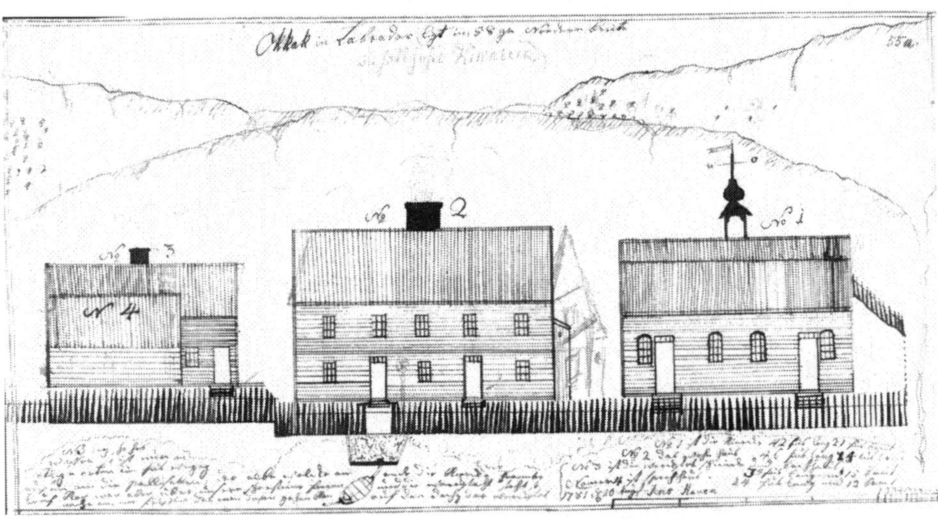

**Drawing of Okkak mission buildings, 1781 (Jens Haven, Fotosammlung zu Labrador und Grönland, Labrador Inuit through Moravian Eyes collection)**

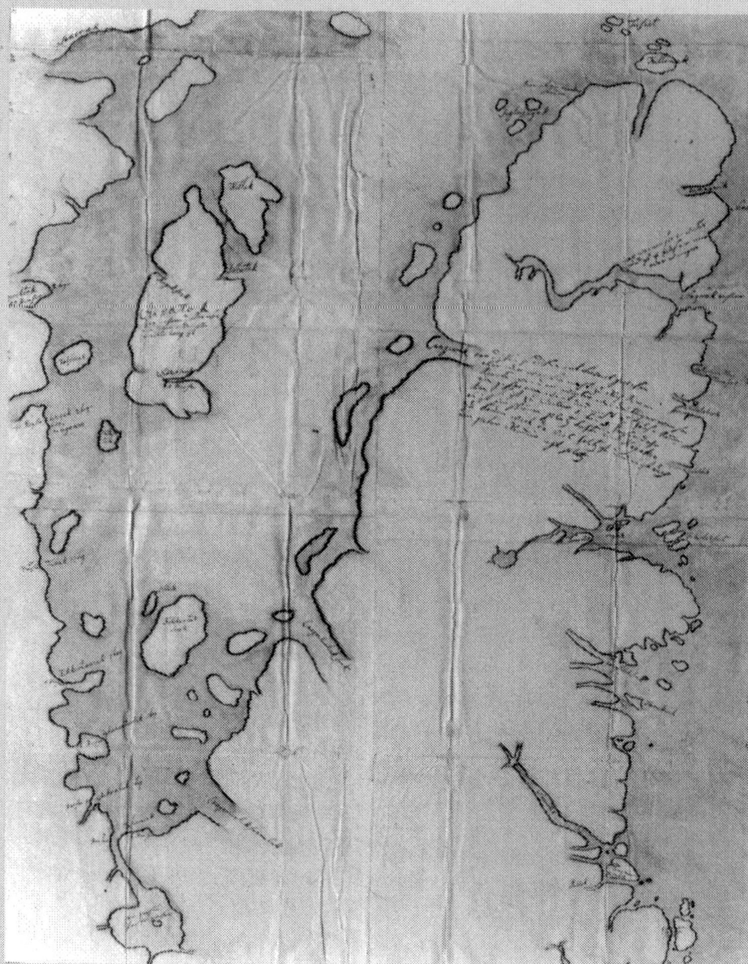

**MAP 4.** **Hand-drawn map depicting the coastline of the northern Labrador Peninsula, Ungava Bay, and the western entrance of Hudson Strait, late eighteenth century (Unity Archives, Herrnhut)**

**NOTES:** This hand-drawn map was discovered in the Moravian Archives at Herrnhut. The sketch was attributed in a pencilled note to Haven's preliminary exploration of the Labrador coast in 1765 and described as the Davis Inlet area. However, this designation was evidently false because the diary of the 1765 voyage does not mention the map, as would be expected for such an important document, and the area outlined extends northward from

Cape Mugford in Okkak Bay. The map appears to have been drawn in the late eighteenth century because it contains information on community place names and the number of dwellings at sites that compare with details compiled by Haven and Lister. As well, the handwritten script conforms to late eighteenth-century style.

The orientation of the map suggests it was drawn by an Inuk from the western Ungava coast where the most details on inhabited communities are shown. Two more settlements are identified between Aupaluk and Aiviktok than were noted by Haven, and several place names and a sizable community are described as located on Akpatok, a large island off the western coast of Ungava Bay. The proportions of the island are greatly exaggerated, compared to its known size on contemporary maps, which suggests that the island had some significance for the cartographer, perhaps because he came from there or was particularly familiar with its resources.

---

Along the western Ungava shore, notes are handwritten in German about place names, the number of dwellings, and travel time in days between seven communities from Tesiauiak (Tasiujak) to Aiwiktok (Aiviktok). These communities contained a total of 111 houses, with an additional 10 houses at a settlement called Neliksawik on Akpatok Island; the travel time between places ranges from one to two days. The largest population concentrations are shown at Ungak (Ungavak) and Aiwiktok (Aiviktok), each with 40 houses. These dwellings were likely snow houses (illuvigait) since Lister confirmed Haven's remark that at Aiviktok, Inuit "here don't know anything about earth and wood houses, but remain until it snows in tents" (Lister, 1775: 13281–82). No figures are indicated for dwellings in places north of Aiviktok.

Aspects of other areas depicted on the map are also significant. A lengthy note adjacent to Cangiwak (Kangivak) describes the occasional nature of residence at the site:

> Formerly this place has been inhabited, but only when they could not get home. When winter, or more accurately, when they were frozen in and can not make it home, there are at times 1–5 houses there.

> It is a good place for building boats and kayaks since there is much wood, and it is a good place to hunt reindeer [caribou].

This explanation seems to be referring to the occupation of Kangivak by Inuit from the western shore of Ungava where forest resources were scarce, particularly since Kangivak is shown to be diagonally across from Akpatok and Aiviktok.

---

The relative location of Kangivak to Nachvak and Saglek on the northern Labrador coast also appears to be misrepresented, perhaps reflecting the cartographer's perception of the landscape from the travel route followed to reach the eastern fiords. The only place on the Labrador coast where several dwellings are clearly indicated is at Nachvak, where a note states "here they live in winter and there are more or less 4 houses." Figures are indicated at four other sites (Nulattatok, Saglek, Kangidlusuak, and Napâttuk) and very likely refer to the number of dwellings.

At its northwestern extreme, the map indicates only general locations for places beyond Aiviktok, suggesting that the cartographer was not personally familiar with the area. This impression is reinforced by the location of the final site on the coastline, Illibliarsuk, which resembles the place "Ittibime" that Haven identified as the terminus of Inuit settlement but is shown to be on the southern shore of Hudson Strait. A second familiar place name, Igloarsuk, is indicated off a headland north of Nuvok and adjacent to a collection of six small islands called Tutseit (Tutjat), with a note explaining that the islands "lie at the entrance of Hudson Strait." The same place name is used for three small islands north of Killinek at the eastern entrance of the strait. In addition, two place names are inscribed on the land mass north of Hudson Strait: "Comberland islands," and in the east, a small cove called "Sawitz Bay," below which is a note also describing it as "Heathen Bay."

As the map begins at the southeastern extreme with the Cape Mugford region north of Okkak, it is likely that its author was an Inuit trader who travelled to barter at the Moravian store in Okkak and provided information to one of the resident missionaries.

In 1775, Moravian officials in Germany approved the construction of a new station at Okkak, chosen after missionaries surveyed the region in 1774.[68] The mission house opened the following year. A site for a third station was selected in July 1775 in the Agvitok region, about 190 kilometres south of Nain. Hoffenthal (Hopedale) was founded in 1781. Both stations were better located than Nain, as they were adjacent to existing large Inuit winter settlements and in productive hunting areas, thus increasing the missionaries' opportunities of making contact with local inhabitants.[69]

Okkak was located on an island near the mouth of Okkak Bay, a rich habitat for marine and terrestrial life at the northern limit of the treeline. Whales, seals, walrus, caribou, and fish were plentiful, and fur-bearing animals and timber could be found in the interior.[70] Missionaries encouraged Inuit converts to live at Okkak during the winter months, but again the high degree of Inuit mobility presented an obstacle for the Moravians in their efforts to centralize their flock at the mission stations and to isolate them from their unbaptized family members and neighbours.[71] From spring until late fall, both Christian and traditional Inuit dispersed to various seasonal camps, where they supported themselves by hunting and fishing. People travelled most frequently, either for trade or social purposes, in the winter period from January to April, when snow and ice conditions were ideal for journeys by dog team and Kamutik. Considerable travel also occurred by boat in summer, especially in July and August, when the sea was generally free of ice and storms.

## Trade at Okkak

After the Okkak mission began operations, Inuit residing at Saglek, Nachvak, and more northerly locations who had previously obtained trade goods from Inuit dealers based at Napâttuk had easy access to articles at the Okkak store. Despite being near the new mission store, however, Inuit continued to exchange goods among themselves and maintained their prior trade associations. Okkak was not the only destination for northern Inuit who stopped at the mission station "in passing up and down the coast" in 1806.[72] They also travelled to visit Europeans living south of Hopedale who offered to trade foodstuffs and other articles that were not stocked at the Moravian stores.[73]

By 1793, trade at Okkak was a regular activity for Inuit living in the immediate vicinity of the station and from northern settlements along the coast to Killinek. Resident missionaries became familiar with many northern Inuit traders, but some of their visitors were newcomers and probably originated from Ungava Bay. Between 1796 and 1798, the Okkak missionaries reported that many "strange" (meaning foreign) Inuit were among a great number of Kamutet passing to and from the north. As they had done in the past, Ungava Inuit continued to make trade expeditions to the coast. Instead of stopping at Nachvak, they extended their destination to trade directly in the Moravian store at Okkak or at other stations, but they came only to trade, returning home after their commercial transactions were completed.

Moravian missionaries frequently commented that northern and Ungava Inuit were only interested in trade and were not attracted by sermons on Christianity.[74] On February 2, 1798, a trading party on four Kamutet arrived at the station from Nachvak. With them were two Inuit "from the Ungava region, who had lived in Aupaluk, had wintered in Aulatsivik, behind Nachvak, this past winter, and had come the past summer to Nachvak."[75] Ungava Inuit, called "Ungawakker" in the original German account, made another visit from Nachvak on March 8. The Okkak missionaries remarked:

> Since they had never been here, they had much to marvel at. Their behaviour was not wild but rather friendly. They did not express much desire to move to this area. They want to move back again from Nachvak to their previous dwelling places.[76]

The missionaries were pleased to have northern and Ungava Inuit visit Okkak, but they worried that these "strangers" who maintained their traditional beliefs and customs might influence Inuit who had converted to Christianity. In their annual letter dated September 6, 1801, missionaries stated that they intended to build a small house in the autumn "for the reception of Esquimaux strangers, when they come here on a visit, as they otherwise become troublesome guests, in our people's houses."[77]

## Missionaries Look to Ungava Bay

The Moravian Mission aimed to develop a strategy for engaging the northern Inuit population. But without travelling to the region and seeing the situation firsthand, it was difficult for the missionaries to document who lived where. Periodic reports from travellers provided only a partial picture, and northern and Ungava Inuit travelled frequently. While missionaries required Christian Inuit to maintain a permanent winter dwelling at the mission station, northern Inuit were free to move their winter residence when local game became scarce.[78]

Resident missionaries learned about the northwestern region stretching to Hudson Bay from Ungava Inuit visiting Okkak. The visitors provided many details, based on their own experience in going as far as the Hudson Bay coast and Igloarsuk. After several conversations with Ungava Inuit, missionaries recorded the following comment in the Okkak diary on May 8, 1800:

> All their extensive communications, in which they reported to us the number of the dwelling places of the Inuit as well as their houses, agree with each other, that the greatest number of this nation are found in those areas and in the adjacent islands. Eivektok [Aiviktok], which place is supposed to be from us a 3–4 day's journey on the farthest tip of the entrance of Hudson Bay, is supposed to be the most inhabited place on the whole coast. As well, the island Igloarsuk, which lies in a northern direction adjacent from the tip, [is] a 2 days journey distant (on the map Nottingham Isle [Resolution Island]), [and] where the Hudson Bay ships pass by, is supposed to be inhabited in very large numbers. One of those people had lived there several winters, and had seen the Hudson Bay ships.[79]

The use of the phrase "this nation" ["dieser Nation" in the original German account] to describe the population distribution indicates that the Okkak missionaries believed that Inuit occupying the Ungava region composed a separate entity from the Inuit population on the Labrador coast.

At the core of the Ungava society was the community at Aiviktok, which hosted the largest number of inhabitants; the site was apparently located near present-day Kangiqsujuaq.[80] With only a few days of travel needed to visit either the Labrador coast or Igloarsuk, Ungava Inuit could easily maintain contact with other Indigenous populations. However, even when they remained for a few seasons or years in another region, they kept an allegiance to their original territory and ultimately returned to it.

Knowing that Ungava Inuit would not remain for long on the Labrador coast, the Okkak missionaries offered to go to Ungava to instruct people in Christianity. Inuit welcomed their proposal:

> Upon our queries, whether it were desirable to them and their countrymen if Europeans came to them to acquaint them with their creator and saviour and to show them the way to salvation, how they could be saved and satisfied human beings, they all said that they would be happy if we came to them. . . . All of them want to return again this summer to their regions and return here in a few years.[81]

Launching an actual expedition to Ungava Bay, however, would prove more difficult to organize than the Okkak missionaries may have imagined.

## Kohlmeister and Kmoch Visit Ungava Bay

In 1799, when the captain of the Moravian supply ship *Harmony* learned of the many northern Inuit who visited Okkak for trade, he proposed a survey of the coast beyond the mission station to determine the size and distribution of the Inuit population in the area. Captain Fraser believed the Inuit population between Okkak and the Button Islands in Hudson Strait was large, and he hoped the Mission might draw them into its fold. The expedition was approved for the summer of 1800 and the missionary John Hasting, who was fluent in Inuktitut, was assigned to lead it. However, the voyage was not undertaken because of strong prevailing winds.[82]

The missionaries soon realized they needed Inuit cooperation and expertise for a successful journey to Ungava Bay. Two Ungava Inuit, Arnaujak and Uttakiyok, agreed to share their geographic knowledge of the region with an Okkak missionary named Benjamin Kohlmeister. Arnaujak and Uttakiyok were middlemen traders whose travel circuit between Ungava Bay and the northern Labrador coast usually took two years. Arnaujak lived at Kikkertaujak, a small island west of Akpatok, and frequently visited the northern Labrador coast to trade. Based on their descriptions of the coast from Okkak to Hudson Bay, Kohlmeister drew a sketch with notations on the location and size of settlements, and on the best route and anchorages for a European ship (Map 5).

Kohlmeister's information generated much excitement among Moravian authorities in England and Germany about the possibility of making direct contact with northern Inuit. In 1803, they endorsed an expedition to Ungava Bay. However, internal debate on the kind of vessel to use for the voyage and obstacles caused by the Napoleonic Wars in Europe delayed the venture until 1811.[83] In the meantime, the Okkak missionaries regularly reported having visitors from the north arriving to trade, bringing such goods as oil, skins, and baleen to barter either for articles in their store or for items obtained from local people.[84]

Beginning in 1804, many Inuit living near the mission stations decided to adopt Christianity. The religious awakening caused the congregations of Hopedale and Nain to rapidly increase in size, as they absorbed virtually all the immediate Inuit population. By the 1810s, Okkak was the only station where groups of unconverted northern Inuit regularly visited to trade. Contacting the majority of the Inuit population in the northwest was the major challenge left for the future of the Labrador mission.

In May 1810, Kohlmeister was directed to organize and lead an expedition to Ungava Bay. Understanding the importance of Inuit knowledge in the success of the venture, he asked Jonathan, "the principal person, or chief of his nation" at Hopedale, to be captain of the journey.[85] Jonathan

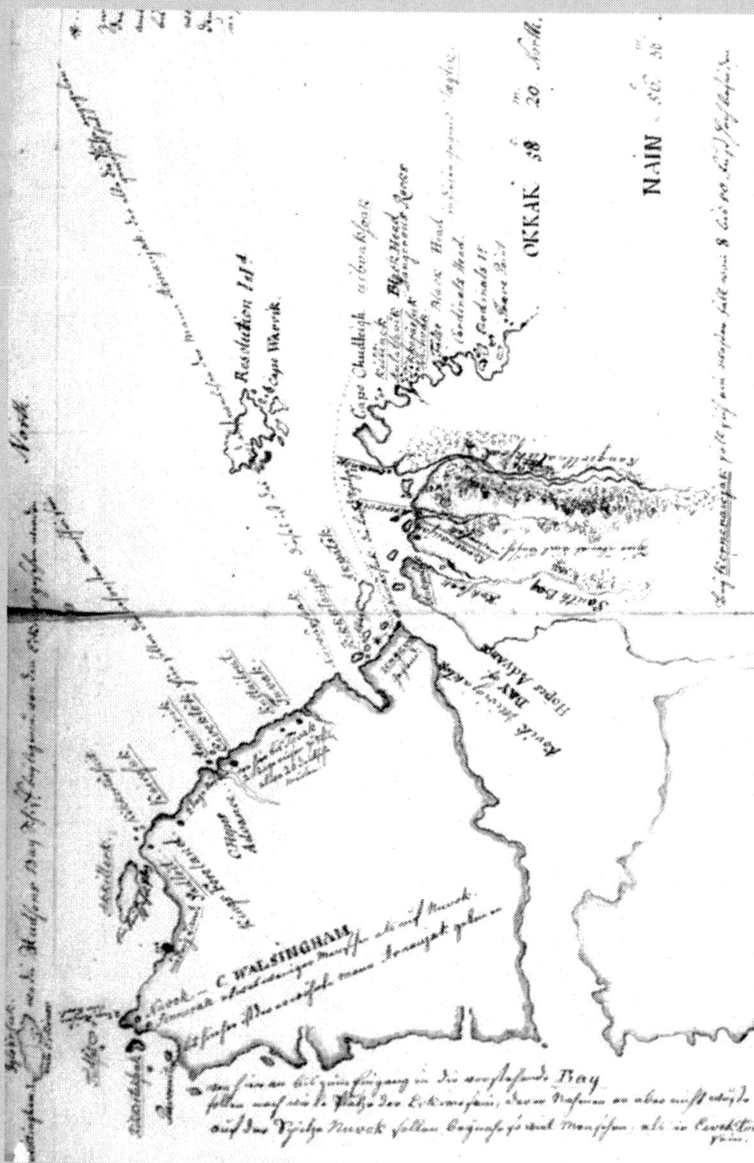


**MAP 5.** Sketch of Inuit settlements and place names in the Labrador–Ungava region drawn by Benjamin Kohlmeister, c. 1800 (Centre for Newfoundland Studies, MUN)

**NOTES:** Kohlmeister's rendition of the Inuit information on the map severely distorts the proportion of the coastline and relative locations of occupied settlements that were documented in earlier sketches of the northwestern region. This result may be due to Kohlmeister's poor comprehension of descriptions given by Inuit or simply to the small scale of the map. It may also be due to different Inuit approaches to map-making that incorporate travel time into distances on maps, as described by Fossett (2003). Kohlmeister seems to have been unaware of the previous maps drawn by Haven and Lister, which provide more accurate renditions of the region. Original copies of these drawings were apparently sent to Europe and forgotten, as no reference is made to them. Major misrepresentations on Kohlmeister's map include the compression of the peak of the northeastern peninsula between the Labrador Sea and Ungava Bay to an irregular knoll, the extension of the Bay of Hopes Advance to a strait leading to Hudson Bay, and consequently the isolation of the northwestern peninsula as an island.

Nevertheless, the sketch and a lengthy commentary inscribed below it provide some useful information on place names and the location of additional Inuit communities, as well as descriptions of the geography of the region. The commentary states:

> From Kings Foreland or Sadloit to Tuvak the land is largely low and the flood extremely wide. The Inuit did not know anything about a harbour or where a ship could enter, but with their skin boats, they can go everywhere. Between Kings Foreland and Nuvok, the farthest point in Hudson Bay, the land is also supposed to be very low, but nevertheless also high in a few places, where the water is also deep. But they couldn't indicate those places. Arnaujak had travelled up the entire coast to the most northern tip in his boat, but also in the winter by sled, and could indicate very precisely all day journeys from one place to another, as well as how many winter houses can be found in each place, according to which he indicated the approximate number of people in each place. From Ungava on to the northern tip of Hudson Bay they have only snow houses in winter, since on the coastline there are no bushes. Also on the entire coast, from Okkak to the farthest Point in Hudson Bay, they do not see any boat, only on Igluarsuk.

The final remark on the absence of boats undoubtedly refers to ships that were known to anchor only at Igloarsuk, which was identified on this map as Resolution Island.

Arnaujak and Uttakiyok recommended that the best entrance to the bay was a route from Cape Chidley across to the point of Akpatok Island and ending off the coast near the communities of Ungava and Kikkertaujak, Arnaujak's home. While this location provided the most secure anchorage for a ship, they also stated that good harbours could be found in other places around the head of the bay, particularly at the island of Arvervik on the eastern Ungava shore, midway along the route. Arvervik was shown on the map to be located between two large rivers, George River in the east and Koksoak River, also named South Bay, in the west.

was "one of the most skilful commanders [seafarers] on the whole coast of Labrador," and the owner of a 45-foot boat.[86] He and his wife Sybilla, both between 50 and 60 years old, were the first people baptized in the community. Okkak missionary George Kmoch and four Inuit families from Hopedale joined Jonathan's family and Kohlmeister, adding another 13 people to the party.[87]

Jonathan was a devout Christian who supported the objective of spreading the Gospel to Inuit in remote regions. However, the Moravians recognized that participating in the long voyage was "no small sacrifice" on his part in having to leave his home.[88] As they explained:

> An Esquimaux is naturally attached to the place of his birth; and, though he spends the summer, and indeed great part of the year, necessarily, and from inclination, in roving from one place to another in quest of food; yet in winter he settles, if possible, upon his native spot, where he is esteemed and beloved.[89]

Jonathan and the other Inuit families from Hopedale moved to Okkak in the fall of 1810 to make renovations to his boat and to leave for the north as soon as the ice cleared from Okkak Bay. Spending the winter at Okkak for Jonathan meant living "among strangers, having no authority or pre-eminence," and he faced the possibility of being absent for a second winter on "an unknown shore" in Ungava Bay.[90] His travels had not previously extended to that area.

The expedition left Okkak on June 24, 1811, and stopped to visit Inuit families camped in several places along the coast north towards Killinek, meeting both Christian converts from the Okkak congregation and traditional Inuit along the way. Many Inuit were also travelling from place to place; the Moravian party encountered several boats from Nachvak and Killinek between Kangidlusuak and Okkak, two families from Killinek camped at Saglek, and a family from Saglek going to the Killinek area for the summer (see Map 6).[91] At Oppernavik, near the tip of the peninsula, they found Uttakiyok and his entourage from Ungava Bay waiting for their arrival.

Like Arnaujak, Uttakiyok was a trader from Ungava Bay. He had last been to Okkak in 1809, travelling from Killinek where he spent the winter. He had intended to return to Ungava Bay in the summer of 1810, but the illness of his son detained him. Hearing of this, the Okkak missionaries sent him a message asking him to guide their boat through the strait at Killinek and along the uncharted coast of Ungava Bay. Uttakiyok agreed to be their pilot and said that he would adopt Christianity if the Moravians went to live with his people and formed a settlement in his country.[92] "For this service Uttakiyok was eminently qualified," the missionaries later wrote:

> and without such a steady, faithful guide, we should have been wandering in the most painful and dangerous uncertainty in the desert regions to the West of Cape Chudleigh. . . . Among his countrymen he is well respected, on account of his superior sense, and skill in all Esquimaux arts, and possesses great influence among them.[93]

Uttakiyok told the missionaries that the island of Killinek and several small islands to the north called Tutsaets (or Tutjuat, "Stepping-stone

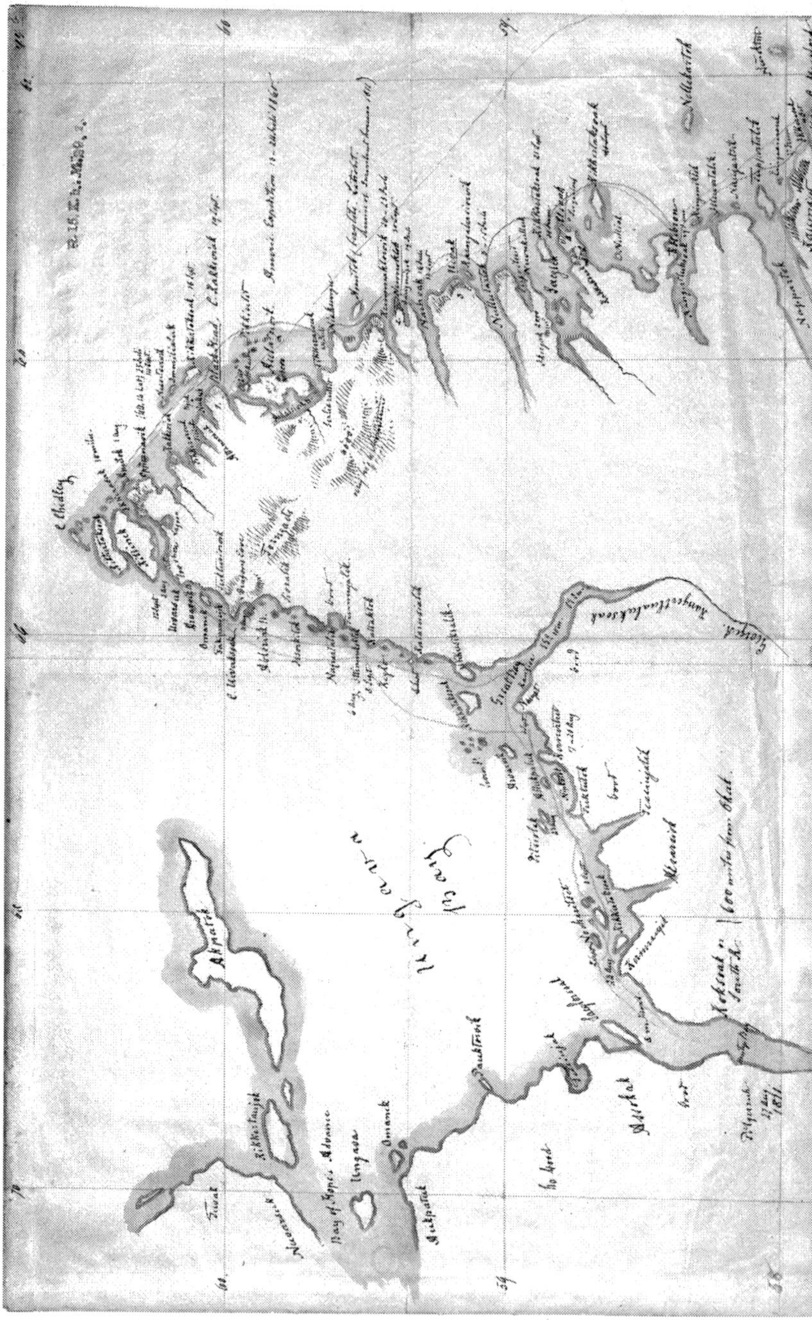


**MAP 6.** Place names and outline of the coast explored in 1811 by Kohlmeister and Kmoch from Okkak to the Koksoak River in Ungava Bay (1814) (Unity Archives, Herrnhut)

islands," later called the Button Islands[94]) were visible from Oppernavik. He stated that a large island called Igloarsuk and inhabited by many Inuit could be seen from the Tutsaets to the north-northeast; the Moravians assumed this place was Resolution Island in the eastern entrance to Hudson Strait.[95] Uttakiyok then named all the bays, points, and islands from Cape Kakkeviak to Killinek, which Kohlmeister noted on a sketch map.[96]

When the party sailed through the narrow strait between Killinek and the mainland and could see Ungava Bay for the first time, the Moravians were astonished by the contrast in the landscape. The low gentle hills replaced the high rocky terrain of the Labrador coast and the waters of Hudson Strait seemed calm compared to the turbulent Atlantic. Travelling southward, they overtook a family from Saglek who were going to their summer camp in a bay called Arvavik[97] and stopped to visit a camp on Omanek Island, where about 50 people from the Ungava area were staying.

Some of these Inuit were familiar to Kohlmeister and Kmoch because they had formerly lived in different places north of Okkak and had visited to trade, but "the rest were perfect strangers."[98] They told the missionaries they intended to return to the northern Labrador coast and "remain some time in that country, for the sake of trade."[99] The report further explained:

> Some of the Ungava people have come to Okkak, and carry on a trade between their countrymen and that place. They are a kind of middle men, bring fox and bear skins, and exchange them for European goods. These they carry back, and sell at a very advanced price in the Ungava country. They spend two years on such a trading voyage.[100]

Most of the Inuit were described as "quite ignorant heathen, who never before seen a European" and closely scrutinized the missionaries' physique.[101]

Farther south at Uivaksoak, a cape forming the northern point of a deep bay called Abloviak, the Moravians could see a large island a very great distance to the west, which Uttakiyok told them was Akpatok. It was a prominent feature defining the Ungava region:

> They say, that it encloses the whole bay or gulf towards the sea, and consists of high land: also, that it is connected with the western continent at low water by an isthmus. The north coast of this island appears to be the line laid down in maps and charts as the coast of America, to the south of Hudson's Straits. But the district of Ungava is separated from the island by a very large bay, extending southward to the 58° N.L [north latitude]. North of Akpatok, the Esquimaux speak of islands well peopled by their countrymen, who have never seen Europeans.[102]

Uttakiyok informed Kohlmeister of the Inuit names for the major points, bays, and islands as the expedition proceeded along the eastern Ungava coast. About 140 miles south-southwest of Cape Chidley, they entered the estuary of a large river called Kangiqsualujjuaq. Reaching the river had been one of their major objectives, and they spent five days exploring the area. They had heard about this river from Inuit from Okkak and Nain who occasionally travelled far inland to hunt caribou and had described rivers flowing to the northwest and wooded slopes leading into the valley of this river.[103]

Uttakiyok advised the Moravians that game was very plentiful in the area during both summer and winter, and that many Inuit from different places would join them if they created a settlement there. A party of Inuit from Killinek subsequently arrived. They stated that they hunted in the vicinity every summer and would consider making a permanent move to live with the Moravians. As there was plenty of wood, fresh water, and a good harbour for a European ship, Kohlmeister and Kmoch decided that it was an ideal place for a mission station. They held a solemn ceremony claiming the territory for the King of England and the preferential right of the Moravians to create a settlement there. In a final act of symbolic possession, the missionaries announced a new name for the Kangiqsualujjuaq River, calling it George River in honour of King George III.[104]

Strong winds and poor weather delayed their progress southward, but 10 days later they entered the estuary of a river called Koksoak, which was the principal aim of their journey. The missionaries estimated that they were about 600 or 700 miles from Okkak and at approximately the same latitude as the mission station. Beyond the river, the coast veered west-northwest, making the estuary the most southerly point of the Ungava coast; Inuit called country to the west Assokak. The Labrador party first encountered residents of the area about six miles up the Koksoak at a camp with three tents. Fourteen families were there, including some people visiting from another campsite farther upstream who came from a distant region called Aiviktok and customarily spent the summer on the river.[105]

Uttakiyok's brother was with the Aiviktok people and had warned them of the impending arrival of Europeans. They were therefore not alarmed at seeing the Kallunât strangers (non-Inuit, people of European descent), but they were very curious. Most of the Inuit had never seen a European before and they examined the missionaries as if they were "a new species of animal."[106] However, the Moravians were well treated and an elderly Inuit man from Aiviktok told Kohlmeister that his name was often mentioned in his community.

Kohlmeister reported that Ungava Inuit were very apprehensive about contact with Innu, who were said to approach the coast frequently in the vicinity of the Kangiqsualujjuaq and Koksoak rivers from the interior and from Hudson Bay. Encounters between the two Indigenous groups were apparently cautious and unpredictable; tokens of friendship were often exchanged but misunderstandings occasionally ended in bloodshed. Inuit described Innu as "a more nimble and active race" and expressed uncertainty about meeting them.[107] The missionaries found several abandoned Innu campsites along the banks of the river but they did not meet any people.[108]

Inuit told the Moravians that the best hunting area in the whole country was located around the Koksoak River. Families from different places congregated there every summer and frequently extended their stay over the winter. However, they added that they were "prevented from making this place their constant residence by their fear of the land-Indians, which cause them to quit it sooner than they otherwise would wish to do."[109] Nevertheless, most of the group, including five families from Aiviktok, said they intended to remain in the area for the winter.

Kohlmeister and Kmoch found a suitable place for a mission station in a small bay surrounded by low forested hills about 24 miles up the Koksoak River. They decided against continuing their explorations along the western Ungava coast because Uttakiyok informed them that the region lacked woods, had no large rivers like the Kangiqsualujjuaq or Koksoak where a European ship could safely approach the land, and probably had no residents at that time of year, as Inuit would have all gone into the interior to hunt caribou.[110] Near the mouth of the Koksoak, the missionaries held a ceremony similar to the one on the Kangiqsualujjuaq River, claiming possession of the territory and bestowing a new name, South River, on the Koksoak.[111]

Since it was early September and weather conditions were deteriorating, the expedition quickly retraced its journey along the coast back to Okkak. On their way back, they found traces of sod houses at Komaktorvik. Earlier in the voyage, they had also seen ruins of houses on a small island called Amittok, northwest of Komaktorvik. The Moravians reported that Inuit believed these structures to be those of Greenland Inuit:

> The Esquimaux have a tradition, that the Greenlanders came originally from Canada, and settled on the outermost islands of this coast [Labrador], but never penetrated into the country, before they were driven eastward to Greenland. This report gains some credit, from the state in which the above-mentioned ruins were found. They consist in remains of walls and graves, with a low stone enclosure round the tomb, covered with a slab of the same material. They have been discovered on islands near Nain, and though sparingly, all along the whole eastern coast, but we saw none in Ungava bay.[112]

The missionaries had no scruples about robbing wooden utensils from old Inuit graves at Oppernavik to burn as cooking fuel, remarking that wood decayed very slowly on the coast.[113]

The expedition returned safely to Okkak on October 4, 1811, receiving a rousing welcome from the mission's annual supply ship in the harbour. Kmoch was instructed to proceed immediately to England. He took his journal, along with extracts from Kohlmeister's diary, to report on the voyage to the Society for the Furtherance of the Gospel (SFG), the Moravian committee overseeing the Labrador mission. These documents were translated into English and a precise map was drawn based on Kohlmeister's nautical calculations and the sketch of the coast made during their voyage. The SFG secretary, Benjamin LaTrobe, edited the documents and completed an account of the voyage in February 1812.[114] This report was published in 1814 and copies of it, as well as the map of the region, were sold to the public. The account drew attention to the economic potential of the Ungava region, and many, including officers of the Hudson's Bay Company, read it with great interest.

CHAPTER TWO

# The Moravian Mission and the Hudson's Bay Company, 1814–1842

## Impact of Moravian Trip to Ungava

Kohlmeister and Kmoch's report about their trip to Ungava Bay impacted many people, including Inuit of the region. After the Moravians returned from their expedition, a rumour spread among Ungava Inuit in 1812 that the missionaries were planning to create a settlement in their area. The next summer, many Inuit from as far as Igloarsuk made the journey to the Koksoak River, expecting to meet the missionaries. The Inuit communication network was obviously effective, and Inuit sought direct contact with Europeans who were a source of desired trade goods.

The Moravian Mission learned of this gathering from Ungava Inuit who later travelled to the Labrador coast. Two men, Atsugarsuk and Aveinek, had left the Koksoak River the previous spring and spent the early winter at Nachvak before arriving at Okkak in the winter of 1815. As Kohlmeister informed the SFG's secretary in a letter dated August 1815, they stated that:

> During the summer of 1813, twenty-one boats full of people, with their goods, had arrived in the Koksoak, anxiously waiting for our return. They spent the winter partly on the banks of that river, partly in its neighbourhood. In the spring of 1814, about the time these two men were preparing to depart, [an]other thirteen

> boats arrived, and more were expected, under a certain persuasion that they should meet us there.[1]

Among the group was the expedition's pilot, Uttakiyok, who had waited for the arrival of the Moravians on the outer islands to guide them into the bay. He was also determined to travel by boat to Okkak in the summer of 1815 if they failed to return.

The Ungava envoys reported that 20 of the boats arriving at Koksoak came from the immediate area. Many of the vessels were very large but the largest came from "the Island of Igluarsuk [Igloarsuk], which lies right before Cape Walsingham, in the entrance of Hudson's bay." According to their account:

> It was full of people, several of them old men and women, who had never seen a tree grow and were exceedingly astonished when they saw a wood for the first time. They construct their boats and implements of drift-wood, which now and then reaches their coast. They report that the said island has a great many inhabitants, and that, for want of wood, many of the old grey-headed people there had never been in possession of a kayak. From Cape Walsingham, they have half a day's sail to some smaller islands, called by them Tutsaets, and again, a long day's voyage with a favourable wind to the great island of Igluarsuk [Igloarsuk]. They live on the south side, and have never seen a ship; but say, that on its northern coasts many Esquimaux have their dwellings, whom they sometimes meet, when they go far into the country, to hunt raindeer [caribou]. From these people they had heard, "that in summer ships are sometimes seen at a great distance out to sea."[2]

The two Ungava emissaries also stated that even the Innu, who called Europeans "Appasimik," apparently expected the Moravians to return and "had made many friendly signs from off the hills, pointing towards the sea, and signifying, that they would be visited from that quarter."[3]

Kohlmeister calculated that nearly 300 Inuit, based on an average of 20 people in a regular boat and 30 in a large one, were waiting for the Moravians to return on the Koksoak.[4] Kohlmeister concluded that "the Ungava country is not so destitute of inhabitants, as one might be led to suppose." He offered to make another voyage to the Ungava region to bring the Gospel to "those poor people."[5]

Kohlmeister and Kmoch's 1814 report also alerted the Hudson's Bay Company (HBC) to the economic potential of the Ungava region. The British Crown had granted a charter in 1670 that gave the Company a monopoly on trade and the exclusive possession of "Rupert's Land," defined as the drainage basin of Hudson's Bay and Hudson Strait, including Ungava Bay. By the early 1800s, the HBC had established trading posts throughout the subarctic region, centred around James Bay. Its governing board had long desired an expansion of trade into the northern and interior areas of the Ungava Peninsula, but the region was unknown and difficult to access.[6] Kohlmeister and Kmoch's expedition served to clarify the HBC's rights by revealing that Ungava Bay could be entered through Hudson Strait and by describing its coastal geography.[7] Their map was the only source of exact knowledge on the outline of the coast for about 60 years,[8] and it ultimately opened Ungava Bay to European exploitation. However, the HBC was slow to act. It launched several exploratory journeys northwest from James Bay, but Company officials were not convinced that the Ungava region could support a profitable fur trade.[9]

Kmoch and Kohlmeister's report proclaimed the Moravian Mission's interest in Ungava Bay, but the missionaries also did not take immediate action. Since 1791, when the Moravians had first proposed a northern expedition, the Society for the Furtherance of the Gospel knew that the HBC might prevent the Mission's plans for trade and a mission station in the vicinity of Hudson Strait. Although the SFG decided in 1812 to proceed with creating a settlement in Ungava Bay, they recognized that they needed HBC consent, as the region formed part of Rupert's Land. No concrete plans were made for a community because the Napoleonic Wars

JOURNAL

OF A VOYAGE FROM

OKKAK,

ON THE COAST OF LABRADOR,

TO

UNGAVA BAY,

WESTWARD OF CAPE CHUDLEIGH;

UNDERTAKEN

*To explore the Coast, and visit the* ESQUIMAUX *in that unknown Region.*

BY

BENJAMIN KOHLMEISTER, AND GEORGE KMOCH,

MISSIONARIES OF THE CHURCH OF THE

*UNITAS FRATRUM or* UNITED BRETHREN.

London:

Printed by W. M'Dowall, Pemberton Row, Gough Square, Fleet Street,

FOR THE BRETHREN'S SOCIETY FOR THE FURTHERANCE OF THE GOSPEL AMONG THE HEATHEN.

AND SOLD BY J. LE FEBVRE, 2, CHAPEL-PLACE, NEVILS-COURT, FETTER-LANE;
L. B. SEELEY, 169, FLEET-STREET; HAZARD AND BINNS, BATH;
AND T. BULGIN, AND T. LAMBE, BRISTOL.

1814.

Title page of Kohlmeister and Koch's 1814 report

continued to disrupt transportation and communication in Europe. Finally, in 1815, the SFG secretary met with Lord Selkirk of the Hudson's Bay Company in London to ask permission to establish a mission station in Ungava. Selkirk was supportive of the Moravian interest in spreading the Gospel, but when he heard that the missionaries would also run a trading post at the station, he refused to grant them permission.[10]

## Hard Times and a Growing Congregation at Okkak

The SFG decided instead to build a new community north of the existing mission stations on the Labrador coast. Many felt that this was a more practical alternative, as Kohlmeister and Kmoch had seen only a small Inuit population along the eastern coast of Ungava Bay. The missionaries had many reasons for establishing a northern station, but the rapidly growing Inuit congregation at Okkak was the main incentive.

In the 1810s and 1820s, Inuit moved to Okkak in large numbers, mainly due to a changing climate, a shortage of game from European overexploitation, and epidemic disease. After 1811, climatic conditions along the Labrador coast deteriorated significantly as the Little Ice Age (*c.* 1450–1850) peaked in the North Atlantic. The sea ice formed earlier than normal in the fall, and heavy snowfalls and severe cold persisted during the winter. The land-fast ice was slow to break up in spring and extensive accumulations of drifting pack ice developed in the summer. These conditions had an immediate effect on Inuit hunting activities, particularly for sea mammals such as whales and seals, which were a primary source of food for both people and dogs and provided staple trade commodities in the form of baleen and blubber.

The whale populations had also diminished due to overharvesting by European and American whalers, who had exploited the bowhead whale and walrus stocks in the Davis Strait and Labrador Sea since the late sixteenth century.[11] Moravian reports indicate that the number of whales captured or sighted along the entire Labrador coast declined significantly in the early nineteenth century. The greatest reduction took place in the vicinity of Okkak and in the northern fiords, which had been the best whale hunting areas in the late eighteenth century; the last successful capture of a whale was reported at Nachvak in 1821.[12] Inuit associated with all three mission stations experienced hunger from a scarcity of game and Inuit residing in remote northern areas were likely severely affected by the failure of whale hunting.[13] With the disappearance of the whales, Inuit needed to focus on other species, especially seals, caribou, and fish. New hunting technology provided by European traders and missionaries, such as nets and guns, offered Inuit easier and more efficient harvesting techniques.

Christian converts had two advantages over unbaptized Inuit during food shortages: they had access to better seal harvests from using the Mission's nets in peak periods of seal migrations, and they could appeal to Mission charity. Although other social dynamics were likely happening as well, the missionaries noticed in their early experience with Inuit that people expressed a greater concern about their spiritual state when they faced economic challenges.[14] Okkak missionaries remarked in 1819 that the "rough, wild and proud heathens" were becoming more

**Okkak, 1800 (Unity Archives, Herrnhut)**

responsive to adopting Christianity.[15] After a widespread famine left families destitute in the winter of 1822–23, 59 Inuit joined the Okkak congregation in 1823 and another 23 people moved from Kangidlusuak to Okkak in 1824.[16] Severe famine was again reported north of Okkak in the winters of 1825 and 1826, and about 30 more "new people" had settled at Okkak or outside the station by 1828.[17]

Epidemic disease also plagued northern Inuit in the 1820s. In a rare reference to Inuit from Ungava, Okkak missionaries reported learning in 1826 that "a great mortality" had occurred a year earlier at the Koksoak River:

> Three boats full of people (ten at an average being reckoned to a boat) were taken ill and died. The rest of the inhabitants immediately fled from the place, that is, all those who were not already seized, and could still escape. Whoever was taken ill at night, was dead in the morning; we were told, that all the sick crept into one tent, and there breathed their last. Their bodies lay unburied, and were devoured by dogs. . . . Several of those who escaped, came hither, but they all intended to return to that country.[18]

Disease was also becoming a major cause of death at Okkak, where 10 adults and four children died from "a violent cold in the head, cough and pleurisy" between April and July 1824; the same illness led to the death of several Inuit in the north.[19]

By the end of 1829, almost four times as many Inuit were wintering at the mission stations compared to the early 1800s, and the largest community was Okkak with 391 inhabitants.[20] The significant size of the Okkak population prompted the Moravian Mission to establish a new northern community. The missionaries searched for a suitable site north of Okkak where Inuit were known to be numerous and a ship could easily approach the coast.[21] In August 1814, Kohlmeister, Okkak missionary Stuermann, and Captain Fraser of the *Harmony* had briefly surveyed three bays north of Okkak. They discovered numerous winter house ruins at Saglek, Kangidlusuak, and Napâttuk, indicating that these places had been inhabited by a large Inuit population and were productive hunting areas. The largest concentration of ruins was located on a small flat island inside the mouth of Saglek Bay, which was evidently the core of the area because its place name was also Saglek. This site was:

> [t]he actual dwelling place of the Inuit . . . their winter houses are standing, but [we] found no humans here. But we found many collapsed winter houses, mostly built from whale bones, which are covered with sod. Generally, in the area around the houses, everything is covered with whale bones, which attests to the previous frequent catching of whales, carried out by the Inuit here. For the place was heavily inhabited, because among the 13 or 14 old collapsed houses, we found ca. 3 that are inhabitable.[22]

The number of house ruins at Saglek and the other two sites indicated that the resident population in the area had recently declined. Kohlmeister noted that Inuit had not lived at Kangidlusuak for a year "since a good part have moved to Okkak and the rest to other areas," and Napâttuk had been deserted a few years earlier when several families had moved to Nain.[23] The party recommended Saglek to the SFG as the best site for a mission station, although ultimately the Mission decided to create the station about 95 kilometres north of Okkak at Kangidlusuak.[24]

## Hebron (1830–31)

The new Moravian community was established in 1830–31 and was called Hebron. The deep and wide fiord at Kangidlusuak was rich in marine life, including seals, beluga whales, and char, and caribou could often be found in late fall and early winter just west of Hebron.[25] The missionaries hoped that some Okkak residents, especially those who customarily fished and hunted in the Kangidlusuak area, would relocate to the new station.[26] Within two years, 72 Inuit moved from Okkak and formed the nucleus of the permanent Hebron population. More

**Drawing of Hebron mission station in 1864 (Carl Linder, copied by L.T. Reichel in 1866, Unity Archives, Herrnhut)**

people from Okkak were interested in settling at Hebron but the missionaries discouraged them because they hoped instead to attract new converts from the northern trading parties to adopt Hebron as a main trading centre.[27]

Aside from reducing the population of Okkak, the creation of Hebron did not alter the economic status of the Labrador Mission. The shift of both baptized and northern Inuit to Hebron simply meant that trade revenues were transferred principally from Okkak to the new station. Nevertheless, Moravian officials assumed that the proximity of Hebron would ultimately stimulate more trade relations with northern Inuit, just as the Mission's trade had expanded when the middleman role was eliminated in earlier periods.[28] They had not anticipated, however, the opening of an

HBC trade post on the Koksoak River in the same year as Hebron was established, nor did they foresee its effect on commercial transactions as well as on the distribution of Inuit in the northern coastal region.

## The Rise and Fall of the Hudson's Bay Company in Ungava, 1830–1842

Kmoch and Kohlmeister's 1814 report had piqued the Hudson's Bay Company's interest in the Ungava region. Based on this new information, the HBC governor, George Simpson, was determined to expand trading posts into the Quebec–Labrador Peninsula, despite concerns about the viability of the fur trade in Ungava Bay.[29] Simpson was anxious that the Moravians might become trade competitors and he pushed the Company to establish an HBC presence in the region before any other traders arrived.[30] On his orders, a group of HBC traders and Indigenous guides travelled in 1830 from James Bay overland to the Koksoak River in Ungava Bay. There they built a post called Fort Chimo and commenced trade with the Inuit and Innu hunters of the region.

The HBC Fort Chimo post at Kuujjuaq intercepted many of the goods that Inuit had previously taken to Moravian stores on the Labrador coast.[31] Inuit residing at "Tayooyak Bay" (Tasiujak), 20 miles west of Kuujjuaq, no longer needed to make the two-year journey to reach Okkak. The HBC agent reported in 1835 that several Inuit acted as middleman traders with Inuit living farther west, possibly in the Richmond Gulf region of Hudson Bay. Three families also announced that they intended to cross Hudson Strait "to see their friends and pass the news among them" about the HBC desire for fox pelts.[32]

With the HBC post providing Inuit in Ungava Bay with access to European articles, trade expeditions to Okkak and Hebron decreased significantly. Ungava Inuit largely stayed away from the northern Labrador coast during the 1830s, partly because of new trading opportunities, but also because of frequent shortages of game due to consistently poor environmental conditions. Heavy drift ice both in spring and in late fall severely reduced seal harvests, especially from 1831–33 and from 1835–37 along the entire coast. During a famine extending as far as Cape Chidley in the winter of 1837, Hebron had few visits from northern Inuit, as they were said to have nothing to trade.[33]

Many Inuit were drawn to trade at the two HBC posts in Ungava Bay, thus reversing the movement from Ungava to the Labrador coast. Inuit from both eastern Ungava and northern Labrador could now choose between making a familiar journey to trade at Hebron or trying the novelty of the new store at the Koksoak River. Inuit had even greater options after 1838 when the HBC opened a second post in Ungava Bay called Fort Siveright on the George River (now called Kangiqsualujjuaq). According to Cooke, the HBC established this post with the specific intention of interfering with the Moravian Mission's trade.[34]

However, as the novelty wore off, the Hudson's Bay Company was not successful in securing all goods that Inuit produced in Ungava Bay. The Company had constant trouble in trying to supply its post at Fort Chimo (Kuujjuaq), and word would spread when the store had little to trade.[35] Inuit took advantage of the new competition and took their business elsewhere. In 1834, the agent at Fort Chimo complained that the Moravian traders could sell guns for less than the HBC, and suggested that the Company find a cheaper source of guns for its store.[36] Some Ungava Inuit decided to continue trading at Hebron because the Moravians offered them better prices for furs.[37] As HBC factor John McLean commented in 1838, Inuit of Ungava had been initially enthusiastic about the new traders in their midst, but when they saw little benefit from the HBC posts at Fort Chimo and George River, "they soon became indifferent about us, and proceeded to the Moravian settlement with the produce of their hunts, where they obtained their little wants at a far cheaper rate than our tariff allowed."[38] The Moravian traders were also said to spread rumours about the poor quality of HBC goods, which HBC staff vehemently denied.[39] McLean's frustration with the Moravians was evident:

> [Inuit traders] admit that our Goods are cheaper, but say that the Brethren represent them to be of inferior quality. Now this is false;

> our goods are in every respect equal to theirs. I know not whether the propagation of falsehood be consistent with the propagation of Christianity according to the Moravian Creed. Be that as it may, such conduct does not accord with the profession of evangelical rectitude they publish in the World as the Rule of Life.[40]

Moravian missionaries at Hebron reported a number of Ungava Inuit visiting their station through the 1830s, including a man from Kangertluluaksoak [Kangiqsualujjuaq] who said that he preferred to travel to Hebron to trade than go to Fort Chimo, as the Kallunât in Ungava Bay "are hostile to Eskimos."[41] In 1838, the missionaries noted a "sledge-company" arriving from the Koksoak River to trade, but made no other references to visitors from the area.[42] Inuit living in the vicinity of George River (Kangiqsualujjuaq) also continued to trade at Hebron. An elderly man named Atataksoak arrived at the station in 1840 after an absence of two years; he and his people had spent the winter and summer hunting caribou in the interior.[43]

Similarly, Inuit residing at Killinek, on the peak of the Labrador Peninsula, traded at both the HBC posts in Ungava Bay and the Moravian store at Hebron. When Inuit from Saglek told the Hebron missionaries in February 1841 that many Inuit at Killinek had died from a disease arising from trade at Fort Chimo, the missionaries were quick to share the report with the Mission's supporters in their *Periodical Accounts*:

> It was supposed, that the infection had been communicated by means of old clothes, which they had received in barter from the Europeans on the Koksoak river. Akkusanna, a man well known to us, had fled from the pestilence to Saglek; but the people there, afraid of taking the infection from him, had compelled him to return again to the north.[44]

Many Killinek Inuit were said to have died in the epidemic,[45] but starvation rather than disease was the cause of extreme hardship for Inuit living around the Koksoak River and George River in the early 1840s.[46]

Caribou were scarce from October 1840 until February 1841, when large herds finally appeared in the region. The following winter, a quarrel between Koksoak Inuit and a group farther west was reported to have caused the death of five or six people.[47]

Moravian reports from 1830 to 1842 indicate that parties of northern Inuit continued to trade at Hebron. The majority originated from settlements on the far northern Labrador coast. The most regular visitors were Inuit living at Saglek, the closest site to the Hebron station, although people also arrived from Nulattatok, Nachvak, and Killinek or Cape Chidley. Although they appreciated their northern customers, Hebron missionaries were dismayed by their absolute lack of interest in conversion, stating "our northern visitors visit us only for the sake of trade, and seem to care nothing for the gospel."[48] Very few people decided to become converts; those who did were mainly elderly or individuals who had difficulty supporting themselves.[49]

In 1842, the Hudson's Bay Company decided to close its two posts in Ungava Bay because they were unprofitable.[50] In its 12 years of trading in the region, the Company had failed to convince Inuit and Innu hunters to bring them large quantities of furs and other products. Several factors likely contributed to the slow business, including low wildlife populations, dangerous travel conditions, competition from the Moravian traders in Labrador, the Inuit desire to preserve their lifestyle, and their minimal need for European goods.[51] Fort Siveright at Kangiqsualujjuaq closed in 1842, and trading at Fort Chimo at Kuujjuaq ceased in 1843.[52] The Company shifted its focus instead to Hamilton Inlet in central Labrador, where it established posts at North West River and Rigolet.[53]

CHAPTER THREE

# Inuit Interactions with the Moravian Mission, 1842–1863

## Impact of HBC Closures in Ungava Bay

After the Hudson's Bay Company closed its posts in Ungava Bay in 1842, Inuit from the region began returning en masse to trade on the Labrador coast. Hebron missionaries reported an unusual number of visitors arriving during the winter and spring of 1843, amounting to about 39 Kamutet, which included several Inuit arriving from the Koksoak River around Easter.[1] They noted the presence of three Kamutet with 13 people "from the far side of our district," referring to the Abloviak Fiord area in northeastern Ungava Bay, in January 1844.[2] A party of 52 people, followed by another group of 13, arrived from the George River area in February 1845, and another 19 Kamutet from unspecified locations reached the Moravian community to trade by the end of the winter.[3]

Hebron missionaries reported that the journey from George River took about 10 days and that Inuit often spent a few weeks at Saglek before returning home. Inuit from Ungava were conspicuously prosperous:

> To judge by their clothing and appearance, as well as by the articles they brought for barter, they would seem to be in comparative affluence. They likewise gave us to understand, that their neighbourhood is much more populous than ours.[4]

Described as comparatively affluent, the Ungava people were evidently better off than Inuit on the Labrador coast. As the missionaries feared, they had no material reason for wanting to stay at Hebron to become Christian converts. A group visiting the station in 1844, for instance, stated that "they would never be converted, because our land was not so rich in reindeer [caribou] as their own."[5] Apparently the migration pattern of caribou had shifted, causing the species to be more abundant in the Ungava region than in northern Labrador, where at the same time sea mammals were also scarce. In March 1845, Okkak missionaries observed that "all land animals seem this year to have vanished, and our hunters constantly return with empty pouches, declaring that every living thing – hares, foxes, partridges – have all died out."[6] Caribou were also reported to be very scarce at Hebron.[7]

Descriptions of the wealth and size of the Inuit population in Ungava Bay served to rekindle the interest of the Moravian agency in London, the Society for the Furtherance of the Gospel, especially after the HBC closed its trade posts. In 1845, the SFG instructed Hebron missionaries to travel overland following the route taken by trading parties and make another survey of the region.[8] Missionary Jonathan Mentzel responded to their request by explaining that such a trip would be impractical. In his view, a European could not endure the hardships and privations of a six-week winter journey in freezing temperatures, with a risk of starvation if the party was caught for any length of time by snowstorms. In addition, he believed the journey would not be worthwhile because very few Inuit would be found in the Ungava region during late winter. Mentzel gave this outline of Inuit seasonal activities:

> The Esquimaux are a wandering tribe; in summer, they are engaged in the reindeer hunt, often till the month of October. In November and December, they are usually occupying their winter habitations. In January, they not unfrequently set out to bring their wares to this place, on which occasions they travel with their wives and families. From this place they proceed to Nachvak

> or Saglek, where they remain till the end of April, and where we occasionally visit them. They are said to put up mere snowhouses, for dwellings, in the Ungava district. Last year some of them told me that they should not visit us this winter, as they wished to spend it in their own country, for the sake of catching foxes, but in two years we should see them again.[9]

Mentzel added that Hebron missionaries had preached to the Ungava Inuit while they were present on the Labrador coast so a visit to the region could not accomplish anything more.[10] His comments ended discussion on the matter.

Inuit living permanently on the northern Labrador coast were not as fortunate as people in Ungava Bay at the time; they were often hungry and had little or nothing to barter for goods at the Moravian stores. Adverse ice conditions continued to reduce seal harvests periodically after 1838, and their economic condition progressively worsened through the 1840s. Many Inuit living at Saglek were driven by hunger in late April 1840 to ask Hebron converts for food, since those at Hebron had ample supplies of seal and caribou.[11] In the summer of 1841, only one Inuit party walked from Saglek to trade at Hebron, "the fishing in the north having turned out so badly that they have little to barter."[12] Killinek Inuit lost all their dogs after game was scarce between 1842 and 1844, so three men had to walk in order to trade at Hebron in January 1844, dragging their goods on a polar bear skin for nearly 200 miles.[13]

Due to the difficult conditions, the Inuit population living north of Hebron declined in the 1830s, as Jonathan Mentzel described in a letter written in 1840:

> It would appear as if the coast immediately to the northward of us were becoming more and more bare of inhabitants. Fifteen years ago, there were, at least, 300 Esquimaux living at Nachvak. Two years ago, none were found there, and last winter, only one winter-house was to be met with. Last summer [1839], two boats' companies left those parts, for the Ungava country, where

> Europeans have settled, with whom they are inclined to traffic. They speak, however, of coming back again. We are much concerned at their tendency to emigration, as it threatens to frustrate one main object of our establishing ourselves at this place.[14]

Mentzel added in August 1841 that 20 to 30 people at most inhabited the two winter houses at Nachvak and that the number of Kamutet arriving at Hebron to trade had fallen from an average of eight or 10 to only four the previous winter, with three Kamutet originating from Saglek.[15] Three winter houses and an illuvigak were occupied at Saglek in March 1841, making the population there larger than at Nachvak.[16]

In the winter of 1847, Ungava Inuit trading parties visited Hebron, bringing with them news of famine in their region. Several Kamutet, including 50 Inuit, arrived from Ungava, Koksoak, and Kangiqsualujjuaq in February.[17] The group from Ungava occupied four Kamutet and expected to be away from their home for a year. Jonathan Mentzel observed, "since the Europeans [the HBC traders] have quitted the shores of the bay, these people are more disposed to frequent this place."[18] Hebron missionaries heard about the consequences of a recent famine:

> They brought the distressing intelligence, that a number of Esquimaux, about forty in all, had died of hunger beyond Koksoak, in the course of last autumn, and that one man had killed and eaten his wife and several children. His mother, for whom he was meditating a similar fate, had escaped just in time. But he perished at length, of famine, like the rest. One man with his two wives and children were the only survivors in the whole district; they had witnessed the whole scene, and were now amongst our visitors. But though the more distant do not shew such an obstinate aversion to the Gospel as those who live nearer to us, their visit gave us little hope of seeing any of them come to settle here . . . .[19]

After completing their commercial transactions, the Ungava Inuit went to Saglek, where they planned to remain until departing on their homeward journey in late April. However, a scarcity of food led three families to return to Hebron in the middle of March; baptized Inuit readily provided them with hospitality but later complained when some of their guests began practising "their heathen conjurations."[20]

### Nangmayo

One member of the Ungava party remained at Hebron when the others departed. Nangmayo was a tall and robust elderly woman who died at the mission station several years later. The missionaries at Hebron described her as follows:

> At her own special request, she was left here, and found a home in the family of our late brother, the well-known native assistant, Renatus, who faithfully cared for her, till her death. Her language was very different from that of the people here, and she even had difficulty in making herself understood by the Northlanders. She probably did not comprehend much of what was said to her here, particularly respecting the salvation of her soul. The Northlanders stated, that she came from a country, which lay opposite to theirs, and which was called Iglorarsuk [Igloarsuk]. They further said, that this region could be approached from their country in boats, that ships came there every year to catch whales, and that there were many people there.[21]

This is the only reference in the Moravian accounts examined here to an Inuk from Igloarsuk on the Labrador coast. It further suggests that contact between Inuit from Igloarsuk and Ungava Bay continued well into the nineteenth century. The account also indicates that the dialect spoken by the different populations was an obstacle but did not prevent communication, and that guests were treated well by neighbouring groups.

Nangmayo apparently never became a Christian convert, as her name was not listed as a candidate for baptism nor was the date of her death recorded in the Hebron Church Book. Recalling memories of her in 1860, Hebron missionaries thought that she may have originated from

Northumberland Inlet,[22] which was an early place name for Cumberland Sound, located on the eastern coast of Baffin Island. A British whaling ship visited the region for the first time in 1840 and Captain Parker of the vessel *True Love* visited in 1846 and 1847. Parker reported that the bay was "inhabited by a tribe of Esquimaux, in numbers exceeding 2000," and that all the people were suffering from a widespread famine which caused many deaths.[23] Nangmayo may therefore have been a member, or the survivor, of a party that left southern Baffin Island in search of food in Ungava Bay.

## Saglek: Inuit Independence

Trade expeditions from Ungava Bay usually stopped at Saglek to rest from their journey across the Labrador Peninsula. Saglek had the largest Inuit population north of Hebron in 1844; missionaries visiting the village in March counted 64 people occupying three houses.[24] The permanent Inuit inhabitants of the area had winter houses on Saglek (Rose) Island and Upernavik Island in the mouth of the deep fiord, and they hunted game year-round in the local area. Fish, seals, and other marine mammals abound in the region during seasonal migrations and at the sina (the edge of the sea ice). Bounded by mountains on either side, the two arms of Saglek Fiord reach 53 km inland into the caribou calving grounds.[25] The rich resources of the Saglek Bay region supported local Inuit residents; they were hostile to pressure from missionaries to adopt Christianity and to relocate to the nearby Hebron mission station. Moravians described them in 1847 as showing a greater "obstinate aversion to the Gospel" than other groups with which they had regular contact.

The independence asserted by Saglek Inuit was primarily due to the authority of the community leader, a man named Joas, whose winter house was distinguished from others in 1841 by a floor boarded with narrow planks.[26] Joas's parents had been converts at Okkak, where he was baptized as a child, but they had subsequently renounced their faith and moved to Saglek. Kohlmeister and Kmoch met Joas there in 1811 and urged him to rejoin the congregation; he resisted, claiming that his mother "kept him back," although he added that "he still intended to be converted."[27]

Thirty years later Hebron missionaries continued to appeal to Joas, as a decision by the chief of a community was customarily followed by all the families in the group. But Joas remained opposed to conversion.[28] One missionary describes how Joas urged his followers to stay faithful to traditional Inuit beliefs by telling them, "If you abide by the customs of your fathers, your souls will continue in this country after death, and want for nothing."[29] His son, Kangaktanak, became the leader of the group in 1841, but he apparently lacked his father's authority, as several families defected from the community soon after.

Inuit living at Saglek could most readily compare their living conditions with those of the converts at Hebron, who could access the social support services provided by the Moravian Mission. The strain of persistent poverty likely led two families to leave Saglek between 1840 and 1842 to join the mission congregation, and several others announced that they intended to move soon.[30] As Joas told the missionaries, he continued to "defend the customs of his forefathers," but his death in February 1847 prompted the erosion of the Saglek people's determination to resist adopting Christianity.[31] Immediately after he died, one of his wives moved with her two children to Hebron.[32] Kangaktanak remained at Saglek, affirming that he had promised never to become a convert.[33]

People's economic condition influenced their attitude towards conversion, as the situation at Kangidlusuak in the 1820s and other instances demonstrated. Food was scarce at Saglek in the winter of 1847 and was likely to be scarce again the following winter, because seal harvests were small all along the coast in late fall due to drift ice blocking the usual harp seal migration route.[34] Two Hebron missionaries visited Saglek in mid-February 1848 to invite Inuit to join the congregation. They were given a cool reception, but their efforts evidently did have an influence on the community. About a week later, two men from Saglek arrived at Hebron and informed the missionaries that several families wanted to move to the mission station. They asked for help with transportation, as they had few dogs of their own; several Kamutet quickly departed and brought back two groups of 16 people each.[35] The remaining inhabitants

**Saglek fiord, 1932 (The Rooms Provincial Archives)**

promised to follow by boat after the sea ice cleared in late spring; another 39 people arrived on July 13th, making a total of 71 emigrants from Saglek. In addition, a family of eight people relocated from their home north of Saglek and two widows from Koksoak decided to remain at Hebron.[36]

With these moves, the population of the mission station suddenly increased by 81, raising the size of the congregation from 248 to 329 members. Hebron missionaries were elated, not only because an impressive number of new converts had finally joined their station, but also because they had gained control of a rich resource area that they had coveted before Hebron was established.[37] They triumphantly proclaimed this new order in the *Periodical Accounts*: "You will rejoice with us when you hear that Saglek is no longer a heathen settlement.... Saglek is now a fishing place for our people, nor are any heathen allowed to reside there."[38] The area had been included in the original Moravian land grant for Hebron but the missionaries did not previously have any means to prevent unconverted Inuit from inhabiting the region.

The older generations, often "the least accessible to the preaching of the Gospel," had yielded to the will of Saglek's younger generations in settling at Hebron, according to Mentzel: "Of many we know, that they would not have thought of removing hither, had they not been compelled to follow their children, in order to secure the means of subsistence."[39] According to the missionaries, the young people believed that residence at Hebron and the adoption of Christianity offered them an opportunity for a better life than continuing at their traditional place.

Two families who were living at Saglek but "did not properly belong to it," according to Mentzel, preferred to remain unbaptized so they moved to Nachvak.[40] With a resident population no longer living at Saglek, Nachvak became the major centre for traditional Inuit living closest to Hebron. People also lived at other places along the coast north of the mission station, but the total population remained relatively small. Visitors at Hebron in January 1850 reported that about 120 Inuit lived along the coast as far as Killinek, with about 30 to 40 people residing at Nachvak.[41]

Inuit at Nachvak displayed a strong independence from the Moravian Mission. "The people from Nachvak now opposed the truth the most," lamented a missionary in 1858:

> One man said, that they knew the same things of their Torngak, which we told about our Jesus, as the former had recalled to life not a few angekoks who were quite dead, etc. . . . He then remarked that some of our people were in their conduct little better than himself and his companions. . . . Upon this, the man cut the conversation short, by saying, laughingly, that they had heard enough of such matters, and would like to see some of our European articles.[42]

Many traditional Inuit expressed "the old spirit of opposition and contempt of all that is holy."[43] One group of northern Inuit traders offended the missionaries when, "on conversing with them about their souls, we

Saglek Bay (courtesy of Maria Merkuratsuk)

were greatly pained by the levity of two of the number, who turned all we said into ridicule."[44] Even those who were open to Christianity could clearly see that moving to the mission station was not ideal; they explained "the impracticability of their settling here, on account of the difficulty of getting a living."[45]

Every year a few more Inuit joined the Hebron congregation. In February 1848, a family consisting of three people who had been living at Komaktorvik, a bay north of Nachvak, asked to stay at the station, and nine other people living farther north said they were considering a move to Hebron.[46] Poverty seemed to be the main factor prompting Inuit to settle at the station, but the missionaries were satisfied with this motive. As Mentzel remarked, "Though some should be driven to us merely by the impulse of hunger, we will not the less cheerfully receive them, nor will we despair of their conversion. The ways of the Lord are not as our ways."[47]

## Ungava Visitors and Resistance to Moving to Labrador

After 1848, most people visiting Hebron to trade originated from Ungava Bay. Inuit living in the vicinity of George River were regular guests, usually arriving at the station during the winter months, while expeditions from places further west appeared every second year or so.[48] According to the Hebron missionaries' records, the number of people travelling from distant areas increased after 1850, and many of these Inuit had not been to the mission station before.

Among the 130 visitors at Hebron in January 1850 were several groups who had travelled from "Hudson's Straits," likely referring to the northwestern coast of the Ungava Peninsula. The Inuit visitors charmed the missionaries, who stated that "their childlike, simple and confident manners, could not fail to gain our attention."[49] Okkak Inuit were equally fascinated by the group when several Kamutet arrived to visit the station and the resident missionaries tried to induce people to remain in Labrador. They described the response of one man in the station diary: "He attentively listened to all [our] speeches and often repeated to himself what was said. But to leave his land and exchange the well-being of his body with that of his soul, <u>that</u> was impossible for him at present."[50] The visitors told the missionaries they would not leave their country because game was more plentiful than in Labrador, but they would become converts if a teacher were sent to live with them.[51]

Okkak missionaries believed the Ungava Inuit had already been in contact with Europeans because they were "not altogether ignorant of the Word of God."[52] The Wesleyan Methodist Missionary Society had established a mission in 1840 at the HBC's Moose Factory post in James Bay, which had been in operation since 1673.[53] Inuit living along the northeastern coast of Hudson Bay traded at the post and likely met a minister there. In December 1852, the Bishop of Rupert's Land (comprising the area under the HBC Charter) asked the SFG in London for copies of the Scriptures in Inuktitut to assist ministers in preaching to Inuit populations living west of Labrador.[54] An Anglican ministry first began in 1852 at Fort George, another HBC post in James Bay, and was extended to Little Whale River on the northeastern Hudson Bay coast in 1879.[55]

The Moravian Mission's hopes for a Moravian station in Ungava endured. In February 1851, William Kennedy, the former HBC agent at George River, had a meeting with the SFG Committee in London and suggested that the facilities remaining at the site were sufficient to form a mission community. He also advised them that the HBC board might respond more favourably to a Moravian proposal for opening a station since the HBC had abandoned its post. The SFG raised the topic with HBC board's secretary, who informed them that further discussions would depend on the views of the HBC governor.[56] Once again, the SFG asked Hebron missionaries to visit the area. Jonathan Mentzel gave a similar response to their request in 1845, arguing that Inuit at Kangiqsualujjuaq dispersed in the winter and that the journey would be too difficult for the missionaries to undertake.[57] The small population in the area hardly justified the effort of a journey or the expense of creating a mission station there, he argued, but the SFG persisted with its interest in having a foothold in Ungava Bay.

Meanwhile, Ungava Inuit continued to travel to Hebron to trade, and shared stories of difficult times. After a harsh winter in 1852, about 50 people visited the station to trade in the spring and summer once economic conditions had improved. From them, Hebron missionaries learned that Killinek was the only place where people had a supply of food and that several people had died from starvation, as well as from murder and abandonment. In one incident, a daughter was the only survivor of a family who had starved to death. Another case involved an old grey-headed man named Akkorluk, who was the father of one of the two families that had refused to join the Saglek Inuit departing for Hebron in 1848 and had instead moved farther north. As a result of the famine:

> [He] returned to Saglek, in the hope of supporting himself by fishing in the river, which last winter abounded in trout. On his way, he abandoned his wife and child, who were unable to proceed on their journey, their feet having been frost-bitten. This man, named Akkorluk, sent us a message in spring, that he would come to us and be converted. He did indeed spend about two days here, having accompanied other Esquimaux, but without any desire after spiritual instruction. He then resolved to return

> to the north in search of his wife and child, in case they should still be living.[58]

The following year, at the end of March 1853, a company of Ungava Inuit arrived at Hebron. They travelled on seven Kamutet with 50 people, "many of whom had never seen a European before,"[59] which suggests that the group originated from the far northwestern area of the Ungava Peninsula. Jonathan Mentzel discussed the possibility of visiting them at their own homes, as he had been informed that the western region could be reached by crossing the sea ice, although the route was unreliable due to the strong current.[60] The Ungava Inuit assured Mentzel that the journey was impossible for a European and also not worthwhile because "they wander about from one place to another, in quest of the means of subsistence, and live in snow-huts."[61]

Beginning in 1855, parties of Inuit from Ungava Bay began appearing at Hebron every year. Although the frequency of the expeditions increased, they often comprised fewer than 100 people. This pattern suggests that different communities were alternating their visits, with groups from some places arriving one year and from other places the next, while keeping to the two-year interval between the long journeys. Travelling to Hebron in this way would have ensured a constant supply of European articles in the region, which no doubt previously became scarce in the year between expeditions. It perhaps also provided a surplus of trade goods that Inuit could barter at a profit with communities farther west. The greater frequency of the expeditions implied a higher demand for European merchandise that could only be obtained from the Moravian store at Hebron.

This explanation would also account for comments by the Moravian missionaries that some of their guests had never seen Europeans or visited the mission station. One of the Ungava Inuit at Hebron in February 1860 had not returned to trade there for 16 years but nevertheless accurately recollected many details from the Scriptures that had been described to him in a five-hour lecture by a missionary. The discussion evidently made a strong impression on the man, who, much to the missionaries' amazement, did not wear any amulets "or other articles of a superstitious character" and asked them for further instruction.[62]

Other Ungava Inuit, however, did not share his interest in religious matters. Despite having given many sermons over the years, Hebron missionaries were dismayed by the single-minded attitude of Ungava Inuit who visited their station "as usual, only to trade, not to hear the Gospel."[63]

> Some of the heathen from the Ungava and Kangiva districts found their way hither from Saglek, but their minds were so full of their superstitious practices and sorcery, that it was difficult to gain their attention, for anything said to them concerning Christ and His salvation. As soon as they had procured the articles they wanted, they hurried back, some of them declaring that the Torngak was angry with them for listening what was told them of Jesus. "We want presents," said some of them; "of Jesus we do not want to hear."[64]

Only in extreme circumstances would people remain at Hebron or Saglek after the trade expeditions departed for Ungava Bay, and they often rejoined their companions as soon as possible. An exceptionally severe famine along the entire Labrador coast during the winter of 1856 prompted 14 Ungava Inuit to stay at Hebron because they were afraid of dying from starvation if they attempted to travel across the peninsula. One family, consisting of seven people, went to Saglek in April and died there.[65] The following year, in 1857, fewer than 60 Inuit in the trade party reached Hebron; they had halted their journey the year before at Kangivak, near George River, as their provisions were low, and they had spent the summer hunting there.[66]

The Moravian missionaries strived in vain to urge Inuit from Ungava to remain at Hebron and adopt Christianity, but people always "repeated their usual excuse, that they could not leave the land which they inhabit."[67] Reflecting on their consistent resistance to abandon their homes, a Hebron missionary made this observation in 1864: "What Bishop

Spangenberg said of the Indians of North America holds true of these heathen Esquimaux: 'It is harder for a native to leave his country than for a king to depart from his kingdom.'"[68] Even when the Moravians gave assistance to desperate people, as they did on several occasions, the visitors would not remain at the mission station longer than necessary. In 1865, Hebron missionaries gave food to a widow with three children in a half-starved condition who asked to stay in the community, but "as soon as the woman regained her strength, she left us to return to her heathen countrymen."[69]

Ungava Inuit had a sound economic reason for not wanting to stay on the Labrador coast and become Christian converts. As the Hebron missionaries reported in 1857:

> The Northlanders will not hear of coming to live at this place, because they will not leave their homes, where they meet with reindeer [caribou] in abundance, and appear, on the whole, to suffer from want of provisions less frequently than the Esquimaux in this neighbourhood. On the contrary, they say if teachers came to them, they would soon be converted.[70]

This attitude, and perhaps also the independence of the Ungava Inuit, impressed Hebron missionaries. In the Moravians' view, the Ungava Inuit were good-tempered, orderly, and friendly people, "and by no means such importunate beggars as those who live nearer to us, in the neighbourhood of Killinek and Saglek, usually are."[71]

## Ungava Inuit Who Stayed in Labrador

Only five references have been found to people from Ungava Bay who chose to live permanently at a mission station on the Labrador coast in the 1800s. Two men and one woman became members of the Okkak congregation, and two women joined the Hebron congregation. Of the five people, Boas was the most prominent individual; he served as a chapel servant at Okkak for 39 years until his death in 1867 and was called "angojokavut" (meaning "our leader") by Inuit in the community.[72]

Boas was an orphan when he arrived at Okkak from Ungava Bay in 1812. Originally named Mammak, he became a baptismal candidate in 1814. When he was baptized in 1818, he was given the name Boaz (Boas).[73] He remembered seeing Kohlmeister and Kmoch during their visit to Ungava Bay in 1811 and described surviving a famine in his early childhood.[74] Br. Reichel wrote about Boas with great respect when he met him in 1861:

> Boaz is undoubtedly the most influential man of his nation, whence he bears the title Angajokavut, our chief. He was born at Ungava Bay, where some of his heathen relatives still live. He . . . has raised himself by his talents and exertions to the position he now holds. He is fifty-six years of age, and a head taller than the rest of his people. He assists in holding meetings for the children, as does Frederick, the second assistant.[75]

The missionaries further stated that Boas "paid but little attention to the praise or blame of men" and "from early years he was diligent and skillful in all Esquimaux pursuits. Consequently, he never suffered want."[76] At the time of his death in 1867, Boas was one of the few Inuit who owned a seal net, and he was well off.[77] His Ungava ancestry was reflected in his stature, and his lineage was traced in the Okkak Church Book until 1918, when all his descendants died in the Spanish influenza epidemic.

Boas is reported to have raised Levi, who apparently travelled with him from Kangivak on his journey to Okkak. Levi also became a chapel servant, and this description was made of him in 1876: "He has generally orphans or poor dependants in his large house, for whom he cares: during the summer he fishes in order to have a supply of food, when the time of scarcity comes on in May."[78] Levi's lineage has not been traced in the Okkak Church Book; his descendants may also have perished during the influenza epidemic.

The third individual at Okkak was a woman named Clementina, who, at her death on October 9, 1885, was the oldest person in the community. This description was made of her: "Clementina was at least seventy-four

**Saglek Bay (courtesy of Maria Merkuratsuk)**

years old, for she knew that she was born at Koksoak in the Ungava District, when Br. Kmoch was visiting the heathen there. That was in 1811. When grown up she came to Okkak and was baptized in 1828."[79] Clementina's lineage was traced in the Okkak Church Book to the fourth generation (i.e., great-great grandchildren, born as late as the 1930s) and her descendants are represented in the Tuglavina and Kojak families.

Of two widows reported to have stayed at Hebron in 1848,[80] one woman was named Kaunak, who was baptized in 1852 and called Tabea. Her lineage was traced in the Hebron Church Book to the fourth generation, and it appears that her descendants died either in the influenza epidemic of 1918 or from other causes. More research will be needed to confirm Tabea's family history as well as to identify the other widow.

## Shipwreck Stories and the Moravian Mission's Interest in Ungava Bay

The Moravian Mission often made use of stories about non-Christian Inuit to justify to the SFG and to their benefactors the "civilizing" efforts in Labrador and their continuing interest in expanding into Ungava Bay. One story about a shipwreck of British sailors served the Mission's purpose especially well by illustrating murderous Inuit behaviour towards

Kallunât. In early November 1859, five shipwrecked British seamen were rescued by Inuit near Okkak and brought to the mission station. They had been part of the crew of the *Kitty*, an HBC ship carrying supplies from England to York Factory in southern Hudson Bay, when their vessel was heavily damaged by violent winds and drift ice in late August near the Middle Savage Islands in Hudson Strait. As the ship foundered, it was approached by six Inuit in Kajait; the British survivors described the encounter as follows:

> They were savage beings, who had evidently never been in contact with civilized people before, and were quite unacquainted with bread, gunpowder, etc. Their clothing was, however, in pattern, like that of our Esquimaux. They endeavoured to obtain some pieces of iron in exchange for articles of clothing, and, not satisfied with that, tried to appropriate everything that was not made fast. As soon as any one of them had secured something which he coveted, he licked it and concealed it under his fur jacket, with gestures which seemed to forbid its requisition.[81]

The crew were terrified and decided to abandon the ship; Captain Ellis and 10 sailors boarded a large longboat while the first mate, Mr. Armstrong, and four sailors boarded a smaller boat.

After the *Kitty* sank, the crew agreed to leave the site and steer for York Factory, but the two boats were separated in a snowstorm. Armstrong's party recognized that they would unlikely make the long journey to the HBC post in a small boat, so they decided to head for the coast of Labrador, aiming for a place marked on their map north of Okkak Bay called Port Manvers, which they thought was a French trading station. They sailed for 63 days until they were sighted by a group of Okkak Inuit at a sealing camp. Initially, the emaciated and half-frozen seamen were very apprehensive about approaching the Inuit group, but their attitude relaxed as they were well cared for and fed. The Inuit families then transported them to Okkak where the missionaries gave them medical treatment. Two sailors remained at the station until the following summer, when they returned to England on the mission's ship, *Harmony*, while Armstrong and the other two seamen left during the winter and travelled to the south coast looking for a ship to take them back to Britain.[82]

Over the next two years, missionaries at Hebron learned about the fate of Captain Ellis and the missing crew members from visiting Inuit traders. In January 1860, a party of 30 northern Inuit arrived at Hebron, the men wearing European clothes and seeming "not a little proud of their dress."[83] Apparently they had found the clothing on an island and the Moravians assumed the articles had belonged to Ellis's party.[84] In February 1862, a man named Serpalo arrived with a trading party from Ungava Bay carrying a number of printed pamphlets that he had found in a box washed ashore near Akpatok Island and now offered for sale at a high price. The material consisted of missionary accounts and scores for religious music, which the Moravian missionaries subsequently discovered had been sent by the Anglican Church to ministers working at HBC posts. They told Serpalo that the pamphlets had no value but offered a gift in exchange for bringing them such a distance.[85]

Serpalo also described the murder of two groups of Europeans in northwestern Ungava Bay. One case involved a group of nine men who landed in a boat near Orkok in the autumn of 1859. According to his account:

> The Esquimaux received them kindly, and provided them with food for several months; but as they did not part with everything they had saved in exchange for food, and their blankets proved special objects of attraction, they conceived the murderous plan of killing them with their spears, and of seizing all they possessed. The spot where this foul act was perpetrated is, according to the description given, about a day's journey to the north of Ungava. We believe them to have been part of the crew of the *Kitty*.[86]

Serpalo told the Hebron missionaries that three men named Pagiuk, Kaunaluk, and Kammatouk had taken the men away by force and were responsible for killing them, but the Moravians thought that most of the people residing at Orkok were involved in the crime.[87]

When Serpalo began altering details of his story, Hebron missionaries began to think he was afraid of being accused as an accomplice in the murders and of being punished by Europeans. He specifically asked the missionaries to mention his name in their report to Europe so that he and his family would not be penalized.[88] The missionaries asked other Inuit in the trading party about the incident. They corroborated his account and further stated that Kammatouk had since died, which they considered as punishment for his evil deed. They also added, "If the Kablunaet (Europeans) had come to them, they would have afforded them shelter, protection, and assistance, that they might have reached their country people, as they were more used to Europeans, as well as better instructed."[89] Their kind attitude towards Europeans was demonstrated by one family living near Cape Prince of Wales who cared for a surviving sailor with badly frozen feet; the man died of his wounds the following spring. This additional detail was related in an account of the incident by a meteorological observer who was stationed in the area in 1884. F.F. Payne was also told by the son of the man who sheltered the sailor that the crew's guns, as well as blankets, were sought by the three Inuit men committing the homicide, and that one man was fatally shot during the fray.[90]

A second case of murder reported to the Hebron missionaries concerned a large ship, possibly an American whaler, that had anchored off the coast north of Orkok. According to the Inuit visitors:

> Here they appear to have traded with the Esquimaux, and, unconscious of any evil design, to have left their ship, and followed them on shore, where they were surprised, and killed with spears like the former company. The ship, whose masts were long after seen above the water, they no doubt scuttled; but to clear themselves of the suspicion of having been guilty of this crime, they declare that a sea monster had taken hold of the ship, and drawn it down to the bottom of the sea.[91]

Evidently the entire ship's crew was murdered because the Inuit stated that the number of people involved "was twice as many as a man's fingers and toes, i.e. 40."[92] The people who had committed the massacre described details of the incident to Inuit living at Ungava when they arrived at their settlement wanting to barter European clothing. The Ungava Inuit were curious about the origins of this clothing because they knew that these people did not have any contact with Europeans.[93] The Hebron missionaries closed their report with this remark about Inuit from Ungava:

> And we beg to observe, that most of the heathen who come to us from Kangiva, Koksoak, and Ungava are traders, who exchange goods which they obtain from our store, for articles which [they] receive from those Esquimaux that live at a still greater distance.[94]

In making this statement, the missionaries may have sought to dispel any notion that the Inuit families with whom they had contact were in any way like the people who had committed the atrocities, but they also defined the unique role of their visitors in a notable way.

Once reports of these murders reached Europe, they became the sensation of newspapers and revived the interest of Moravian officials in extending Christianity to the inhabitants of Ungava Bay. In March 1863, the Moravian Mission Board in Germany formally sanctioned an SFG application to the HBC Board for permission to establish a mission station in its territory. The Moravian Board also approved an expedition to explore the Ungava region and asked the SFG to determine if any of the Labrador missionaries would be willing to live in "such an isolated spot among heathen barbarians."[95]

CHAPTER FOUR

# Trade Competition and Expansion, 1863–1898

## Moravian Trade and Evangelism

The Moravian Mission continued to dream of extending its reach farther north and northwest. In 1863, the Society for the Furtherance of the Gospel asked the Hudson's Bay Company for permission to establish a station in Ungava Bay. The HBC Board responded that it would not concede any of its exclusive trading rights in the region.[1] However, two years later, the HBC Board offered a startling counter-proposal by offering to buy the entire Moravian trade operation on the Labrador coast.[2] The proposal provoked extensive discussion within the Mission.

Debate about the Moravian Mission's involvement in trade had been simmering for years. The combination of trade and evangelism had posed an ethical dilemma for the missionaries when the Labrador mission was founded in the 1770s, but they had rationalized the situation by arguing that trade attracted potential converts and subsidized the expenses of its stations.[3] By the 1860s, however, the trade operation had become a divisive factor. Inuit were actively hostile towards the Mission's repressive trade and credit policies and independent traders and fishermen were providing Inuit with new imported goods and better prices for their produce. The competition for trade exacerbated Inuit debts and reduced the Mission's profits. As a result, trade had become a source of resentment and conflict for both the resident missionaries and Moravian Inuit.[4]

In 1861, Levin Reichel, a bishop of the Mission Board in Germany, visited the coastal stations to evaluate the Labrador mission. Reichel's findings shocked the organization. He argued that the Moravians' primary religious objective had been compromised by the SFG's barter trade and that the missionaries ran a de facto mercantile colony.[5] He recommended a complete reorientation of the Mission's economic and social affairs: the separation of trade functions from missionary work, and the training of Inuit as assistants in spiritual, educational, and commercial aspects of the Mission. Missionaries could then focus solely on spiritual matters without implicating their economic relationship with Inuit. Reichel suggested raising prices for furs, providing Inuit with equipment and more credit, and sharing more of the Mission's seal harvest.[6] He also believed that the Mission would only be successful if Inuit could eventually look after their own affairs without depending on the presence of European ministers.[7] As he said, "One must not forget that the purpose of the mission is to become, in time, dispensable. . . . In earlier times the mission was too much a colony, the brethren did everything themselves and kept the people in tutelage."[8] His recommendations were fully endorsed by the SFG, the Mission Board, and the missionaries based in the region. As a result, the SFG decided in 1865 to separate trade interests from missionary activities by appointing a trade superintendent and by employing men solely to work as storekeepers.[9]

Thus, a variety of trade reforms and other changes to the Labrador Mission were well underway when the HBC approached the Mission Board with an offer to take control of the Moravian trade operation in 1865. While German members of the Moravian Board were inclined to accept the offer, SFG officials wanted to retain control over the 90-year-old trade operation in northern Labrador. They argued that trade was vital to sustain the Mission and the HBC could not be compelled to support the social and economic goals of the Mission. The SFG recognized that serious problems occurred due to the Mission's involvement in trade, but its members believed that even greater difficulties would arise if it relinquished its trade operation.[10]

Labrador missionaries agreed with the SFG's position. Although some were uncomfortable with the Mission's involvement in bartering, they insisted that the trade operation provided Inuit with useful goods and the Mission with operating funds. To pay for its stations in Labrador, the Moravian Mission needed to make a profit from trade.[11] Samuel Weitz, a minister at Hebron, also believed that conducting trade was particularly important in establishing a relationship with northern Inuit. As he explained to the Mission's supporters,

> Our only aim in carrying on this trade is to benefit the poor Eskimoes, and raise funds for carrying on the missionary work to the glory of God: the trade forms a sort of outward bond of union between us and the natives, which is valuable, especially as long as God's Spirit has not wrought a spiritual union.[12]

Ultimately, the Mission's trade interests prevailed, and the HBC offer was rejected.[13]

## Competition for Inuit Trade Begins

The Hudson's Bay Company's offer to acquire the Moravian Mission's trading posts may have been prompted by the knowledge that its legal situation would soon change. Since 1670, the HBC had asserted land rights and a trade monopoly in Rupert's Land, a territory comprising the entire watershed draining into Hudson Bay and Hudson Strait, which included the Ungava District. But shortly after the Dominion of Canada was established in 1867, the HBC sold its territorial rights to Rupert's Land to the new nation. In exchange for £300,000, the Company relinquished its rights to both the land and its trade monopoly.

Moravian officials in London initially saw the transfer of land as another potential opportunity for the Mission in Ungava Bay. "Should this [transfer] take place, the Co. would doubtless remain in competition with us as a trading corporation. But its right to exclude other traders would cease. This might be of great bearing on the extension of our mission work in the north & north west."[14] With the dissolution of the HBC trade monopoly in Rupert's Land, the missionaries would be free to establish their own trading and mission posts in Ungava Bay. However, increased trade competition along the Labrador coast would soon prove to be a source of much anxiety for the Mission.

Once the Moravian Mission had declared its commercial priorities by refusing to sell its trade operation in 1865, the HBC doubled its efforts to attract Inuit business. The Company aimed to expand into the Labrador–Ungava region and started by purchasing other trade enterprises on the Labrador coast. For the first time, it competed aggressively with the Mission for access to furs and other resources produced by Inuit. The transfer of property to Canada eliminated the Company's monopoly on trade in Rupert's Land but also provided it with considerable capital resources to expand its enterprises.[15] In the Labrador–Ungava region, this resulted in the establishment of a series of new posts promoted by Donald Smith, chief factor of the Labrador District. Smith was keenly aware of the profitable trade that the Moravian Mission had with Inuit from Ungava Bay,[16] as well as at its stations on the northern Labrador coast, and he was determined to compete vigorously with the Moravians to increase the HBC's profits. Although Smith had once hoped to cooperate with the missionaries by encouraging them to establish a mission in Hamilton Inlet, he now saw their reluctance to give up trading as reason to treat them solely as competitors. "The 'United Brethren' on this Coast appear year after year to be more and more laying aside the character of Missionaries of the Gospel and assuming that of ordinary merchants or traders," he wrote in 1863.[17]

HBC traders had branched out into the fishery at their central Labrador posts at North West River and Rigolet, and they were eagerly eyeing potential cod, char, and salmon fisheries in Ungava Bay and northern Labrador.[18] Now equipped with boats powered by steam instead of sail, the Company could more easily access and supply posts along the coast.[19] As this chapter describes, the HBC launched its campaign in 1866 by reopening Fort Chimo at Kuujjuaq, after which it established a new outpost called Fort Lampson at Saglek in 1867, built another outpost at Nachvak in 1868, and reopened Fort Siveright at Kangiqsualujjuaq in 1869.[20]

**Fort Chimo (Kuujjuaq) on the shore of the Koksoak River, 1909 (McCord Stewart Museum)**

With the operation of these posts, Inuit from Ungava Bay once again stopped making long trading expeditions to the Labrador coast. While the Moravian stores had provided them with the goods they wanted, most preferred to trade closer to home. When the HBC trader arrived at Kuujjuaq in 1866, he was surprised to see Inuit with guns, ammunition, and cloth obtained from Mission posts in Labrador. They told him, however, that they were pleased that the Company had re-established a trading post in their own hunting grounds.[21] Large parties of Ungava Inuit would no longer be regular annual visitors at Hebron.

## Saglek

The Moravian Mission felt competition from traders all along the coast. After the mid-1850s, a growing number of non-Moravian traders and fishermen began appearing in the vicinity of the mission stations. The newcomers often took possession of good char fishing areas or sought to barter imported foods, liquor, and household articles for char and salmon caught by Inuit. The missionaries strongly resented this invasion of their domain by competing traders and harvesters. They also believed that the purchase of unessential goods, and especially the consumption of alcohol, would damage the economic, physical, and spiritual welfare of Inuit. However, they could not prohibit the fishermen's activities, as a clause in their land grants stipulated that they could not interfere with fisheries.[22]

Hebron missionaries were especially upset by the presence of traders in Napâttuk Bay and Saglek Bay. Napâttuk was the main source of timber for the Mission, while Saglek was a primary fishing area for Hebron Inuit as well as a customary place for northern Inuit.[23] Since more Inuit lived at Saglek than at Napâttuk, the missionaries were particularly concerned about retaining control of that bay and preventing traders from corrupting Inuit with "their evil communications."[24]

The Mission therefore decided to build an outstation "in order to retain a firm footing at Saglek, on account both of its importance to our people as a fishing-ground, and the advantage of holding it as a point of contact with the yet remaining heathen in the north."[25] With a base at Saglek, missionaries could more easily visit Hebron congregation members as they fished in the deep fiord during the summer, as well as have closer access to unconverted Inuit living in Nachvak.[26] Materials for a blockhouse were transported to Saglek in the spring of 1867. However, when two missionaries returned to the bay in early October to begin erecting the structure, they discovered that an HBC post had already been constructed there.[27]

Given the Mission's misgivings about independent traders, the sly way in which the HBC post was built in Saglek only heightened the missionaries' anxiety about newcomers threatening the established order of trade. Chief Factor Donald Smith had been on board the Company's steamship *Labrador* when it travelled north along the coast in August 1867 carrying building materials and supplies for the Saglek post. The ship had anchored at Hopedale, where the crew hired a pilot for Saglek, and at Hebron, where Smith had a cordial visit with the resident ministers. The missionaries believed that the ship was only transporting freight to Fort Chimo and did not suspect the real purpose of the voyage.[28]

Smith evidently did not intend to repeat the experience of the HBC posts on the Koksoak River and George River in the 1830s. At that time, Inuit had capitalized on the competition between the HBC posts and the Moravian station in Hebron by strategically deciding where to barter their furs and other produce. Having trading post options was an advantage to Inuit both financially and practically, but the competition had reduced profits for the HBC. Thirty years later, Smith wanted instead to ensure that the Company's posts succeeded by cutting off Inuit trade at Hebron.

The HBC achieved this objective by opening two outposts, the first at Saglek and the second at Nachvak. Both places were key terminals on Inuit travel routes to Hebron where goods destined for the mission station could best be intercepted. At Saglek, the HBC post was situated on the northern shore of the bay near a winter Kamutik trail leading north to Nulattatok, while the Moravian Mission outpost that was later built was located on Saglek (Rose) Island in the mouth of the bay, close to places where Inuit camped.[29] In August 1867, Smith reported preparations "for getting up a station near to the Moravian settlements where I think a profitable business may be expected to be done in course of a year or two and it will be a convenient halting place on the way to Ungava."[30] In addition to interfering with the Hebron trade, the HBC posts also disrupted its social program by having closer contact with Inuit in both fiords. Once their trade needs were met, northern Inuit would not likely travel to Hebron solely to hear the missionaries' religious sermons.

The social interactions between Inuit and HBC agents at Saglek likely contributed to the store's appeal. The HBC often staffed its posts throughout Labrador and Ungava with Labradorians of mixed ancestry who spoke Inuktitut fluently, including the Ford, Edmunds, Voisey, Lane, Lyall, and Saunders families.[31] The agent at its Lampson Post in Saglek, Solomon [Salomo] Lane, was "partially of English extraction," and his "Eskimo wife and two grown-up children" all spoke Inuktitut.[32]

Descendants of British men and Inuit women, these families often self-identified as socially distinct from Inuit, but with their linguistic abilities, local knowledge, and familial relations, they could exert a social influence on local Inuit that European missionaries could not.[33]

The HBC strategy was a brilliant manoeuvre that isolated Hebron and confounded the Moravian missionaries' complacent attitude about their relationship with both the Company and northern Inuit. Once again, the Mission had no recourse for expelling the intruders from Saglek. Although its land grant for Hebron encompassed Saglek Bay, the Mission only had a right to occupation of the territory and not possession.[34] With an HBC post at their doorstep, Hebron missionaries were convinced in 1869 that having independent traders at the mission stations "whose sole object would be to drive a paying trade, would be most injurious, if not fatal, to [their] missionary work."[35]

## Nachvak

Once Moravian missionaries realized that the HBC had beaten them to Saglek in 1867, they sought another location farther north to maintain their contact with northern Inuit. In February 1868, an Okkak missionary, Johann Schneider, was appointed to visit Inuit living at Nachvak and to make a preliminary survey of its prospects for a mission station.[36] Heading north, he held a service attended by about 40 people at Saglek and visited two groups of Inuit on his journey to Nachvak. One family group with 11 members occupied a winter house at Sorviluk, a bay located between Saglek and Nachvak.[37]

When he arrived at Nachvak, he found all the residents, consisting of 20 to 30 people, were living in "remarkably well constructed" snow houses (illuvigat) at a cove called Naksariktok.[38] This winter settlement was located on a headland, south of the mouth of the fiord and close to the open sea where hunters pursued seals. Nachvak fiord is long and narrow, framed by the Torngat Mountains on either side. Its waters were rich in seals, walrus, and other marine mammals, and the rivers that flowed into it provided good habitat for char.[39]

When Schneider asked the Nachvak Inuit whether they would like to have missionaries live with them, they informed him that Tuglavina was their chief (angajukKâk), and they would follow his decision on the matter. Tuglavina was away on a trip to Saglek, but Schneider believed that he would agree to having missionaries living among them. Tuglavina was not "a decided opponent of the truth," the missionary surmised, although he thought the leader clung to traditional customs because he was "afraid that if he became a Christian, he would lose his power."[40] Schneider found the same ambivalence towards Christianity at Sorviluk. While an elderly man there stated that he would like to live near the Moravians, his family expressed little interest in converting. His two adult sons told the missionary that they "liked their own country too well and have no desire to become Christians. They said that, if they were instructed, they would not be able to understand what was told them, as they were very ignorant."[41] This comment likely referred to their apprehension about learning how to read and write, which was a common fear among adults.

**Ships and a Kajak, Nachvak, August 1897 (Them Days Archive)**

At a general mission conference held at Nain in March 1868, the missionaries decided to leave the HBC in "undisputed possession" of Saglek Bay and to begin a new station at Nachvak, where the greatest number of unconverted Inuit were permanently settled.[42] Unless they leapt ahead of the HBC, the missionaries feared that northern Inuit "would be prevented from coming down to Hebron, if they could dispose of their skins and blubber at a trading station which they would pass on their way, and where they could obtain almost any article they might wish for."[43] The arrival of several small groups of northern Inuit at Hebron in March and April 1868 relieved the missionaries' fear of having all their trade taken by the Saglek HBC store,[44] but their trade losses were serious nonetheless.

Schneider's brief survey was followed by another visit by two Hebron missionaries, Samuel Weitz and Ernst Beyer. The two men travelled to Nachvak in early August 1868 to select a location for erecting a small house that would serve as an initial base for a mission station.[45] Finding a suitable site within the deep fiord proved to be more difficult than the missionaries expected. On the north shore, towering peaks block the sunlight while cliffs drop into the sea. On the south shore, however, the low-lying terrain is exposed to the bitterly cold north wind. The missionaries finally found an adequate place about 20 miles inside the fiord on the north shore, close to two inlets branching into the hinterland, where they began constructing a foundation for their house.[46] About 32 people were camped in six tents near the site; each tent included a married man who owned a Kajak and all of the families shared the use of a skin boat (umiak).[47] Weitz described the members of one family as a man named Panionayak, his wife, mother, crippled brother, and two children.[48] The other five tents in the encampment were likely composed of similar extended family households. Tuglavina was the group's leader, and his position was hereditary, "his father having been the chief of the tribe living in the Nachvak district, and probably also angekok or sorcerer, an office now devolving on the son."[49] Tuglavina listened to the missionaries' descriptions of their religion but he resolutely refused to "make use of the books," as Weitz explained, "meaning that he would not go to school, and learn to read."[50]

Leaving Beyer to complete the erection of their dwelling with the aid of several Hebron Inuit, Weitz sailed out of Nachvak and headed north to determine the number of Inuit living along the coast as far as Cape Chidley.[51] He had hoped to find a pilot among the Nachvak Inuit but left without one, stating that "none of them knew much of the coast to the north."[52] At a place called Attanarsuk, in the northern entrance of a strait separating the island of Aulatsivik from the mainland coast, Weitz met a prominent Inuk from the region and his family returning from a hunting expedition.

> We found a man and his wife with her infant in her hood at her back and two elder children sitting on a rock. They had just returned from a reindeer chase, all laden with fresh meat, even the dog not excepted, and were on their way home further down the coast. The stranger proved to be Kajuasiak, well known to us . . . a lively and active man.[53]

Kajuasiak directed him to the place where people were living.[54]

Weitz noted that the encampment consisted of about 21 people, the only inhabitants along the 60- or 70-mile coastline between Nachvak and Killinek. Kajuasiak's household at the site was the largest and included his three wives and six children. The other residents were his father-in-law, Auvek, with his two sons, and an Inuit evangelist from Hebron named Gottlob who, with his wife and daughter, had been living with northern Inuit since February. Weitz added that a family of nine people who had resided at Killinek had recently moved somewhere between Saglek and Nachvak.[55] Furthermore, some members of this family were reported to be living in Saglek, close to the HBC post, which Kajuasiak had also visited in the spring to barter his furs.[56] Auvek and his sons stated that after spending one more winter in the north, near Killinek, they would go south in the spring to be instructed by the Moravians. Kajuasiak refused to join his relatives at a mission station, saying he would not leave his country.[57]

Weitz returned to Nachvak in late August with the intention of remaining there for the winter with his wife, when an HBC vessel arrived and landed materials for a post close to his house.[58] Despite the limited means of communication in northern Labrador, the HBC was remarkably well-informed about the Mission's plans, doubtless from information obtained from its Saglek agent's conversations with Inuit. The speed with which the Company countered the Moravian move to Nachvak was essential to preserve its strategic advantage in intercepting northern Inuit at Saglek and elsewhere. HBC employees built a post at the junction of the two arms of the fiord, near an ice lead and an Inuit winter sod house (illusuat) settlement.[59]

With the appearance of the HBC post, Weitz abandoned the Nachvak outstation and suggested that Hebron missionaries could periodically visit the area by Kamutik during winter.[60] He recommended instead that Nulattatok Bay was a better site than Nachvak for a mission station.[61] The Moravian dwelling at Nachvak was deep within the fiord, he argued, and far from the region where Inuit spent most of the year hunting.[62] As Weitz explained in his German diary, Nachvak Inuit would not likely interrupt their subsistence activities to remain with the Mission; the Nulattatok Inuit could just as easily trade their goods at Saglek as at Nachvak, as the travel distance was similar.[63] In light of his comments, the missionaries did not regret abandoning their site at Nachvak, expecting that they would find a more appropriate location at Nulattatok.[64]

Immediately after Weitz returned to Hebron, he boarded the *Harmony* and went to Europe as the Labrador delegate to a General Synod at Herrnhut, Germany, in 1869.[65] His observations were undoubtedly instrumental in leading the Mission Board to endorse the creation of a new station at Nulattatok and may have also persuaded them to make a remarkable suggestion to the SFG. To avoid unpleasant rivalry with the HBC, the Board proposed that trade should not be conducted at the station. The response from the SFG Committee was categorical; its members unanimously rejected the policy as they argued that the Mission's interests would be harmed if it abandoned its trade.[66]

## New Hudson's Bay Company Posts

The Hudson's Bay Company seemed to be winning the trading competition with the Moravian Mission. Its two new posts at Saglek and Nachvak effectively drained trade from the Hebron store. "The whole winter no northerner visited here," a Hebron missionary complained in early 1869, "so that the plan of the Hudson's Bay Company to completely cut off northern heathens from us through both their trade stations . . . was unfortunately quite successful."[67] The report in the *Periodical Accounts* outlined the same problem: "Hitherto the heathen Eskimoes from the north brought their furs to Hebron, and heard the Gospel preached, now they come no farther south than the nearest trading station, where they dispose of their goods."[68] Without the need to trade at Hebron, unbaptized as well as Christian Inuit living in the northern fiords could avoid the missionaries' religious sermons if they wished.

Several families belonging to the Hebron congregation spent almost all their time living in Saglek and, although they promised that they would maintain contact with the mission station after the HBC post opened in 1867,[69] they did not do so. Christian Inuit living in Saglek were absent even for Christmas services in 1868, prompting the missionaries to complain, "These [Inuit] had already abundantly shewn that they preferred the irregular life which they can lead at that place, under the evil influences proceeding from the new trading-post, to the privileges obtainable at a mission station."[70] Some families did not visit Hebron for a whole year, while others made only one short visit.

In response, the missionaries sent an Inuk assistant, Philip, to Saglek in February 1869 to hold a service and determine if the people wished to continue as members of the Hebron congregation. Although some residents were absent when Philip arrived, the remaining inhabitants stated that they wished to retain a connection with the Mission. Philip was subsequently appointed to take charge of their spiritual welfare and keep school for their children.[71]

The missionaries blamed the HBC agents for contributing to the indifferent attitude of Saglek Inuit, as well as northern Inuit, towards

**View from Hudson's Bay Company post in Nachvak, 1884 (Library and Archives Canada)**

Christianity. Their reservations about the influence of the traders were reinforced by two incidents. During Easter 1869, the Saglek and Nachvak agents visited Hebron and the missionaries chastised the Saglek trader, Solomon Lane, for "very improper conduct towards a married woman" who was a member of their congregation.[72] Almost a year later, in March 1870, resident Inuit threatened the Nachvak agent with murder due to disagreements over trade dealings. A native evangelist named Daniel, who was living in Nachvak at the time, intervened and prevented an assault against the HBC agent, but the man was so frightened that he sought refuge with his colleague at Saglek.[73] To the missionaries, these events served to confirm that independent traders were incapable of maintaining a responsible relationship with Inuit, and that the Mission was needed for its moderating Christian influence in the region.

To the Hudson's Bay Company agents, however, the missionaries' attempts to convince Inuit to spend extended periods of time at the mission station conflicted with their trading interests. They saw this time as wasted opportunity and lost productivity, and consequently encouraged

Inuit to spend time instead on the land trapping for furs to trade.[74] Like the Moravian Mission, the Hudson's Bay Company desired loyalty from its clients and the two trading companies used persuasion, credit, and threats in their battle for Inuit business and allegiance.

## Inuit Evangelists in the North

One of the Mission's newest methods of persuasion, prompted by Bishop Reichel's 1862 report, was to engage Inuit as Moravian ambassadors.[75] Daniel, the man who had intervened in the assault on the HBC agent, was one of the first Moravian Inuit to assume the role of a Moravian evangelist. Daniel had arrived at Nachvak with his family in the spring of 1869 after spending over a year living with Inuit on the northeastern coast of Ungava Bay to encourage them to adopt Christianity. Originally from Hopedale, Daniel had offered his services in spreading the Gospel among northern Inuit at the 1867 general mission conference held at Nain. Another man named Gottlob, who was born in Nachvak and spent his adult life as a convert at Hebron, also volunteered for the task.[76]

Daniel and Gottlob were both upstanding Inuit leaders and devout Christians who served as Moravian evangelists and Inuit liaisons between unconverted Inuit and the Mission. In their home communities, they had served as leaders in the church, conducting religious services, holding school classes, resolving disputes, and generally monitoring the behaviour of congregation members. The men were known as native helpers or national helpers (National-Gehülfe), a position established by the Mission to give Inuit more responsibility in church affairs. Inuit assistants' duties were largely confined to the mission stations, although they also held services at seasonal camps.[77]

The role of evangelist offered Inuit leaders even more scope in influencing the changing Inuit society. As Hans Rollmann has argued, "Being Moravian was for many Labrador Inuit since the beginning of the nineteenth century an inseparable part of their personal identity and social self-definition and resulted in some indigenous missionary efforts by aboriginal Moravians to reach their fellow Inuit through evangelization and worship."[78] The missionaries recognized that Inuit were the best proponents of adopting Christianity among other Inuit, as they could speak with conviction of their personal experience and the benefits of converting to a new religious and social order.

Inuit evangelism also offered the Mission a way of conducting a survey of the northern region. The SFG had requested such surveys on numerous occasions, but the Labrador missionaries had always opposed the idea on the pretext that visiting the small transient population was impractical. The missionaries knew that they would not be able to endure the rigours of travel and the winter climate. However, when the Mission Board approved an expedition to the Ungava region in 1863 to investigate the possibility of extending the Mission in the northwest, the Labrador missionaries needed to take concrete action. They recognized that Inuit helpers possessed the expertise and experience necessary to make long and arduous journeys northward, and they likely encouraged their native assistants to volunteer for the task. According to the mission superintendent, however, Daniel proposed the endeavour independently.[79]

In volunteering to live among traditional Inuit, Daniel and Gottlob may have been influenced by stories about another Indigenous evangelist.[80] John King, a native of Suriname, helped the Moravian Mission spread the Gospel among peoples in his region of South America, and the missionaries shared his example with their congregations around the world.[81] As the first Inuit evangelists for the Labrador Moravian Mission, however, Daniel and Gottlob faced a challenging task. They had to prove themselves and the strength of their faith not only to the resident European missionaries but also to their fellow Inuit, especially those who continued to resist conversion.

With the aim of bringing Christianity to Inuit living as far as the Koksoak River in Ungava Bay, Daniel and Gottlob left Hebron with their families in late July 1867 on a 26-foot boat loaded with provisions, Kajait, a Kamutik, and several dogs.[82] Their report on the journey illustrates the interaction between Christian and traditional Inuit, and the ways in which Inuit incorporated both Christianity and traditional Inuit beliefs.[83]

Their first stop was at Silukpak in Saglek, a popular char fishing area. They asked Inuit there for a guide to take them along the far northern coast, and an unconverted man named Seneraluk agreed to join them with his family.[84] Continuing along the coast, the party did not meet any Inuit until mid-August when they landed at Attanarsuk, an isthmus near the peak of the Labrador Peninsula. Here they found two tents occupied by 13 members of the families of Siksiarsuk and his younger brother Kajuasiak, including four women (three of whom were Kajuasiak's wives) and seven children.[85] Daniel and Gottlob described the meeting:

> We were very glad to see them, and after speaking with them for some time, asked whether they would like to be taught or not. Thereupon Siksiarsuk thanked us and said: "Oh how good that is for me and for every one here, for I know in what you trust and also on what we rely; what we believe in is not unimportant, but what you trust in can alone make [one] happy." Some years ago he was the sole survivor of a party who died in consequence of eating reindeer meat, and he attributed his safety to the Lord Jesus. These people live at Ikorliarsuk, and treated us most kindly.[86]

Although Kajuasiak, called "the sorcerer" by the missionaries,[87] expressed no particular interest in the Moravian endeavour, Siksiarsuk decided to join the travelling party. He piloted them through the dangerous narrow strait between Killinek Island and the mainland and showed them where to stay on the Ungava coast during the winter. At the western end of the strait, they discovered that two family groups were occupying the area; Siksiarsuk had not expected to find anyone living in the strait and was apparently surprised to see Auvek's family there.[88] Auvek and the head of the second family, called "old Serkuak, the chief," were both elderly men.[89] After hearing the party's objective in travelling to the region, the two leaders welcomed the idea of having teachers to provide instruction to their families, but they clearly expected teachers to live with them rather than having to move to a mission community. As Serkuak stated, "Let them come and teach the young people and furnish them with powder and shot: we will not leave our own country, for there is no other like it."[90]

In early September, the party continued southwest to a bay called Taqpangajuk where they stayed for four days before proceeding to a place farther south with ample wood and game for settling during the winter. Here they were visited by Kajuasiak, who, despite their differences in religious beliefs, nevertheless helped the evangelists' families by providing them with food to supplement their diminishing supplies.[91] As Daniel wrote, "Kayuatsiak is also worthy of thanks because he helps us very much as far as physical needs are concerned."[92] When Kajuasiak's brother Siksiarsuk died from influenza in late September, Daniel and Gottlob moved to Kajuasiak's hut "since we despair of our life on account of hunger."[93] They described the camp as located "on the other side" of the land from the winter site they had chosen and as having a more reliable quantity of seals.[94] Soon after, another Inuk living in the area named Sokortai convinced Seneraluk and his family to leave the Labrador group; apparently he was displeased by Seneraluk's inclination to become a convert.[95]

It was not easy for Daniel and Gottlob's families to spend the winter months in Kangivak, as the coast between Killinek and Koksoak was called, and to live with Inuit to whom they were not related. The experience was especially difficult for Gottlob and his wife, who were both over 50 years old, and for their disabled daughter. After only a few months, Gottlob's family decided to return south, fearing the effects of the severe climate on their daughter's health. The family joined a trading party travelling to Hebron and arrived at the mission station in January 1868. While the missionaries were surprised by their early return, the information Gottlob gave them on the distribution of the northern Inuit population was very opportune in helping them decide on another location for an outpost after the HBC occupied Saglek. Based on his report that about 60 people lived at Nachvak and another 50 or more people were dispersed between Nachvak and Killinek, the missionaries Schneider, Beyer, and Weitz visited Nachvak in 1868.[96] After a brief stay at Hebron, Gottlob and his family resumed their evangelical mission by going to live with unbaptized Inuit north of Nachvak. They were welcome residents at a campsite occupied by Kajuasiak and Auvek at Attanarsuk when Weitz arrived there in August 1868.[97]

Daniel and his family continued to live in Kangivak, but they too faced many challenges. The family spent a second winter in the area, but their relationship with the local population deteriorated after August 1868. Accused of evil intentions, the family was constantly under surveillance and threatened with murder. Their alien religious devotions and the fact that they were strangers led Ungava Inuit to completely ostracize them.[98] As Daniel reported:

> In the land where we are now sojourning as strangers, we have to endure manifold afflictions. . . . We often pray in our house, even with tears, because we desire to be preserved amid the many temptations which surround us, and to cleave to our Lord Jesus. We also desire that the people among whom we dwell may become acquainted with our Saviour's love, and be freed from the bondage of their sorcerers and the service of Satan. But when we pray, they believe that we wish to kill some one of them. They have therefore come three times into our house, to make inquiry what we were doing. They said, "We come because the torngak (evil spirit) has commanded us to come. He says you design to make some one ill, and to bring about his death." When an old man was ill, they blamed us as having caused his sickness. We try to convince them that we did not come hither to do any person harm, but that we rather wish that they all should be saved from injury. But our words appear to have no effect. . . . We are now treated as hateful persons, and our names are dishonoured. . . . Because I do not take part in their heathenish practices and customs, we have many difficulties to contend with, and because I will not allow my children to join in their wicked play, I am disliked.[99]

Daniel also believed that four men wanted to kill him and then kidnap his wife, Josephine.[100]

Daniel and his family left Kangivak with a trading party in early January 1869 and travelled for 10 weeks, stopping frequently due to bad weather and to hunt for food before they finally reached Nachvak. The Ungava Inuit were originally destined for Hebron but, when they discovered an HBC post at Nachvak, they bartered for goods there and returned home, leaving Daniel's family to make their own way to the mission station. After describing their experiences to the missionaries, Daniel offered to go to Nachvak where Inuit had responded more positively to his presence; he was reluctant to return to Kangivak without a European missionary. The missionaries agreed with his proposal and suggested that he retrieve the boat he had left at Killinek during the summer.[101]

Like Gottlob, Daniel was determined to persevere in his efforts to encourage northern Inuit to become Christian converts, but he and his wife eventually chose to leave their isolated position in Nachvak society. In December 1869, Daniel wrote a letter to the Hebron missionaries stating that he could no longer preach to Inuit because he had joined in a traditional dance and his wife had committed adultery with the HBC agent. Both of them were sincerely penitent but their service at Nachvak was terminated.[102] Leaving the fiord to return to Hopedale, they stopped at Hebron in early March and reported that Nachvak Inuit had threatened to murder the HBC agent as well as Daniel because they blamed him for a scarcity of seals in the autumn.[103] Daniel eventually regained his stature as a respected leader in Hopedale, and in 1876 ministered among the settlers in the Hopedale region with another Inuit assistant, Titus.[104] Gottlob steadfastly persisted in acting as an evangelist among Inuit living north of Hebron, and he and his family were church leaders and teachers in the new station of Ramah.[105] The efforts of these first two Inuit evangelists later inspired other Inuit leaders to spread the Gospel in central Labrador.[106]

## A New Moravian Station: Ramah (1871)

After 1868, native assistants from the Hebron station periodically visited Inuit at Saglek,[107] but concrete plans for a new community at Nulattatok were not made until 1871. That summer, the missionaries landed at Nulattatok and chose a site to erect three blockhouses for a residence, store, and church.[108] They named the site Ramah and referred to it as the Jubilee station, as its establishment coincided with the 100th anniversary of the Labrador Mission.[109]

The house built in Nachvak three years earlier was dismantled and reconstructed at Nulattatok.[110] Located about 95 km north of Hebron, Ramah was situated on the north shore of a sheltered harbour close to the mouth of Nulattatok Bay. Open to sunshine due to a low range of hills surrounding it, Ramah's scenery was described by missionaries as tame and romantic compared to the formidable landscape of Nachvak.[111] Once Ramah was established, the Moravians had a secure base for reaching northern Inuit. Ramah replaced Hebron after 1871 as the primary com-

**Ramah mission buildings, 1906 (photo by Karl Filschke, Unity Archives, Herrnhut)**

munity visited by unbaptized Inuit, just as Hebron had earlier succeeded Okkak, although northern Inuit still occasionally went to the older stations to see relatives and friends. Two Inuit families living in Nulattatok, headed by Kaksungaut and Nochasak, became the mission's neighbours and were among its first candidates for baptism. As other Inuit joined them, the congregation of Ramah slowly grew.[112]

CHAPTER FIVE

# Many Names, Many Relations: Inuit Families North of Hebron, 1868

Between 1867 and 1871, officials from both the Moravian Mission and the Hudson's Bay Company made detailed records about Inuit who lived north of Hebron. Missionaries at Hebron, hoping to establish a new northern station, documented residents of the area, and traders at the new HBC posts at Saglek and Nachvak remarked on Inuit and their families in their journals. Based on these records, this chapter will reconstruct the distribution and kinship relationships of Inuit in the region during that time.[1]

To appreciate the kin relationships within the northern Inuit population of this period, it is useful to know something about Inuit naming practices. Traditionally, Inuit personal names are non-gendered and can be given to either male or female children.[2] Children are often named after other relatives, a practice that acts as a symbolic means of continuing the person's life beyond their death. As a Ramah missionary noted in 1897, Inuit customarily gave a newborn child "the name of the person, irrespective of sex, who was the last to die in the family."[3] The traditional practice of giving children a namesake, called "atitsiak" by Labrador Inuit and "saunik" by Ungava Inuit, is still followed by families today.[4] Inuit names therefore often reappear in multiple generations for either gender. Until the late 1800s and early 1900s, many Inuit in Labrador used only their personal names. If they joined a Moravian congregation and became baptized, Inuit adopted a Christian name.[5] On the recommendation of Moravian missionaries, families also began to adopt surnames after 1893.[6] The surnames that Avanimiut chose were often the names of prominent men in their families, such as Onalik, Tuglavina, Semigak, or Kajuasiak. This chapter describes the genealogies of families during the period just before they adopted surnames. In some cases, it therefore provides detailed portraits of the male leaders after whom their families were later named.

The Inuit population living north of Hebron in the winter of 1868 consisted of approximately 100 people, grouped into three major kinship groups headed by Serkuak, Tuglavina, and Kavanga. In the Killinek area, Serkuak and his extended family numbered 26 people. Another 13 of his relatives lived in the Tessiujaluk and Aulatsivik areas. In Nachvak fiord,

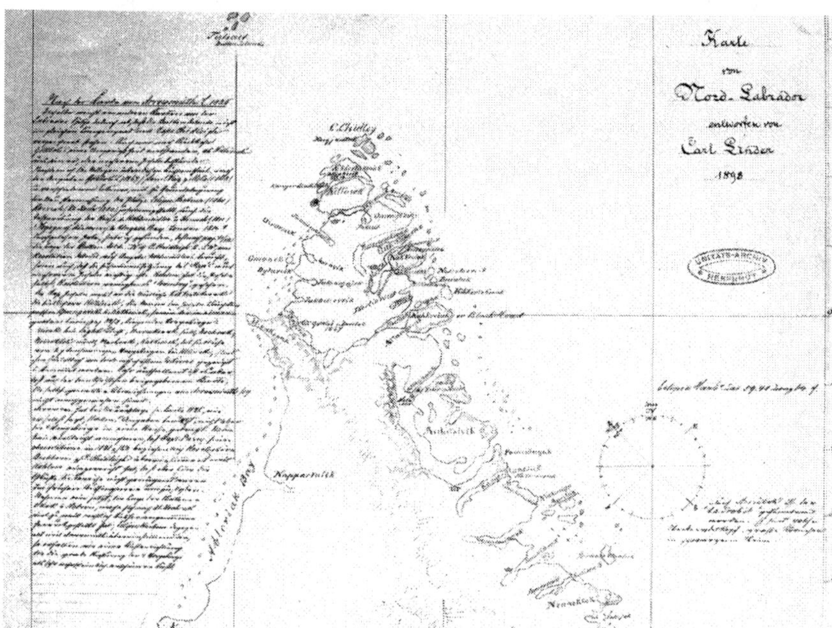


**MAP 7.** **Location of Inuit winter dwellings in northern Labrador identified by Gottlob and Daniel in 1868, and drawn by Carl Linder in 1898 (Unity Archives, Herrnhut)**

Tuglavina's family lived with other families in a community of 32 people. At Nulattatok Bay and Sorviluk, Kavanga led a group of 28 people (Table 2).

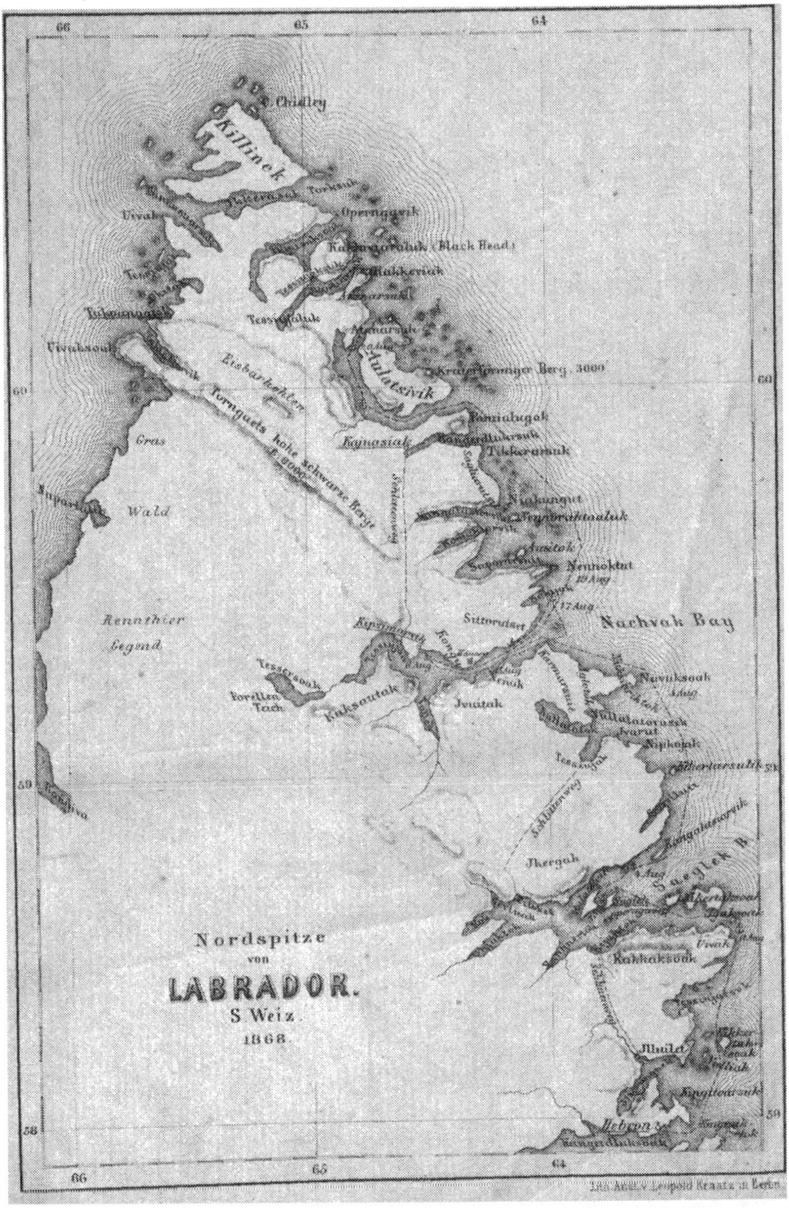


MAP 8. The northern extremity of Labrador drawn by S. Weitz in 1868 (in Packard 1891: 226)

**TABLE 2.** **Distribution and Composition of Inuit Family Groups North of Hebron, Winter 1868.**

| | | |
|---|---|---|
| **Killinek: total 26** | | |
| Auvek | 8 | son: Akpik<br>wife: Ujaratsiak<br>son: Arnasuk<br>son: Terrieniak<br>wife: Paingo<br>dau: Noggasak<br>son: Kingatsiak |
| Serkuak | 18 | wife (unnamed)<br>son: Kemmanek<br>wife: Okak<br>girl aged 12 years (unnamed)<br>son: Terriak<br>wife: Kajaluk<br>son: Komigak<br>son: Siniksit<br>son: Kasuk<br>wife: Safiale<br>Lorijak<br>female: Attataksoak<br>son: Nochak<br>wife: Akpajok |
| **Tessiujaluk/Aulatsivik: total 13** | | |
| Kajuatsiak | 10 | wife: Kingak<br>2nd wife (unnamed)<br>3rd wife: Aniortama<br>6 children (unnamed) |
| Koliligak | 3 | wife (unnamed)<br>child (unnamed) |
| **Nachvak: total 32** | | |
| Tuglavina | 5 | mother (unnamed)<br>wife: Pitsuratsuk (later called Sabina Tuglavina) ca. 1849–1923 (KCB)<br>daughter (unnamed)<br>son: Sekepa |
| | 2 | Tuglavina's younger brothers:<br>Paksaut<br>Semigak [Jr] |
| Semigak | 4 | wife: Nangmartvarsuk (later called Eugenia Semigak) b. 1855 (KCB)<br>son: Kudjaijok 1868–1905 (RCB; NHBC)<br>son: Anatsiak d. 1904 (NHBC) |

| | | |
|---|---|---|
| Paniunajok | 6 | mother (unnamed)<br>crippled brother: Tuglavina<br>wife: Makkijok<br>2 children (unnamed) |
| Nochasak | 9 | wife: Akusanna<br>son: Manek<br>son: Paungana<br>dau: Ikinek<br>dau: Itinguk<br>dau: Aninasuak<br>dau: Komigiak<br>young man: Koversak |
| Ikera | 3 | wife (unnamed)<br>son (?): Kudlo |
| Ikauja | 3 | wife: Sakkiarak<br>son: Ajaluk |
| | | Swansi (later called Matthew)<br>wife: Akkusane (later called Verone)<br>Paksaut<br>husband: Ajaluk |
| | | Kauksuk<br>Putak<br>Anautak<br>Apaluk<br>Okiuk |
| **Nulattatok/Sorviluk: total 28** | | |
| Kaksungaut | 7 | wife: Nippissa<br>wife: Simigak<br>son: Panigoniak<br>son: Arnigasak<br>son: Itinguk / Ilinguk(?)<br>son: Mamangin |
| Kavanga | 11 | wife/wives (unnamed)<br>eldest son: Angutaunek<br>son (unnamed)<br>other children (unnamed)<br>dau (?): Onalik |
| Aivearsuk | 4 | wife (unnamed)<br>children (unnamed) |
| Amaukiliak | 4 | wife (unnamed)<br>children (unnamed) |
| Atsugarsuk | 2 | wife: Omaluk |

NOTE: Some details on the size and composition of families are specific, originating either from observations by Daniel and Gottlob or by Weitz, from comments in the Ramah Church Book, or from notations on Linder's 1898 map (Map 7); the structure of other families is surmised from references cited in the discussion. Young men and the women who became their wives have not been included in the figures, as they would be accounted for in families with children who are not specified by number or gender. However, the names of the young people are noted with families affiliated with particular areas.

## People of Killinek

The inhabitants of the Killinek region consisted of Serkuak's household, Auvek and his family, and Kajuasiak's household.[7] Kajuasiak was likely the son of Serkuak and the son-in-law of Auvek. Serkuak [or Sikoak] was described as the angajukKâk (leader) at Killinek. He and his wife lived with the families of his adult sons Kemmanek, Terriak, Nochak, and Kasuk at Okiakivik, on an island north of Killinek Island.

Most of Serkuak's family eventually joined the Ramah congregation. Serkuak's son Terriak moved to Ramah in 1881 with his wife Kajaluk, her son Komigak from a previous marriage, and their sons Siniksit and Serkuak.[8] The fact that Terriak gave his son Serkuak's name indicates they had a close kinship relationship. The elder Serkuak evidently died sometime after 1868 since no reference is made to him in later reports; Terriak's son Serkuak was born in about 1873.[9] The couple also named a daughter born later Kemangnak,[10] which resembles Kemmanek, for whom she may have been named.

The Ramah Church Book indicates that Terriak and his family originated from Killinek, but when they settled at the mission station in 1881, they travelled from Komaktorvik.[11] Several references by the HBC agent at Nachvak to "Tunuck," "Tenjok," and "Terrijok" in 1871 and 1872 confirm that Terriak and his family spent the winter at Komaktorvik from this time.[12] Terriak [baptized Daniel] and his family left for Hebron in 1890; he died in 1892 and his descendants chose his Christian name for their surname.

Serkuak's sons Nochak and Kasuk joined the Ramah congregation a few years after Terriak's family. Nochak and his wife Akpajok arrived at the mission station in 1884.[13] They later had two sons who adopted the surname Nochak (or Nugak); one of their sons moved to Killinek and

**Inuit at Ramah between 1882 and 1902 (Paul Lundberg fonds, Labrador Inuit through Moravian Eyes collection)**

married an unbaptized girl before they joined the congregation of the new Moravian station established there after 1904.[14]

Kasuk, his wife Safiale, and young son Paunyana became candidates for baptism at Ramah in 1887.[15] Kasuk (baptized Kleofas) moved his family to Hebron in 1892 where they subsequently adopted the surname Serkoak,[16] which alludes to a close kinship relationship with the elder Serkuak's household at Killinek.

Kemmanek and his family appear to have been the only members of the elder Serkuak's group who remained in the Killinek area. Kemmanek and his wife Okak had a 12-year-old daughter in 1863.[17] Another person associated with Killinek was a female named Attataksoak, who was born near Killinek in about 1866. When she later became a candidate for baptism at Ramah, she was the widow of Kudjaijok, the eldest son of Semigak from Nachvak, and had five children.[18]

Auvek lived with his wife and adult sons' families south of Killinek Island. His younger son, Kingatsiak, was unmarried, while his two elder sons, Terrieniak and Akpik, each had a wife and one child.[19] Auvek stated that he, and presumably his sons, would move from Killinek to the vicinity of Ramah after the winter of 1869. They had moved south by 1871, when Br. Weitz noted that Terrieniak and Akpik lived at Sorviluk, a bay south of Ramah.[20] The brothers occasionally visited the mission station to trade, but they had no interest in religious matters, according to a Moravian report in 1874, because they were influenced by "an old man, whom the others regard as their model in everything."[21]

Terrieniak and Akpik left Sorviluk in 1874 because they believed that "if they staid there any longer, one of them would be sure to die."[22] Inuit traditionally left a place after someone died so Auvek's death may explain their departure; his name is not mentioned in any subsequent reports. The two brothers and their families then moved to Nachvak; a comment in an 1876 Moravian report states that they were "not natives of Nachvak."[23] References to the activities of "Acpic" and "Tenginiak" in the HBC journals for 1874 and 1875[24] undoubtedly refer to them and confirm their presence in Nachvak.

The brothers told the Ramah missionary during a trade visit in 1876 that they wanted to live at the mission station.[25] When they continued to live at Nachvak, the missionary believed that the HBC trader had prevented them from leaving.[26] However, in 1878, Akpik, his wife Ujaraitsiak, son Arnasuk, and younger brother Kingatsiak finally joined the Ramah congregation; they died from infectious diseases in 1880 and 1886.[27] Terrieniak (or Tiggianiak), his wife Paingo, and daughter Noggasak remained in Nachvak until August 1880, when they decided to be part of a Hagenbeck ethnographic exhibition in Europe. They died a few months after arriving in Germany from smallpox, as described in the diary of their fellow Inuk traveller, Abraham Ulrikab.[28]

At approximately the same time as Serkuak's relatives and Auvek's family departed from Killinek, Kajuasiak began spending the winter there and probably remained in the area during other seasons as well. He became the chief at Killinek after Serkuak's death and was also known as the paramount shaman in the northern region. If the same practice of hereditary leadership was followed at Killinek as at Nachvak, Kajuasiak's accession to the role of chief suggests that he may have been Serkuak's senior son, following the death of his elder brother Siksiarsuk.

Before he lived at Killinek, Kajuasiak and his family resided on both the Labrador and Ungava coasts of the peninsula at the head of Kangerdluarsuk Bay, located immediately south of Aulatsivik, as well as at Tessiujaksuk, a small bay adjacent to Tessiujaluk on the northern Labrador coast, and at Taqpangajuk on the northeastern Ungava coast (see Weitz's 1868 map [Map 8] and Chapter 11).

Kajuasiak rarely traded at the stores, but his presence evoked comment due to his stature as the pre-eminent shaman on the coast and the quantity of goods he brought to barter at the HBC post. In January and December of 1874, for instance, the HBC journals from Nachvak note that "Karyatsiak" arrived from Killinek to trade. On both occasions, he brought a considerable quantity of goods, including, on one visit, four fox pelts, 10 seal pelts, 52 fathoms of sealskin line, two pieces of polar bear hide, and 80 pounds of seal blubber.[29] Kajuasiak appears to have intimidated the HBC agent, who described him as "the wicked man from Kidlinek," which was likely an allusion to his role as a shaman.[30]

Missionaries at Ramah described Kajuasiak in 1878 as "the chief sorcerer or medicine-man on the coast."[31] He undoubtedly considered the Moravians to be intruders and he strongly opposed the adoption of Christianity by Inuit in the northern region. In 1885, a member of a Canadian scientific expedition at Cape Chidley, Charles Tuttle, described Kajuasiak in his notes:

> Old chief Ki-ur-chur, the last of a long line of illustrious Uttericks [attanek, meaning chief], who have ruled the Cape Chidley natives for centuries and who, in late years, takes up his summer residence on the extreme north point of the cape, resides, in winter, with his two wives and large family of children, in one of those caves, at the seat of power of his royal ancestors.[32]

The occupant of another house was a family headed by "Komikan" (Komigak) and included his brother, his wife, two sons, a daughter, and an infant.[33] Komigak's daughter "is waiting, it is said, until the chiefs son, at the cape, her cousin, gets old enough to take a wife; for it must be nicer to be the wife of an Utterick than the slave of an ordinary hunter, especially the first one, as the first always rules the second."[34] If their children were cousins, Komigak and Kajuasiak were either brothers, step-brothers, or possibly brothers-in-law. Despite Tuttle's ethnocentric and derogatory tone, his observations suggest that Kajuasiak was the chief of several people sharing close kinship relationships and that the position was hereditary. Tuttle also described Kajuasiak's appearance:

> He is man of over fifty, of the usual high cheek-bones, black hair and eyes, and insufficient beard. He wears a great cap of bright red cloth, decorated with beads and precious stones, polished from pieces of latrobite and labradorite, and other gems indigenous to that rock-bound coast, and is otherwise attractively clad. His cap is stuffed with the down from many ducks, until its diameter will measure twenty inches. He has put away skins, except for the severity of winter, and wears a sort of common cloth of European manufacture, procured, no doubt, at Fort Chimo [or Nachvak or Ramah].[35]

Kajuasiak's family resided on both the Labrador and Ungava coasts that formed the peak of the peninsula. He seems to have hunted seals on the northeastern Ungava coast at Kangivak and Abloviak in the early fall and spent the winter and summer with his family on the Labrador coast.[36] Kajuasiak is certainly the "Kaiguatstuik/Kaiyuatshick" mentioned in HBC journals to be trading goods at the Nachvak post in 1869. One reference indicates that he and his family arrived "from inland," which implies that they came from the northeastern Ungava coast.[37]

When Daniel's party and Weitz met Kajuasiak at Attanarsuk, in August of 1867 and 1868 respectively, close relatives were staying with his family, which included three wives and six children. Kajuasiak and his elder brother Siksiarsuk, with his wife and child, appear to have lived together at Ikorliarsuk as well as at Attanarsuk in 1867.[38] During the summer of 1868, Auvek and two of his sons travelled from Killinek to visit his daughter, one of Kajuasiak's three wives.[39]

In 1894, Kajuasiak was murdered by Koliligak in the high mountains north of Ramah.[40] His youngest wife, Aniortama, then left the area with two of her children and joined the Ramah congregation in February 1895.[41] One of his senior wives, Kingak, remained at Killinek and was baptized in 1908 at the new Moravian mission station there. Six adult men described as Kajuasiak's sons were reported to be living at Killinek in 1900; four of them had wives at that time.[42]

Koliligak, Kajuasiak's slayer, is a perplexing character because he appears to have lived with Kajuasiak at periods of time, which suggests that they had a kinship relationship. References in HBC journals from Nachvak to "Kolleleyok/Kolleliak" indicate that he had a wife in 1869[43] and a family in 1871. They were said to have arrived at the post from "the next bay to the north" in 1871, which suggests that they were living in the vicinity of Komaktorvik.[44] Br. Weitz observed a striking change in Koliligak's physical appearance and attitude in 1873:

> [He wore] ragged, filthy garments, his long black hair hanging down over his face and neck to the middle of his chest and back, occasionally pushed aside with his hand or by a shake of his head, to afford his restlessly rolling eyes an opportunity of seeing more distinctly. Although we may not always judge correctly of the mind and heart from the appearance of the person, in this sad case we could very soon perceive that the outward appearance was but a faint picture of the inner state of this wretched man; at least no Eskimo has ever yet so decidedly stated to me his determination not to be converted, and has so coolly assured me that he has no fear whatever of hell or everlasting damnation.[45]

Weitz also noted in 1873 that Koliligak had moved farther northward and was then living near Aulatsivik.[46] Koliligak appears to have remained in this region and may have been with trading parties from the north who travelled to the HBC post in Nachvak. Apart from a brief reference to his presence with northern Inuit trading at Ramah in 1884,[47] his name is not mentioned in Moravian reports until 1895, when he was identified as the person who murdered Kajuasiak.[48] Koliligak's death at Aulatsivik was reported in 1900.[49]

## Inuit at Nachvak

The second prominent figure in the northern region was Tuglavina, who was the leader and the shaman at Nachvak. References in various reports indicate that in about 1868, his family included an elderly mother,[50] a wife named Pituratsuk,[51] a daughter,[52] and a son named Sekepa, who died in 1880.[53] He had younger brothers[54] named Semigak and Paksaut,[55] who were probably half-brothers, as his father likely had several wives due to his stature as chief. In addition, he had a married brother who was also named Semigak and probably shared the same mother because they were closer in age. The HBC agent referred to the younger brother as "Simmica Jr."[56]

The older Semigak had a wife and family,[57] including two sons named Kudjaijok and Anatsiak. Kudjaijok ultimately married a woman called Attataksoak, who was born about 1866 at Killinek,[58] and Anatsiak married a woman named Paniguniak, who was born about 1869.[59] In 1871, Semigak's family included a daughter who died in the kitchen of the HBC post and was buried nearby. Her body was wrapped in a caribou skin with a piece of bone,[60] which suggests she was an infant. Semigak's wife was named Nangmartvarsuk and was believed to have been born in about 1855.[61]

Tuglavina may not have had another son, after the death of Sekepa, to inherit the position of chief. Instead, he was succeeded, perhaps due to his advancing age, by his brother Semigak, who was recognized as the headman and also shaman of Nachvak after 1895.[62] His younger brother Semigak and his wife Ikinek moved to Ramah in 1881 and became members of the Moravian community; their descendants later adopted the surname Paniguniak.[63] Tuglavina had three wives in 1898[64] and never

**Inuit summer camp, Nachvak, 1890s (The Rooms Provincial Archives)**

became a convert, although members of his immediate family adopted Christianity after his death in 1910; they chose Tuglavina as their surname when they were baptized.

Semigak ultimately had a large family that included two wives, with three sons and a daughter in 1901.[65] Like Tuglavina, he opposed conversion to Christianity. After his death during an influenza epidemic at Komaktorvik in the fall of 1904, members of his immediate family joined Moravian congregations and chose Semigak as their surname when they were baptized.

Following Semigak's death, his brother Paksaut became the recognized chief and shaman of Inuit residing at Nachvak.[66] He was an intimidating man, said in 1896 to be "feared by almost everyone,"[67] and he had a large family including three wives in 1905.[68] Paksaut and one of Semigak's sons were the last members of their lineage to be permanent residents of Nachvak when they finally left the fiord in 1909.

Another family inhabiting Nachvak in 1868 was led by a man named Panigonayak and included his wife, mother, a crippled brother, and two children. The HBC agent referred to Panigonayak's brother as "Tugklavina Cripple"[69] and described activities by "Panyingajok" from 1873 to 1875 in the Nachvak area.[70] After Panigonayak died from an accidental gunshot wound in September 1884, his widow Makkijok took her two young daughters to Ramah, where she had lived as a child and had relatives.[71] Both of her daughters were born after 1879 but whether her two previous children survived cannot be determined. She appears to have been the daughter of Kaksungaut (baptized Boas, see below) because her family joined them when they moved to Hebron in 1886.[72]

Two other men with families who were active hunters in the Nachvak area, according to references in the HBC journals from 1869 to 1875, were "Ikauyok/Ekangak/Ekaujak" and "Ikera/Iksa/Ikra." In April 1882, Ikauja, his wife Sakkiarak, and their son Ajaluk, who had a wife named Paksaut at that time, left Nachvak and became members of the Ramah congregation. They were all baptized and subsequently adopted the surname Suarak.[73] Ikauja was reported to have had a brother among the people at Ramah who were not yet candidates for baptism in March 1883.[74] His brother may have been Swansi, who had moved to Ramah three months before Ikauja.[75] Following Ikauja to Ramah was a young man named Tivua, who became his foster son and joined the Ramah congregation in 1888; he was baptized Ludwig and later adopted the surname Alasoa.[76]

Ikera and his family lived in Anillusuak near the HBC post in 1873 and frequently assisted the staff with tasks to maintain the post.[77] A man named "Kudlo" also worked for the HBC agent and, after he died following a brief illness in February 1875, Ikera's family became ill, which suggests that Kudlo lived in their house and may have been Ikera's son. Ikera died due to illness a month later and was survived by his wife and daughters; at the HBC agent's request, they were taken to a camp elsewhere with help from Tuglavina's brothers.[78]

Several other men mentioned in the HBC journals from 1869 to 1875 appear to have been single at the time and were likely related in some way to the families already described because their activities centred in the Nachvak area. One such man was called "Shipanesi/Sjevanca/Sjevanesi"

The Tallek fiord in Nachvak Bay, 1905 (The Rooms Provincial Archives)

Inuit tent at Nachvak, 1910 (The Rooms Provincial Archives)

in the HBC journals.[79] This unusual name may correspond with Swansi, who left Nachvak with his wife Akkusane and infant daughter Sekkinek and joined the Ramah congregation in January 1882. They were baptized as Matthew, Verone, and Magdalena, but then left the mission station with their children in 1898 and returned to live at Nachvak, where Swansi (or Matthew) and his wife died from illness in 1907–08.[80] Two of their daughters, Sekkinek (Magdalena) and Lena, ultimately became joint wives of one of Semigak's sons and, after the youngest one separated from him, she was described by the surname Tuglavina,[81] which indicates a close connection between her natal family and the former chief of Nachvak.

The HBC journal in 1869 makes one reference to "Nokashuk" and to "Kakshingout," whose names correspond with Nochasak and Kaksungaut, both of whom were residing at Nulattatok in 1871 when the Moravian missionaries arrived to establish Ramah. Nochasak's family probably occupied one of the six tents in Nachvak noted by Weitz during his survey of the fiord in the summer of 1868 because they appear to have moved frequently between Nulattatok and Nachvak. The family was living at Nulattatok in the summer of 1871, but they spent the winter of 1873 residing with other Nachvak families at Naksariktok, a site at the mouth of the fiord.[82] After walking overland from Nachvak in July 1873, the family appears to have remained in the vicinity of the mission station.[83] They became candidates for baptism after 1875.[84]

In 1868, Nochasak's family would have been composed of nine people, including two daughters named Itinguk and Aninasuak and a son named Manek from a previous marriage, his wife Akusanna, their son Paungana and daughter Komigak, as well as a young man named Koversak who was likely related to them.[85] Nochasak (baptized William) was described as a daring walrus hunter and the most skillful seal hunter at Ramah in 1876.[86] After he died in 1894, his sons adopted Nochasak as their surname.

Kaksungaut's family would have been composed of seven people in 1868, including his first wife Nippisa, her sister and his second wife Simigak, and four sons, Panigoniak, Arnigasak, Itinguk, and Mamangin.[87] References in 1871 to a man named "Akialsjuk" and "Alualskuk" in the

HBC journal were likely to Kaksungaut's son, Arnigasak. Kaksungaut (baptized Boas) and his family were the first Inuit to be baptized at Ramah. In 1886, 18 members of his extended family, including his married children and grandchildren, moved to Hebron;[88] they subsequently chose Obed as their surname.

## Inuit of Nulattatok/Sorviluk

A third prominent figure living in the region north of Hebron in the late 1860s was a man named Kavanga. Both Gottlob and Weitz reported meeting him in 1868 during their travels on the northern coast,[89] and the HBC agent at Nachvak noted that Kavanga's family lived at "Nofituktu" or Nulattatok in the winter of 1869.[90] Kavanga's large family then appears to have settled at Komaktorvik, a fiord just south of Kangalaksiorvik fiord, where they were reported in 1873.[91] By then, some of Kavanga's sons were travelling independently to trade at the HBC post,[92] indicating that they were adolescents or young adults and that Kavanga was a mature man.

The HBC agent called him "Kovanga Chief"[93] and the Ramah missionary described him as a "headman" in 1875.[94] Like Serkuak at Killinek, Kavanga was the leader of a group of several families related to him by blood or marriage. One family was headed by Atsugarsuk, who, according to a statement made by him to Weitz in 1873, was given permission by Kavanga to move with his family to Ramah where they became converts.[95] Atsugarsuk must have been related to Kavanga in some way to be subject to his authority; he may have been a younger brother, nephew, or son-in-law as he was born about 1840 at Komaktorvik and was likely younger than Kavanga.

Atsugarsuk travelled from Nachvak to Ramah in 1872 with his wife Omaluk and three children; their eldest child was born in 1870.[96] When Weitz asked the reason for his desire to become a Christian, Atsugarsuk stated that he hoped to catch more seals. His ambition reflected his background, according to Weitz's description of him: "He appears always to have lived in needy circumstances, and never to have been clever or successful in fishing and hunting."[97] His lack of skill may have accounted for Kavanga's approval of the family's move to Ramah.

Atsugarsuk's baptism was delayed for several years when he took another woman, named Onalik, as his second wife. Following Onalik's death during childbirth in 1885, Atsugarsuk was baptized Friedrich.[98] He evidently appreciated his relationship with the missionaries because his family later adopted the surname Kohlmeister, after the missionary who led the expedition to explore the northern coast in 1811.

Kavanga visited Ramah in 1874 to arrange a marriage for a man living with him named Kauksuk.[99] The young woman they hoped would become his wife was Itinguk, the daughter of Nochasak (baptized William), one of the first converts at Ramah.[100] Since Kavanga acted on Kauksuk's behalf in arranging his marriage, Kauksuk may have been one of Kavanga's sons or a younger brother. References in the HBC journal to Kautchuck indicate that he spent most of 1873 hunting in the Nachvak area with other men living there.[101] In 1878, Kauksuk travelled with his wife and infant son, Tuglavina, from Nachvak to Ramah and became members of the congregation; they later chose the surname Tuglavina.[102]

Another member of Kavanga's group was a man named Aivearsuk. Gottlob lived with Aivearsuk and his family in 1868, and Weitz met the household during the summer on his tour of the north coast. Versions of his name appearing in HBC journals indicate that he traded regularly at the Nachvak post after 1869, and that he frequently came from Komaktorvik.[103] He was also reported to have travelled from Komaktorvik when he visited Ramah to trade during the winters of 1872 and 1873.[104] He had a family,[105] travelled once with his father from Komaktorvik,[106] and had a brother named "Amauliliak" or "Amauklilik"[107] who also had a family.[108] Aivearsuk and his brother were often travelling companions, and on one occasion he and Kavanga made trade exchanges together at the HBC post,[109] which suggests that the two men were related.

Kavanga stated in 1873 that he would become a Christian if teachers went to live in his neighbourhood.[110] The missionaries also reported his comment that the HBC trader "would not let them" move to Ramah.[111] Like Kavanga, Aivearsuk also expressed an inclination to become a

Christian convert and claimed in 1873 that the HBC trader would not allow him to move to Ramah. Instead, the trader urged him to live at Nachvak and help with tasks around the post; the Ramah missionary later heard that Aivearsuk had moved to Nachvak.[112]

Considering the close association between Aivearsuk, Amaukiliak, and Atsugarsuk with Kavanga, the three men and their families likely followed Kavanga to the Nulattatok area in the winter of 1868 and were among the 28 people estimated by Weitz to be living in the bay at that time. Aivearsuk's family, and perhaps other families in Kavanga's group, apparently moved north of Nachvak in the spring or summer of 1868, where Gottlob reported staying with them.

Kavanga and Kajuasiak were probably similar in age, since they both had sizable family groups, but they may not have met frequently because they usually lived in areas far distant from each other. Nevertheless, the men were occasionally together, and were travelling companions in January 1874 on a journey to trade at Nachvak.[113] Around this time, they apparently agreed on a marriage between their children: in 1880, Kajuasiak's daughter was said to be the wife of Kavanga's eldest son Angutaunek and the couple already had some children. By then, however, a serious strain had developed between the two families.

Kavanga told the Ramah missionary that Kajuasiak threatened to take back his daughter and her children and would probably kill Angutaunek if Kavanga and his people adopted Christianity. Kavanga's desire to become a convert, along with the conversion of two families associated with his group, may have driven Kajuasiak to prevent any further defections. The missionaries reported that Kavanga had considered murdering Kajuasiak in response to his threat, but they had dissuaded him from doing so. At that time Kavanga's household was living at the northern extremity of the peninsula,[114] possibly near Killinek where Kajuasiak was based.

Kavanga and Angutaunek never became Christian converts, although Kavanga continued to appear sympathetic to the Moravian religious theology. He must have been an elderly man by 1883 because, after suffering a severe illness while visiting the mission station, he anticipated his death. His parting comment revealed his attitude to conversion and to the future:

> It is too late for me to come and live amongst the Christians, but perhaps my children, who frequently speak of these things, may in time to come be converted. Your doctrines are not strange to me, but here in the North we have been trained to certain customs and practices which we should be very reluctant to give up.[115]

Kavanga's foresight was accurate; he must have died soon after because his name disappears from the historical records.

## Kinship Bonds and Leadership

As this chapter has described, the three major kinship groups on the northern Labrador coast in 1868 were headed by Serkuak, Kavanga, and Tuglavina. These men were all described as chiefs or headmen of several families living with them; following Serkuak's death, Kajuasiak assumed his position. Based on the size of their families, Kajuasiak and Kavanga were probably similar in age, and Tuglavina may have been younger as his family was relatively small. Both Kajuasiak and Tuglavina were described as shamans but Kavanga was never portrayed as performing this function. On a unique occasion at Ramah in late January 1884, the missionary noted that three Inuit who occupied "the position of chieftains amongst their countrymen on this coast" were present together for the baptism of the HBC agent George Ford's son, James.[116] One of the men was identified as Kavanga, and the other two men were undoubtedly Tuglavina and Kajuasiak.

The information gathered on the composition of local groups indicates that the predominant kinship relationships underlying them were bonds between fathers and sons and between brothers. Serkuak and Auvek were the only men in the region described as elderly in 1867–68. Since they were both based at Killinek and Serkuak was the recognized chief, Auvek may have been his younger brother or a relation by marriage. They both kept their sons close to them, even after they were married, and their sons continued living together following their father's death. The same close relationships were particularly evident at Nachvak, where Tuglavina's father had exerted a dominant influence over his sons, who remained living together after his death. The prevalence of these male bonds was a common feature of traditional Inuit society a century earlier.[117]

The control exercised by fathers over their sons and by elder brothers over their siblings was one of the greatest obstacles that Moravian missionaries faced in trying to convince Inuit to adopt Christianity. They noted that people responded to invitations to settle at Ramah "with the usual excuses: 'I should like, but on his deathbed my father told me to live and die where he had done,' or 'I always do what my elder brother does,' and the elder brother professes to have no will of his own, but always to follow someone else's lead."[118]

Statements by Serkuak and Kavanga cited above, in 1867 and 1883 respectively, clearly indicate that Inuit elders were determined to remain in their traditional areas and to preserve their customary beliefs and practices. However, as Serkuak and other Inuit added, if a missionary went to live with them, they were willing to have their children taught how to read and write, as well as listen to Christian doctrines. Literacy skills were especially valued, according to Br. Weitz, because they were "a supernatural acquirement."[119] Tuglavina, the chief or angajukKâk of Nachvak, similarly explained to the missionaries in 1871 that "they neither could nor would leave their homes, but if a teacher would come to live among them, their conversion would follow."[120]

Tuglavina's brother, Semigak, candidly explained the need for a compromise to Weitz in 1875 as follows:

> It is wrong of us to yield to the influence of Tuglavine, who prevents us from accepting Christianity, but I will tell you how it is. We promised our father, when he was dying, that we would never leave Nachvak to reside elsewhere. If a missionary were to come and live among us, then we would forsake heathenism.[121]

Inuit might consider converting to Christianity if a European missionary lived with them. A Moravian might exploit a difference in attitude towards traditional spiritual beliefs that existed between old and young generations of Nachvak Inuit, Tuglavina and Semigak implied, but it would have to be on their own terms; they were unwilling to leave their homeland.

Mature Inuit were able to defend their cultural heritage and control their families' allegiance in a subtle but basic manner. They were the primary practitioners of customary beliefs and practices, and the main suppliers of necessities for their families. While young people were more inclined to adopt Christianity, they would have had to rely on their own skills to support themselves if they moved to Ramah to become converts. The predicament of Nachvak Inuit was described by Weitz in 1877:

> To their minds the idea of "conversion" is associated with coming here to reside, and with this they know must be inseparably connected the abandonment of heathen practices, which seems to be more difficult to the older than the younger people: but the latter are dependent upon the former, who are experienced hunters, and provide food for the whole family.[122]

However, the dependence of young people was not absolute. After 1880, several young couples left Nachvak to settle at the mission station at Ramah. The next chapter provides context for these decisions by describing Inuit life at both the traditional settlement at Nachvak and at the new Christian community at Ramah.

## CHAPTER SIX

# Traditional Inuit Life and Colonial Interactions, 1870s–1890s

### Inuit Life at Nachvak

Nachvak was the core area of Inuit settlement in the northern region before and after outposts were established in the vicinity by the HBC and the Moravian Mission.[1] Various historical accounts dating from the late eighteenth century consistently describe Nachvak as having the largest concentration of Inuit on the coast. However, as Weitz noted in 1868, the Nachvak population consisted of family groups living in two places, within the fiord and on the outer coast at Nulattatok Bay. Inuit families occupying Komaktorvik, a fiord on the outer coast north of Nachvak, were also closely affiliated with the Nachvak population.[2]

According to the HBC journals, Inuit living in Nachvak and Komaktorvik interacted frequently. Virtually all the adult males living in Nachvak went to Komaktorvik for seasonal fishing or hunting activities, and the residents of Komaktorvik, including Kavanga, Aivearsuk, and Amaukiliak, spent periods of time with their families hunting and living in Nachvak and trading at the HBC post.[3] Komaktorvik fiord and Kangalaksiorvik fiord flow into Seven Islands Bay, a rich area for marine mammals, char, and caribou.[4] Inuit at Nachvak often went to Komaktorvik in March and April to fish for char at the head of the fiord. In April 1873, the Inuit evangelist Gottlob counted 54 adults and children assembled near a river in Komaktorvik when he visited the area. He reported seeing Aivearsuk and Kavanga with their families, as well as other people from Nachvak and from Nachasak,[5] which may be the name of the winter site in Komaktorvik. When char were scarce in the rivers and ponds near Ramah in the spring of 1875, Gottlob travelled to Komaktorvik and returned with his Kamutik loaded with fish.[6]

The main early winter settlement in Nachvak was located at a place called "Aklavi," according to the HBC journals. Tuglavina resided here[7] along with other families, as people were frequently described as travelling "from below" or "up from the winter houses" to trade at the post.[8] Ruins of at least eight sod houses (illusuat) found on a point named Aklavik, southeast of the HBC post, confirm the location of this site.[9] Families occupied the illusuat from October until early January. Once ice had formed over the waters of the fiord, they would all move to a cove called Naksariktok on the southern headland at the mouth of Nachvak, close to the open sea.

**Inuit in northern Labrador, ca. 1901 (Them Days Archive)**

Naksariktok, or "Naksautok" in HBC journals, was the primary place where Nachvak Inuit hunted for walrus and seals.[10] The site was only about 25 km or a journey of three hours by Kamutik from Ramah, so people frequently travelled to trade or to appeal for gifts at the mission station.[11] In February 1873, two missionaries visited the site and met with women and children in the six illuvigat while the men were away hunting or fishing.[12] The area was important as walrus and seal blubber were major trade items, while the fresh meat was a vital food source for families and their dogs. The hides were also essential for making a variety of items such as Kajak covers, tents, bedding, clothing, and boots. Fox furs, which Inuit hunted or trapped on the high hills during the winter, and seal pelts had the greatest value in trade exchanges.

In April, Nachvak Inuit returned inside the fiord where they became involved in a variety of harvesting activities. Many families appear to have camped at this time at the head of the fiord in Tallek Arm and Tasiujak Arm, which were located west and south, respectively, of the HBC post. Inuit remained in these areas until May hunting caribou in the interior, fishing for char on the ice near rivers, and hunting seals that were in open channels or basking on the sea ice.[13] The same activities were conducted at Komaktorvik by families visiting that area.[14]

In May, as the ice cleared from the sea, Nachvak Inuit once again headed for places outside the fiord to hunt seals.[15] They continued pursuing seals in open water further inside the fiord in June and July, and gradually returned to Tallek and Tasiujak where they resumed fishing for char.[16] A few caribou were taken as well, but the critical period for hunting these animals was in late summer, during August and September, when new fur on their hides provided the greatest warmth for winter clothing and bedding. At this time of the year, however, dog teams could not be used for transportation, so hunters had to walk into the interior and carry heavy loads on their backs to their camps.[17]

The main area where Nachvak Inuit sought caribou was around a large lake emptying into Tasiujak.[18] Hunters usually found enough game there, but animals were scarce in 1874 and 1877. The HBC agent noted in April that hunters had caught only a few caribou "in the woods" near the lake, and a party returning in October after hunting for two months had a small number of animals.[19] In 1877, several hunters from Ramah joined a party of Nachvak Inuit to hunt caribou in the interior. The missionary reported that "they had wandered over to the George River in the Kangiva district (on the western side of the peninsula of Labrador) and had found great difficulty in making their way home, on account of the fresh-fallen snow and the absence of reindeer [caribou]."[20] This is the only reference to a hunting expedition to the Ungava coast. After caribou hunting ceased in early fall, Nachvak Inuit pursued seals, made repairs to their illusuat, and generally prepared for the coming winter and the repeat of their harvesting cycle.

In 1880, the Norwegian sailor Johan Jacobsen travelled to Nachvak to recruit Inuit participants for ethnographic shows in Europe. He described his first impressions of the people in a book published in 1894:

> The men wore their hair long, hanging down to their eyebrows, and in the back, it flowed unkempt and wild over their shoulders. Short jackets of reindeer skin and sealskin trousers were their traditional costume. The women wear a jacket of sealskin which reaches down to their ankles in the back somewhat in shape like a beaver's tail. The hair is braided and rolled up around the ears; braided into the hair they wear a long dangling tassel of pearls, which often hangs down over the shoulders in more than half an ell's length.[21] The forehead is tattooed with stripes, running parallel with the eyebrows. The rest of the traditional costume: pants and short boots.[22]

## Inuit Life at the Mission Station at Ramah

Inuit living at Ramah, as well as families residing in other areas along the northern coast, followed the same seasonal pattern of activities. While Nachvak Inuit oriented their pattern of movements to places inside and outside the fiord, Ramah Inuit centred their activities around the mission station. But members of the Ramah congregation had a significant advantage in their pursuit of food. Soon after the station was

**Ramah mission station, 1900 (Hettasch family collection, Them Days Archive)**

formed, the Moravian missionaries introduced the use of nets, which significantly increased the harvest of harp seals migrating south along the coast in the fall. Inuit crews used seal nets at all mission stations and received a share of the animals caught in return for setting them. Initially, the Mission owned all the nets, but after 1861 the gear was offered for sale at the mission stores. Nets were expensive items so only prosperous Inuit could afford to buy them.[23]

Early experiments in setting nets near Ramah in 1874 were not very productive,[24] but better netting areas were found by 1876.[25] The increased seal harvest provided Ramah Inuit with a larger and more secure food supply for the winter than could be obtained from traditional hunting techniques. As one missionary noted in 1879:

> Those who have only what they can take by pursuing these animals in the kayak were, as usual, just able to obtain the necessary

> supply of meat, &c., while those who could afford to use nets did well. About 360 seals were taken, and we can look forward to a winter free from the usual care and anxiety in regard to food-supplies.[26]

Nachvak Inuit quickly realized the difference in their situations, and during the winter of 1877 they made frequent visits "mainly to share in the blubber-riches" of Ramah Inuit.[27] Over the following years, they regularly took advantage of the large seal catches to supplement their own resources.

Inuit from the north desired other assets at Ramah as well. A party visiting in January 1878 expressed an interest in becoming converts, but the missionary recognized that their motive was not spiritual. "Two men found that they might get wives here, which they cannot in their own homes, owing to the small number of females: others cast a longing glance at our wood for sledges, kayak-frames, &c."[28] Kavanga, for example,

**Ramah, before 1910 (Adolph G. Stecker collection, Them Days Archive)**

**Inuit at Ramah, 1900 (F.W. Peacock fonds, Labrador Inuit through Moravian Eyes collection)**

had obtained a bride for Kauksuk from Ramah in 1874, despite the missionary's insistence that the couple could only be married if they agreed to live at the mission station;[29] after living elsewhere, they eventually moved to Ramah.

The shortage of eligible young women appears to have been the result of several mishaps and deaths due to disease. In 1875, the Ramah missionary reported that six adults in the northern region had died from a severe influenza epidemic. He also described three incidents involving the death or abuse of women:

> A mournful event was the suicide of a native woman at Aulatsivik, with whom Gottlob was in the habit of staying on his northern missionary tours. Having hanged her two children, she put an end to herself by the same means. Another woman, who left home with the intention of coming to Ramah, has not been heard of

**Inuit sawing wood at Ramah, 1900 (F.W. Peacock fonds, Labrador Inuit through Moravian Eyes collection)**

> since, having no doubt miserably perished by the way. A third case was that of a young woman, whose husband had maltreated her and then sent her away. Having sought refuge with us, Gottlob hospitably received her into his house, where she remained for several months. . . . When her husband lost his second wife he became desirous of recovering the one whom he sent away, and as she was willing to go back to him, the affair was soon made up.[30]

While suicide was a rare act in traditional Inuit society, missionaries had noted sexual disputes between spouses and the abuse of women as relatively common occurrences in the late 1700s.[31]

A low ratio of males to females and a high incidence of polygynous (or plural) marriages were also characteristic of Inuit society in the late eighteenth century.[32] When mature men commonly had two or three wives, the marriage prospects of young men were significantly limited. Due to the small size of the population in the region, few women were left for young men to marry, so eligible girls were in high demand. Even men who already had a wife or wives took extreme measures to secure an additional spouse.

According to missionary reports, the shaman Paksaut prevented a widow named Kuttukitok and her three children from moving to Ramah from Nachvak in 1896 because he wanted her as his third wife. The family managed to leave in January 1897 when Kuttukitok's brother, a Ramah convert, arrived to transport them to the mission station. However, Paksaut waylaid the party and seized the widow's box of provisions and bed. Several months later, he appeared at Ramah and abducted the widow's 12-year-old daughter; she was brought back to the community about a month later.[33]

Paksaut's elder brother, Semigak, the chief of Nachvak Inuit, was reported to have three wives at the time and wished to find a wife for his son. In August 1897, he demanded the crippled eldest daughter of a Ramah convert in payment for a debt owed by her father, but the family managed to escape without having to forfeit her.[34] The Ramah missionary reported in 1900 that two of Kajuasiak's adult sons "cannot get wives because there are none to be had. There is a great lack of women on the coast between Ramah and Killinek."[35]

Despite the resources and benefits available at Ramah, people in Nachvak often displayed little interest in the missionaries' attempts to change their beliefs or way of life. In 1872, a missionary reported that traditional Inuit did not show "the least desire after spiritual things; all their thoughts were upon other matters."[36] While some professed to believe in Jesus, "when we further endeavoured to teach them wherein real faith in Christ consists, they were either silent, or attempted to turn the conversation to other subjects, by asking such questions as: 'Have you no tobacco?' 'Have you not a pipe?' 'Will you give me some bread?'"[37]

## Competition between the Hudson's Bay Company and the Moravian Mission

The Ramah mission station was not the only colonial influence in the region. The HBC post at Nachvak competed vigorously with Ramah to attract clientele and the two stores countered each other's tactics for obtaining products from Inuit. Both trading posts advanced credit as well as the use of equipment, such as fox traps, to northern hunters. However, since the travel route to Ramah involved passing through Nachvak, on occasion the HBC agent acquired pelts that were intended for the mission store in return for borrowed traps.[38] He seems to have been less successful at intercepting silver fox pelts, because the Ramah storekeeper offered a gun, spyglass, and other articles for one pelt; the HBC trader considered this to be too high a price to pay.[39]

Another strategy employed by both agencies was to use Inuit as advocates. The HBC agent depended on Ikera and his family, who lived next to the post, as he remarked after Ikera's death in 1875:

> I am sorry not to have at least one Esquimaux family at our place. There is none except ourselves to recommend the company to the Northerners now. With their assistance I was able to keep the Northerns from trading at Ramah but I trust I will never see one of the Northerns at this place if they are able to keep them about Ungava.[40]

**Hudson's Bay Company post at Nachvak, ca. 1910 (McCord Stewart Museum)**

Ikera's role in furthering the interests of the HBC compared with Gottlob's role in advocating conversion to Christianity among northern Inuit. While Gottlob and the Moravian missionaries urged people to settle at mission stations, Ikera helped the HBC by advising Inuit to either remain in their territories or move to Nachvak.

Local bilingual HBC staff also could influence Inuit to trade with the Company. The interpreter at the HBC Nachvak post, starting in 1877, was George Ford, a Labradorian.[41] Born in Cartwright to British parents in 1857, his father, John Ford Sr., had 14 children in two marriages. Many members of the Ford family worked for the Hudson's Bay Company throughout the Canadian Arctic, including at Kangiqsualujjuaq (George River), Kuujjuaq (Fort Chimo), and Killinek.[42] George Ford married Harriet Merrifield Ford, who had Inuit ancestry through her mother's Lane family,[43] and they had three children, Henry, Solomon, and Sarah Elizabeth.[44] In 1880, George helped convince Abraham Ulrikab, an Inuk from Hebron, to travel to Europe with his family as part of an ethnographic show. As mentioned in the previous chapter, Terrieniak (or Tiggianiak), his wife Paingo, and daughter Noggasak from the Nachvak region also participated in the journey, and all died in Europe of smallpox.[45] Abraham Ulrikab kept a diary during the voyage, which has recently been published.[46] George Ford acted as postmaster at Nachvak from 1880 to 1887, and as clerk from 1889 to 1910.[47] His bilingual abilities and local knowledge made him an invaluable source of information and advice for both HBC and Moravian authorities.

The Moravian missionaries' determination to proselytize the entire northern Inuit population seriously concerned the HBC agents. They knew that Inuit would trade at the most convenient store for them and that they would lose their clients if another mission station were established farther north. Commenting on the value of trade with Indigenous inhabitants, the commander of the Canadian Hudson's Bay Expedition in 1884 noted that a "good Eskimo family" could be worth about $500 a year to a trader.[48] Although the Moravian Mission emphasized that evangelism rather than trade was its primary aim, congregation members were expected to show loyalty to the Mission by trading exclusively at its stores.[49] There were no further plans, however, to expand the Mission into Ungava Bay due to reports of a small and widely dispersed Inuit population on the eastern coast.[50]

Despite the HBC agents' efforts to keep Inuit trading at their posts, they often had fewer articles for sale than at the Ramah store. The Nachvak and Saglek posts, as well as those in Ungava Bay, were supplied annually with merchandise by an HBC vessel. Ramah also received goods each year from a Moravian ship sent to the Labrador coast from England, but the Mission's shipments were apparently more reliable. After the HBC supply ship failed to arrive in the fall of 1870, the agents at Nachvak and Saglek left in January 1871 to seek information further south about their stock.[51] They learned that the HBC steamer had been wrecked,[52] and although they may have obtained some supplies from other HBC posts, the Nachvak post ran out of gunpowder and shot in August of that year. Inuit travelling to Nachvak from Abloviak reported that supplies were also very scarce in Ungava Bay. When Nachvak Inuit needed ammunition, they obtained it from Ramah.[53]

In 1873, Inuit sought tools and tin kettles from the Ramah store[54] and the Nachvak agent even purchased tinware himself at Hebron.[55] During the next winter, the HBC post again lacked articles that were "indispensible" to northern Inuit, and the agent noted that they "therefore are going where they can get proper supplies."[56] Inuit took advantage of the competition between the Moravian Mission and the Hudson's Bay Company, taking their business where it best suited them.[57] In 1876, the competition and perpetual supply problems led the Hudson's Bay Company to close its Saglek post, less than a decade after it had opened. The Nachvak post faced the same supply issues but remained open, as it was slightly more successful in attracting trade.

Problems with supply plagued all the HBC posts in the region. Northern Inuit traded at Ramah when merchandise was not available at the Nachvak post or at the posts on the George River and Koksoak River in Ungava Bay. During the winters of 1880 and 1881, missionaries reported

Hudson's Bay Company buildings, Nachvak (Them Days Archive)

having unusually frequent visits from Inuit originating from the northern Labrador coast, Kangivak, and Ungava Bay.[58] As people were solely interested in trading, Ungava Inuit must not have been able to obtain supplies from the HBC posts in their region.

## Inuit from Ungava Bay

Problems with the trade supply were not the only difficulties in the 1880s and 1890s. A scarcity of game and the low price of furs caused hardship for Inuit on both the Labrador and Ungava coasts. In 1880, the Ramah missionary learned that many Inuit had died of epidemic disease in Ungava Bay.[59] Two years later, he was told that severe cold and stormy weather had prevented hunters in the Kangivak area from pursuing game, and seven people had consequently died from starvation during the winter.[60] Caribou populations decreased, and many Inuit and Innu families in Ungava faced severe famine in the late 1880s and early 1890s. The Hudson's

Bay Company's sole focus on trade often exacerbated the situation, as visiting Canadian geologist A.P. Low wrote in 1892 from Fort Chimo:

> This deplorable state of affairs might to a great extent [have] been averted by a more generous policy of the H.B. Co. who trade and make a good profit out of these poor people. The rules at present are that no debt or advances are to be made without prompt payment and I am sorry to say in the present case the rules are strictly and too strictly kept up. . . . It must be mistaken policy to allow these people to die off wholesale as it is the profits of the fur trade (and fishery) that keeps up the post.[61]

Low's fierce critique of the HBC policies eventually forced the federal government to provide food rations to the Company to give to struggling Indigenous families.[62]

Throughout this difficult period, Inuit in Ungava Bay navigated between different spiritual beliefs and religious authorities. HBC officials at Fort Chimo described how Inuit relied on shamanism to treat illness and disease in the early 1880s.[63] In 1881, Kangivak Inuit described to a Moravian missionary how an old shaman named Sappa fused Christianity with traditional Inuit religion:

> He preaches vigorously to his people, exhorting them to abstain from a variety of gross sins, which are commonly practised by them, such as adultery, theft, &c. He states that he receives revelations from Jesus, with whom his spirit has intercourse in heaven, while his body on earth remains in a kind of trance-like condition, the limbs rigid as in the corpse. He tells his followers that Jesus is mightier than the devil, but that, as the latter gives him more assistance in some things, he finds it advisable to apply to one or the other, according to the nature of the thing desired. Light and darkness are singularly mingled in this man, and I should be very glad to speak with him; but I fear there is little likelihood of this, as he lives so far off and is aged and weakly.[64]

Sappa's fusion of Christian and Indigenous spiritual practices may have been a common Inuit approach towards the new religion. According to anthropologists Fréderic Laugrand and Jarich Oosten, shamans/angakkuit often incorporated Kållunât beliefs and practices into their own, and they played a leading role in deciding if, how, and when the people should convert.[65]

More information about Sappa is provided in an account by Lucien Turner, a meteorologist employed by the Smithsonian Institution to conduct scientific research at Fort Chimo [Kuujjuaq] from 1882 to 1884. According to Turner, the shaman "Sápa" accompanied a trading party travelling to Fort Chimo from the east coast of Hudson Bay in the spring of 1883. Sappa was "renowned throughout the land. . . . His power over the spirit controlling the reindeer is widely believed in and invoked by the other shamans."[66] In treating sick Inuit at an encampment near the Koksoak River, he tried to force married couples to separate, which led several people to flee the area so as to avoid this order. However, at the Fort Chimo post, Sappa repudiated shamanistic practices and announced his conversion to Christianity.[67]

Turner was the first European to produce a detailed description of the distribution and characteristics of the Inuit population occupying the Quebec–Labrador Peninsula. He identified three groups of people who inhabited specific areas on the mainland and described their ethnic, linguistic, and socio-cultural traits and their degree of contact with European traders. Turner was most familiar with Inuit residing in the immediate area surrounding the Fort Chimo HBC post at Kuujjuaq. He reported that these people called themselves "Sukhinimyut" and occupied the territory extending eastward from the mouth of the Leaf River (Tasiujaq), on the western coast of Ungava Bay, as far as Hamilton Inlet on the central Labrador coast.[68] Turner also noted that this population could be further subdivided into several communities, each of which was known by a name derived from the locality in which people resided. While his major report referred to the three such place-groups in the region, based at the Koksoak River, George River (Kangiqsualujjuaq), and

Cape Chidley (Killinek),[69] an earlier publication offered a more detailed and different perspective on social arrangements.

In an 1887 article, Turner stated that three "subtribes" of the Sukhinimyut were recognized, "solely on account of the stress laid by an Innuit upon the land of his birth."[70] The divisions focused on the three primary rivers in the region, consisting of "Tasyuyak" (Tasiujaq), Koksoak River, and Kangiqsualujjuaq. The people of Killinek were added to the Kangiqsualujjuaq group.[71] His subsequent report allotted the Tasiujaq inhabitants with an adjacent northwestern population of "Tahagmyut" and accorded a separate status for Killinek residents.[72] These changes suggest that Turner was uncertain about the actual range and boundary of Inuit social groupings in the region.

Aside from acknowledging the presence of Moravian mission stations on the Labrador coast, Turner had very little information on the size or characteristics of the Inuit population there, compared with the details on groups who traded at Kuujjuaq. He estimated that about seven families, with fewer than 40 people, lived from Hebron to Killinek, and another eight families resided between Killinek and Kangiqsualujjuaq, amounting to fewer than 50 people. The coast between Kangiqsualujjuaq and Koksoak River was said to be uninhabited, and only four or five Inuit families, totalling fewer than 30 people, lived in the Koksoak area.[73]

Turner's estimate of the Inuit population north of Hebron was grossly inaccurate. He was evidently unaware of the Moravian community at Ramah, which had 82 members in its congregation at the end of 1884;[74] approximately the same number of people occupied the region from Nachvak to Killinek, according to Moravian accounts. Since Turner did not spend any time outside Kuujjuaq, besides a few days at Rigolet on his trip north, he must have relied on reports from Inuit visiting or living at Kuujjuaq for his estimates of the population residing to the northeast.[75] The low figure given to him suggests that his informants were not familiar with all Inuit occupying the area from Hebron to Killinek. Similarly, the discrepancy in his designation of Tasiujaq and Killinek, at the periphery of the Sukhinimyut area, suggests that he had either inadequate or conflicting information about their status.

Garth Taylor, an ethnohistorian who has conducted extensive research on traditional social and economic features of northern Labrador Inuit culture, has disputed Turner's use of the name "Sukhinimyut" for Inuit occupying the Atlantic coast of Labrador. Noting that this term was not generally known in the Labrador region, Taylor suggests that a broad traditional name does not appear to have been used to describe coastal inhabitants, who commonly "refer to themselves simply as Labrador Inuit or as Labradorimiut."[76] He further states that "prior to the arrival of Europeans in the Ungava region, Inuit of the Atlantic coast had relatively little contact with those of Rivière aux Feuilles [Tasiujaq] from whom they were separated by wide uninhabited and sparsely populated areas on the south and east coasts of Ungava Bay."[77] In the early historic period, relations between the Inuit population in Ungava Bay and on the Labrador coast were limited to trade exchanges, as this book has illustrated.

The second subdivision of Ungava Inuit described by Turner was composed of the inhabitants of the southern shore of Hudson Strait extending north beyond the mouth of the Leaf River at Tasiujaq. This population was known by the name "Tahagmyut" and had the least contact with white traders, who called them "Northerners."[78] Compared to their eastern and western neighbours, these Inuit were unusually tall, had a paler complexion, spoke a different dialect, had distinct customs, and retained more traditional practices.[79] A meteorological observer stationed at Cape Prince of Wales in 1884 also noted that the pronunciation of words was more similar to the language spoken on the north side of Hudson Strait than to the dialect of Inuit living at Killinek.[80]

Turner provides a detailed description of annual expeditions coordinated by the Tahagmyut to obtain imported goods from Kuujjuaq. The trade party consisted of individuals from different camps in the region who formed a caravan of three to five Kamutet, with the first Kamutik originating from the most western settlement and joined by others proceeding along the coast. The participants acted as intermediaries or middlemen in making purchases for people remaining in the community:

> Certain persons are selected from the various camps who have personally made the trip and know the trail. These are commissioned to barter the furs of each individual for special articles, which are mentioned and impressed upon the mind of the man who is to effect the trade.[81]

The traders would be responsible for 30 or 40 parcels of furs sent by different families and apparently only relied on a few toothmarks made on trade goods to identify their owner.[82]

Inuit living along the southern shore of Hudson Strait commonly traded among themselves, as well as at distant trade posts, and used a white fox pelt as a standard of exchange. They took their furs to two trading stores: a post operated by a Captain Spicer located across the strait on the Baffin Island coast (in the vicinity of Kimmirut) and the HBC Fort Chimo post at Kuujjuaq.[83] Inuit traders made frequent journeys to both places over a year.[84] Pelts of foxes, wolverines, and wolves were the primary commodities exchanged for such items as ammunition, guns, knives, files and other hardware, and tobacco. About two-fifths of all the furs traded at Fort Chimo derived from expeditions originating on the southern Hudson Strait shoreline. Trade parties began their journey with the first snowfall in November and usually reached the HBC post in early May; they returned to their home communities by the middle of summer or the following winter.[85]

Inuit made the same kind of expeditions to the Moravian stations on the Labrador coast during the late eighteenth and early nineteenth centuries, as well as to Fort George on the southern Hudson Bay coast before the Fort Chimo HBC post was established at Kuujjuaq. Despite the long period of time during which these trade ventures were made, Turner reported that many Inuit participating in them had never seen white men until they visited Fort Chimo.[86] This suggests that the individuals acting as trade middlemen held the position for lengthy intervals, perhaps throughout their lifetime. As late as 1903, a Canadian vessel landing at Sugluk Bay on the southern shore of Hudson Strait reported meeting three Inuit families who had never had direct contact with white men. They exchanged their furs with neighbours to the east or west for guns and other articles rather than visiting a distant trade post.[87]

A third Inuit group called Itivimyut, who lived on the eastern coast of Hudson Bay, also made an annual trade expedition to the post at Fort Chimo.[88] While these families traded mainly at an HBC post located at Fort George on James Bay (current-day Chisasibi), a party consisting of the same six individuals regularly travelled across the peninsula to barter furs and bags of partridge feathers at Fort Chimo. Turner described Itivimyut as having a shorter stature, more oval facial structure, and darker complexion than northern Inuit, and speaking with a different and harsher dialect than used by Koksoak Inuit. The Itivimyut had less contact with other Inuit than their neighbours to the north and east, although they had a longer history of relations with traders and missionaries based in the southern Hudson Bay region.[89]

## Ramah and Its Decline

The trade at Fort Chimo (Kuujjuaq) provided a link between the three Inuit groups in the Ungava region but did not involve Inuit living on the far northern coast of Labrador. Inuit in Labrador do not appear to have had a tradition of long-distance trade ventures in the nineteenth century; instead, they relied on obtaining trade goods from the nearest store. With two stores in the area, at Nachvak and Ramah, northern Inuit had convenient outlets to barter their furs and other resources and so had no reason to travel elsewhere to trade. Moreover, increasing illness, food shortages, and recurrent social disputes in the late 1800s prompted people to become Christian converts at Ramah. Compared to the hardships they faced, the mission station may have offered more security and material comforts than could be found at traditional camps.

Families at Ramah often had easier access to food and social assistance than those in traditional camps. The Moravian missionaries and their trading post provided food supplies and trade merchandise, as well as access to medicines, gifts of food, and protection from abuse. All these factors likely influenced the decision of five young couples to move from Nachvak to Ramah, regardless of the approval of their elders, between 1881 and 1887. One of these couples included Tuglavina's youngest brother, Semigak. The Ramah missionary "feared the influence of his elder brother will still draw him towards heathenism,"[90] but Semigak and his family persevered as converts. The departure of young people from Nachvak replicated a pattern that had occurred at Saglek 40 years earlier.

The movement of families into Ramah, along with deaths due to illness or mishap, significantly reduced the resident population at Nachvak during the 1880s. The Ramah missionary hoped in 1885 that the HBC post would be closed; as the Nachvak population would then likely resettle at Ramah, the closure would offer the only prospect for further growth of the mission station.[91] However, a change of staff was all that occurred; George Ford, the HBC's agent since 1877, was given a leave of absence and temporarily replaced, and Solomon Lane, who was previously the agent at Saglek before that post closed in 1876, retired from HBC service.[92]

The Moravians could only anticipate a trickle of new converts at Ramah from the small population of Inuit occupying the northern coast. In 1890, about 70 people were estimated to be living in the region;[93] the HBC agent at Nachvak was reported to have 84 Inuit on his list in 1895.[94] The mission station also lost a significant number of its congregation. Between 1886 and 1892, three families headed by Boas, Daniel, and Kleophas moved from Ramah to Hebron;[95] no explanation for their departure is given in the annual reports. As a total of 30 people were included in these three families, their absence accounted for a loss of over one-third of the station's population.

This reduction in numbers may have seriously affected the labour force and viability of the community. In contrast to early annual reports, which noted the success of seal harvesting and other land-use efforts, reports from Ramah in the 1890s refer to the failure of sealing, hunting, and fishing activities, and the growing poverty of its residents.[96] While poor seal harvests had occasionally occurred in previous years, environmental conditions appear to have deteriorated and caused greater hardship than was ever known in the community.

Adolf Stecker, a young missionary appointed to Ramah in 1893, attributed the slow rate of settlement by northern Inuit at the mission station to its poor location for resource harvesting.[97] He questioned the value of erecting a new mission house and church at Ramah, and instead proposed moving the station further north, stating that "the Christians would willingly go, and the heathen would then come and live near the church."[98] As an alternative to moving Ramah, Stecker suggested opening an outstation with an Inuk evangelist to convert the last Inuit "on the well-nigh christianized Atlantic coast of Labrador."[99]

Stecker communicated his ideas on the future of Ramah to the SFG Committee in London and argued that a site farther north, such as Komaktorvik, would attract more converts and lead to better engagement with Ungava Inuit. In a letter dated November 1894, Benjamin LaTrobe, the SFG's secretary, informed Stecker that the Committee supported his proposal for relocating Ramah, although a location other than Komaktorvik would have to be found because they had heard that the bay was too shallow for their supply ship. The Committee considered Nachvak as a possible site and was prepared to cease trade activities if the HBC post remained there but left the final decision on the matter to the Mission Board in Germany.[100]

The other Labrador missionaries responded differently to Stecker's proposal.[101] Gathered at a general field conference in Nain in March 1896, his more experienced colleagues did not agree that starting a new northern station or moving Ramah farther north would be necessary, possibly because episodes of decline and growth occurred at every mission station.[102] Their reaction, however, contradicted the SFG's support for the idea, and created a problem for the superintendent of the Labrador Mission, Carl Albert Martin.

In a report on the status of the Labrador Mission, Martin strongly challenged Stecker's claim that more contact would occur with Ungava Inuit:

> A not insignificant factor, in support of Br. Stecker's plan, was the view, that one could establish relations from Komaktorvik with the Ungava inhabitants. But this view is entirely erroneous. As long as we can remember, it has happened only ONCE, that some families have come over here from Ungava. One can thus not speak of an actual connection, least of all a connection on which one could base missionary activity. Should at some time Ungava be considered, it could only be done on its own and independently of the work in Labrador.[103]

Martin's reference to a single occasion in which Ungava Inuit settled on the Labrador coast may allude either to some residents at Ramah, or to the individuals who settled at Okkak and Hebron earlier in the nineteenth century. The records from Ramah consulted for this study do not specifically refer to any person or family originating from Ungava Bay; however, a passing observation suggests that some people of Ungava ancestry were long-term residents at the mission station.

In the summer of 1888, Benjamin LaTrobe, the editor of the *Periodical Accounts*, visited all the mission stations along the Labrador coast and described his experiences in the journal. At Ramah, he remarked that some Inuit were about 5'10" tall, while others were much shorter.[104] As the Ungava ancestry of Boas at Okkak was displayed by his greater height compared with other Inuit in the community, the implication of LaTrobe's observation is that the tall Ramah Inuit were also of Ungava ancestry; people of greater height were known particularly along the southern coast of Hudson Strait, according to Turner.[105] LaTrobe made his comment after passing houses belonging to John (Ikauja) and Matthew (Swansi), but before reaching "little" Paul's (Simigak's) house, which he noted had a very low door.[106] Thus Ikauja and Swansi may have been the taller Inuit who elicited LaTrobe's remark.[107] The place of birth for these men is not noted in the Ramah Church Book.

In the end, Stecker's proposal to relocate Ramah was not supported. The Mission erected new buildings at the station in the late 1890s, but the community was destined to have a brief future. Ultimately, Stecker was correct in foreseeing that the resolute northern Inuit would not convert to Christianity until a new mission station was established in the region beyond Ramah. The impetus for this development, however, only emerged when another missionary society expressed an interest in proselytizing Inuit in Ungava Bay. The appearance of a minister from the Anglican Church Missionary Society at Killinek in 1899 threatened the Moravian Mission's sole authority on the northern Labrador Peninsula and finally dashed their hopes of expanding into Ungava Bay.

CHAPTER SEVEN

# The Moravian Mission and the Anglican Church in Ungava Bay and Port Burwell, 1899–1904

## A Religious Awakening in Ungava

In the final year of the nineteenth century, Inuit arriving from the north to trade at Ramah told the resident Moravian missionary, Adolf Stecker, that a Christian awakening had occurred among Inuit living along the shores of Ungava Bay and southwestern Hudson Strait. People were said to have made confessions of sins and abandoned traditional rituals and were very eager to learn to read. Stecker heard more about the movement when he received a letter from Mr. Guy, the HBC agent at Kangivak. Guy believed the awakening was thoroughly genuine and stated that almost all Inuit in his neighbourhood were affected by it. He appealed for a visit from a Moravian missionary, as the Inuit families wanted to be baptized and asked for a teacher.[1]

Stecker left Ramah to investigate these reports in April 1899 and joined the HBC agent, George Ford, at Nachvak and a man named Kangerarsuk, who acted as their guide. The party crossed the fiord into Tallek Bay, followed a valley uphill to several ponds, and after reaching the top of a ridge, descended into the valley of the Koroksoak [Koroc] River. Flowing westward from Nachvak and with high hills on both banks, this river formed a natural corridor for travel to Kangivak, which could be reached in one day under ideal conditions.[2] Normally in winter a good Kamutik track could be found on the river ice, but an early thaw that year had made the route extremely difficult. After seven days of rough travel, the party finally reached the coast and the HBC post.[3]

Only three Inuit families lived near the HBC post, although the agent estimated that a total of about 70 people inhabited the Kangivak area. Stecker held several meetings with the residents and discovered that their introduction to Christian matters came from a small book sent to them by Reverend Edmund James Peck, an Anglican missionary based in eastern Hudson Bay. The tract was written in syllabic characters representing phonemes [sounds] in the Inuit language and contained passages of Scripture, prayers, and hymns.[4] Stecker was not familiar with this writing system but he had little difficulty communicating with Inuit, as only their accent and some words differed from the language spoken by Labrador Inuit.[5] Kangivak Inuit understood some Moravian hymns that were sung by Stecker and his travelling companions, and they wrote the words of the hymns in syllabics so they could repeat them later.[6]

Guy provided Stecker with a guide named Kannikitok, who originated from Kuujjuaq and was the oldest man in Kangivak, to take him along the coast to visit Inuit families living as far north as Abloviak Bay. As they travelled, Stecker observed two differences in Kannikitok's habits compared to Labrador Inuit. Instead of using a whip to drive his dogs, Kannikitok threw a stick about two feet long at any dog that did not keep pace. He was also accustomed to stopping at noon to prepare a meal whereas the Labrador travellers went from early morning to evening without anything to eat or drink.[7]

Kannikitok stated that all the people of Ungava–Akpatok, as well as those living on the opposite side of Hudson Strait, had rejected shamanistic rituals and adopted Christian beliefs. They stopped at four settlements, of which the two largest consisted of five families living in a big sealskin tent and a village of six snow houses (illuvigat) where a man named Kena was the chief. Only two families resided at each of the other places, one of which was the home of a man named Akpik, who was the most renowned shaman in the region.[8]

**"Old Tuglavi's iglu," Killinek, ca. 1905 (S.K. Hutton collection, Them Days Archive)**

The Inuit families showed Stecker their religious tracts, including material they had copied or written themselves, and he reported that they were very anxious to learn more about achieving salvation. Stecker was impressed by the people's profound resolve to become Christians and was convinced "this awakening is of God."[9] However, he added:

> Of course, it is not all gold. Some only follow the others, without themselves knowing exactly why. All the same, no Christian can help but rejoice with what is here to be seen . . . they look you in the face with far more frankness and candour than is customary with their people; they observe the Sabbath; they count the days until the seventh, when all work ceases. Their zeal to learn whatever they can is astonishing.[10]

Stecker noted that some people from Ungava had first taught Kangivak Inuit to read and write using syllabics in the spring of 1898, and practically everyone had since acquired literacy skills.[11]

At Abloviak, Kannikitok left Stecker's party, and they continued on their own back to the Labrador coast. The party journeyed inland following tributaries of the river emptying into the bay and the ridges of hills leading eastward to the Komaktorvik River. After three days of strenuous activity, they reached Nachvak; Stecker continued to Ramah, arriving there on May 4.[12] The venture was a unique occasion when the HBC agents and a missionary had collaborated and relied on each other in pursuing a common interest. Both agents offered to assist a Moravian missionary in every way possible to return to the region the following winter and provide instruction to Kangivak Inuit. Stecker's conclusion that "the work is the Lord's, and He will find ways and means in due time" would shortly be realized, although in a different manner than he may have imagined.[13]

## Anglican Church in Ungava

Inuit enthusiasm for conversion in Ungava may have originated with the Anglican minister Edmund Peck's visit to Fort Chimo in August 1884,[14] but they were more likely influenced by other Inuit converts. Two Inuit families from Whale River (Kuujjuarapik), who had been converted by Peck, arrived to trade at Fort Chimo in the winter of 1895 or 1896.[15] Three women in the group were very active in teaching people to sing hymns and pray, and held services in which they explained the basic principles of the Gospel. The religious movement among Inuit at Fort Chimo developed immediately after this visit.

Twenty years earlier, in 1876, the Anglican Church Missionary Society (CMS) had assigned Rev. Peck to Little Whale River, where he ministered to Inuit trading at HBC posts in James Bay and on the southeastern coast of Hudson Bay.[16] Earlier missionaries had focused their attention on the Cree population in the region but the bishop of the diocese wanted to extend Christianity to Inuit, who began visiting Fort George to trade in 1839.[17] Two decades before Rev. Peck arrived, two other ministers named Horden and Watkins had adapted a syllabic writing system to produce religious literature in the Inuit language.[18] Syllabics had first been developed for the Cree language by collaboration between Cree and Methodist minister James Evans in northern Manitoba in the 1830s, and the writing system quickly spread throughout northern Canada.[19] Horden and Watkins distributed to Inuit in 1856 the first small Inuktitut books containing Gospel verses printed in syllabic characters, after which the Lord's prayer, Ten Commandments, and portions of Scripture were published.[20]

Unlike the Anglicans, Moravian missionaries in Labrador used Roman characters for transcribing Biblical material in the local Inuktitut dialect. From the beginning of their work in Labrador in the late eighteenth century, all Labrador missionaries were expected to become fluent in Inuktitut. Their publications, particularly an 1840 edition of the New Testament in the Labrador dialect, were the basis for the first transliterations made by Anglican ministers for Inuit in Hudson Bay.[21] The literacy instruction given by the Moravians to Labrador Inuit also benefited the Anglicans. In 1862, a man originating from the Labrador coast named Gustave Lutolf, who was employed as an interpreter by the HBC at Little Whale River, wrote out the Inuktitut text of a catechism in Roman characters, which was then converted into syllabics.[22] The CMS also engaged a retired Moravian missionary in 1874 to adapt sections of a Labrador Inuit prayer book for Hudson Bay Inuit, but the book proved to be useless because of the way it was written or translated.[23]

Rev. Peck began learning Inuktitut by studying words in the Moravian New Testament, although he was uncertain as to the extent of similarity between the language spoken by Inuit on the eastern Hudson Bay coast and the Labrador dialect. With assistance from another HBC interpreter from Labrador named Adam Lucy, Peck discovered that the dialects varied principally in pronunciation and not in words or idioms.[24] He gradually mastered the Inuit language by memorizing words and deciphering its syntax over a period of seven years; he later produced a grammar of the eastern Hudson Bay dialect.[25]

Rev. Peck and earlier Anglican ministers discovered that Inuit could learn to read syllabic characters in a shorter period of time than it takes to learn the Roman writing system.[26] Within eight or nine weeks, people were able to read with ease and often became keenly interested in obtaining printed material to advance their knowledge.[27] Peck noticed that having the ability to read the Scriptures themselves strengthened people's understanding of Christianity when they were living away from a minister's influence.[28] Moravian missionaries made the same observation about the significance of literacy to Labrador Inuit converts.[29]

The greater ease of learning the syllabic system resulted in an independent and widespread movement among Inuit in the Hudson Bay region to acquire literacy skills. Inuit who learned the syllabic system at Whale River began teaching it to other people who had no personal contact with Peck's mission.[30] As late as 1903, Inuit residing in Kangiqsujuaq on the southeastern shore of Hudson Strait, who had never seen a missionary, had been taught to read by people at Fort Chimo.[31]

Inuit converts also played an active role in advocating the adoption of Christianity. An elderly convert named John Molucto agreed to assist

**Women and children outside the entrance to an illuvigak (snow house), 1908 (photo by Berthold Lenz, Unity Archives, Herrnhut)**

Rev. Peck in his work,[32] and even unbaptized Inuit spread information about the Gospel. Peck learned that a man named Titikgak had promoted conversion after returning to his home area, 1,250 km from Little Whale River, and convinced many people to abandon their traditional spiritual customs.[33] Peck also trained young Inuit converts to become teachers, who provided instruction to residents during the minister's absence. While Peck considered the development of a native ministry to be a vital component of his program,[34] Moravian missionaries working on the Labrador coast were often more reluctant to encourage Inuit to serve independently as spiritual leaders.

Working alone and without many facilities, Peck's approach to attracting Inuit to Christianity was much less intrusive and demanding than the Moravian strategy; his ambition was simply to gain people's faith in Christianity. In contrast, Moravian missionaries required Inuit converts to reside for the winter at their mission stations, attend instructional classes for long periods, and make numerous changes to their customary social and economic practices. The Moravian missionaries' role was also compromised by their involvement in trade, whereas Peck was independent from the economic relations of Inuit and the HBC. With a character described as patient, humble, prudent, loving, and diligent, Peck was an ideal missionary[35] and readily gained the respect of Inuit. His personal qualities may have been an instrumental factor leading to the rapid spread of interest in conversion among Inuit in the region.

From his base in Little Whale River, Rev. Peck met Inuit who travelled as much as 1,000 km to trade at the HBC post.[36] They originated from places throughout the Ungava Peninsula, but particularly from the southern shores of Hudson Strait.[37] Hearing that a relatively large Inuit population was centred in Ungava Bay, Peck became determined to visit the area. He made three attempts, between the summer of 1882 and winter of 1883, to travel overland from the eastern Hudson Bay coast, but each time severe weather, ice conditions, or a scarcity of game forced him to abandon the journey.[38]

In the summer of 1884 Peck finally reached Ungava Bay, travelling by canoe with a party of four Cree from Little Whale River to Richmond Gulf on the Hudson Bay coast, then following rivers and chains of lakes to Seal Lake and taking the Larch and Koksoak rivers leading to Kuujjuaq.[39] The journey lasted 25 days. After spending three weeks preaching to Inuit, he boarded the HBC steamer for a year's furlough in England. Except for mentioning that he taught several Inuit living at or near the HBC post to read, a detailed account of his experiences was apparently not recorded.[40]

Peck returned to the Hudson Bay region in 1885 and continued working from a new base at Fort George until 1892. That summer, he proposed starting a new mission at Fort Chimo (Kuujjuaq) in Ungava Bay, as he had heard that the Roman Catholic Church was planning to open a station to attract Inuit as well as Innu trading at the HBC post.[41] However, the HBC refused to allow a mission to be started in the region and Peck had to return to England because of his wife's poor health.[42] While on the journey, he met a ship's officer who had visited Cumberland Sound in Baffin Island on a whaling vessel and described the condition of the Inuit inhabitants. His account inspired Peck to extend his work to that region instead.[43]

After another leave in England, Peck began planning a new ministry at Cumberland Sound, supported by the owner of two whaling stations there. This venture occupied him after 1894 and eventually expanded to include mission stations at Frobisher Bay [Iqaluit] and at Lake Harbour [Kimmirut], on the northern coast of Hudson Strait.[44] When Peck first arrived at Cumberland Sound in 1894, Inuit were amazed that he could speak their language. He found only minor dialectical differences between the language spoken there and the Inuktitut spoken by Inuit at Little Whale River and Fort George.[45] A similar observation was made by a Moravian missionary from Greenland, Mathias Warmow, who lived for a winter in Cumberland Sound on a whaling ship in 1856 and was able to communicate with Inuit in the Greenlandic dialect.[46] Peck continued to use Moravian texts as the basis for his translations of scriptural material for his missions in southern Baffin Island.[47] His booklets in

**Family outside a tent, 1908 (photo by Berthold Lenz, Unity Archives, Herrnhut)**

Inuktitut were widely distributed, sometimes reaching Inuit communities via ships surveying Hudson Strait.[48]

Peck was informed in 1899 of the religious awakening in Ungava Bay in a letter from Benjamin LaTrobe, the secretary of the Moravian Mission Board. LaTrobe described Stecker's visit to the Kangivak area and commented on the "astonishing" progress that Inuit had made in learning to read and write in syllabics within one year.[49] The underlying purpose of the Moravian's letter was revealed in a question he posed: "Whose is the privilege and duty to take up the work thus begun in the Divine leading of Providence?"[50] Answering his own question, LaTrobe argued that the Moravian Church had the prerogative of developing a mission in Ungava Bay as an extension of its existing work with Inuit on the Labrador coast. He hoped that Peck and the CMS Committee would agree, adding that a committee member had indicated support for the Moravians' interest in Ungava at a meeting held in 1897.[51]

LaTrobe was obviously trying to prevent the CMS from placing a missionary in Ungava Bay. If the Anglicans proceeded, the Moravians would be obliged to stand aside, despite their long history of contact with Inuit from the Ungava region. According to Stecker, the religious awakening had really created "an open door" for missionary work.[52] The Moravian missionaries wanted the entrance reserved for them so they could claim a large number of new converts.[53] Responding to LaTrobe's correspondence, Peck acknowledged that the CMS lacked the capacity to create new missions in Ungava Bay and Hudson Strait, as they were fully occupied with Inuit in Cumberland Sound, and he welcomed the Moravians to "spread the light in these dark wilds."[54]

## The Anglican Church at Killinek and Tension with the Moravian Mission

While these discussions were occurring among church officials, a Newfoundland fisherman was trying to secure a missionary to evangelize Inuit at the very northern tip of the Labrador–Ungava Peninsula. The Job Brothers merchant firm of St. John's had established a fishing station at Port Burwell on Killinek Island in 1898. Its agent, Captain Samuel Blandford, was a Newfoundland fisherman who had learned of the rich cod grounds around the Chidley Peninsula in about 1893. The site at Port Burwell was previously used for a meteorological observation post by the first Hudson's Bay Expedition in 1884–85, and its crew had named the site after Herbert Burwell, the officer in charge.[55] Port Burwell's harbour was the only safe port on the western side of Killinek Is-

**Inuit women, Killinek, 1910 (The Rooms Provincial Archives)**

land.[56] The Job Brothers' premises served as a base for harvesting cod and narwhal and was also a trade centre for obtaining fox and seal pelts from local Inuit.[57]

Anxious to convert and "civilize" Inuit living in the vicinity, Blandford approached the Anglican diocese of Newfoundland for a missionary; when they showed no interest in the Ungava region, he applied to the Anglican bishop of Quebec.[58] Upon hearing this, Bishop Jones of Newfoundland relented and agreed to supply a missionary.[59] Blandford was a devout Christian who instructed his employees to do everything in their power to assist a missionary.[60] In the summer of 1899, Rev. Samuel Milliken Stewart accompanied him along the coast to examine the area, and he returned the following summer to work from the Job Brothers' station, which was thereafter called "Bishop Jones' Village."[61] Stewart hired Samuel Ford, the son of Nachvak HBC agent George Ford, as his interpreter among the Killinek Inuit.[62]

The Moravian SFG Committee first learned of Stewart's appointment to Port Burwell from a Newfoundland newspaper article in November 1899. Hearing that the Colonial and Continental Church Society in Newfoundland had sponsored him for a seven-year term, the Moravians assumed that the door to the Kangivak–Ungava area was closed to them.[63] No doubt disappointed, the SFG abandoned plans for further surveys of the region as they wanted "to avoid running rival missions alongside of any other Society."[64]

Stewart's assignment was a severe blow to the Moravians, especially after they were informed that he would be visiting and providing religious instruction to Inuit residing along both coasts south of Killinek. The terminal points of his field included Nachvak on the northeastern Labrador coast and Kangivak on the northwestern Ungava coast,[65] which was also the target area for the Moravian mission at Ramah. Rather than creating a new mission with a different population of Inuit, as he would

**Children at the entrance to an illusuak (sod house), Killinek, 1919 (McCord Stewart Museum)**

have done if he had been based at Fort Chimo or elsewhere in Ungava Bay, Stewart was encroaching on the Moravians' work with northern Inuit, particularly on the Labrador coast.

When Blandford learned of the tension between the Anglicans and Moravians over Stewart's appointment, he wrote to LaTrobe explaining his role and assuming responsibility for the situation.[66] However, nothing could be done after Stewart was installed at Killinek, although the Moravians doubted that he would be able to last the full seven years.[67] With their experience and knowledge of the northern region, Labrador missionaries were well aware of the hardships facing a minister working alone from a remote station and having to travel in frequently difficult environmental conditions. The SFG anticipated Stewart's resignation and envisaged opening new stations at Killinek as well as at Fort Chimo (Kuujjuaq), if they could come to an agreement with the HBC.[68]

In the spring of 1900, Moravian missionary Stecker reasserted the extent of Moravian territory by venturing north along the Labrador coast to Cape Chidley, visiting Inuit at two sites in addition to people living near Captain Blandford's station at Port Burwell.[69] Stecker followed the Kamutik trail from Nachvak to Sagliarusek, a cape north of Komaktorvik, where he counted 41 people occupying seven large snow houses (illuvigat). The residents were very short of food, as they had been unable to obtain game for a considerable time. At Aulatsivik, another seven illuvigat were inhabited, which would have included approximately 35 inhabitants based on an average of 5 occupants in an illuvigak.[70] They apparently had ample provisions because Stecker noted that, although they were all quite ready to become converts, they could not be persuaded to leave that part of the coast. He understood their position, stating, "nor can we expect it of them with good conscience, for at Ramah they would not be half as well off as here."[71]

Stecker was met at Sagliarusek by the manager of Blandford's station, Julius Lane. Lane was the son of Solomon Lane, the former HBC manager at Saglek, and a native Labradorian of mixed Inuit ancestry originally from the Davis Inlet area who now lived with his family at Port Burwell.[72] He accompanied Stecker to the station where the missionary held services attended by 21 people. Stecker noted that the core of the population was composed of the families of Kajuasiak's six adult sons, four of whom were married.[73]

Stecker described a scheme for a missionary in the area that corresponded precisely with the program later adopted by the Anglican Church, which involved visits to Inuit occupying the Labrador and Kangivak coasts. He believed that the residents of the two districts could not "well be gathered into congregations, for there are not enough of them, and they are obligated to live scattered in order to make a living."[74] Nevertheless, Stecker thought they could assemble at Blandford's station during Christmas and Easter. He was amazed at the richness of game in the Port Burwell area, stating "it is almost incredible what quantities of seals and birds are to be found up there, but there are not enough people to secure them."[75] Stecker concluded that another mission station would have to be formed at the Koksoak River to provide services for people living there and further north at Akpatok Island.

In the summer of 1900, Stecker left Labrador for a new posting in Alaska. He was replaced at Ramah by Sigmund Waldmann, who attempted to retrace his journey to Killinek in March 1901. Waldmann headed for Semigak's summer residence in Komaktorvik, where he met one of Semigak's sons-in-law and his "old cast-off wife."[76] Semigak and two of his sons soon arrived and guided Waldmann's party to Sagliarusek, where five illuvigat were built, of which at least three were occupied by the families of Semigak's sons.[77] After Waldmann lost his sealskin trousers, sleeping-bag, and other articles in a severe gale, he decided to curtail his trip and return to Ramah.[78] He repeated the journey in January and again in April 1902, halting on his first trip once more at Semigak's residence after a fierce storm prevented further travel northward along the coast. He reported that Semigak's elderly brother Tuglavina was a member of the kinship group and had built a sod house (illusuak) for his family in Komaktorvik.[79]

Waldmann pressed the two Inuit leaders to adopt Christianity but they both adamantly refused to leave their dwelling place. Tuglavina was quoted as stating: "We are as good as the Christians and have to eat what we need, also, we are not sick. Thus we want to remain what we are."[80] Semigak demanded an allowance of food every year as a condition to becoming a Christian: "I have told you already last year and say it again, if you give me something to eat each year, as bread and flour, I don't demand very much, then I'll come to you immediately and become a Christian. If you don't give it to me, then I'll not become a Christian."[81] When Waldmann rejected his ultimatum, Semigak stated that he did not believe in a living God and preferred the Torngait (helping spirits),[82] adding:

> I don't need this [Christianity]. I have done nothing wrong. I want to stay with the one who has taken care of me all my life and fed me. I don't want to leave him . . . I don't need a God or saviour, for if someone among us needs anything, then I'll heal him and make him alive and the Torngaks help me. I can do everything, and if you don't want to come to us and build a store, then it's no use.[83]

Providing a local store was the primary benefit of a Moravian presence, in Semigak's opinion. He concluded the interview by commenting that Christian Inuit did not behave better than his people and that he protected single girls, as the missionaries did at Ramah.[84]

Waldmann learned in January that visiting Killinek would also have been futile since a group of Inuit living at Aulatsivik had already left their winter place and Stewart, his interpreter Samuel Ford, and Blandford's manager Julius Lane were absent on a tour to the Kangivak region.[85] In late April 1902, Waldmann finally succeeded in reaching Killinek and meeting with Stewart; he also preached to about 25 Inuit staying at Ikkerasak, a campsite nearby.[86]

Waldmann's visit was very briefly described in the *Periodical Accounts*. He was said to have had a "friendly reception" from Stewart,[87] but their relations were not at all amiable according to the original report on the journey. Waldmann fiercely criticized the Anglican minister's efforts and approach. He noted that Stewart could not speak Inuktitut well and that his interpreter wanted to stop working for him. He belittled Stewart's reliance on a few books written in syllabics – a "script invented by a monk," Waldmann claimed.[88]

The Moravian missionary was particularly irritated by Stewart's assertions that Inuit living near Nachvak belonged to his district and were considered "Church people" by the Anglican diocese in Newfoundland. Waldmann countered that the Moravian Church viewed Inuit living north of Nachvak as "belonging to us."[89] Although he observed that conducting regular tours would be expensive for the Anglicans, he also noted that the HBC Fort Chimo manager at Kuujjuaq had offered Stewart a small vessel that would enable him to visit people frequently during the summer. The Company's support of Stewart dismayed Waldmann, but he recognized that the HBC had a different attitude to Stewart's interactions with Inuit compared to its attitude towards the Moravian missionaries.[90] As Stewart had no interest in trade, HBC agents were willing to provide him with practical assistance to advance his ministry, while they could hardly be expected to offer help to the Moravian competitors in trade.

Stewart may have wanted to press his advantage by deciding to join Waldmann on his journey back to Nachvak, but the Moravian minister slyly checked this manoeuvre by proposing that they jointly visit Semigak's encampment when they approached the Komaktorvik area. Stewart declined the invitation, saying that he preferred to stop there on his return trip, and continued to Nachvak.[91]

Waldmann spent only one hour with Semigak and his family at Tupervialuk and then briefly visited a group of people camped near the Komaktorvik River. Upon meeting a young woman who had learned to sing hymns and pray when she was a child living at Ramah, Waldmann asked her if she still sang and prayed to Jesus. She replied that she did not. Other people affirmed her statement, adding that "praying and singing and ABC is not good for us."[92] The girl was likely the daughter of Mattheus and Verone (Tuglavina), who left Ramah with their family in 1898.[93]

## The Moravian Mission Considers a New Station at Killinek

The Anglican missionary's presence in Killinek provoked the Moravian Mission to renew its attention to the northern and Ungava region. The Moravians had been considering expanding south into the Rigolet area, but, as Bishop Benjamin La Trobe told the Anglican Bishop Llewellyn Jones in 1902, "our Church has given up the thought of a station at Rigolet. We are turning our attention to the Ungava Bay."[94] Initially, not all Moravian missionaries supported the idea. Waldmann thought at first that forming a congregation at Killinek would be impossible unless food was supplied to Inuit for several months in the winter, as they depended on distant hunting grounds.[95] The location became more attractive, however, after the Job Brothers firm offered to sell its entire establishment to the Moravian Mission in May 1902, citing high operating expenses. The property included a two-storey dwelling, provision store, large fuel shed capable of storing 3,000 gallons of oil, boats, and equipment, as well as their remaining trade stock.[96]

Bishop Jones of the Anglican diocese was not immediately ready to relinquish the Anglican mission at Killinek. In a letter to LaTrobe, he noted that the Moravians were not established in the region and that their prior objective had been to create a station in Kangivak, which he assumed was quite distant from Killinek. Jones offered to transfer Stewart to a location south of Cape Harrison and place him in charge of the Anglican mission at Rigolet and Cartwright if the Moravians were prepared to occupy Killinek and continue his work in Ungava Bay. A meeting between Canon Pilot and Bishop Martin, the Moravian superintendent of the Labrador Mission, was proposed at Nain during the summer to arrange matters to their mutual satisfaction.[97]

LaTrobe presented Jones's suggestion to the Central Mission Board at Herrnhut and consulted the Moravian agency in London. In a letter addressed to Bishop Jones in June 1902, he stated that the Moravians wanted Stewart's mission transferred to their church, although they did not intend to take over Killinek and would more likely settle in Kangivak. Labrador missionaries would make an exploratory voyage before a final decision was made on the location of a new station.[98] Bishop Jones replied to LaTrobe in July 1902, stating that he had received a letter from Stewart indicating that his mission work could only be conducted from a more central location than Killinek. Stewart planned to relocate under HBC auspices to George River (Kangiqsualujjuaq), where he would be able to continue providing services to Inuit residing at Killinek, Nachvak, and Kuujjuaq. Bishop Jones erroneously assumed that an Anglican presence at Kangiqsualujjuaq and a Moravian one at Kangivak would be quite distant from each other and not cause any conflict.[99] LaTrobe responded by sending Jones a sketch map showing that Kangivak and Kangiqsualujjuaq River were in close proximity and noting Stewart's agreement with the Moravian view that the location of Killinek was inappropriate. Adding that Inuit in Kangivak had appealed to the Moravian Mission after their spiritual awakening, LaTrobe made it clear that Stewart was unwelcome in the area and should be transferred to Rigolet.[100]

Waldmann and Walter Perrett, a missionary from Hopedale, made a brief visit to further investigate the prospects at Killinek in the summer of 1902. They learned that the largest family at Aulatsivik had moved to Killinek and that people migrated in summer to fish on the Kangivak coast. There they met Inuit who traded at HBC posts and had a kinship relation with families from Labrador.[101] If Stewart departed, Waldmann speculated that Killinek could become a "connecting station" linking Inuit from the Atlantic and Ungava shores.[102] He argued that missionaries based at Killinek could make more frequent and longer visits with families living at Aulatsivik, compared to Ramah, while missionaries from both stations could visit people at Komaktorvik. Waldmann also expected that the residents of Komaktorvik would be more willing to become converts and move to a mission station after the deaths of Semigak and Tuglavina.[103]

Waldmann's enthusiasm for opportunities at Killinek was not shared by the second missionary at Ramah, Otto Eckhardt, or the store manager, Wilhelm Merten, who advised the Moravian Board in Germany not to proceed hastily with creating a new station there. In January 1903, they approached George Ford, the HBC manager at Nachvak and a member of the Ramah congregation, for his advice on the best site for a station. With over 20 years' experience in the northern region, Ford was better equipped to evaluate the prospects. He thought that Killinek was a poor location due to its rough terrain, lack of firewood, and limited resource availability. Strong tides and ocean currents create turbulent waters in the Killinek region, providing good habitat for seals, walrus, and other marine mammals, but rarely allowing a floe edge to form.[104] The channel separating Killinek Island from the mainland, McLelan Strait, was called Ikirasagatuk or "Big tickle with strong tides" in Inuktitut, and could be extremely dangerous for boats and ships.[105] While the marine life is abundant, terrestrial wildlife is scarce; caribou are only occasionally available when their population is plentiful, and other animals are rarely seen.[106] The area's resources were insufficient for a large population, he argued, as shown by the small number of people residing there at the time [about 25 people]. Ford estimated that the total Inuit population between Ramah and Killinek amounted to about 60–70 people, which compared with the size of the Ramah congregation.[107] He told the Moravian missionaries that the largest number of Inuit living between Ramah and Killinek were based at Aulatsivik because it was the best area for harvesting game.[108] The Aulatsivik region was home to nesting eiders, seal populations, char, fox, and often caribou, and featured broad valleys among the towering Torngat Mountains.[109]

Waldmann and two other missionaries conducted a second survey of the Killinek area on the mission's ship *Harmony* in August 1903. The party had originally planned to travel as far as George River (Kangiqsualujjuaq), but after reaching Fort Chimo (Kuujjuaq), they had a long conversation with Stewart that convinced them to terminate their journey. Stewart admitted that he had never intended to stay at Killinek/Port Burwell and preferred a base in southern Ungava Bay, but he could not refuse Job Brothers' invitation to reside at their premises. In the interim, his living conditions had become intolerable after he was obliged to share accommodations with the station manager, Julius Lane. He claimed that Lane's "unchristian" way of life caused their personal relations to seriously deteriorate, and that he was determined to move to southern Ungava Bay, where the HBC had promised him a private dwelling.[110]

The Moravian missionaries thus concluded that travelling to Kangiqsualujjuaq was futile. Once Stewart relocated to one of the HBC posts, the small Inuit population on the eastern Ungava coast would not justify having another station in the region. As well, they were not interested in creating a Moravian mission at Kangiqsualujjuaq because the area had no connection with northern Labrador. It represented a new mission territory that would have to be administered separately from their established field, as Martin had stated in 1899.[111]

Despite George Ford's counsel against settling at Killinek, the Job Brothers' premises provided an immediate base for a mission station. The site would quickly secure the Moravian Mission's position in the far northern region and define its constituency in relation to the Anglican Church; these advantages seem to have outweighed any drawbacks for the Mission. Superintendent Martin presented Killinek's geography as an asset, providing an opportunity for the Moravians to extend their mission westward along the Ungava coast to Kangiqsualujjuaq, as well as southward along the Labrador coast to Ramah. He expected that a station there would "most certainly" lead to a migration of Inuit families from both areas to join the 44 people occupying five houses and a few tents found at Killinek in 1903.[112]

Martin noted the rich seal and sea bird resources in the area, as Stecker had in 1900, but he did not question why the resident population was so small. The option of selecting Aulatsivik, the site favoured by Ford and many Inuit, was never pursued. Moravian surveys of the coast had focused on Killinek and consequently lacked information to properly assess the Aulatsivik area and compare it to Killinek. Martin acknowledged that Killinek's rough terrain limited building space, but he added that there was enough ground for a small station and a cemetery, adequate fresh water in surrounding ponds, and a good harbour for their annual supply ship. Although Martin did remark on the absence of firewood and brush as a troublesome problem, he did not speculate on how fuel would be provided or the cost of heating facilities in the cold environment.[113]

The status of Ramah was an additional factor for the Moravian missionaries in promoting the creation of a new station at Killinek. Very few new converts had moved to Ramah in the previous decade and not many were expected because game harvests had declined. The missionaries recognized that they were unlikely to convince Inuit families in the north to adopt Christianity by visiting them occasionally from Ramah. With another station at Killinek, Ramah missionaries could concentrate on the coast extending south to Hebron while their Killinek counterparts devoted themselves to the northern region.[114]

Martin's recommendation to locate a new station at Killinek was endorsed by Moravian officials. Negotiations to purchase the Job Brothers' property followed, and the SFG paid $4,000 for its assets in an agreement concluded in November 1904.[115] Martin wanted to distinguish the station, commonly known as Port Burwell, with a new name and proposed calling it "Kikkertaujak," meaning "peninsula" in Inuktitut.[116] Other Labrador missionaries thought the word was unwieldy and not sufficiently distinctive, as it was used for many places along the coastline. Instead, they decided to call their mission Killinek, meaning "the land nearest the ocean," which was the name of the island where it was located.[117]

On September 24, 1904, Sigmund Waldmann, his wife, and Sam Voisey and his family arrived at Killinek to establish the mission station.[118] The next day, the Moravians held their first meeting, at which the missionary preached and two Inuit helpers from southern communities spoke. Thomas from Hebron told the gathering that "it was God's will that they (the heathen) can also learn the way to salvation," while Joel asked people to show obedience towards the missionaries, since they were there for the good of the Inuit.[119]

## Uncertain Jurisdictions at Killinek

From the start, it was unclear whether the new station at Killinek was built on Newfoundland or Canadian territory. Labrador missionaries had raised the question of jurisdiction in the spring of 1904 but received conflicting information. They asked the SFG to request a land grant for their mission from the Canadian government, and to ask if customs duties would be levied on goods imported and exported by their store.[120] A month later, A.P. Low of the Geological Survey of Canada arrived at Killinek on the steamship *Neptune* and told Waldmann that the Moravian station was on Canadian territory and that a customs house would soon be built.[121]

Low was the leader of a Canadian government expedition aiming to assert sovereignty over Hudson Bay and the Arctic Islands. The limit of Newfoundland's jurisdiction was considered to extend a few miles inside Cape Chidley, the northern point of the Atlantic coast, while Canada's jurisdiction extended westward.[122] Thus, according to federal officials, the Moravian mission station was in Canadian territory as it was located on the western side of Killinek Island, within the entrance to Hudson Strait and therefore part of the HBC territory ceded to Canada. Low advised that the location and good harbour at Killinek made it an ideal site as a port of

**Fishing premises, Killinek (The Rooms Provincial Archives)**

entry for installing a Canadian police and customs station to regulate commercial shipping entering and leaving Hudson Strait.[123]

A year later, the governor of Newfoundland, Sir William MacGregor, visited Killinek during a tour of the Labrador coast and observed that Newfoundlanders residing there always believed the colonial government had "unquestioned" jurisdiction over the area.[124] He noted that Inuit living near the mission station were all natives of the east coast, except for one woman from Kangiqsualujjuaq. He was told by Julius Lane that "no people other than the Killinek natives" hunted or trapped in the vicinity. MacGregor reported that the entire area from the Chidley Peninsula to the Button Islands appeared to belong exclusively to the Killinek Inuit, who composed a population of 48 people in six families at the time.[125]

Lane described the area of land used by Killinek Inuit as extending to the west about five miles beyond a second cape called "Oivuk," located approximately 25 km from Killinek, and encompassing the Button Islands to the north.[126] MacGregor was told that the Button Islands were formerly inhabited, as many graves were found there, and Inuit oral history referred to a resident population. However, the current Killinek Inuit rarely hunted on the islands because crossing the channel to reach them was very dangerous.[127] MacGregor was also informed that a man named "Kuber" claimed ownership of the Button Islands, although exclusive individual or family rights to defined areas were uncommon because Inuit hunters frequently hunted or fished together over the same land.[128]

MacGregor was aware that the Moravian Mission had a historic exemption from customs duties, awarded to them by the British government and recognized by Newfoundland officials. He believed this privilege would be extended by the Canadian government, if it ultimately had jurisdiction over the territory, because of the nature of the Mission's work; a customs exemption was also given to Wilfred Grenfell's Mission to Deep Sea Fishermen.[129] However, MacGregor may not have been informed of the conflict caused by the Moravian involvement in trade transactions, particularly with its long-standing rival in the northern region.

The HBC and other commercial enterprises, such as the Job Brothers firm, had to pay customs duties on goods imported to Newfoundland, which increased their costs. Supplies shipped to Labrador for HBC posts in the region, as well as for its posts in Ungava Bay, were landed at Rigolet, where Newfoundland authorities collected customs duties on the ship's entire invoice. Although Ungava Bay was in Canadian territory, the HBC had to pay Newfoundland duties on goods destined for Fort Chimo when its cargo was transferred to a small steamer at Rigolet.[130]

Uncollected customs revenues in Ungava Bay, as well as throughout the Hudson Bay area, prompted the Canadian government to sponsor several surveys of Hudson Strait and Hudson Bay after 1884. Many American whaling vessels were active in Hudson Bay and traded illegally with Inuit inhabitants, using imported goods for which duties were not paid. Their trading activities constituted unfair competition with existing HBC posts, which paid a considerable sum annually in duties to Canadian authorities.[131] Killinek, at the entrance to Hudson Strait, was a strategic location that was vital to Canadian interests in regulating shipping and collecting customs duties from vessels destined for Hudson Bay. As a result, Job Brothers was notified by Canadian officials in 1903 that it would have to pay duties in the future.[132] This threat may have been the primary reason underlying its desire to sell the station to the Moravian Church.

Despite MacGregor's opinion that the Moravian Mission would likely continue receiving a customs exemption, Canadian authorities were not so lenient. In 1907, a customs officer on board the *Neptune* made an inventory of goods subject to duty at the mission station.[133] Canadian officials continued to levy the Killinek mission with customs duties over subsequent years, although the Moravian missionaries consistently protested paying them because jurisdiction over the area was unresolved.

In addition to speculating about the customs and jurisdictional issues, Governor MacGregor provided other advice during his trip. He was impressed with the healthy state of Killinek Inuit, but he was concerned that the Inuit population at the other mission stations was seriously declining, as rates of infant mortality and deaths from infectious epidemics were very high. As a result, he strongly recommended changes to the design of Inuit houses and to sanitation facilities to promote better health.[134] Like MacGregor, many Moravian missionaries also connected physical health and healthy morality to issues of housing and they sermonized on the benefits of cleanliness and European-style houses.[135] The same views were more forcefully expressed by Dr. Wilfred Grenfell, who dispensed medical care on his tours along the northern coast. Grenfell severely criticized the Moravian Mission for neglecting the state of Inuit housing at its stations and for maintaining a conservative barter system of trade.[136] His comments provoked hostility between his agency and the Moravian Mission that lasted for many years.

While the Moravians were establishing themselves at Killinek, the Anglicans were moving into Ungava. In September 1904, Grenfell provided transportation to Rev. Stewart as far as the HBC post at Nachvak, and that winter, Stewart travelled by dog team to George River (Kangiqsualujjuaq) and Fort Chimo (Kuujjuaq).[137] He established his headquarters at Fort Chimo and spent the next 28 years ministering to the Indigenous population in the Ungava Peninsula.[138] Once Stewart was diverted to this region, the Moravian missionaries commonly described him as a "courageous pioneer" and welcomed his visits when he stopped at their stations during his later travels to and from Newfoundland.[139]

With Stewart's Ungava mission removed from Killinek, a definite boundary was established for the Moravian constituency in northern Labrador. A southern limit at Cape Harrison had been recognized since the 1870s with the Anglican and Methodist churches, which ministered to residents of Inuit and mixed European ancestry living in the Hamilton Inlet area and further south. In April 1908, the superintendent of the Moravian Mission, Bishop Martin, informed delegates attending a general mission conference at Nain that the Moravian sphere of influence was "co-extensive with the coastline from Cape Harrison in the South to Killinek, and a little beyond, in the North."[140] He confirmed, for the final time, that further extension of the Moravian Mission's work beyond these "boundary stones" with unbaptized Inuit elsewhere was out of the question.[141]

CHAPTER EIGHT

# Inuit Living between Ramah and Killinek, 1904–1908

In the summer of 1904, Moravian missionaries calculated that approximately 100 Inuit lived on the coast between Ramah and Killinek, based on information provided to them by the Nachvak HBC agent, George Ford.[1] Killinek was occupied by about 35 people, and about 15 people were settled at Aulatsivik. All the families residing permanently in the region were related to Semigak, the recognized chief of the band, and include the families of his sons, his elder brother Tuglavina, and his younger brother Paksaut. The largest number of Inuit close to Ramah belonged to Semigak's family and included about 30 people residing at Komaktorvik. Another 20 or so people lived near Nachvak.[2]

This chapter provides a detailed outline of these individuals and their kinship relationships between 1904, in the months before a deadly influenza outbreak swept through the region, and 1908, as the impacts of the epidemic on families became apparent. The Inuit population living at Nachvak and Komaktorvik can most easily be identified because they were in frequent contact with the HBC agent and Ramah missionaries, who recorded abundant information about them in their reports. Fewer details are available concerning the inhabitants of Aulatsivik and Killinek, where families were reported to be settled permanently.[3] Farther from the HBC and Moravian stores, Inuit living in these locations made

**Inuit in front of large illusuak (sod house), Ramah, 1908 (The Rooms Provincial Archives)**

only occasional visits to barter resources for imported goods. Hunters in these areas were not dependent on the Nachvak post since they could trade their furs at the Job Brothers' fishery station at Killinek or with ships stopping in the harbour during the summer season.

## Inuit of Aulatsivik

Aulatsivik was home to about 35 people in 1900. By 1904, the population had dropped to about 15, as many had moved north to Killinek, and the families of Onalik and his son-in-law Sekepa were the primary residents of Aulatsivik Island (see Table 3).[4] Onalik lived with two or more wives,[5] children, and his aged mother.[6] Sekepa was married to Onalik's daughter, Tuglavina.[7] The two families resided at Aulatsivik, a site located on a narrow neck of land joining Aulatsivik Island with the mainland coast.[8] Another daughter and granddaughter of Onalik were both called Koliligak. His daughter was born about two years after the man named Koliligak of Kavanga's family group died at Aulatsivik in 1900, which strongly suggests that she was named after him.[9] The genealogy of Onalik's family group is outlined in Figure 1.

**FIGURE 1: Genealogy of Onalik's family group in 1904**

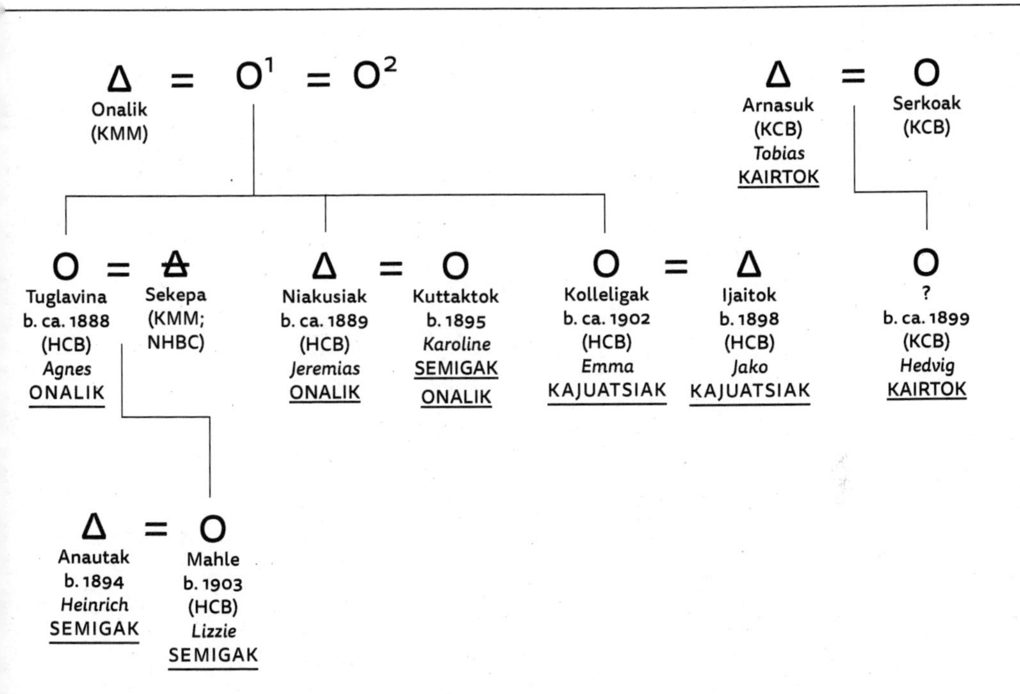


**Key to genealogies:**

O / Δ: male / female

O$^n$: first wife, second wife...

ϴ or ∆̶: deceased

=: married

≠: divorced

**(HBC), (KBC), etc:** source of information (see Abbreviations on page ix)

**Name**: Inuit name

***First Name*:** Christian name

**LAST NAME**: chosen last name

**b.** or **d.**: date of birth or death

**b. ca.**: born *circa* (approximate year of birth)

**TABLE 3. Composition of Inuit Families Inhabiting Aulatsivik and Killinek in 1904.**

| | | |
|---|---|---|
| **Aulatsivik (est. 15)** | | |
| Onalik | 6 | wives (2?) (unnamed)<br>mother (unnamed)<br>son: Niakusiak (Jeremias Onalik) b. ca. 1889 (HCB)<br>dau: Kolleligak (Emma) b. ca. 1902 (HCB) |
| Sekepa | 3 | wife: Tuglavina (Agnes Onalik) b. ca. 1888 (HCB)<br>dau: Mahle (Lizzie) b. 1903 (HCB) |
| Arnasuk (Tobias Kairtok) | 3 | wife: Serkoak<br>dau: Hedvig b. 1899 (KCB) |
| **Killinek (est. 35)** | | |
| Avigiak (Nicodemus) b. ca. 1860, d. 1906 (KCB) | 8 | wife: Kajoe (Caritas Onalik) b. ca. 1860 (KCB)<br>son: Kajuatsiak (Benjamin Onalik) b. ca. 1887 (KCB)<br>son: Omiak (Klemense Onalik) b. ca. 1892 (KCB)<br>son: Tivoa (Boas Onalik) b. ca. 1893 (KCB)<br>son: Ikka (Samuel Onalik) b. ca. 1898 (KCB)<br>dau: Tullugaksoak (Hildegard Onalik) b. ca. 1901 (KCB)<br>son: Onalik (Herman Onalik) b. ca. 1905 (KCB) |
| Koktok (William Jararuse) b. ca. 1871 (KCB) | 6 | wife: Sappa (Mary Jararuse) b. ca. 1875 (KCB)<br>dau: Attua (Emily Jararuse Onalik) b. ca. 1891 (KCB)<br>dau: Simigak (Susana Jararuse) b. ca. 1894<br>dau: Kuper (Klara Jararuse) b. ca. 1902 (KCB)<br>son: Angutaunek (Paulus Jararuse) b. ca. 1904 (KCB) |
| Anga (Jako Jararuse) b. ca. 1875 (KCB) | 3 | wife: Pingoak (Rahel Jararuse) b. ca. 1880 (KCB)<br>son: Martin Jararuse b. 1900 (KCB) |
| Paujunge (Tomas Jararuse) b. ca. 1877 (KCB) | 3 | wife: Nipissa b. 1880 (HCB)<br>son: Ungerdlek (Jefta Jararuse) b. 1902 (KCB) |
| Kavanga (Henry Jararuse) b. ca. 1889 (KCB) | 2 | wife: Paungak (Sara) b. ca. 1873 |
| | 3 | brother: Serlek (Konrad Jararuse) b. ca. 1887 (KCB)<br>sister: Pullanersoak (Selma Jararuse) b. ca. 1894 (KCB)<br>brother: Sekkinek (Lukas Jararuse) b. ca. 1897 (KCB) |
| Paksau | 5 | mother: Kingak<br>wife (unnamed)<br>son: Kajuasiak<br>son (?): Ijaitok (Jako Kajuatsiak) b. 1898 |
| Kupa (d. 1906) | 3 | wife: Annekordluk<br>dau: Kajuasiak (Elizabeth) b. 1901 (KCB) |
| Serlek (d. 1906) | 3 | wife: Louisa/Lucy<br>dau: Sara b. 1904 (KCB) |

Onalik made two journeys to Killinek during the winter of 1905 to visit and trade. He stated that he would move to Killinek and abandon his old ways in the future, but he was rich that winter, apparently because he made a large catch of fox pelts.[10] Even if he did move to Killinek, he added, "he would always return for some time to his place."[11] Onalik also spent some time at Nachvak in 1905. According to a missionary, he considered moving there but he "was ordered back from Nachvak to his old place" by "our people on the eastern side," presumably meaning members of Semigak's extended family group who customarily resided in the fiord.[12]

The third family at Aulaksivik in 1904 consisted of Arnasuk, his wife Serkoak, and their young daughter whose Inuit name was not recorded.[13] In 1908, Arnasuk became a candidate for baptism at Killinek. He was later baptized Tobias and adopted Kairtok as his surname. Following his wife's death in 1912, he married a widow, Tabea (Arnatuk), who had been Tuglavina's youngest wife.[14]

## Inuit of Killinek

Inuit sometimes moved between Aulatsivik and Killinek when game was scarce at one location and plentiful at the other. The large family that left Aulatsivik in 1902 probably included a man called Avigiak, who was baptized on his deathbed at Killinek in March 1906 and given the name Nicodemus.[15] His wife, Kajoe, and seven children later became candidates for baptism and chose Onalik for their surname,[16] which implies that the family was closely related to the headman Onalik at Aulatsivik. Avigiak and Onalik may have been brothers, and Kajoe may have been Kajuasiak's daughter.[17] The genealogy of Avigiak's family is outlined in Figure 2. Table 3 summarizes Inuit known to be residing at Aulatsivik and Killinek in 1904.

Another family at Killinek consisted of a man named Koktok, his wife Sappa, and four children.[18] Koktok was reported to have travelled several times to trade at the Nachvak HBC post from "Berwell" (Port Burwell).[19] He and his family were the first candidates for baptism recorded

**FIGURE 2: Genealogy of Avigiak's family**

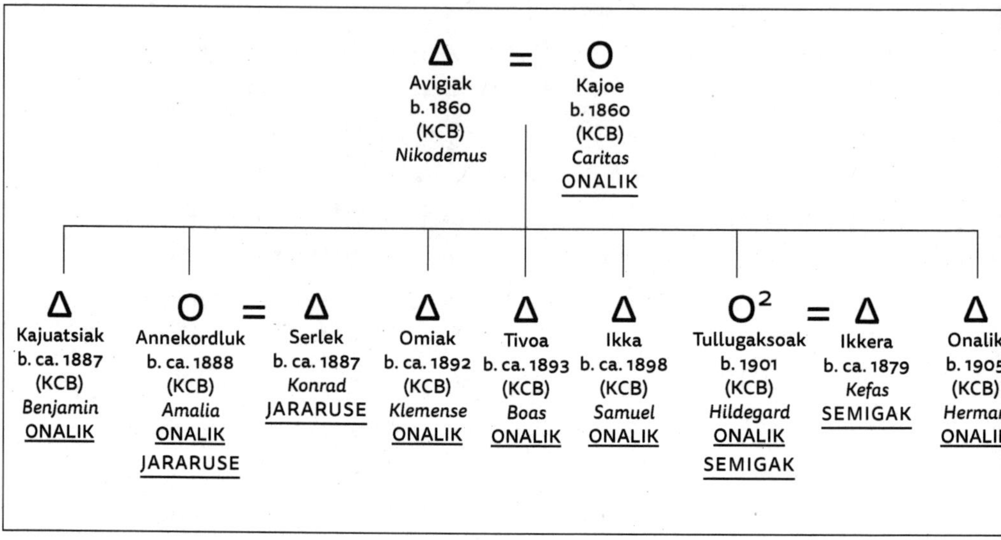


in 1905 after the Moravian Church opened at Killinek (see photo of William (Koktok) and Maria (Sapa) Jararuse). Koktok's family may have also resided at Aulatsivik prior to 1904 because he appears to have been very familiar with Onalik. Koktok went to the camp in April 1905 and asked Onalik to join the congregation, but he refused to leave.[20] During the winter of 1917, Koktok made another attempt to urge Onalik to become a convert and received the same response.[21]

Koktok had five brothers and a sister, all of whom became candidates for baptism by 1908 and formed the initial core of the Moravian congregation at Killinek. Koktok was born about 1871 and was the eldest sibling; three of his brothers, Anga, Paujunge, and Kavanga, had wives and children by 1904.[22] The genealogy of Koktok's siblings is outlined in Figure 3.[23] After Koktok and his brothers were baptized, they all chose the surname Jararuse.[24]

A widow named Kingak also lived at Killinek. She became a candidate for baptism in March 1908 and was likely one of Kajuasiak's three wives because when her son Paksau was baptized in 1912, he adopted

Kajuatsiak as his surname (see Figure 4 and photo of David Kajuatsiak [Paksau]).[25]

Paksau's mother, Kingak (The Rooms Provincial Archives)

Of the eight married men living at Killinek in 1904, three of them had wives who originated from the vicinity of Kangiqsualujjuaq or elsewhere along the northeastern Ungava Bay coast.[26] As Stecker remarked in 1900, eligible women were very scarce on the coast between Ramah and Killinek, so finding a wife from the eastern Ungava region appears to have been a common practice for men in the Killinek area.[27] A few more marriages involving partners from the two regions occurred after the Moravian Mission was established at Killinek, as it attracted families who had previously lived a distance apart. Aside from these couples, other families at Killinek appear to have derived primarily from marriages between the descendants of Tuglavina, Semigak, Kavanga, and Kajuasiak.

## Inuit of Komaktorvik and Nachvak

Semigak and members of his large family lived at Komaktorvik at the beginning of the twentieth century. He lived with his two wives and children, as well as with five grown sons and one grown daughter and their families, numbering approximately 30 in total (see Table 4). Semigak's older brother, Tuglavina, the former chief, and his younger brother, Paksaut, lived at Nachvak with their families.

Many of these Inuit firmly refused to convert to Christianity. Missionaries at Ramah made little progress in trying to convince them to abandon their traditional beliefs and customs. In April 1904, a missionary visited Semigak's group and discussed conversion privately with

FIGURE 3: Genealogy of the Jararuse family

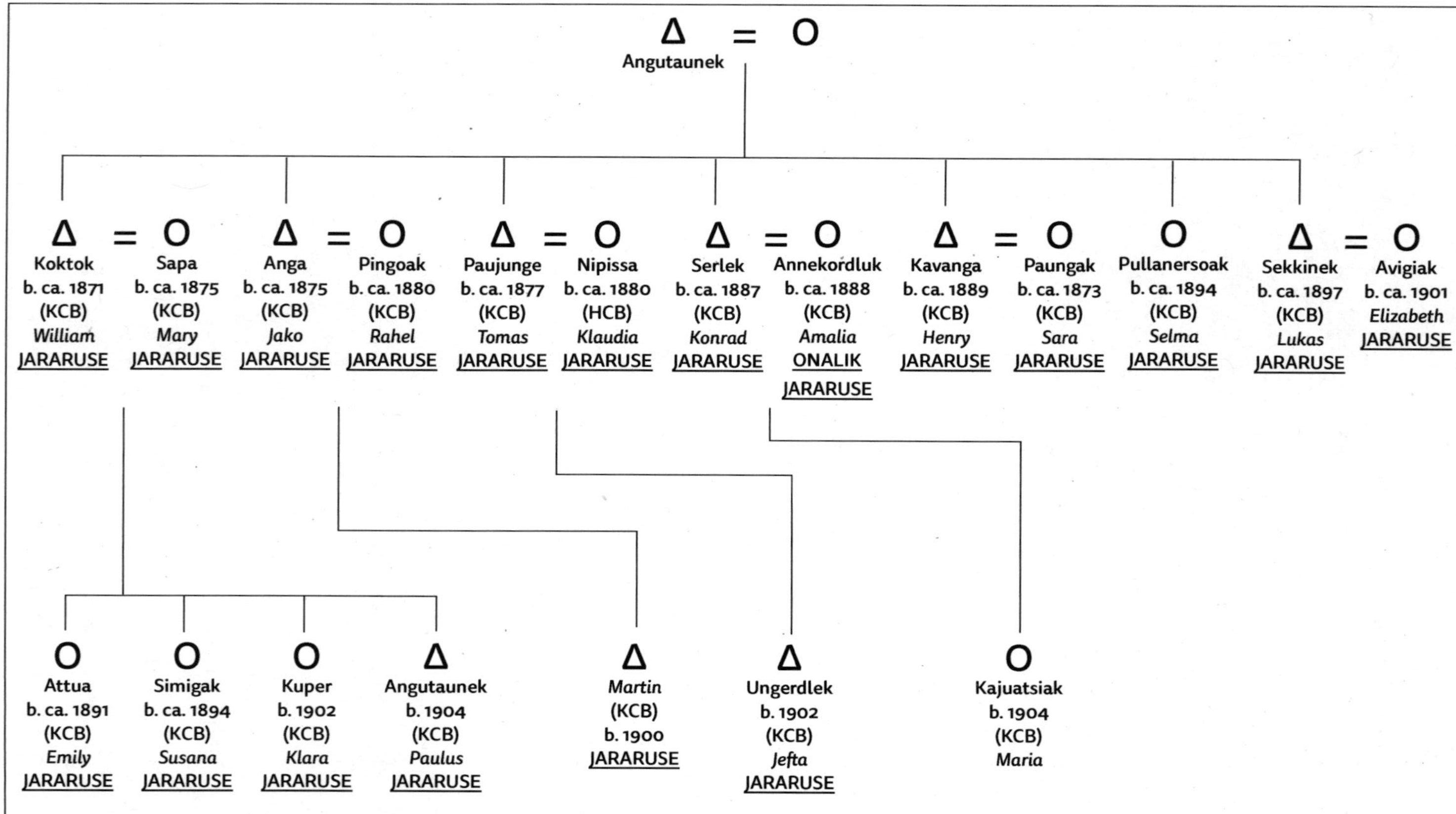

**FIGURE 4: Genealogy of the Kajuatsiak family**

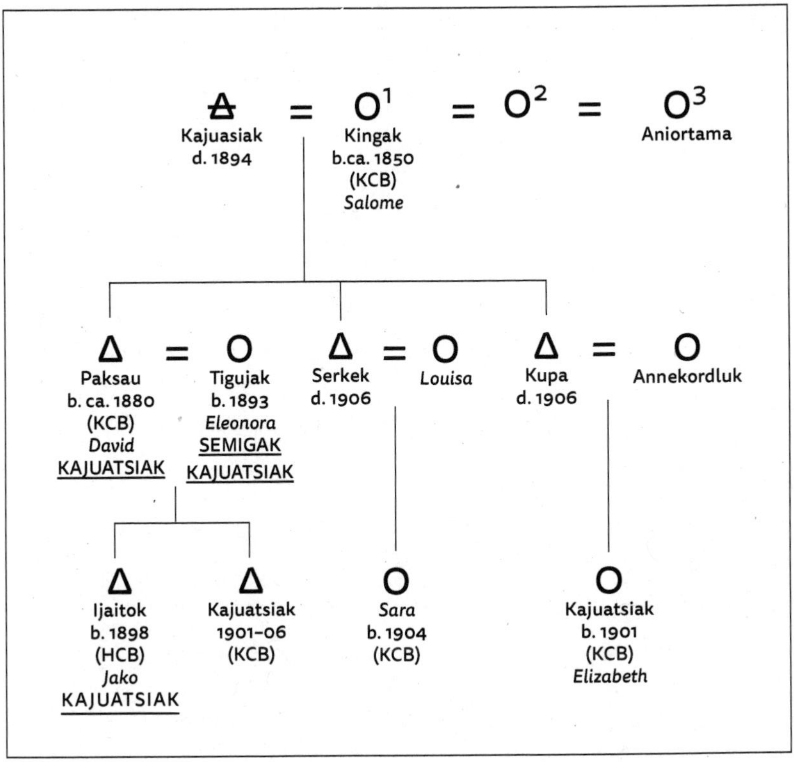


"the heathen chief in the North."[28] Semigak told him that a Christian life at a mission station offered him little of interest:

> Semigak remains firm in his determination not to relinquish his heathen beliefs and ways – nor does the life of most of the native Christians at Ramah tend to influence him in favour of the change. He finds most of them to be but little better than himself, and prefers to remain as he is.[29]

Inuit who had left the church for their own reasons also lived in the Nachvak area. Nine people were nominally members of the Ramah congregation. They had been either candidates for baptism or baptized but chose not to continue their association with the Ramah mission. One family consisted of Mattheus and Verone (Tuglavina), with three daughters and

**TABLE 4.** Composition of Inuit Families Inhabiting Nachvak and Komaktorvik in 1904.

| **Nachvak (est. 20)** | | |
|---|---|---|
| Paksaut | 9 | wife: Inumanek (HCB)<br>wife: Nippisa (HCB)<br>wife: Paniguniak (KMM)<br>son: Puttoruk (Jako Jens) b. 1890 (HCB)<br>son: Silligarsuk (William Jens) b. 1896 (HCB)<br>dau: Pamiok (HCB)<br>dau: Niakotsiak b. 1903 (HCB)<br>young man: Kippinguk (Jako Kippinguk) 1885–1910, son of Aniortama (HCB) |
| Kangerasuk | 2 | wife: Sofie [Tuglavina] |
| Tuglavina | 8 | 1st wife: Pitsuratsuk (Sabina Tuglavina) ca. 1849–1923 (KCB)<br>2nd wife: Kedlek d. 1904 (NHBC)<br>3rd wife: Arnatuk (Tabea) b. 1874 (KCB)<br>son: Attataksoak (William)<br>wife (unnamed) d. 1904? (NHBC)<br>son: Kuttaktok (Renatus Tuglavina) b. 1896 (KCB)<br>son: Omanatsiak (Josef Tuglavina) b. 1902 (KCB) |
| **Komaktorvik (est. 30)** | | |
| Semigak d. 1904 (NHBC) | 5 | 1st wife: Nangmartvarsuk (Eugenia Semigak) b. 1855 (KCB)<br>2nd wife (unnamed) d. 1904 (NHBC)<br>dau: Tigujak (Eleonora) b. 1893 (KCB)<br>dau: Kupa (Pauline) 1900–1914 |
| Kudjaijok (son) 1868–1905 (RCB; NHBC) | 7 | wife: Attataksoak b. 1866 (RCB)<br>son: Nippisa b. 1883 (RCB)<br>son: Inuluk (RCB)<br>son: Inukulluktok b. 1891 (RCB)<br>dau: Inurulluk b. 1893 (RCB)<br>child: Serkoak b. 1901 (RCB) |
| Paniguniak (son) d. 1904 | 4 | wife: Kutaktok (Zipora Semigak) b. ca. 1880 (HCB)<br>son: Anautak (Heinrich Semigak) b. 1894 (HCB)<br>dau: Kuttaktok (Karoline Semigak) b. 1895 (HCB) |
| Anatsiak (son-in-law) d. 1904 | 7 | wife: Paniguniak (Harriot Semigak) b. ca. 1869 (RCB)<br>dau: Sikepa (Sabina Semigak)<br>dau: Kuttaktok 1894–1906 (RCB)<br>dau: Kupa (Luida Semigak) b. 1899 (KCB)<br>dau (unnamed) d. 1904 (NHBC)<br>son: Pitsiango (Levi Semigak) b. 1901 (KCB) |
| Koganak (son) (Raymond Semigak) b. 1876 (HCB) | 2 | wife: Sekkinek (Magdalena) b. 1877 (RCB) |
| Ikkera (son) (Kefas Semigak) b. 1879 (KCB) | 3 | wife: Agnes [Nipissa] 1887–1920 (RCB; KMM)<br>son (unnamed) |
| Nikkatok (son) (Gustav Semigak) b. 1889 (KCB) | 2 | wife: Kristine Semigak b. 1891 (RCB) |

a son, who were formerly communicant members of the congregation. They had severed their relationship with the Moravian missionaries in 1898 following a disagreement and had avoided going to Ramah thereafter.[30] The missionaries predicted in 1904 that their children would eventually marry unbaptized spouses,[31] a forecast that was partially fulfilled.

Another former convert was a man named Kangerarsuk. He had been a candidate for baptism but left Ramah in 1896 with his baptized wife Sofie (formerly Tuglavina), who had been born in Nachvak.[32] Kajuasiak's widow Aniortama and her two children also left Ramah with Kangerarsuk, but she and her young daughter went to live at Hebron in 1898 and were baptized there.[33]

## The 1904 Influenza Epidemic and Movements North

The familiar pattern of life at Nachvak and Komaktorvik changed radically after late September 1904, when an epidemic of influenza rapidly infected Inuit living in the region. George Ford, the HBC agent, noted the death of 10 people, including "the good old hunter" Semigak, one of his wives, and a child in his household.[34] Most of the deaths occurred in October, but the final victim of disease was Semigak's eldest son, Kudjaijok, who passed away the following July.[35]

These sudden deaths devastated the cohesion of Semigak's family group and threatened their resolve to remain in the area. Most of the survivors gathered in Nachvak but some people moved to Ramah or went to live with relatives in other areas. A missionary travelling from Ramah to Nachvak in the winter of 1905 reported that Semigak's younger brother, Paksaut, was the chief and shaman of five families inhabiting the fiord; his own family included three wives. The group of 30 people were the only inhabitants of Nachvak.[36]

In the late spring of 1905, Paksaut led some of these families to the Killinek area and stayed there with relatives for about two years. During this time, his third wife, Paniguniak, separated from Paksaut and lived with her brother at an outlying campsite called Terrekok (Tiggekok).[37] Although the couple reconciled for a short period, the relationship did

**Aulatsivik (photo by Berthold Lenz, Unity Archives, Herrnhut)**

not last because she did not accompany him when he returned to Nachvak in 1909.[38]

One of the families joining Paksaut in travelling from Nachvak to Killinek included Semigak's surviving widow, Nangmartvarsuk, and a widow named Paniguniak, whose husband Anatsiak and a daughter had also died during the influenza epidemic;[39] they provided care to six children.[40] Two years later, the two widows and their children became members of the Killinek congregation.[41] Both Paniguniak and Nangmartvarsuk, who were baptized Harriot and Eugenia respectively, and their children adopted the surname Semigak.[42] The genealogy of Semigak's family is outlined in Figure 5.

When these two widows became converts, they were joined by the youngest widow and children of Tuglavina, the elderly former chief of Nachvak, who had lived with his brother Semigak's family as his age advanced. In April 1905, Tuglavina's family was at Aulatsivik staying with three families headed by Onalik. That year, Tuglavina decided to move to Killinek, so he arranged transportation for himself, his two wives, Pitsuratsuk and Arnatuk, and their children to be taken to the mission station; he was then almost blind.[43] When Moravian doctor Samuel King Hutton arrived at Killinek in 1908, he was told that Tuglavina was a "famous old heathen chief" who was now in his "second childhood," and prone to exploring the missionaries' living quarters, uninvited.[44] When the missionaries started locking their doors to prevent him from entering, he simply used a knife to "lift the latch and let himself in."[45]

Tuglavina never surrendered his resistance to adopting Christianity and died at Killinek in March 1910.[46] His wife, Pitsuratsuk, who was born in about 1849, became a candidate for baptism in 1909; when she was baptized a year later, she adopted the name Sabina Tuglavina.[47] After Tuglavina's death, his youngest wife, Arnatuk, married Tobias Kairtok and was baptized Tabea in April 1914; her three sons adopted the surname Tuglavina.[48] The genealogy of Tuglavina's family is shown in Figure 6.

Kutaktuk, the widow of Semigak's son, Paniguniak, and her two children also moved to live with Onalik and Sekepa at Aulatsivik after the 1904 epidemic.[49] This choice suggests that Kutaktuk was related to one of the adults there; she may have been Onalik's daughter. Over the follow-

**Three women, with Paksau's mother on right (The Rooms Provincial Archives)**

FIGURE 5: Genealogy of Semigak's family group in 1904

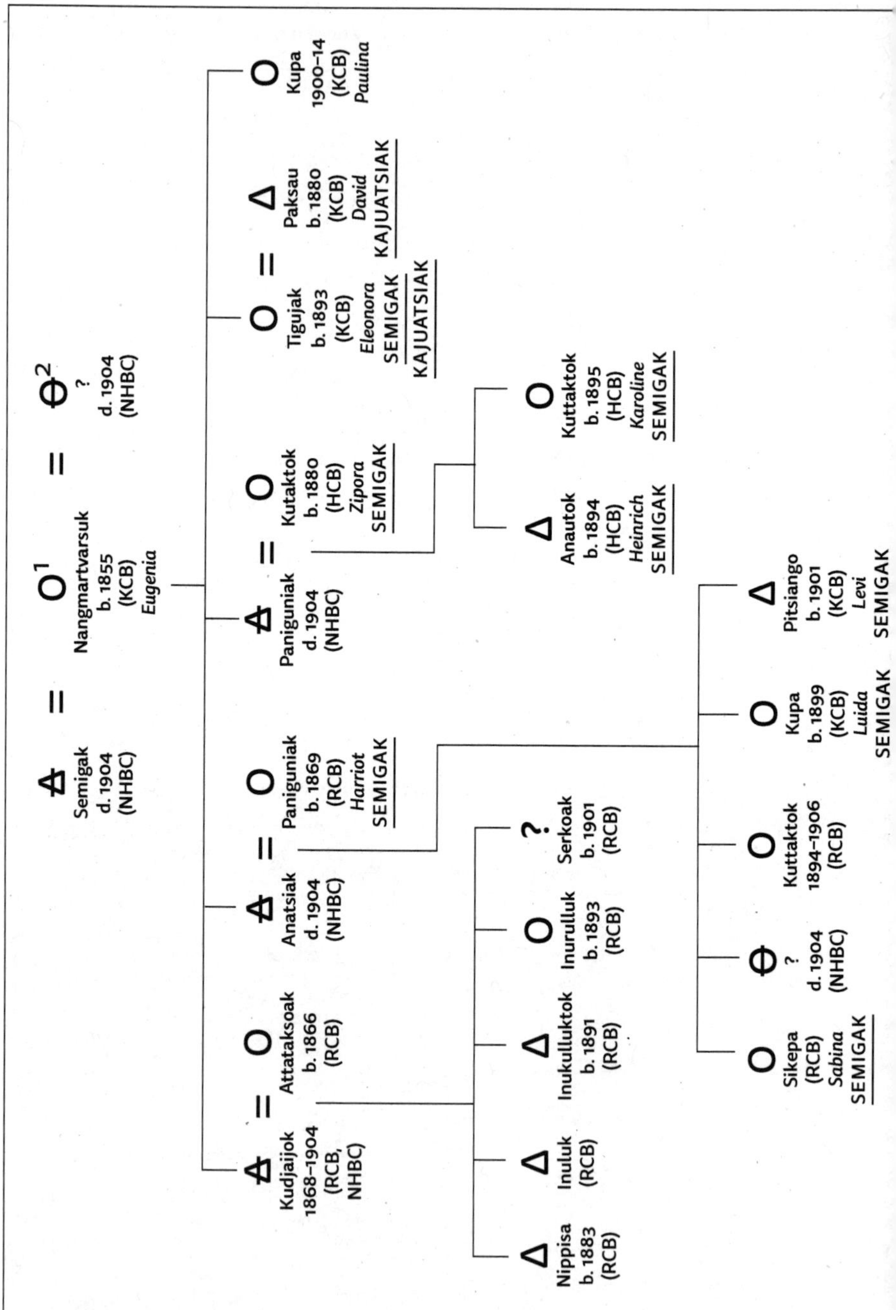

ing years, Onalik and Sekepa occasionally visited Killinek, but as a Moravian missionary commented in 1912, "when they come, it is only because there is a store here."[50] Onalik was the leader of a group that included his mother, son, son-in-law, and two young men living at Aulatsivik in 1917:

> They come here to trade occasionally. Onalik controls them & is satisfied with himself & his manner of life; he is very good to his old mother who is alive, blind & helpless. We & our Helper, William Jararuse have talked with him, Onalik, but he sees no reason to turn from his present mode of life. The son & the other young men sometimes attend a Service in the Church, but the father, never.[51]

The families at Aulatsivik were a very close-knit family group and remained together at the site after Sekepa and Onalik died in the 1920s.

Members of Onalik's family group were still residing at Aulatsivik

**Inuit family from George River (Kangiqsualujjuaq), Nachvak, 1905 (Them Days Archive)**

**FIGURE 6: Genealogy of Tuglavina's family**

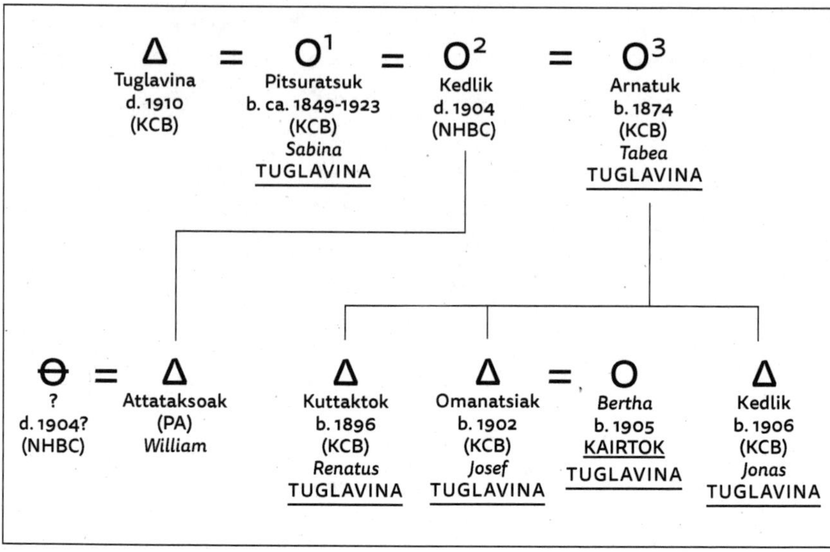


in 1933, and were the last remaining traditional Inuit on the northern Labrador coast to become Christian converts.[52] When Kutaktuk and her children were ultimately baptized in 1933 at Hebron, they adopted the surname Semigak.[53] Onalik's son, Niakusiak, chose the surname Onalik when he was baptized at Hebron, as did Sekepa's widow, Tuglavina.[54] The genealogy of the family groups who moved to Hebron from Aulatsivik in 1933 is presented in Figure 10.

## Inuit at Nachvak and Komaktorvik after the 1904 Epidemic

While some of Semigak's relatives at Nachvak and Komaktorvik moved north with Paksaut after the 1904 epidemic, others stayed in the area or travelled south. Some decided to join Moravian congregations, while others strongly resisted Christianity. Tuglavina's second wife, Kedlik, died at Nachvak during the influenza epidemic.[55] She had a son named Attataksoak who left Nachvak in 1905 and travelled to Nain, where he joined the congregation as a candidate for baptism.[56] He had visited the mission station in March 1904 during a journey with George Ford to the

HBC post at Davis Inlet.[57] At that time, he informed the missionaries that he wanted to settle as far south as he could "in order to be out of reach of his heathen relations and companions, who would do all they could to induce him to return to his former life and beliefs."[58] Attataksoak was baptized in January 1906 and took the name William.[59]

A member of Semigak's extended family who made a similar decision to join a mission station was a widow also named Attataksoak, the wife of Semigak's eldest son, Kudjaijok.[60] The HBC agent described "Kugjaijok" as an old man in 1904 and noted that he was ill before the start of the influenza epidemic.[61] Ramah missionaries believed that Kudjaijok was sympathetic to Christianity before his death.[62] After he died, Attataksoak remained in Nachvak when the rest of Semigak's relatives went to Killinek and lived with other Inuit staying in the fiord. In June 1906, she travelled from Nachvak with her five children and arrived at the Ramah mission station in a very poor state; they later became candidates for baptism.[63]

Kangerarsuk also left Nachvak following his wife's death in the epidemic and settled at Ramah, where he married a baptized widow with

**Ramah, ca. 1905 (S.K. Hutton collection, Them Days Archive)**

three sons in 1905. A year later, he was baptized Tomas and adopted the surname Kangerarsuk;[64] in the summer of 1908, they moved to Hebron.[65] Sometime in 1906 Aniortama's son Kippinguk departed as well because he married a baptized girl at Hebron in February 1907. He was then baptized Jako and adopted Kippinguk as his surname; he died at Hebron in 1910.[66]

Among the people staying with Paksaut at Nachvak in the winter of 1905 were three brothers named Koganak, Ikkera, and Nikkatok. They were likely Semigak's sons because when they were all ultimately baptized, they chose Semigak as their surname.[67] Koganak, born in about 1876,[68] was the eldest brother and was living with a wife in 1906.[69] Nikkatok was noted to have a wife in 1901[70] and a family in 1904,[71] which included a son.[72] Ikkera, born in about 1879 at Komaktorvik,[73] had a wife in 1906.[74] Their detailed genealogies are outlined in Figure 7.

The three brothers did not accompany Semigak's surviving relatives to Killinek in 1905.[75] At least two of the brothers, Ikkera and Nikkatok, occupied a place in Nachvak called Kudlutak during the winter and early spring.[76] In 1909, they decided to leave the area and spent the winter at

**Ramah mission station from the southwest, 1907 (photo by Paul Schmidt, Unity Archives, Herrnhut)**

Aulatsivik;[77] at that time, they intended to settle at a campsite called Operngevik, near Killinek.[78] Nikkatok and his family joined the Moravian congregation at Killinek in 1912; he was baptized Gustav and adopted the surname Semigak.[79] His wife Kristine had been baptized at Ramah in 1897[80] and they had two children, a son, Amos, and daughter, Selma.[81]

Ikkera was married to Kristine's sister Agnes, who was also baptized at Ramah,[82] and they had at least one son, named Wilson.[83] In 1912, Ikkera had a second wife, who was not baptized, but she either left him or died in 1917.[84] Ikkera and his family were likely among the 26 Inuit reported to be living in the vicinity of Aulatsivik and Komaktorvik in 1914.[85] Following the death of his wife Agnes after she was badly burned in a fire at Nachvak in October 1920, Ikkera became a candidate for baptism in early March 1921 at Killinek. His motivation for becoming a convert may have derived from his desire to marry a young widow who was a member of the congregation. His baptism and marriage coincided later that month; his name became Kefas Semigak.[86] He and his new wife Hildegard, along with his son Wilson, moved to Hebron in 1924. He died there two years later.[87]

**Ramah mission station from the northwest, 1907 (photo by Paul Schmidt, Unity Archives, Herrnhut)**

The third brother, Koganak, was also married to a woman baptized at Ramah. His wife Magdalena (Sekkinek) was the eldest daughter of Matthew (Swansi) and Verone (Akkusane) (Tuglavina) who left Ramah in 1898 (see Figure 7). After Matthew died in 1907, followed by his wife in 1908, Magdalena's siblings lived with her and Koganak. They and Paksaut's family, following their return from Killinek in 1908, were the sole remnants of Semigak's kinship group occupying Nachvak.[88]

Koganak's and Paksaut's families were entirely alone in the fiord and lived apart from other Inuit. They also lived far from a trade store, as the HBC post at Nachvak closed in 1906. A poor seal catch during the fall led them to visit Ramah frequently during the winter to obtain food because a good harvest was made there.[89] In May 1909, the two families decided to leave Nachvak and move to Saglek;[90] at that time Paksaut had two wives and four children[91] while Koganak's family, including his wife's relatives, amounted to six people. Paksaut's genealogy is described in Figure 8.

Paksaut remained at Saglek after his eldest son, Puttoruk, married a baptized girl named Augusta Menzel belonging to the Hebron congregation in 1911. Puttoruk was then baptized Jako and adopted the surname Jens; another son also married a Hebron girl and was baptized William Jens.[92] Although Paksaut's three eldest children joined the Moravian congregation, he and other members of his family did not become converts. The death of his entire lineage was noted in the Hebron register during the Spanish influenza epidemic in November 1918.[93]

Koganak stayed in Saglek until the spring of 1911, when he moved north with his immediate family and took one of his wife's sisters as his second wife.[94] They lived at Aulatsivik before moving to Killinek in 1914, at which time the family had six children. Because of their father's continued resistance to becoming a Christian convert, none of the children were baptized.[95] Koganak's second wife separated from him in 1921 and moved to Hebron in 1923, where she married a convert who was originally from Killinek.[96] After the Killinek mission station was closed, Koganak

**TABLE 5. Composition of Inuit Families Inhabiting Nachvak, Winter 1905.**

| | | |
|---|---|---|
| Paksaut (HCB) | 9 | wife: Inumanek (HCB)<br>wife: Nippisa (HCB)<br>wife: Paniguniak (KMM)<br>son: Puttoruk (Jako Jens) b. 1890 (HCB)<br>son: Silligarsuk (William Jens) b. 1896 (HCB)<br>dau: Pamiok (HCB)<br>dau: Niakotsiak b. 1903 (HCB)<br>young man: Kippinguk (Jako Kippinguk) 1885–1910, son of Aniortama (HCB) |
| Nangmartvarsuk (Eugenia Semigak) b. 1855 (KCB) | 3 | dau: Tigujak (Eleonora) b. 1893 (KCB)<br>dau: Kupa (Pauline) 1900–1914 (KCB) |
| Paniguniak (Harriot Semigak) b. 1869 (RCB) | 5 | dau: Sikepa (Sabina Semigak)<br>dau: Kuttaktok 1894–1906 (RCB)<br>dau: Kupa (Luida Semigak) b. 1899 (KCB)<br>son: Pitsiango (Levi Semigak) b. 1901 (KCB) |
| Koganak (Raymond Semigak) b. 1876 (HCB) | 2 | wife: Sekkinek (Magdalena, daughter of Matthew and Verone) b. 1877 (RCB) |
| Ikkera (Kefas Semigak) b. 1879 (KCB) | 2 | wife: Nipissa (Agnes) 1887–1920 (RCB; KMM) |
| Nikkatok (Gustav Semigak) b. 1889 (KCB) | 3 | wife: Kristine b. 1891 (RCB)<br>son (unnamed) |
| Attataksoak b. 1866 (RCB) | 6 | son: Nippisa b. 1883 (RCB)<br>son: Inuluk<br>son: Inukulluktok b. 1891 (RCB)<br>dau: Inurulluk b. 1893 (RCB)<br>child: Serkoak b. 1901 (RCB) |
| **Total** | **30** | |
| Other | | |
| Matthew (Swansi) [Tuglavina] | 5 | wife: Verone (Akkusane)<br>dau: Mathilda<br>dau: Lena b. 1887 (RCB)<br>son: Thomas |

returned to Aulatsivik with his family. They remained there until 1926, when they moved to Hebron and finally joined the Moravian congregation; he was baptized Raymond and his family adopted the surname Semigak.[97] The genealogy of Inuit who moved from Aulatsivik to Hebron in 1926 is outlined in Figure 7.

FIGURE 7: Genealogy of three other sons of Semigak

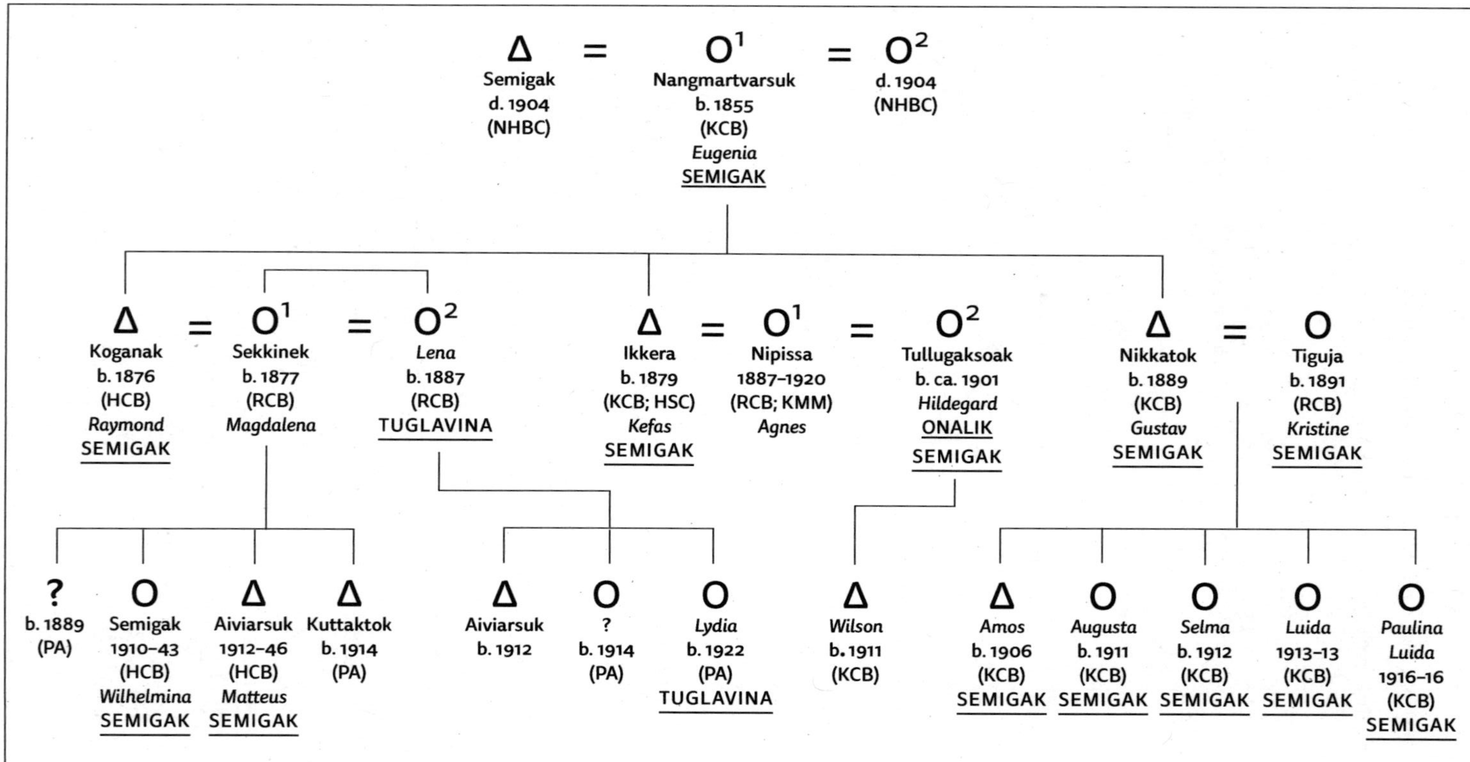

## Inuit Traders from Ungava Bay

The record of Inuit from Ungava Bay during the same period is scant. Journals from the HBC post at Nachvak dating from 1898 to 1906 indicate that most people mentioned by name to be trading there originated from places along the Labrador coast, including the Killinek area.[98] HBC records list only three examples of people making a journey from the George River area solely to trade at the HBC post in Nachvak.

One case involved a man named "Ettegaituk/Ellegaituk," a trader at George River, who went to Port Burwell before reaching Nachvak.[99] Another man, named "Emadlak," also from the George River area, travelled from Aulatsivik when he traded at the Nachvak post in May 1904.[100] In a third case, two men named Naggolak and Nashak from "Ablogelik" (or Abloviak fiord) on the "George River side" arrived at the Nachvak post in December 1903 to purchase ammunition and tobacco. They had no fox pelts as no animals had yet been trapped, and they apparently returned home after obtaining supplies.[101]

Unlike Inuit from the vicinity of George River who appeared at Nachvak briefly to trade, one large family group headed by Ananak remained in the region for two years. Ananak was called "an Ungava man" by the HBC agent when he first arrived at the Nachvak post in July 1901, accompanied by Koktok and Onalik and their families.[102] Ananak appears to have confined his trading activities to the HBC post because his presence was not mentioned by Ramah missionaries until May 1903. His aged mother was the first member of the group to visit the Ramah mission, after which Ananak arrived with his two wives and children. Described as "a big, portly man," he received some pictures and articles of clothing as a gift from the missionaries.[103] Ananak departed for the Koksoak River in Ungava Bay in June 1903.[104]

Another man from George River named Nicodemus arrived in Nachvak at approximately the same time as Ananak.[105] Nicodemus spent periods of time between 1901 and 1903 at both George River and Nachvak.[106] Some of his travel was related to HBC business. He took George Ford on visits from Nachvak to George River,[107] carried mail to Nachvak[108] and

Port Burwell,[109] and acted as a guide for Rev. Stewart from Nachvak to Cape Chidley.[110] In March 1903, Nicodemus and his wife left Nachvak for Hebron.[111] He and his family spent the winter of 1905–06 at Killinek, along with several other families from Kangiqsualujjuaq, but they left the area during the summer.[112]

Inuit from the Ungava region had few incentives to travel to Nachvak. According to the George River HBC journals, Inuit living in the vicinity of the post from 1898 to 1912 generally had access to ample supplies of game and had better harvests of fur-bearing animals and caribou than were reported at the HBC post in Nachvak. Inuit trading at the George River post primarily hunted game in the immediate area encompassing southern Ungava Bay, just as Inuit based at locations along the northern Labrador coast principally harvested resources close to their encampments. After the Moravians established a station at Killinek, several Inuit from George River spent periods of time living in the area.

**A widow with her three children, Ramah, 1907 (photo by Paul Schmidt, Unity Archives, Herrnhut)**

A comparison of names recorded by agents at the HBC posts in George River and Nachvak illustrates the extent of travel between northern Labrador and Ungava Bay. Table 6 outlines the names of Inuit cited in HBC journals from George River dating from September 1898 to December 1904 and from Nachvak from April 1898 to June 1904. The George River agent gave Christian names to people whom he baptized and referred to other Inuit either by their traditional name or by descriptive terms, such as "Curly Head" and "Mooch." Although it is not possible to determine, these nicknames may refer to the same people mentioned also by a traditional or Christian name. In addition, the names recorded by the Nachvak agent related only to men appearing at his post, while the George River agent mentioned a few women, whose names are shown at the end of the list.

Table 6 shows that, of the Inuit individuals described by name in the HBC journals from George River and Nachvak, only seven people known to have lived in the Ungava area visited the Nachvak post, and only two people known to have resided in the Labrador region visited the George River post. Labrador Inuit would have little reason to travel to George River to purchase supplies, since they had the option of trading at the Moravian store in Ramah, which was closer to their encampments and generally had a better stock of goods than the HBC posts. Inuit living in the Killinek area could also trade at the Job Brothers' fishing station after 1898, and later at the Killinek mission station.

## Trade Competition between Nachvak and Ramah

The HBC trader at Nachvak, George Ford, did his best to ensure that the post remained profitable while competing for Inuit business with the Moravian trading post at Ramah. He loaned fox traps and fish nets to several men; in return, they were expected to bring their produce to trade at the post. If people violated this trust by selling their fur or fish elsewhere, he often refused to lend equipment to them again.[113] Ford also kept strict control over the amount of credit that he advanced to hunters. He was not easily intimidated when people pressed him for a higher limit and used violence to assert himself. In 1901, for example, he and Paniguniak began fighting after he refused to increase Paniguniak's loan; when Paniguniak tried to trip him, Ford gave him a blow on the "smeller" that made him "know his place."[114] However, Ford also made a special effort to assist certain people to obtain items not normally sold at the post. In 1898, he promised Tuglavina that he would obtain a boat for him from Newfoundlanders who were fishing cod along the northern Labrador coast.[115]

When the Nachvak post ran short of essential items like ammunition, its commercial rival at Ramah gained an advantage that, not surprisingly,

FIGURE 8: Genealogy of Paksaut's family

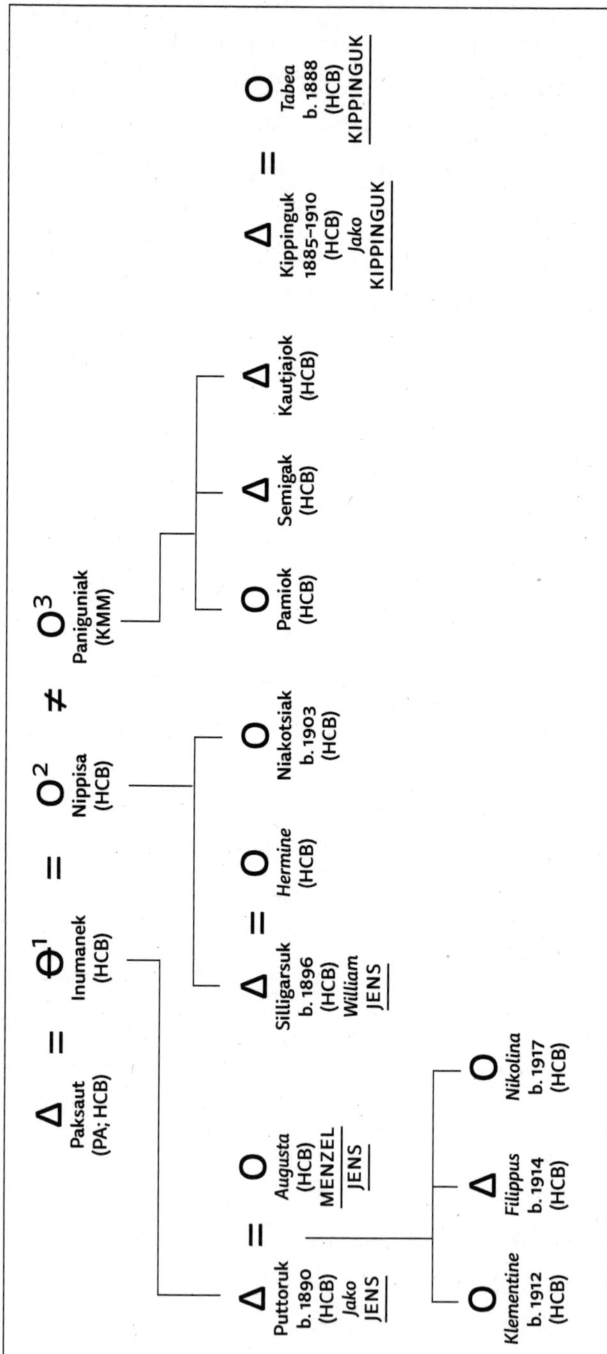

it sought to retain. In 1905, the Nachvak post had a limited supply of cartridges. George Ford sent Nippisa to purchase some from Ramah, but he bought the wrong ones.[116] A month later, Nippisa returned to Ramah and purchased "Snider" cartridges for Paksaut and Ikkera. When Ford tried to buy the same ammunition, however, "he was told by the storekeeper they had none to spare."[117]

**Ramah, before 1910. Back (l-r): Frederich and Conrad; front (l-r): Henrietta and Sussana (Adolph G. Stecker collection, Them Days Archive)**

An absence of chewing tobacco at the Nachvak post in December 1898 led Koliligak and Paniguniak to travel to Ramah to obtain a supply. However, George Ford managed to secure Koliligak's furs in exchange for other goods, leaving him to trade seal fat for tobacco at the Moravian store.[118] Paniguniak and Ikkera also went to Ramah in 1901 to obtain a Kajak and dogs, two articles that were probably not sold at the HBC post.[119] George Ford could not object when Inuit obtained items from the Ramah store that were not available at his post; otherwise, he did his utmost to protect HBC interests.

## Closures of Nachvak (HBC) and Ramah (Moravian Mission)

After 1904, Ford's HBC post at Nachvak quickly became unviable. The influenza epidemic had claimed many lives and had prompted others to move away, so only a few Inuit remained in the Nachvak area. With a lack of clients, the Hudson's Bay Company decided to close the trading post. HBC staff prepared to cease store operations in 1905 and the post physically disappeared in September 1906 when they dismantled the buildings at the site.[120] Soon after, George Ford left with his family.[121] At

**FIGURE 9: Genealogy of Inuit Families moving to Hebron from Aulatsivik in 1926**

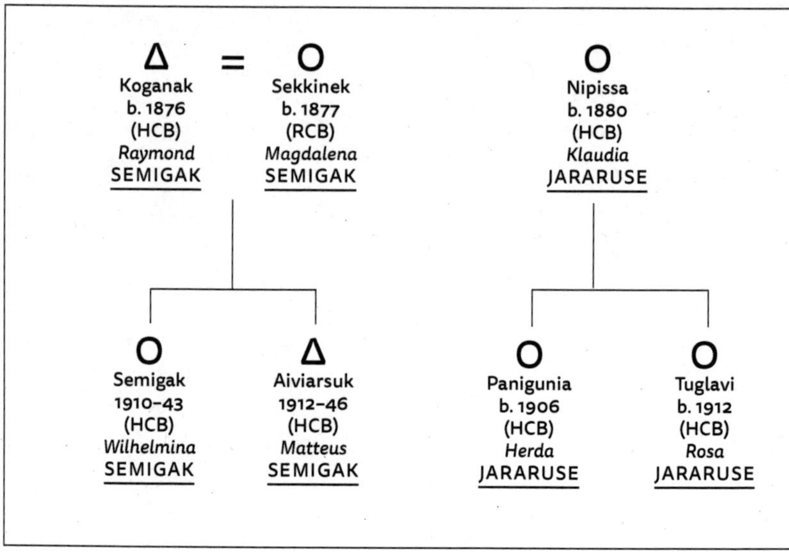


the same time, Moravian officials were forced to make major reductions in their own trade operation, due to the poor financial state of the SFG. One of their measures was to assign only a single missionary, rather than two, to each station on the Labrador coast.[122] This decision led to the transfer of a Ramah missionary to another community in 1907.[123] However, this was only a first step in the policy of retrenchment, as the missionaries also decided that one Labrador station had to be abandoned.

Ramah was selected for closure because it was the smallest station and the least important of the seven communities sponsored by the Moravian Mission.[124] Although facilities were just being established at Killinek, Moravian officials were committed to keeping this newest station to accomplish their goal of converting the last traditional Inuit families on the Atlantic coast. They anticipated that some Ramah families would move to Killinek after the station was abandoned, but they expected most people to migrate southward and join the Hebron congregation.[125]

**Nochasak father and child, Ramah, ca. 1905 (S.K. Hutton collection, Them Days Archive)**

The missionaries recognized that if the HBC post at Nachvak had not closed, some of the Ramah Inuit would have moved to its vicinity after their station was abandoned.[126] But with no trade store existing between Hebron and Killinek, the missionaries were fully aware that Inuit would be forced to vacate the area, observing that "where the stores are, there, or near there, the natives will and do congregate as a rule."[127] While the Moravian Mission and the HBC had originally pursued the permanent Inuit population north of Hebron in strategically establishing their posts, a number of factors now influenced Inuit to reside near the traders. Firmly embedded in the trading economy and deeply impacted by wildlife fluctuations, uncertain global markets, and infectious disease epidemics, Inuit increasingly chose to align their movements and pursuits with the colonial agencies.[128]

Hearing of Ramah's impending closure, Dr. Grenfell of the Mission to Deep Sea Fishermen wrote to the editor of the Moravian newsletter. He argued that closing Ramah would be "a great disaster" because the station was "a stepping-stone in the long distance" between Hebron and Killinek, and he urged the Mission to keep a modest facility operating at Ramah.[129] But despite all calls against the move, the Moravian Mission abandoned Ramah in September 1908. The missionaries demolished the buildings and used the material for construction in other communities, particularly for a new church at Nain.[130] They erected a small chapel at Ramah, where an Inuk helper could hold services for people spending periods of time in the area.[131] Thirty-three people left Ramah for Hebron, either travelling by boat or walking overland, and settled mainly in

FIGURE 10: Genealogy of Inuit families moving to Hebron from Aulatsivik in 1933

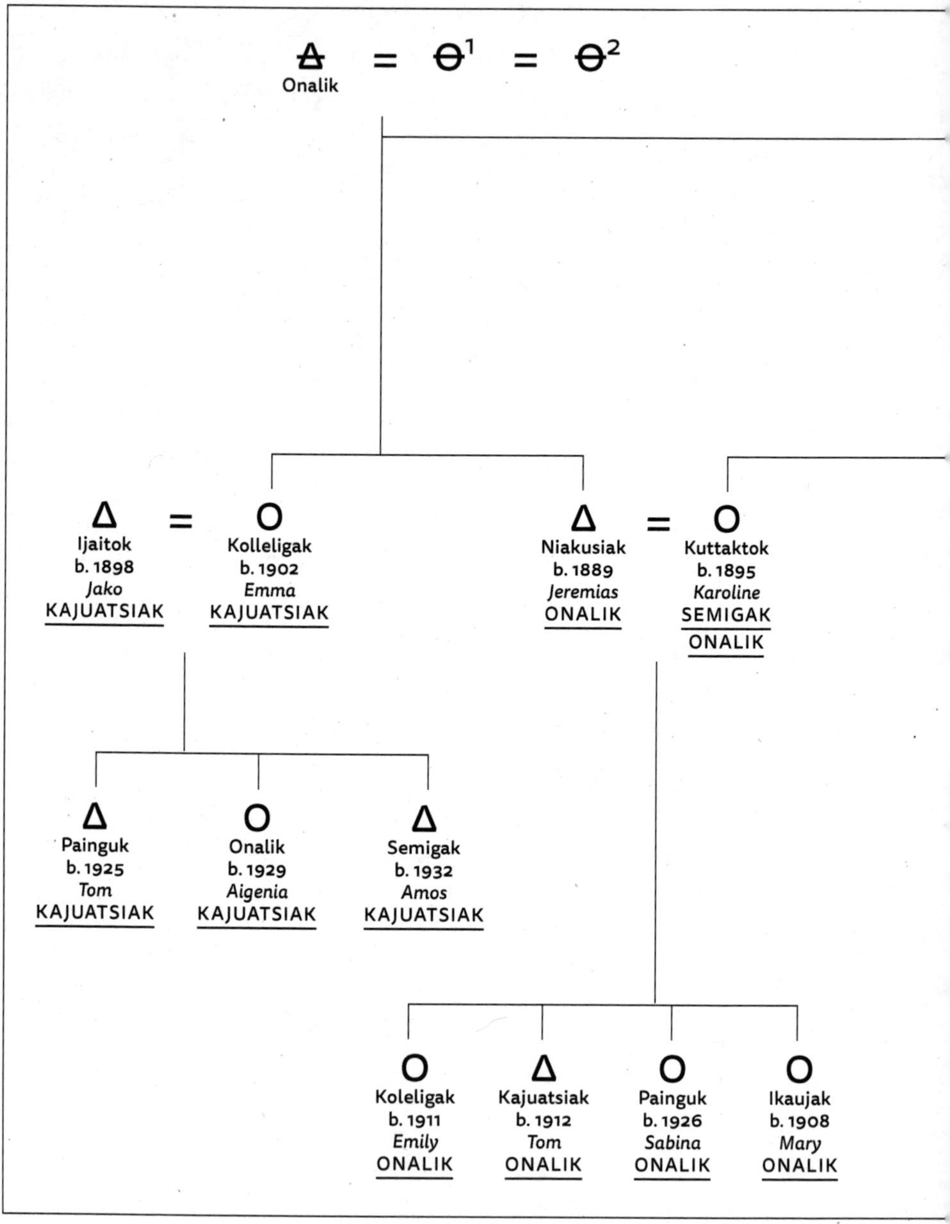

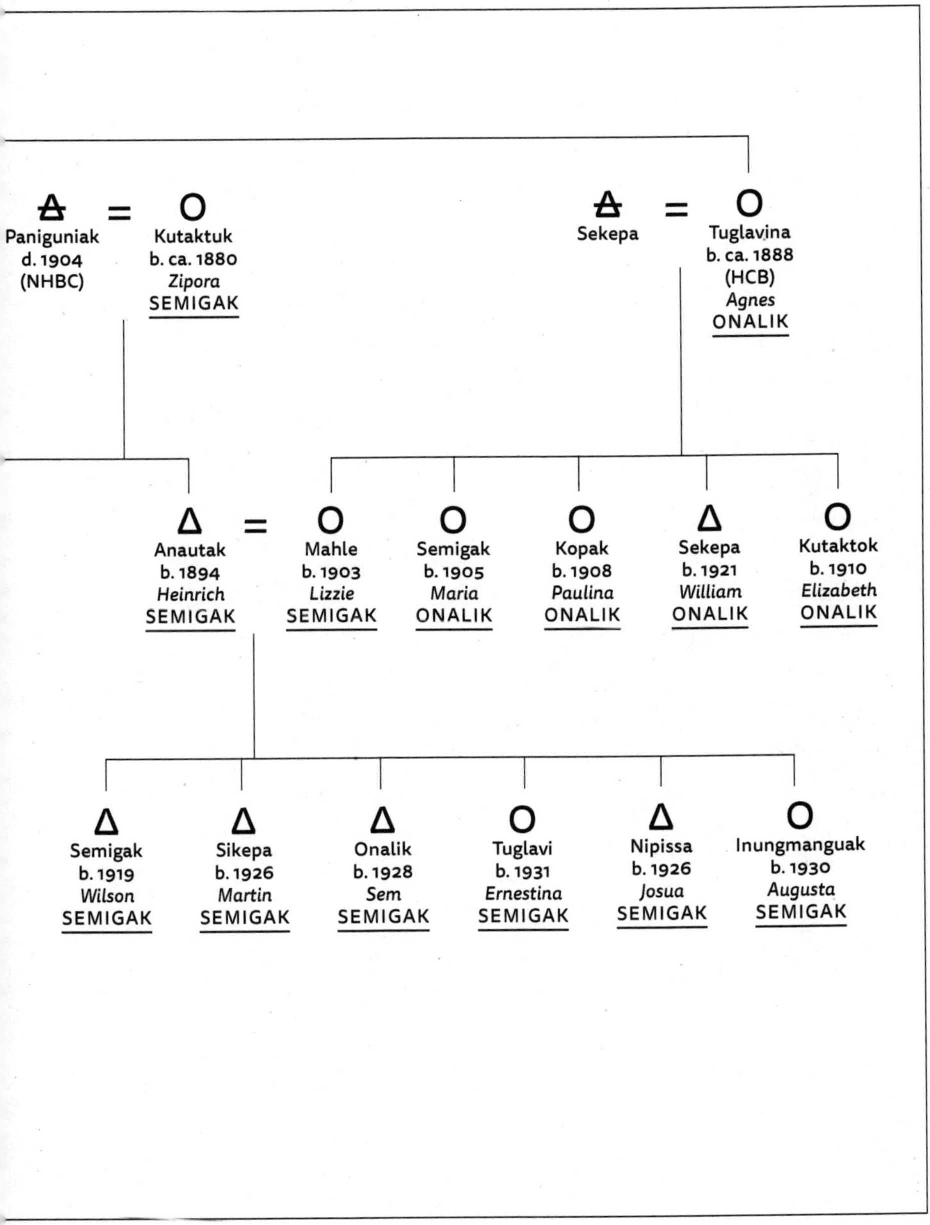
Paniguniak
d. 1904
(NHBC)
Kutaktuk
b. ca. 1880
Zipora
SEMIGAK
Sekepa
Tuglavina
b. ca. 1888
(HCB)
Agnes
ONALIK
Anautak
b. 1894
Heinrich
SEMIGAK
Mahle
b. 1903
Lizzie
SEMIGAK
Semigak
b. 1905
Maria
ONALIK
Kopak
b. 1908
Paulina
ONALIK
Sekepa
b. 1921
William
ONALIK
Kutaktok
b. 1910
Elizabeth
ONALIK
Semigak
b. 1919
Wilson
SEMIGAK
Sikepa
b. 1926
Martin
SEMIGAK
Onalik
b. 1928
Sem
SEMIGAK
Tuglavi
b. 1931
Ernestina
SEMIGAK
Nipissa
b. 1926
Josua
SEMIGAK
Inungmanguak
b. 1930
Augusta
SEMIGAK

**TABLE 6. Names of Inuit Cited in HBC Journals from George River and Nachvak, 1898–1904.**

**George River**

Akojak

Ambros

Angnatok (Angonatook, Angnatook, Angmatook, Angnatsoak, Anogssatok)

Anhattick (Anhattiek, Annakatak, Anakatuk)

Annanak

Apongnelak

Assevak (Assevak Moony, Assivak)

Bob (Babble, Bobby, Bobie)

Big Boy

Carpenter

Charlie (Charley)

Cooper

Curly Head

Ekutuvik

Ettak (Etook, Iktook, Ektook)

Ettigaitook

Ettoksasook

Ettolat

Euttick

Harrie

Hunter

Ingalook (Inogaloak)

Inuulook (Inoulak)

John Ponjuk (Punjak)

Jonas

Joseph

Kalesiek

*Kamikomtook

Kaneketuk (Kanikitook)

Kennie (Kenneth, Kainnie, Kain)

Kilsoik

*Kogjijook

Komak (Konick)

Lukas

Maugrow (Mugrun)

Mooch (The Mooch, Mutch)

Morgan (Mugson)

Nakarlak (Nakatek, Nakolak)

Nasak (Nashak)

Nicodemus (Naskineus)

Okoaksiak

Okpik (Apkick)

Pakujak (Poktajiok)

Peter

Poneuk (Paneuk)

Senungnack (Siunungnuk, Sinosungnuk)

Sokatie

Toxpick

Tukkapik (Tukapek, Takiakpik, Tukeapik)

Uncle

**Females**

Annie

Lizzy

Mary

Kalotok (his widow)

Pugvick

The Hammer

**Nachvak**

| | |
|---|---|
| Anga | Kollelligak (Kolleliak, Kolellajak) |
| *Annanak | Kottaktok |
| Attatotsoak (Attaksuak) | Kugjaiyuk (Kogjaijuk) |
| Arnashuk (Annashuk) | Matheus (Mathew) |
| Arnatseak (Arnatsiak) | *Naggolak |
| Angotaunek (Anyotaunik) | *Nashat |
| Baksauk | Nekartok (Neksituk, Nekkootuk) |
| *Echluk (Echalluk, Ekalut) | Nepisha (Nepesa) |
| Ekera | *Nicodemus (Nekudemas) |
| *Emadlak | Onnalik (Omalik, Onalek) |
| *Ettegaituk (Ellegaituk) | Panegonack (Panegoneak, Pane-goniak, Paneyoneak) |
| Kangegatsuk (Kangegatauk, Komegatsuk, Komgigatsuk) | Paujunge |
| Kasunganeak | Semmegak (Simmica) |
| Kipenguk (Kepengok) | Sekepa |
| Kogannak (Kogammik, Kogeinnak) | Tugslavie |
| Koktok | |

* Denotes someone trading at a post who normally lived in the opposite region.

Saglek; most of them went to Hebron only for the winter months.[132] A few others moved to Killinek and to Okkak.[133]

One extended family of about 20 people headed by Jako Nochasak decided to remain at Ramah. Nochasak and his wife were both highly respected chapel servants,[134] and he was appointed to be the Inuit leader responsible for holding religious services.[135] Ten years later, Jako was a victim of the 1918 Spanish flu epidemic, but his descendants continued to live at Ramah after his death.[136] Levi Nochasak, who was born in Ramah in 1894, recalled the 1908 exodus from the community in an interview in 1977:

> There weren't too many people living there then, a whole lot less than a hundred altogether. It's no wonder the people had to be moved from there, there were so few. When it was time to move

out to Hebron, the people had to take off on foot because they couldn't get aboard the *Harmony*. They tried to get aboard the ship, but they couldn't get close because of the waves, so the *Harmony* took off without them. That's why they started walking to

**TABLE 7. Moravian Mission Stations and Hudson's Bay Company Trading Posts on the Northern Labrador–Ungava Peninsula.**

| Year | Moravian Mission | Hudson's Bay Company |
|---|---|---|
| 1776 | Okkak | |
| 1830 | Hebron | Fort Chimo at Kuujjuaq |
| 1838 | | George River/Kangiqsualujjuaq (Fort Siveright) |
| 1842 | | George River/Kangiqsualujjuaq (closed) |
| 1842–43 | | Fort Chimo (closed) |
| 1866 | | Fort Chimo at Kuujjuaq (reopened) |
| 1867 | Saglek (attempt & closure) | Saglek (Fort Lampson) |
| 1868 | Nachvak (attempt & closure) | Nachvak |
| 1869 | | George River/Kangiqsualujjuaq (re-opened) |
| 1871 | Ramah | |
| 1876 | | Saglek (closed) |
| 1904 | Killinek | |
| 1906 | | Nachvak (closed) |
| 1907–08 | Ramah (closed) | |
| 1916 | | Port Burwell/Killinek |
| 1919 | Okkak (closed) | |
| 1924 | Killinek (closed) | |
| 1926 | Moravian Mission sells Labrador trading rights to HBC | |
| 1938 | | Port Burwell/Killinek (closed) |
| 1942 | | HBC closes all Moravian trading posts; Newfoundland government takes over |
| 1952 | | George River/Kangiqsualujjuaq (closed) |
| 1956 | Nutâk (closed by provincial government) | |
| 1959 | Hebron (closed) | |
| 1978 | Killinek (closed by federal government) | |

> Hebron. I don't remember how long it took to get there. I was only young when they moved.[137]

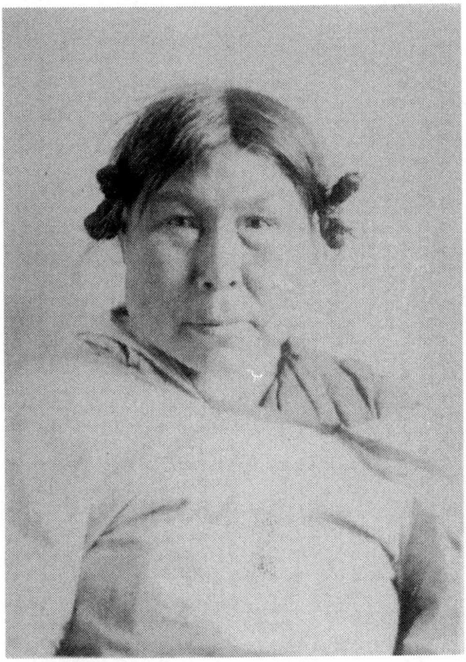

**Inuit woman from Ramah district, ca. 1905 (S.K. Hutton collection, Them Days Archive)**

The closure of the Ramah mission station and the Nachvak HBC post triggered a major evacuation of Inuit from the region. As noted above, while most moved south to Hebron, some headed north to the new Moravian station of Killinek. Some 20 years later, they would be faced with further displacement when the Moravian Mission again withdrew from northern Labrador. Table 7 indicates openings and closings of mission stations and HBC posts, which invariably led to migrations of Inuit on the northern Labrador–Ungava Peninsula.

CHAPTER NINE

# The Moravian Mission at Killinek, 1904–1924

## Killinek Mission Station

When the Moravian Church purchased the Job Brothers' fishing premises at Killinek for a new mission station in 1904, Inuit in the region were assured of a continuing trading post. The mission store offered a wider selection of merchandise than the Job Brothers' firm had provided, since the Moravians imported goods for their network of stores along the Labrador coast and were more familiar with the preferences of Inuit clientele. The Moravian missionaries also introduced a significant change in the local economy by introducing the use of seal nets, which were regularly employed at their other stations.

The first experiment in netting seals at Killinek produced a catch of 350 animals in November 1904. The Inuit men hired to manage the nets received 250 seals for their labour while the remaining seals were reserved for the mission store as its share for owning the nets.[1] The high yield of netting seals substantially increased the supply of meat, oil, and skins available to Inuit in the area and, along with good prospects for fox hunting,[2] gave the new station a promising economic start.

There were only two inhabited sod houses (illusuat) near the Killinek mission in the fall of 1904. With the onset of cold weather, the families moved to snow houses (illuvigait), which retained the warmth better. People remained in illuvigait for the five months of winter, unlike Inuit in southerly areas of the Labrador region who occupied sod dwellings (illusuat) for the entire winter season.[3] The closest winter encampment to the mission station in 1905 was located at a place called Terrekok (Tiggekok), southeast of Killinek on the Labrador coast.[4] Beyond this site, the only other major settlement was at Aulatsivik, where families related to Onalik were permanently based.

## Visitors to Killinek

Southwest of Killinek, along the coast of Ungava Bay, the nearest Inuit encampment was in Abloviak; the next settlement further south was the HBC post at George River. People from both places visited the mission station soon after it opened. Two men named Zacharias and Lukas arrived from George River in February 1905 "mainly because of the store,"[5] and in April other people travelled from the Kangivak area to trade.[6] Three families said that they intended to move from George River to Killinek the next summer and a fourth family accompanied them when they arrived at the mission station in October 1905.[7] The group consisted of two sets of brothers, including Zacharias and his brother Nicodemus, and Charley and his brother Bob.[8]

These families were apparently assessing the Killinek area, because in May 1906 they were reported still to be uncertain about whether they would remain.[9] Nicodemus and his family, as well as his mother and her two younger children, subsequently returned to George River.[10] However, they were transported back by boat to Killinek in late September by Zacharias. Accompanying them was another family headed by Peter, who was related to Charley and Bob; the three men were brothers, and their wives were sisters.[11] According to reports, more families would have joined them if Zacharias's boat had been larger. The George River Inuit also wanted to get other people from the Koksoak River to settle with them in the Killinek area.[12]

In addition to these households, an extended family from Abloviak moved to Killinek in the late spring of 1906. The group consisted of a widow named Lucy [or Louisa], who had previously lived at Killinek with her husband Serlek, and her child, mother, sister, and two brothers.[13] Lucy re-established a connection with families originating at Killinek by becoming the second wife of Paujunge, a brother of Koktok, but the relationship was not condoned by the resident missionary as Paujunge was a candidate for baptism at the time. Other Inuit at Abloviak also seemed to be interested in receiving religious instruction without relocating to Killinek. In March 1907, an elderly man named Anakatak travelled to the mission station and invited the Moravians to visit Abloviak and teach people there.[14]

In early July 1907, Ananak led a group on an extraordinary journey from the Koksoak River to Killinek, travelling on the drift ice for six days without ever touching land. About 20 people in his party used a large skin boat (umiak) and a wooden boat to reach Killinek Island. After purchasing foodstuffs and ammunition from the Moravian store, they headed for the Button Islands where they intended to remain for the winter to hunt polar bears. Drift ice surrounding the Button Islands made access to them difficult and the hunting party expected to be isolated on the islands for the entire winter.[15]

Ananak's group was joined by the two brothers, Nicodemus and Zacharias, who had moved to the Killinek area with their families in September 1906 from George River.[16] The Moravian missionary Waldmann was amazed in early February 1908 when several people returned to the station by walking across drift ice in order to buy tobacco from the store.[17] Another group of men arrived in late March to obtain more ammunition and indicated that polar bears were not as abundant as they had hoped they would be.[18] Ananak's party remained on the Button Islands until late July when they returned to Killinek. Shortly after, all headed south along the coast to the Koksoak River. According to Waldmann, Ananak was quite successful in his hunting activities.[19]

The following winter, Nicodemus's family and his brother Zacharias joined Ananak on the Button Islands, and then travelled to the HBC Fort Chimo post at Kuujjuaq in August 1908.[20] The two brothers later went to live near Abloviak Fiord and made trade exchanges at both the Moravian store in Killinek[21] and the HBC post on the George River, where their activities were reported in the company journal from 1906 to 1912.

## A Growing Station

The movement of Inuit from eastern Ungava Bay to Killinek during the first two years of the mission station more than doubled the size of the Moravian congregation. At the end of 1906, the missionaries counted 87 people in the Killinek district. They also included the 18 people at Aulatsivik led by Onalik, who continued to oppose the adoption of Christianity, in their claims of having a total of 105 Inuit under their mission.[22] This population represented three groups of Inuit from different areas who had different degrees of knowledge and opinions about Christian religious practices.

The missionaries believed that the "original" families living at Killinek and Inuit formerly based at Nachvak belonged "entirely" to the station as their "settled, reliable congregation."[23] These Inuit resided along the northern Labrador coast and had some familiarity with Moravian trade and religious discourses. Adults from this group composed virtually all the names of candidates for baptism and baptized adults eventually recorded in the Killinek Church Book; the primary surnames they adopted

**Killinek, ca. 1919 (McCord Stewart Museum)**

were Jararuse, Kajuatsiak, Semigak, Tuglavina, and Onalik. Missionaries frequently referred to this group in reports and letters from the station as "Killinek Eskimos."

The only other adults baptized at Killinek were Inuit from Abloviak who had been influenced by the Anglican movement through contact with other Inuit in Ungava Bay but had not been baptized. They had retained their traditional Inuit names and adopted new personal and family names after they were baptized by the Moravian missionaries. The surnames they later chose included Kallutak, Arnatok, Kannikitok, and Arnakattak.[24]

## Moravian Religious Efforts

In contrast, Inuit from George River settling at Killinek had been baptized by the HBC agent, Mr. Guy, and were known only by their English personal names. The Moravian missionaries were concerned that they had not been properly instructed about the meaning of baptism or other Christian sacraments and were bothered that they had not received a blessing when they were baptized.[25] They addressed these omissions by holding classes to teach people about Christian doctrine, along with literacy and mathematic skills, and by providing a blessing when the adults were confirmed.[26]

The Moravians also consecrated the marriages of George River Inuit after families joined their congregation, baptized newborn infants, and introduced the use of surnames. Two of the three brothers originating from George River (Bob and Peter) adopted the surname Nagolak while the third brother, Charley, became known by the surname Agopivik;[27] their choice of different surnames is probably a reflection of the fact that they had different fathers. When the Moravians referred to people from this group, they usually identified them as coming from George River or belonging to the "George River contingent."[28]

Compared to the apparent ease with which they had been baptized by the HBC agent, George River Inuit were puzzled by the Moravian approach to religious conversion and asked why people were not immediately baptized.[29] This question arose because no one was baptized for several years at the mission station. Except for one man baptized on his death bed in March

1906, the next baptisms did not occur until March 1908 when a group of 11 adults, of whom nine were Killinek Inuit, were accepted as Christians.[30]

A long period of instruction prior to baptism was typical of the Moravian program for conversion. Missionaries taught people to read and write and expected them to understand the precepts of the sacraments before they were fully accepted into the Church. The Mission's emphasis on literacy, however, acted as a deterrent for some adult Inuit in becoming candidates for baptism. Koktok and his wife were apprehensive about their ability to learn to read and write and must have been perplexed when they brought their newborn child to be baptized and found the rite could not be performed because they were unbaptized. When the missionary Waldmann discovered the reason for their inhibition, he admitted that a lack of literacy skills should not be an impediment to baptism and accepted the entire family as baptismal candidates.[31]

George River Inuit were often further advanced in their literacy skills than Killinek Inuit as they had already learned the syllabic method

**Family of William (Koktok) and Maria (Sapa) Jararuse, Killinek. Back row (l-r): Traugott, Klara, Emily, Paulus; middle row (l-r): Susanna, Annie, Maria (Sapa), William (Koktok); front row (l-r): Kate (Kitty), Benjamin, Hanna (postcard, Hettasch family fonds, Labrador Inuit through Moravian Eyes collection)**

of reading and writing and were familiar with religious tracts distributed in the Ungava region by the Anglican Church. The resident missionary was impressed that they regularly attended instruction classes and showed a keen interest in learning about the Bible.[32] In contrast, missionaries reported that Killinek Inuit were unwilling to consider themselves "heathen" and had difficulty comprehending the notion of sin.[33]

One aspect of traditional Inuit society that people were reluctant to concede was the prerogative of having more than one wife. The Moravian missionaries stressed the Christian standard of monogamy among their converts, but some Inuit resisted any interference in their marital relations. After Paujunge, a candidate for baptism, took Lucy from Abloviak as his second wife, a missionary tried to persuade him to separate from her, but without success. In September 1907, the missionaries appealed for assistance from Captain J.E. Bernier, whose vessel, the *S.S. Arctic*, was anchored in the harbour.[34] Bernier was commanding an expedition to assert the Canadian government's sovereignty over the Arctic islands and Hudson Strait. The Moravian missionaries informed him that the Mission had no lawful jurisdiction in the area, and they were concerned that other Inuit in the community might follow Paujunge's example if something was not done to force an end to the relationship with his second wife. Bernier readily agreed to meet Paujunge and to assert sovereignty over Inuit lives as well as land. He informed Paujunge that having two wives was against the laws of the Canadian government.[35] The traditional Inuit custom of plural marriage constituted the crime of bigamy in Canadian conventions.

During a second meeting, Bernier negotiated a separation agreement with Lucy's mother Ikkiake and her two brothers, Pangortok and Kallasek, whereby they agreed to look after Lucy and her expectant child if she and Paujunge severed their relationship and she did not remarry. The missionaries prepared a written contract outlining these terms, and all Inuit involved in the situation signed with a mark.[36] However, as Bernier added, "everybody was satisfied except the first wife, who cried when she saw the other one leaving her."[37]

Tomas Jararuse, 1930s (The Rooms Provincial Archives)

Under this new arrangement, Paujunge continued his religious instruction and was baptized Tomas [Jararuse] in April 1911. A few months later, he renovated his house and brought back his former second wife, much to the missionary's consternation. Paujunge/Tomas refused to discuss the matter with the missionary, who reported that "he was quite indignant at my troubling him with such a subject."[38] Returning with an Inuit chapel servant and other leading male members of the congregation, the missionary told Tomas that "he could not continue to live at the station, if he would not obey the rules."[39] The situation was finally resolved when Tomas's first wife, Nippisa, left him; she eventually became a candidate for baptism at Hebron in 1926.[40]

Moravian rules for proper conduct also prohibited extramarital relations. Zacharias from George River offended the missionaries by resuming an illicit affair in 1908, which he had earlier promised to terminate. They believed that Zacharias moved to the Koksoak River and then settled in Abloviak in order "to evade all problems."[41] In 1910, Zacharias travelled back to the mission station with a trading party and asked the resident missionary if he could once again live at Killinek. The missionary claimed that he was "clever but dishonest" and "demanded that he follow their rules," presumably regarding monogamy, should he want to remain at the mission station.[42] This injunction appears to have dissuaded Zacharias, whose real objective, the missionaries later thought, was to steal a young woman from a Killinek man and give her to his brother.[43]

The Moravian Mission's attempts at controlling social interactions at Killinek created constant tensions with Inuit families. Although the historical record documents only the missionaries' perspectives on the situation, Inuit independence and ability to dislodge and unsettle the Mission's efforts are apparent. Faced with appallingly intrusive demands to change their personal lives and seemingly arbitrary rules about church membership, Inuit families responded to the missionaries through both strategic defiance and measured tolerance.

## Life at Killinek

For most of the year, the Moravian missionary at Killinek was alone and worked at constructing a mission house, church, and other facilities at the new station, while Inuit families lived at outlying camps and harvested game. People visited to trade throughout the year and attended major religious festivals such as Christmas and Easter, but the only lengthy period they spent near the station was during the fall seal fishery. Missionaries did not try to encourage Inuit to spend the winter residing in a central community at Killinek, as they did at other Moravian stations along the Labrador coast. They recognized that people had better opportunities to obtain game away from Killinek and would have a superior lifestyle by continuing their traditional economic patterns.

The advantages of maintaining Inuit cultural practices in the region were explained to Moravian officials by Christian Schmitt, the Labrador trade superintendent who visited Killinek in 1906, as follows:

> It has never been the custom of these people to collect at any given place, but they live scattered in the eastern and western coast or south of the cape.... For certain reasons it is desirable that they should continue to live as they have done. This kind of life becomes them best, they are stronger, healthier and more able to withstand hardships and cold. They are always able to secure something while away from the station, even in mid-winter seals, birds, foxes, walrus etc. can be got, and to secure that livelihood is

> better than if they settled down at the station during the whole winter and lived like their southern countrymen either on debt, or by employment from the missionaries, or on poor fund.[44]

Schmitt's commentary was inadvertently as much a criticism of the way southern Moravian communities had evolved as largely permanent settlements as it was a tribute to traditional Inuit lifeways.

Other colonial agents also recognized the impact of sedentary and mobile ways of life on Inuit associated with Moravian stations. Newfoundland Governor Sir William MacGregor, who visited Killinek in August 1905, was very impressed by the excellent health of adults and their children, and especially by the large number of children in families.[45]As he remarked, their condition contrasted sharply with the high mortality rate of Inuit populations in southerly areas.[46]

Killinek Inuit survived in the most rigorous environment on the Labrador coast. Their lifestyle differed from that of Inuit living in southern communities because they managed without access to forests for firewood, depended mainly on local resources, and resided in snow houses (illuvigait) all winter.[47] People burned seal oil in soapstone lamps as a source of heat and light, although some driftwood was found along the coasts. Their preference for illuvigait had the practical advantage not only of being warmer than sod dwellings (illusuat), but also of enabling families to be mobile during winter. They could readily move to other hunting grounds and build new illuvigait if game was not plentiful in the Killinek area, as occurred during the winter of 1905–06.[48] Illuvigait also tended to be cleaner than illusuat because old structures were easily replaced when they became grimy.[49]

Winter was the longest, and almost continuous, season at Killinek. Its location at the peak of the peninsula, thrusting into Hudson Strait, acted as a hook for heavy arctic drift ice carried south by ocean currents from late spring until fall. This ice often blocked the coastline and at times extended so far seaward that it formed an impenetrable barrier to local travel, hunting activities, and navigation by the Mission's annual supply ship.

Climatic conditions were also affected by the prevalence of sea ice. Squire Joseph Townley, stationed at Killinek from 1916 to 1919, thought the weather was comparable to Iceland, noting in a one-year period the occurrence of 271 damp, snowy, cold, and stormy days compared to 94 days with some sunshine and wind.[50] He added that Killinek Inuit only spoke of two seasons – winter and spring – although in fact they recognized the subtlety of six seasons.[51]

Killinek's location, nevertheless, was also strategic for harvesting marine mammals and other game when ice and weather conditions were not obstacles. Harp seals migrated in large herds from southern Baffin Island during late fall and were the primary species pursued by Inuit hunters. Seals provided a vital source of food for people as well as for the dog teams needed for winter travel, and the seal blubber and skins were traded at the mission store. Another resource that was often abundant in the Killinek area and valuable only for trade was fox. Inuit hunted and trapped white and coloured fox during winter and bartered the pelts for imported goods.[52]

The use of nets in the fall seal fishery produced some very large catches in the first seven years of the Killinek station. Beluga whales trapped in

**Inuit at Killinek, 1919 (McCord Stewart Museum)**

the nets also added to the supply of meat available to Inuit living in the area. The largest catch occurred in the fall of 1909 when 898 seals and 188 beluga whales were netted; the fox catch was equally impressive, with 544 pelts taken during the winter. These returns had a value of $6,000, of which Inuit earned $4,000 and the mission store gained $2,000.[53] But the abundance of marine life in the Killinek region was short-lived.

## A Shortage of Game and Movement Away from Killinek

Despite the promising first few years at the new station, a sharp decline in catches of seals, beluga whales, and fox after 1911 quickly eliminated the prosperity that Inuit and the mission store initially enjoyed at Killinek. The poor harvests confirmed George Ford's 1903 assessment that the resources in the region were unstable. Only 120 seals, one beluga whale, eight sharks, and a single codfish were taken in the mission's nets in the fall of 1912, and even less game was caught by local hunters. Luckily, families did secure several white foxes and were therefore able to purchase food supplies.[54] Inuit blamed the presence of several ships in the harbour during the fall for the small seal catch.[55] In later years, seal catches likely declined because the use of nets had resulted in over-harvesting the seal population. While foxes became scarce at Killinek, they were abundant further south at Aulatsivik and Komaktorvik on the Labrador coast, as well as at Abloviak on the Ungava Bay coast.[56]

**Kajuatsiak (Benjamin Onalik) and Attua (Emily Jararuse Onalik), Killinek, 1911 (Them Days Archive)**

Inuit started to move away from the Killinek area beginning in 1913 due to the shortage of game and resulting poverty. Families originating from places in Ungava Bay departed for Fort Chimo [Kuujjuaq] or George River [Kangiqsualujjuaq].

The first people to leave Killinek were the three brothers, Charley, Bob, and Peter, who had moved to the area in 1906; they were among the 23 people who departed in the summer of 1913. Although they initially intended to move to Fort Chimo, Charley and Peter decided to remain at George River while Bob settled with his family at Abloviak. People living at Abloviak were described as so poor in the winter of 1914, following a scarcity of seals the previous fall, that they had to kill their dogs to survive. Nevertheless, Bob's family appears to have remained there, as his later children were baptized at Killinek. Always anxious about the viability of their stations, the missionaries reported that Charley and Peter considered returning to Killinek because they greatly missed seal meat and thought the mission station was a better place to live.[57]

Other people departing from Killinek were a widow with two children who left for Ramah in the spring of 1914, and two more families who moved to Fort Chimo in 1915.[58] Inuit originating from the Killinek area and from Nachvak dispersed to different places along the Labrador coast during the winter of 1915 and remained away until summer, hunting game from campsites at Cape Chidley, Aulatsivik, Komaktorvik, and Nachvak. An exception was William Jararuse and his family, who accompanied his brother-in-law Josef Suarak in August 1914 to catch foxes along Ungava Bay. Relatives assisted them in returning to the mission station in January 1915 after a poor hunt.[59] The traditional Inuit of Aulatsivik and Komaktorvik were luckier, reported a missionary.[60]

## Newfoundland Game Laws and Canadian Claims of Jurisdiction

During this difficult period, the resident missionary Karl Filschke observed that Inuit had no choice in leaving the area, stating "It is once again the neediness, which expels our people from here."[61] However, the scarcity of game was not the only factor that made Killinek unattractive to Inuit. A new game law introduced by the Newfoundland government in about 1911 prohibited the sale of fox pelts after the hunting season closed on March 15. The mission store was therefore not permitted to accept furs brought by Inuit to trade for supplies after this date, even though, as Filschke remarked, winter conditions continued at Killinek and it was the best time for obtaining foxes.[62]

A comparable game regulation did not apply in the Ungava Bay region, which was transferred by Canada to the jurisdiction of the Quebec government in 1912, so the HBC post at George River was able to accept fox pelts year-round. After March 15, Inuit residing in the Killinek region had to travel to George River to exchange their fox pelts at the HBC post. The Newfoundland game law not only forced the Moravian store at Killinek to forfeit pelts, but it also strained the mission's "poor fund," as demands for charitable assistance increased from families who had no means of earning an income. Filschke strongly believed that the game regulation was unjust, and that the government had "the obligation to provide a substitute livelihood" for Inuit adversely affected by the regulation.[63]

The Canadian government's continuing claim to jurisdiction over Killinek also threatened the Moravian store's competitive position. Canadian officials insisted on charging the Mission customs duties on goods imported for its trade operation, as they had warned the missionaries when the Killinek mission first opened. In 1912, a customs officer arriving at Killinek levied duties on supplies at the station. The captain of the Mission's cargo vessel, the *Harmony*, paid the charges under protest because ownership of the territory was still undetermined. Although missionaries suggested again that the SFG should apply for a customs exemption from Canada, the Committee preferred to wait for a judgement from the British Privy Council, to which the issue had been submitted for resolution.[64] Canadian authorities again demanded customs duties from the Mission in 1915.[65]

## Difficulties for Inuit and the Moravian Mission

The uncertain administrative status of Killinek left the Moravian Mission caught between the exacting policies of two governments, both of which caused losses for Inuit and the Mission. In 1913, Inuit proposed moving the station south on the Labrador coast to Komaktorvik where seals, foxes, and especially arctic char were abundant. The missionary Filschke worried that char stocks might decline if they were intensively exploited, although he agreed that Komaktorvik was a better location.[66] It would also provide better access for the *Harmony*, whose captain did not favour travelling to the isolated Killinek station from Hebron.[67] Voyages along the remote coast were often hazardous due to fields of drift ice, thick fog, and severe gales. These conditions forced the ship off course in 1906, taking it near Resolution Island in Hudson Strait and towards Akpatok Island in Ungava Bay.[68] However, any possibility of relocating the Killinek mission was quickly eliminated with the start of World War I in 1914.

In 1915, Inuit netted many seals and beluga whales at Killinek, providing some relief from hardship; the mission store's share of the catch amounted to 367 seals and 75 beluga whales.[69] Inuit had also been successful for the previous several years in earning high incomes from fox pelts. Receiving $121 for a white fox and more for coloured varieties, Inuit at Aulatsivik were "rich all winter" in 1914–15.[70] The absence of foxes the following year, however, left them with nothing to trade for supplies. Not owning any seal nets, they could not match the size of the catch made at Killinek. They avoided going hungry by frequently going to Killinek during the winter and staying with families who shared their food supply with them.[71] Even if foxes had been abundant, the value of pelts fell to a minimum, while prices for provisions sharply increased due to the war.[72]

In addition to problems caused by various game harvests and market fluctuations, the Moravian Mission also had serious trouble with the management of its trade operation, which was being undermined by its own staff. Missionaries thought that both the store manager and the clerk were dishonest and were trading fraudulently with Inuit. The clerk and interpreter, a Labradorian named Sam Voisey, also infuriated the resident missionary by having an adulterous relationship that lasted for several years. In 1911, the Mission investigated the store's operations and eventually appointed new staff.[73]

After Voisey either was fired or resigned from the store, he and the store manager, John Goleby, continued to undermine the Mission's trading interests. In 1912, Voisey occupied a dwelling that Goleby had purchased from Julius Lane, the former manager of the Job Brothers' fishing station, and worked as a pilot for the *Mento*, a Canadian vessel conducting surveys around the Button Islands led by Captain F. Anderson.[74] Voisey also became an agent for Anderson in conducting trade with local Inuit, exchanging a large quantity of flour, bread, sugar, and guns provided by the captain for fox and polar bear pelts.[75]

As the resident missionary Filschke caustically remarked, "Voisey thus lives in a house of the S.F.G. and is now our competitor."[76] Filschke also believed that Captain Anderson would "try to use his influence to impose customs on all imported goods,"[77] presumably to cause an increase in prices at the Moravian store that would weaken its competitive position. However, Voisey only acted as Anderson's agent for a short period because he left Killinek in 1913 with Inuit travelling to Fort Chimo at Kuujjuaq, and later worked as the HBC clerk at George River (Kangiqsualujjuaq).[78]

**Killinek, 1925 (Fotosammlung zu Labrador und Grönland, Labrador Inuit through Moravian Eyes collection)**

The HBC clerk at George River in 1914, John Caldwell, took a kinder view of Sam Voisey. In his journals, Caldwell described Voisey as an interpreter and handyman "par excellence," and a "master of all."[79] Born in Labrador, Sam Voisey spoke Inuktitut before English, and his two daughters living at home, Alice and Emily, spoke Inuktitut more fluently than English.[80] The family of five lived in one room above the kitchen, while Caldwell and the post's doctor lived in their own rooms in the HBC house. Sam's wife, Nancy Voisey, washed and cooked for Caldwell, and sewed sealskin boots "quite as good as any native could sew."[81]

Other Labrador families of mixed ancestry had close ties with the HBC and the Moravian Mission. Harry (Henry) Dicker and Chesley Ford worked as managers for the Hudson's Bay Company in Killinek / Port Burwell, and Sam Lyall grew up there in the mid-1910s when his father, John Lyall, ran the mission store:[82]

> That was a good place for seals, down to Burwell. Father used to be sealing there for the Mission, and he'd get a thousand seals some summers or some falls. He was working for the Mission. Seal fat them times was a really good price, you know. They'd render all the oil and everything down there. That's what Father used to be doing in the winter, making puncheons to put oil in. He was coopering. There was no HBC at Burwell then. The Mission was the only traders down there then, the Moravian Mission. The boat, the *Harmony*, she used to always go down there and pick up all the stuff.[83]

Sam's brother, Ernie Lyall, also wrote about his memories of Killinek/Port Burwell in his memoir, *An Arctic Man: Sixty-Five Years in Canada's North*:

> We shared a big double house with the missionary and his family in Burwell; they lived on one side of it, and we lived on the other. . . . We couldn't play with the Eskimo kids of course, since they weren't that close to the mission, but Mr. Lenz, the missionary, had three children, two boys and a girl, and we used to play with those German kids. . . .

> My dad used to go netting seals in the fall. My older brother and three Eskimos worked with my dad, and sometimes I got to go along. They used to set eleven seal nets and had to tend those nets every day. The mission didn't have motor boats in those early days, so they had this big boat they had to row out to the nets, and they'd leave about five in the morning and travel about two miles to the nets. They got anywhere from 750 to 1500 seals a year, and the Eskimos were paid by my dad, a dollar a day for getting the seals. . . . Once the skins got dried, any woman that wanted to make sealskin boots, my dad would give them the skins; and when they brought the finished boots back to the store, he used to give them a dollar and five cents, at first. But I can remember that before I left there the boots went up to two dollars a pair. . . . We used to send out thousands of pairs of boots every year from Port Burwell.[84]

Fifteen years later, Ernie Lyall returned to work for the Moravian Mission's trade competitors, the Hudson's Bay Company, which had since established a post at Killinek.

### The Hudson's Bay Company Arrives

Sam Voisey's experience in working at the Moravian store in Killinek made him very knowledgeable about the Mission's trade operation, and he undoubtedly described its value to the HBC managers when he moved to Fort Chimo and George River. Even when he worked for them, Voisey had been critical of the Moravians' trade. In 1910, a Killinek missionary complained that Inuit "are being told lies about the trade practices of the missionary by ruthless people," meaning Sam Voisey.[85] The missionaries also said that he was making the Mission look bad in the eyes of Captain Anderson's crew on the *Mento* in 1912.[86] The HBC agents in Ungava were likely an eager audience for Voisey's insider information about the Mission's trade.

The fierce competition between the two agencies had cooled to some extent. After the closure of the HBC post at Nachvak in 1906, the

Moravians had a virtual monopoly on trade in the northernmost coastal region. The George River HBC post at Kangiqsualujjuaq was vying with the Mission enterprise for furs obtained by Inuit living on the northeast Ungava coast close to Killinek, and it did profit from the prohibition on spring fox sales there. However, the distance between the two trade stores cushioned their competition. But Voisey's information may have roused the HBC's rivalry with the Moravian missionaries and contributed to plans for a direct assault on their monopoly at Killinek.

In the summer of 1916, the HBC appeared on the Moravian Mission's doorstep, setting up a store and residence 10 minutes away from the mission house at Killinek. The Company closed its post at George River (Kangiqsualujjuaq) and transferred its trade and supplies to Fort Chimo (Kuujjuaq).[87] With the traders came many families from Kuujjuaq and Kangiqsualujjuaq. Squire Joseph Townley, the resident Moravian missionary,[88] described the newcomers as members of Rev. Stewart's Anglican congregation and called them "H.B.C. Eskimos," as they apparently traded exclusively at the HBC store. He noted the group of about 60 baptized Inuit had moved to the area, stating that they "have migrated for a time from the George's River District, etc., under the gentle, patriarchal pressure of the H.B.C. Officials."[89] The Ungava Inuit established themselves on the "Canadian side," meaning the coast of Ungava Bay southwest of Killinek.[90]

With the HBC having its own clientele at Killinek / Port Burwell, Captain Jackson of the Mission's supply ship advised the SFG Committee on his return to London that the Company's agent "assured us we should not suffer thereby in our trading operations."[91] The HBC store was initially managed by Julius Lane, the former manager of the Job Brothers' premises.[92] Lane had remained at Killinek with his family after the Moravian Mission purchased the station, but he was frequently absent on jobs as an interpreter or pilot for Canadian ships travelling in northern areas.[93]

Julius Lane and his wife Clara Lane were well known to Killinek Inuit and were likely instrumental in drawing members of the Moravian congregation to trade at the HBC post. Despite the assurance given to Captain

Jackson, competition with the HBC significantly reduced profits at the mission store over the following year. However, Jackson believed that the missionaries could recover their position by setting up a station for fishing cod and char "on the other side of the land," likely meaning the Labrador coast, because "the H.B.C. cannot handle the codfish like we can."[94]

Townley included the Ungava Inuit in his calculation of the total population in the region at the end of 1917, distinguishing them from 126 baptized Inuit belonging to the Moravian congregation and 37 unbaptized Inuit residing on the "Atlantic side" of the Labrador coast.[95] Thus, over 200 Inuit were living in the Killinek district, the largest number of people associated with the mission station since it was founded in 1904. The mix of new people led to four marriages involving people from opposite coasts of the peninsula after 1918, as well as two marriages between people originating from the Abloviak area.[96]

Noah Angnatuk, born in 1910, described his memories of Killinek in a 1985 interview from his home in Kangiqsualujjuaq:

> The Hudson's Bay Company post was already established near our camps when I became old enough to sell fox pelts, as well as a German [Moravian] trading post whose manager was known as "Nuvatutialuk." In those days, Inuit were mostly interested in tea and tobacco. . . . When people were expecting those who went to trade, they listened for dogs barking and when they could hear them approaching, they told each other that they would soon have some tea. Adults took out their pipes and got them ready to smoke tobacco.
>
> The [Moravian trading post] was just across [from] the Hudson's Bay Company post. The two trading posts used to fight over their Inuit customers. Traders went to trade to either one of the posts which had better bargains. . . . If an Inuk trader went to sell his fox pelts to the German post, the HBC took his gun away from him if he had purchased it from the HBC post, no matter how long ago it had been purchased.

> The HBC employees ignored even starving Inuit if they didn't have anything to sell. . . . The German company was good for us and treated us kindly. They had a motorboat and took Inuit people to their spring camps and supplied them with food. On the other hand, the HBC didn't do such things for their people.
>
> The German trading post was also known as "Ingillisi" (English). The English trading post groceries were cheaper than the HBC post's, and gave good bargains for fox pelts. . . . [The Moravians] had their own ship [the *Harmony*] which arrived only in autumn, in October, when snow covered the hills. . . . It was an old ship and every time it arrived, all the people caught colds and sniffles. I think it brought in all the germs! It arrived so slowly and when someone noticed it arriving, every Inuk customer of theirs screamed with joy! I think they looked forward to eating biscuits. It arrived from the other side of the ocean. The crew of the sailboat fished cod and took in oil which had been frozen, pounded with big rocks inside wooden vessels. It was the Inuit who did all the work to make oil.[97]

## Scarcity of Game, 1917–1918

In the years after the Hudson's Bay Company set up operations at Killinek/Port Burwell, returns from sealing and fox hunting were strained by low catches. Townley reported that sealing was "very, very meagre" in the fall of 1917 and seals were difficult to find all winter.[98] When only two foxes were caught on Killinek Island over the winter by people belonging to the Moravian congregation, many families became so desperate for food by Easter that they had to be given assistance from the Mission's "Poor Fund" and program providing "Relief Work" to needy householders. People were often hungry all spring and many dogs died due to the shortage of seal meat. Three families left for Nachvak to try hunting and trapping there, while other families moved to islands off the northern Labrador coast to gather the eggs of nesting eider ducks.[99]

Heavy drift ice blocked the harbour and sea surrounding Killinek all summer in 1918, and Inuit did not make a large catch of seals or foxes over the following months.[100] Several families moved once again to the Atlantic coast south of Killinek in March 1919 to hunt for game because, as Townley described, "there was very little of anything to be caught in our district."[101] Townley added that people were no better off financially than they had been the previous year.[102]

## Spanish Flu Epidemic at Hebron and Okkak

Disaster struck Labrador in 1918 when an epidemic of Spanish influenza swept through many of the communities. A sick sailor on the *Harmony* infected people at Hebron and Okkak when the ship arrived at the stations in the fall.[103] Almost two-thirds of the Hebron population died over the course of about nine days, leaving only 70 survivors of the original 220 residents.[104] In Okkak, the devastation was even worse, as only 59 of the 266 residents survived.[105] However, people in Killinek were spared from the disease. Ice conditions prevented the *Harmony* from reaching Killinek that fall, and its residents only learned about the epidemic from mail that arrived in January 1919.[106]

A full third of the Inuit population on Labrador's north coast died in the epidemic. The Killinek missionary, Joseph Townley, speculated that these devastating events would likely influence the future of the Killinek mission.[107] The Okkak mission station closed in 1919, but Hebron was maintained and quickly attracted new residents from Inuit communities farther south.[108] Two families from Killinek, headed by Abel Nugak and Lucas Jararuse, also went to the Hebron area, but they returned after spending only a year there.[109] The small population of fewer than 100 Inuit at Hebron could barely manage to cope with a catch of 528 seals in the fall of 1919 and about 1,000 seals caught in 1920 at netting sites outside the community.[110] All adults were fully occupied preparing seal oil and skins for markets in Europe and even children were employed to assist in rendering seal oil. The missionaries welcomed any further increase in the local population to assist with the work needed for the

Mission's trade.[111] Over the next few decades, as the next two chapters will describe, northern Inuit gradually moved – or were pushed – south into the Hebron region.

## Financial Difficulties

Despite the industry at Hebron in 1919 and 1920, the Moravian trade operation was floundering. Increasing prices for imported goods, low catches, and fluctuating market values for fish had forced Inuit to accumulate high debts at the mission stations.[112] The Mission's finances were in terrible shape. To add to its troubles, a fire in August 1921 destroyed all the mission property at Nain, including the church, mission house, store, school, and warehouses, adding significantly to the financial burden. The SFG struggled with the task of funding a reconstruction of the community facilities, although many materials were salvaged from Okkak.[113] As it had done previously in 1907, the SFG focused on reducing the number of missionaries and closing another mission station on the Labrador coast to limit its expenditures.

Berthold Lenz, the resident missionary at Killinek, was told by Moravian officials that his station would be the last one considered for closure.[114] After claiming a prerogative to convert northern Inuit in establishing Killinek, the reputation of the Moravian Church would have been tarnished, certainly in the eyes of the Anglican Church, if its mission and new converts were subsequently abandoned. Lenz felt that if the Mission departed, it would surrender all influence it currently enjoyed and many of the Killinek Inuit would quickly "sink back again into the old ways, if left alone."[115] Nevertheless, he suggested that the station could manage without a missionary for a year or two, if a storekeeper could be found who was fluent in Inuktitut, was willing to hold church services, and agreed to monitor people's spiritual welfare.[116] Lenz may also have applied at this time for a furlough in Europe due to his poor health; he was given a leave of absence and left the station in September 1923.[117]

The mission store at Killinek no doubt suffered from competition with the nearby HBC trading post and from the loss of business when

Inuit decided to sell their furs to transient ships anchoring in the harbour during the summer and fall seasons. In 1920, the station also gained a new neighbour when a Royal Canadian Mounted Police (RCMP) post was erected in the area.[118] The Canadian government had established the post to assert its sovereignty over the Arctic region and to collect customs duty from passing ships.[119] The senior RCMP officer of the post also assessed the customs duty on the Mission's goods. He presented the Moravians with a bill for £1500, which the SFG refused to pay, and indeed could not afford. The Committee appealed for support from Newfoundland authorities in London, but they were unable to intervene because the issue of jurisdiction was still undecided by the British Privy Council. Lacking any other recourse, the SFG finally decided to send a letter to the commissioner of customs in Ottawa requesting an extension of the duty-free status that the Moravian Mission had received from Newfoundland.[120]

While a decision was pending on jurisdiction over Killinek, the mission store attempted to cover the duty charges by increasing the price of

**Inuit at Killinek, 1919 (McCord Stewart Museum)**

goods and reducing the value of fox pelts. The HBC agent reported that the missionaries, following instructions from Hebron, reduced the payment they offered for fox from $18 to $16 for a white pelt and from $15 to $9 for a red pelt.[121] Countering these changes, the HBC store lowered its prices for biscuit, cotton, coffee, and other consumer goods;[122] it may also have offered higher prices for fox pelts. The better values were attractive to "mission" Inuit, as the HBC manager called Moravian converts, including one hunter who "snuck over to trade" at his post.[123]

## The Mission's Approach to Inuit Housing

Inuit belonging to the Moravian congregation greatly resented the higher cost of goods, as well as frequent shortages of wood and coal. Lenz reported in 1923 that these two factors led five families to decide to move from Killinek and settle at Hebron. He attributed their discontent to inadequate supplies of home heating fuel after the Mission had encouraged Inuit to build wooden houses.[124]

The issue of Inuit housing was central to many of the Mission's attempts to transform Inuit society throughout its time in Labrador.[125] Although some missionaries advocated for preserving the traditional Inuit practice of seasonal movement and the sod and snow houses that best suited that life, many others were fixated on the social, health, and moral implications of housing. They associated sod houses (illusuat), tents, and snow houses (illuvigait) with unhealthy and crowded conditions, filth, and "improper Christian sexual activity."[126] European-style wooden houses, on the other hand, were thought to encourage the "civilized" habits of cleanliness, morality, and Christian domestic arrangements.[127]

Given the environmental and social conditions at Killinek, missionaries there had been reluctant to advocate for abandoning traditional Inuit housing. They recognized that illusuat, illuvigait, and tents were perfectly designed for life in the region, and that the complete lack of wood made European-style houses unfeasible. But criticism of the poor condition of Inuit homes in southern communities by Newfoundland Governor Sir William MacGregor and Dr. Grenfell in 1905 and

1908 prompted the Mission to slowly change its approach. MacGregor, Grenfell, and prominent Moravian missionaries such as Dr. Samuel Hutton stressed the need for transforming housing and improving sanitation to raise the standard of Inuit health.[128] In 1910, the mission stores responded to the pressure by reducing the mark-up on building materials. As a result, many Inuit families decided to build small wooden houses to occupy during the winter when they visited the mission station from outlying camps.[129]

In retrospect, Lenz recognized that promoting the adoption of wooden dwellings at Killinek was "probably a mistake" because the new houses during winter had definite disadvantages compared to traditional illuvigait.[130] Families were colder and "more miserable" in their wooden cabins than they would have been in illuvigait, as they required more fuel for heat. Initially, Lenz said, some Inuit families viewed living in an illuvigak to be "too great a hardship," after they had experienced the greater space and comfort of a well-heated wooden house. But once they had become "tied down to the spot where their house stands," they were unwilling to move to remote areas with better hunting opportunities.[131] Consequently, people's ability to earn an income from fox hunting and

**Kamutik trip from Killinek to Hebron (photo by Berthold Lenz, Unity Archives, Herrnhut)**

other activities was reduced, and in a poor winter they could hardly afford to pay the high cost of imported fuel.[132]

When Inuit lacked the means to purchase fuel, they complained that the storekeeper failed to provide enough poor relief. Alternatively, when people had good fox hunting returns and could afford to buy fuel to heat their homes, they would deplete the store's supplies of wood and coal well before the end of winter. This shortage made Inuit indignant because they could not get these necessities, even for payment. A greater amount of fuel could not be transported to Killinek as the mission's annual supply ship was too small to handle more stock.[133]

## Inuit Relocate South, 1923

Lenz noted that persistent shortages of fuel had prompted two of the best hunters in the community to move south where fuel was more easily obtained. Two families left Killinek by Kamutik in the spring of 1923, and three other families followed by boat in the summer.[134] The latter group, consisting of 23 people, arrived at Hebron in August, but accommodation could not be found for all of them at the mission station. Sigmund Waldmann, the resident missionary, advised the group to settle at Saglek, where a large house was unoccupied. Lacking bed frames and material to make furniture, the families had to camp on the floor until late autumn.[135]

Lenz provided a rational explanation for the movement of these families from Killinek, and his observations on the consequences of erecting wooden houses may well have been valid for the years prior to 1923. However, reports from the mission station in earlier years indicate that Inuit families frequently left the mission station for long periods during winter to hunt in other areas, particularly when game was scarce around Killinek. Similarly, his account of discontent over the price of store goods and fuel shortages only makes sense if the mission store is viewed in isolation, without reference to the HBC store, a 10-minute walk away. However, Inuit did have the option of obtaining goods at the HBC post. Describing conditions at Killinek in 1923, Waldmann reported that "the

H.B. Company does everything to win over to them the people who are there."[136] Although the Moravian missionaries made no reference to comparative prices or goods offered by the HBC, its trade operation was certainly an alternative for Inuit families living in the Killinek area to obtain essential supplies. If people were unhappy with services at the mission store, they did not necessarily have to leave the area, as the HBC offered lower prices for consumer goods. So why did they relocate to Hebron?

The five families who left Killinek in 1923 mainly consisted of people who were either closely related to the elderly widows of Semigak and Tuglavina, the former Inuit leaders in the Nachvak area, or were associated with their extended families. One exception was the family of Henry Jararuse, who originated from Killinek and whose extended family included relatives by marriage from Ungava Bay. The names of people in these families and of other families who departed from Killinek over the next three years are listed in Table 8. In addition to people's Christian names, Table 8 also notes adults' original Inuit names before their baptism and the women's family surnames prior to their marriage.

The families related to the elderly widows may have had their own motive in wanting to move closer to familiar areas by settling at Hebron. However, the Jararuse household and other families originating from Killinek did not have a strong connection with Nachvak, although some people did hunt there when game was scarce at Killinek; they would have had even less knowledge or experience of the Hebron area. Considering the strong attachment shown by Inuit to their place of origin, as described in many instances in this book, the decision by families to leave Killinek could not have been motivated solely by consumer goods available at the mission store.

An increase in the number of residents at Hebron was welcomed by its missionary, Sigmund Waldmann, who was trying to rebuild the mission community after the influenza epidemic. He was also personally well known to Killinek Inuit, as he had been their first resident missionary. With the addition of 36 people in the five families from Killinek and more households expected to follow, Waldmann remarked that Hebron was "once more populated but unfortunately at the expense of Killinek."[137] He further stated, "this station [Killinek] will likely not exist much longer."[138]

Waldmann's hint that the Killinek mission station would soon be abandoned provides a better explanation for the departure of Inuit

**TABLE 8. Names of Inuit Arriving at Hebron from Killinek, 1923–1926.**

| **1923** |
|---|
| Herman Onalik (Onalik) b. 1905 (KCB)<br>wife: Lena (nee Tuglavina)<br>dau: Lydia Tuglavina (fa: Koganak) b. 1922 (PA) |
| David Kajuatsiak (Paksau) b. 1880 near Killinek<br>wife: Eleonora Kajuatsiak (Tigujak, nee Semigak) b. 1893 near Nachvak (KCB)<br>mother-in-law: Eugenia Semigak (Nangmartvarsuk) b. 1855 (KCB)<br>son: Abia Kajuatsiak (1st marriage) b. 1902 near Killinek<br>dau: Amalia Kajuatsiak (2nd marriage) b. 1914 near Killinek<br>son: Tomas Kajuatsiak b. 1918 near Killinek<br>son: Solomon Kajuatsiak b. 1922 near Killinek |
| Ida Suarak (Paksaut; sister to David Kajuatsiak) b. 1870 near Killinek<br>son: Josef Suarak b. 1893 in Ramah (KCB)<br>wife: Selma Suarak (Pullanersoak, nee Jararuse)<br>son: Gabriel Isaac Suarak b. 1914 near Killinek<br>dau: Rebekka Martha Suarak b. 1920 near Killinek<br>dau: Amalia Onalik (nee Suarak) b. 1886 (KCB)<br>son: Simon Kohlmeister (1st marriage) b. 1905 in Ramah (KCB)<br>son: Nikodemus Thomas Menzel (2nd marriage) b. 1916 in Killinek<br>son: Jonatan Onalik (3rd marriage) b. 1919 near Killinek |
| Henry Jararuse (Kavanga) b. 1888 in Killinek<br>wife: Sara Jararuse (Paungak) b. 1873 near Kangiqsualujjuaq<br>dau: Naemi Jararuse b. 1909 near Killinek<br>son: Tomas Jararuse b. 1913 near Killinek<br>dau: Lizzie Maggie Jararuse b. 1915 near Killinek<br>son: George Jararuse b. 1918 near Killinek<br>mother-in-law: Hanna b. 1850 near Kangiqsualujjuaq<br>son: Michael Kallutak b. 1887 in Kangiqsualujjuaq<br>wife: Hulda Kallutak (nee Suarak) b. 1895 in Ramah<br>adopted dau: Rute Onalik b. 1914 near Killinek |
| Sabina Tuglavina (Pituratsuk) b. 1849 near Killinek<br>Tabea Tuglavina Kairtok (Arnatuk) b. 1874 near Aulatsivik<br>son: Jonas Tuglavina (Kedlik; 1st marriage) b. 1906 (KCB)<br>son: Josef Tuglavina (Omanatsiak; 1st marriage) b. 1902 (KCB)<br>wife: Bertha Tuglavina (nee Kairtok) b. 1905 near Killinek<br>son: Zacharias Kairtok (2nd marriage)<br>step-dau: Hedvig Kairtok (2nd marriage) |
| **Sub-total: 36** |

**1924 (April)**

Lucas Jararuse (Sekkinek) b. 1897 near Killinek
wife: Elizabeth Jararuse (Avigiak) b. 1901(?) near Killinek
son: Henry Benjamin Jararuse b. 1923 near Killinek

**1924**

Filipus Kallutak (Pangortok) b. 1888 near Kangiqsualujjuaq
wife: Sibilla Kallutak (Kuttaktok) b. 1888 near Kuujjuaq
mother: Marta Kallutak (Ikkiake) b. 1864 near Kangiqsualujjuaq
dau: Tabea Kallutak b. 1910 near Killinek
son: Johannes Kallutak b. 1913 near Killinek
dau: Maggi Kallutak b. 1915 near Killinek
dau: Marie Emily Kallutak b. 1920 near Killinek

Konrad Jararuse (Serlek) b. 1887 in Aulatsivik (brother of Koktok)
wife Amalia Jararuse (Annekordluk) (nee Onalik) b. 1888 near Aulatsivik (KCB)

**1924 (summer)**

Kefas Semigak (Ikkera) b. 1879 in Komaktorvik (KCB)
wife: Hildegard Semigak (Tullugaksoak, nee Onalik; 2nd marriage) b. 1901
son: Wilson Semigak (1st marriage) b. 1911 (KCB)

**Sub-total: 15**

**1925**

Boas Onalik (Tivoa) b. 1893
wife: Susana Onalik (Simigak/Jararuse) b. 1896
son: William Onalik (Jararuse) b. 1913 near Killinek
dau: Mary Hildega Onalik b. 1916 near Killinek
dau: Margareta Caritas Onalik b. 1919 near Killinek
dau: Jesika Salome Onalik b. 1923 near Killinek
dau: Faride Jane Onalik b. 1922 near Killinek

Martin Jararuse b. 1900
wife: Maria Jararuse (Kajuatsiak) b. 1904 (KCB)
son: Jako Jararuse b. 1923 near Killinek
mother: Rahel Jararuse (Pingoak) b. ca. 1880
?: Mathilda Jararuse b. 1898
?: Daniel (David?) Jararuse b. 1908

Tomas Jararuse (Paujunge) b. ca. 1877
wife: Lucy Jararuse (2nd marriage; nee Kallutak) b. 1883 at Kangiqsualujjuaq (KCB)
son: Julius Jararuse b. 1908
son: Albert Jararuse b. 1912
dau: Nikoline Jararuse b. 1915

Jefta Jararuse (Ungerdlek) b. 1902 in Hebron (KCB)
wife: Maria Jararuse (Onalik) (Sokkosek/Kallutak) b. 1895 near Kangiqsualujjuaq
dau: Susi Jessi Jararuse b. 1922
dau: Lucy Lavinia Sabina Semigak b. 1924

Gustav Semigak (Nikkatok) b. 1899
wife: Kristine Semigak (Tiguja) b. 1891 near Nachvak
son: Amos Semigak b. 1906
son: August Semigak b. 1911 near Killinek
dau: Selma Semigak b. 1912 (?)

**Sub-total: 27**

**(to Nachvak, 1925; to Hebron 1932)**

William Jararuse (Koktok) b. ca. 1871 (KCB)
wife: Mary Jararuse (Sapa) b. ca. 1875 (KCB)
dau: Emily Onalik (Attua) b. ca. 1891 (KCB)
son: Traugot Jararuse b. 1908
dau: Hanna Jararuse b. 1911
dau: Kate Sofie Jararuse b. 1913
dau: Anni Emili Jararuse b. 1915
son: Jako Benjamin Jararuse b. 1917
son: Paulus Jararuse (Angutaunek) b. 1904 (KCB)
wife: Mathilda (nee Annatok) b. 1905 at Kangiqsualujjuaq (KCB)
dau: Anni Alice Sara

**(to Nachvak, October 1925; to Hebron 1926)**

Mark Kannikitok b. ca. 1887 (KCB)
wife: May Kannikitok b. ca. 1890 at Kangiqsualujjuaq, d. 1926 (KCB)
dau: Lily Kannikitok b. 1914 (KCB)
son: Job Kannikitok b. 1914 (KCB)

**Sub-total: 15**

**1926**

Abel Nugak
wife: Monika (Paniguniak)
son: David

**Sub-total: 3**

***Total: 96***

Source: Hebron Supplementary Catalogue (HSC).

families from Killinek than Lenz's account of discontent over store services. His comment also clarifies why the first five families left Killinek shortly before Lenz's own departure in September 1923. Inuit may have known or suspected that another missionary would not be sent to the mission station and understood Lenz's departure as a prelude to the impending end of the Moravian presence at Killinek. Families belonging to the Moravian congregation were expected to be loyal in only trading at the Killinek mission store, and missionaries likely encouraged Inuit to move south with the Mission.

**Maria Obed Jararuse, Killinek, 1920s (The Rooms Provincial Archives)**

Although the mission store at Killinek continued operating, another 15 people in four families left during the winter. In February 1924, Waldmann expected "almost all of the old Killinek inhabitants" to move to Hebron.[139] He predicted that the only people who would not join the relocation were two families at Killinek "who lived there in our time" and families continuing to reside at Aulatsivik.[140] Members of the latter group could not be pressured to trade solely at the mission store, since they were not Christian converts. Available records from the HBC post after 1920 indicate that men from Aulatsivik, including Sekepa, Anautak, Ijaitok, Niakutsiak, and Onalik, periodically travelled to barter resources at the HBC store both before and after the mission store ceased operating.[141]

Jefta Jararuse, his wife Maria, and their two daughters moved from Killinek to Hebron in 1925. He endured two displacements in his lifetime:

> I lived on the south side of Killinek at Ungalingatsuk. The English manager told us to move so we went on the ship *Harmony* to Hebron. From Hebron, I was told to move again to Nain or Hopedale [in 1959]. Because I now had a boat, I moved to Hopedale. I was one of the last to move [from Hebron].[142]

In the fall of 1924, the Moravian shopkeeper at Killinek was reassigned to Okkak because the station was "largely depopulated."[143] A clerk was sent to handle the remains of the trade operation. The final closure of the Killinek mission station was attributed by Waldmann in 1925 to the fact that "the people moved south."[144] Yet almost as many Inuit left Killinek after the mission store was closed as had departed while it was still operating.

Compared to 51 Killinek Inuit settling in the Hebron area in 1923–24, another 45 people composing eight households arrived there, or chose to live at Nachvak, in 1925 and 1926.[145]

A total of 96 Inuit in 17 family groups left Killinek and moved to Hebron from 1923 to 1926. They were all members of the Moravian congregation and mainly included people who originated from the Killinek area, with two families from the Abloviak region of Ungava Bay. The exclusive nature of this group, consisting of virtually only and all the Inuit families belonging to the Moravian congregation, suggests that their movement to Hebron was not a spontaneous or independent act. With their departure, the only Inuit remaining at Killinek were people who originated from Ungava Bay and traded at the HBC store.

Noah Angnatuk of Ungava Bay recalled the Moravians leaving Killinek when he was a teenager, as he described in a 1985 interview:

> Many Inuit lived in Killiniq while the German traders were there. When the German traders had to leave, HBC traders bought all their buildings. The reason for their leaving was because they could no longer compete with the HBC. They planned to come back north to set up stores but they never did. When they left, many of their Inuit customers followed them, some by dog team and some in summer by boat. The German traders stayed in Iipujuuni (Hebron) for a while so some Inuit moved to that area.[146]

For the Moravian authorities, having their congregation relocate to Hebron would have been desirable for several reasons. First, the Mission would retain its hold on Inuit families, who had been carefully instructed and baptized, thereby preserving the integrity of their social and religious constituency in Labrador. Second, an evacuation of Moravian Inuit from Killinek removed potential customers for the HBC and potential members of the Anglican Church, which might decide to return and take control of the station. Rev. Stewart evidently monitored events at Killinek; he performed the last marriage ceremony at the station and recorded it in the Moravian Church Book on May 8, 1924.[147]

A third factor was that Killinek Inuit were better candidates to repopulate Hebron than people from southern mission stations because they were accustomed to living in a similar environment.[148] Compared to Inuit from the Nain or Hopedale regions, Killinek Inuit would have found getting firewood from a forest 30 miles south of Hebron easier than their experience in the Far North. Finally, by attributing the Killinek congregation's decision to relocate south to their discontent over consumer goods, the Moravian Mission could justify abandoning the mission station without having to implicate their own financial difficulties in the closure.

Moravian officials may have hinted at the mission station's closure to Inuit, but they did not share their knowledge about another element of the situation at Killinek. In April 1921, the SFG had begun negotiations with the Hudson's Bay Company about ceding its entire trade operation on the Labrador coast to its long-time rival.[149] The HBC was essentially the only commercial enterprise capable of and interested in assuming responsibility for the stores in all mission communities. Faced with a debt of $47,000 in 1923, and per capita debts of $600 to $1,000 in 1924, the Moravian Mission's financial situation was dire.[150] The SFG tried to limit its liabilities by terminating credit advances at the mission stores in 1924, and so closing the Killinek station would have reduced operating expenses to some extent. However, the SFG realized that reaching an agreement with the HBC was a necessary step in resolving its desperate financial state.

The relocation of Inuit families from Killinek to Hebron allowed Moravian missionaries to consolidate members of their congregation. Hebron was the last remaining mission station in the northern region, and the community needed a larger population to bolster its revival from the 1918 Spanish flu epidemic. While some Killinek families may have wanted to move to the Hebron area, the departure of practically the entire Moravian congregation suggests that people were influenced to leave by the missionary at the station, Berthold Lenz, before he left on furlough. He likely told people that he or another minister would not return to the community, and that they should therefore move to Hebron where they would have an easier lifestyle and continue their standing in the church.

Lenz's account of discontent among Inuit at Killinek may have supported the interests of the Moravian Mission and masked the looming transfer of its trade operation to the HBC. In August 1926, an official notice announced the finalization of an agreement whereby the HBC purchased the outstanding trade stock, the *S.S. Harmony*, and leased premises associated with the business from the Moravian Mission for a period of 21 years.[151] The HBC also purchased the mission property at Killinek in December 1925 for $5,000.[152] As the editor of the *Periodical Accounts* remarked, "Thus closes an important chapter in the history of the Mission of our Church in that bleak, inhospitable land."[153] Had the Killinek Inuit not moved before the agreement with the HBC was concluded, the Moravian missionaries may have been unable to convince families to leave the area afterwards, since the HBC store could supply them with essential goods.

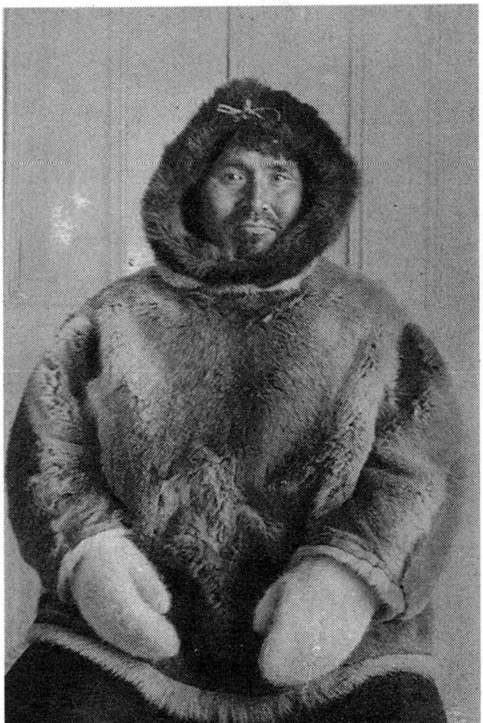

**David Kajuatsiak (Paksau), Killinek (postcard, Hettasch family fonds, Labrador Inuit through Moravian Eyes collection)**

Thirty years later, a similar situation occurred at Hebron, when the Moravian Mission was facing financially ruin and was determined to leave the area. In the late 1950s, missionaries cited a lack of firewood, poor housing, and other difficulties as reasons for removing the Inuit population at Hebron. As in the 1920s, Inuit were also not informed about a scheme designed to consolidate them with the population of southerly communities on the Labrador coast.[154]

After 1926, the area north of Hebron continued to be used by Inuit families based mainly at Ramah, Nachvak, and Aulatsivik, as well as by Ungava Inuit who remained at Killinek and obtained supplies from the HBC store. The people of Aulatsivik were some of the last Inuit to come under the influence of the Moravian Mission. In the winter, about 40–50 people lived in the area, mainly from the Onalik, Semigak, and Kajuatsiak families.

In a 1977 interview, Jako Kajuatsiak described his memories of growing up in Aulatsivik and then moving to Hebron in the 1930s. He speaks here through a translator:

> [He grew up] where there were no Kallunât in Aulatsivik. Two families [lived in the area], and other people outside, like his wife's grandmother, her parents, and her brothers. What they had for their food was char, seal meat, caribou meat, cod, and sculpins. They never had tea.
>
> When they were going to Killinek, they would have to sleep out for two or three nights. It was hard going. They would have to go through rough land. In the springtime, from Aulatsivik they would go to Nachvak, walking all the way, and carrying their belongings on their backs. They would go there to shop for tobacco, gun powder, and gun cleaners and bags.
>
> In the springtime, the men would get caribou by walking, for their clothes. The families would stay home. Sometimes they would have two dogs. The dogs would be carrying their food on their backs. They would be gone for a month and maybe even more. We'd carry the meat on our backs, same as the dogs. The women would make the clothes. They would make pants out of seal skin, boots out of seal skin, and coats would be made out of caribou skin.
>
> [He can remember his wife's father, Onalik] could pull a walrus up, all by himself. Walruses are right heavy, hey? Takes a lot of men, need a lot of men to haul a walrus, but her father, all by

> himself, would haul in a walrus. There's this saying – a man with a lot of sins, he wouldn't be able to even budge a walrus. A man with a clean soul, it would be easy for him to haul one up.
>
> [To fish char], they would use fish forks made of wood and use them for spearing the fish. They never used nets. They never sold any cod, or char, or salmon. All they used to sell to the stores were the fox furs and the seal skins. In the wintertime, they would be sealing with their guns. In the spring and open water, they would go by Kajak. And then when they sold their seal skins, they would get a dollar for the skins. He can remember when seal skins would sell for 20 cents at Hebron.
>
> They started going to Hebron in the 1920s. When they left Aulatsivik, they went to Hebron. They went to Hebron only when there were no more people there because of the influenza epidemic. That influenza never got to Aulatsivik.[155]

Jako's wife, Emma Kajuatsiak, recalled life as a young woman in Aulatsivik at the same period:

**Jako Kajuatsiak (Hettasch family collection, Them Days Archive)**

> In Aulatsivik, when I was just married, I used to stay home when my husband went hunting. I'd stay and clean seal skins while my mother braided caribou sinew. Those sinew, that we used to braid, were really strong. They were used to sew kayaks together and they were good for tapping seal skin boots, too, so they don't wear out so easily. When my mother was making a sealskin tent, I used to help her sew. We'd use the strong sinew that we had braided, three strands. It takes over thirty seal skins to make a good-sized tent, less for a smaller one. . . .
>
> I used to follow my husband when he went caribou hunting. I even used to take my son, Tom, in my back. When we went to the country, we used to take a tent along and I'd stay in the tent while my husband went caribou hunting. When he'd get the caribou, I'd dry them, the deer meat. I used to save every part of the sinew and dry them. . . . Every time my husband got a caribou, I would dry a lot of sinews and make dried meat and cook the fat of it to dry later. When the fat was cooked, I'd put it under flat pieces of rock so that they'd dry nice and flat. . . . [Jako] made a pack of the caribou skin, what he just killed, and put all the dried sinews, meat, fat, and fresh meat into it. Then he would put them into one skin and carry it on his back. He used to carry loads of meat on his back, real heavy ones, too. He was a strong man.[156]

William Onalik also lived in Aulatsivik in the 1910s and 1920s. He described his memories in a 1977 interview:

> I was brought up in a place called Aulatsivik, just outside of Killinek, where we never ever saw any white people. I wouldn't even dare touch the white people's food because I didn't like it when somebody brought a supply of it. I remember everything quite clearly from when I was small. We'd have a lot to eat sometimes and whenever we got hungry, our parents always managed to come up with food. They always did take good care of you and never let you starve. They were never stingy over it either because

we always shared everything amongst us. The men were always out hunting for something, and whenever they killed anything, we all shared it and had a big feed out of it.

They didn't go to Hebron for supplies because Hebron was too far from Cape Chidley and our place (Aulatsivik). We'd have a really difficult time sometimes. When I was a kid, I saw them going through the difficult times with my own eyes. They had some bad years when you couldn't catch anything either on land or on water. There are times when game is scarce. We even went hungry sometimes, and other times game was really plentiful, same as it is now. That's how it went. I can't say everything was perfect either from the place I came from. It was like any other place.

During all the years I've been living, I've never known anybody yet who never shared his catch with anybody after he's been

**Herman Onalik, 1948, at St. Anthony hospital (The Rooms Provincial Archives)**

> hunting. If he came back with any sort of game, they shared it with everybody in the village and they never ever wasted anything either. Like with caribou, if anyone came back with a load of caribou, they'd make sure the widows, widowers, or the older people were the first ones to get their share of the meat, or else they'd invite them for a meal right away. Anyone who was unable to support his own family, like the widows, were always taken care of by other people and given their share of the game. And they weren't expected to pay anything back in return. Anybody who was unable to do anything for himself was always given special attention and given special care. The older folks were the most respected people in those days.[157]

Information about the people who lived in Aulatsivik in the 1920s is incomplete, as they had refused to join a Moravian congregation and were therefore not subject to the missionaries' detailed documentation, but Appendix 2 lists the names and information that Randy Ames collected during land-use research in 1986.

In 1927, a decision made in London by the British Privy Council clarified the exact location of the boundary between the Dominion of Canada (Quebec) and the colony of Newfoundland (Labrador).[158] The border ran right through Killinek Island, putting Cape Chidley on the eastern shore in Labrador, and Port Burwell/Killinek on the Canadian side. The jurisdictional line arbitrarily divided Inuit territory, and although its impact was at first negligible, the boundary eventually had significant implications for the Indigenous residents of Labrador, Quebec, and the Northwest Territories/Nunavut, as the next two chapters will illustrate.

CHAPTER TEN

# The Hudson's Bay Company Era, 1926–1940s

## Hudson's Bay Company Assumes Trade

The transfer of the entire Moravian trade operation in Labrador to the Hudson's Bay Company in 1926 had a radical effect on Inuit land-use activities. Unlike the Moravian traders, the HBC prioritized the purchase of pelts from fur-bearing animals over fish and seal products. This policy compelled Inuit to spread out in winter over wide areas to have a better chance of finding foxes to earn an income from trapping.[1] Families no longer congregated at the mission stations during the winter but instead dispersed to outlying places where they focused on trapping fur-bearing animals and hunting game to provide food for their households. From spring until late fall, people also lived away from the communities, settled at traditional camps where they fished cod and hunted or netted seals to supplement their income through the sale of dried fish, seal pelts, and sealskin boots sewn by women.[2] Some hunters extended their range far into the interior and were equipped for "long distance fur hunting."[3] Inuit from George River also began trapping and hunting in the vicinity of Nachvak, as well as visiting Hebron to obtain necessary supplies.

On the Quebec side of the peninsula, the Hudson's Bay Company also gained control over their main competitors. Revillon Frères, a French company, had established trading posts in the Ungava region in 1903 but by the 1920s was having financial problems. In 1926, it sold 54 per cent of

**Tuglavina, Killinek, 1928 (photo by Heinrich Simon, Unity Archives, Herrnhut)**

its interest to the HBC and agreed to a pricing system that ended the fierce competition between the firms.[4] Indigenous trappers could no longer demand high prices for furs and their trade economy diminished. When the Great Depression of 1929 gutted the markets, Revillon Frères closed its store at Fort Chimo.[5] With no competition, the prices offered for furs dropped dramatically. While a white fox fur once fetched over $100, HBC only paid $2.50 per pelt during the Depression.[6]

The Hudson's Bay Company, now the sole trader in the region, reopened its George River post at Kangiqsualujjuaq in 1930.[7] Travel and communication were frequent between the George River and Fort Chimo posts, as Inuit and staff from the HBC and RCMP visited and journeyed along the coast. Trade focused on fur, seals, and the commercial salmon fishery in the area. During the short summer season, Inuit at various stations along the river were equipped with salmon nets and preserved their salmon catch at the HBC's cold storage plant near the mouth of the river. Within a few years, however, as the economy faltered, the Company dismantled the freezer and shipped it to Rigolet.[8]

On the Labrador coast, the HBC initially allowed families a small amount of credit and was responsible for providing relief or public welfare assistance to destitute families, in return for which the Newfoundland government allowed the Company to import goods duty-free to

Labrador.[9] However, when the markets for fish and seal products dropped during the Depression, trade and credit policies tightened. Credit advances were eliminated in 1932 and the stores began operating solely on a cash and barter basis.[10] Hunters were nevertheless given an "outfit," consisting mainly of a little ammunition and food, to trap during winter, which was deducted from their fur returns after the season was over.[11]

Complaints about the inadequate amount of relief given to impoverished families by HBC managers led Newfoundland authorities in 1934 to assign the administration of welfare assistance to officers of a newly formed rural police force called the Newfoundland Rangers. Constables were stationed at the six communities along the northern coast and assumed the task of determining welfare assistance to needy inhabitants, as well as enforcing game laws and other legal provisions.[12] The government also launched a new program of providing welfare in the form of loans to able-bodied residents. This approach did not significantly improve people's circumstances, however, and both Moravian missionaries and Inuit strongly opposed the scheme.[13]

The increasing restraints in the coastal economy after 1926 and greater poverty resulting from tighter restrictions on credit and welfare allowances appear to have influenced some families living near Hebron to move. Several households left the community in 1926 and moved to the Okkak area, where they could more easily fish and obtain firewood to heat their dwellings.[14] Three families from Killinek who were living in Nachvak decided to go back north in 1927 because they found that the trip to trade at either Hebron or Killinek was too far.[15] Another group of people originally from Nain also decided to return to their home community in 1929, except one family that moved to Okkak. The group from Nain had settled at Hebron after the influenza epidemic, hoping to have a better standard of living, but conditions were more difficult than they had anticipated.[16]

During the same period, the last unbaptized Inuit residing at Aulatsivik left their customary home and moved to Hebron. The first group arrived in 1926 and included seven people in two families. Onalik, the leader at Aulatsivik, was by then an elderly man. After his death, the remaining members of the community, consisting of 26 people in two extended families, left Aulatsivik. When they landed at Hebron in July 1932, the Inuit brass band played hymns for them in welcome.[17] They were all baptized within a year, and joined a congregation of Inuit who had roots throughout the Quebec–Labrador Peninsula.

## A Diverse and Widespread Hebron Congregation

Inuit belonging to the Hebron congregation spent most of the year living at outlying encampments and only visited the station to trade and to celebrate major religious festivals.[18] Augusta Jararuse later recalled, "We spent time in Hebron only during Easter and we returned to our land after Easter. Our land was beautiful back then."[19] Clara Ford's family lived at Napâttuk Bay: "We were always outside [away from Hebron], more up in the bay at Napâttuk. We were always there, but we used to go to Hebron at Christmastime and at Eastertime."[20] The largest number of families were situated north of Hebron, at Saglek Bay and Ramah, and to the south at Napâttuk Bay, but households were also dispersed at other locations within a 50-mile radius of the community.[21] People also continued to hunt and fish along the coast as far as Killinek, where they were reported by the HBC agent in July 1932, although they did not visit the post to trade.[22] Years later, Sabina Nochasak described how her family spent most of the year outside Hebron, as the hunting and fishing were better elsewhere:

> We were always at our hunting places. They were always gone to their hunting places, those who had houses at their hunting camps. Right in Hebron itself, there was nothing, either trout [char] or any other game. In Sillupat, in summertime, we could always get trout.[23]

Dick Kairtok's family also had their own hunting and fishing places: "When we lived in Hebron, we used to go to a little bay in the fall from what I recall. We used to go to Ittilisuak in the fall and in the summer, we used to go around Saglek, Nachvak, and Kangalaksiorvik."[24] Many people identified strongly with their hunting places, as Augusta Erving described:

> We had our own little place which was called Tikkigasukuluk. That is where the Onaliks, Jararuses, and Semigaks lived, in that little place called Tikkigasukuluk, north of Hebron.... Johannes Semigak, Clemence Jararuse, Jako Semigak, Raymond Semigak, Conrad Jararuse, my grandfather, and his wife Agnes.[25]

Although the families had officially moved to Hebron, they continued to spend most of the year in the bays and islands north of the community.

With all the migrations of people into Hebron, the congregation there had a diversity that was not found at other mission stations. As most of their time was spent with their families in their own hunting and fishing places, Inuit of Hebron often focused their lives elsewhere. Rev. George Harp at Hebron commented in 1938 that the mix of people created challenges for the missionaries:

> There is a vast difference between the Hebron and Southern Eskimos. They are made up of Ramah, Nachvak, Killinek, and Aulatsivik people, and there are no original Hebron people here to act as a foundation on which to work. We have four distinct types of Eskimos, and it is very difficult to get them to pull together.[26]

The Spanish flu of 1918 had devastated the core group of families that had originally formed the Hebron congregation.[27] After 1919, the community consisted mainly of families from the north, who may not have been as enthusiastic about supporting the Mission's community goals as the missionaries hoped they would be.

Inuit families displayed their community cohesion in other ways, however. "Life in the Hebron community was everything," Boas Jararuse later commented. "Families were close and everyone knew each other, looked after one another. After returning from the camps, they would be very happy to see each other again."[28] Sophie Lampe also remembers how families would support others:

> People helped each other well I remember; we did anyway. We weren't always close to others. People lived in a place where there was a lot of food. We weren't hungry for wild meat. And those from Hebron who didn't have anything to eat, if we came back and we had something, they would get some meat from the beach. That's how things were back then.[29]

## Inuit–HBC Interactions, 1930s

Inuit supported themselves and others when the wildlife was plenty, but in lean years, one's relationship with the traders played a major role in determining one's circumstances. In the 1930s, when global fur and fish markets plummeted and some wildlife populations declined, the Hudson's Bay Company's restrictive approach to trade and credit in both Labrador and Quebec caused much hardship for Inuit. In response, several trappers found ways to circumvent the trading system, as well as the imposed national border between Labrador and Canada. Lucas, Adam,

**Hudson's Bay Company post at Port Burwell (Killinek), (McCord Stewart Museum)**

and Peter Ukuatsiajuaq/Ukuatsiaq/Okuatsiajoak[30] were brothers who had started trading at George River in 1931, leading the HBC manager to claim "they belong to this post now and call themselves Company's men."[31] In 1933, the George River manager learned that Lucas had traded a fox pelt in exchange for tea and ammunition at the HBC post at Hebron.[32] The following March, Peter "Cud-Luh" and his brothers visited Hebron and traded 20 or more foxes because the price of provisions was much lower than at George River.[33] The brothers had previously bartered their furs with the Revillon Frères traders at Seal River.[34] Having changed their dealings once to a different post, they likely believed they were free to choose where they sold their fox pelts. However, the George River agent was not prepared to forfeit any furs to another post, even if it was an HBC store. "Trading at Hebron will have to be stopped," he wrote, "or otherwise in a year or two, when no furs [are collected,] George River will only be a relieving depot for the destitute."[35]

W.E. Swaffield Jr., an assistant at George River, discussed the issue with Lucas and Adam. He learned that they had sent furs to Hebron residents who had covertly sold them to an independent trader, Richard White, based just outside of Nain. White had encouraged them to send him furs and had paid them $200 in cash for two silver and two cross fox pelts, a higher price than they would have obtained from an HBC post on either coast.[36] Adam also stated that Hebron hunters had offered to sell him an eight-horsepower boat engine in exchange for 15 fox pelts after he cleared his debt at the George River store. Adam was an excellent trapper, as his son, Tivi Etok later described: "The HBC accorded my father special status among the hunters. The HBC observed the practice of designating trappers who could harvest many foxes as 'men of rank.' My father was one of them."[37] While Adam felt entitled to make the transaction because he had more than enough foxes to pay for the engine, Swaffield argued that he had an obligation to sell his entire trapping returns at the George River post. According to Swaffield's account of the discussion, Adam then apologized for his action and said he would not trade elsewhere in future;[38] nonetheless, he obtained his engine by travelling

**Women standing outside the HBC Store at George River, August 16, 1947 (Jardin botanique de Montréal Archives, Jacques Rousseau, A-JAR-003)**

to Hebron via Port Burwell the following year.[39] As a "man of rank," Adam likely had more clout in the negotiation than Swaffield was willing to admit.

Lucas, on the other hand, was unapologetic about his actions. He told the manager that Inuit could act as they wished and were not controlled by the Company's agents. He also stated that he had a notebook in which he had recorded complaints about the manager's business practices and that he intended to continue trading at Hebron until he heard from the district manager.[40] The George River agent became incensed by Lucas's response and considered "his nerve and action [was] unfair to any white man."[41] Countering "with a knock out threat," he demanded Lucas's notebook and kept it for his own reference.[42] The manager decided to withhold credit to Lucas, giving him "nothing except for what he pays for until seeing the District Manager" because he had "proved himself a twister."[43]

Credit may also have been withdrawn from Lucas's younger brother Peter, although the George River journal makes no reference to his status in the conflict. Once Lucas's family had to rely solely on their own resources to make purchases at the store, they would certainly have had more difficulty surviving, particularly during the summer when they could not obtain foxes to barter for provisions. A year later, the George River manager noted that some people had threatened to move to Hebron;[44] the claim was likely made by Lucas's family.

Adam Ukuatsiajuaq's son, Tivi Etok (born in 1929), describes the family's experience during this time in his autobiographical book, *The World of Tivi Etok*:

> As a young boy I remember Killiniq as a large village. There were many Qallunaat at Killiniq back then, working either for the HBC or the Royal Canadian Mounted Police (RCMP). Killiniq was already a big busy village, long before I was born. When I was a boy, we used to go hunting offshore from Killiniq. The area had a lot of marine mammals. There was an abundance of harp, ringed, and bearded seals. Killiniq is located on the migration route of many marine mammals. Our ancestors knew it was a migration route, as did their ancestors. That's why it was such an ancient habitation. I remember Killiniq having a Hudson Bay Company post and the RCMP. Schooners used to go there. I remember a schooner docked there. People from camps around Kangiqsualujjuaq and other communities went to Killiniq to trade. It was a really nice old community. I miss it profoundly. . . .
>
> My father had two younger brothers, Lucassie and Tommy Ukuatsiaq, who both had families. . . . The two families went up to the head of Kuururjuaq [Koroc River] to build a log house. . . . From the log house Father and the other men went inland to the Kuururjuaq Valley to hunt caribou. In the summer they took tents with them. By fall they would have many caches of caribou. We spent quite a long time there at Kuururjuaq. The men were always walking, either caribou hunting or fetching meat from the caches. The men were also learning where they could catch foxes, so that

they had fox pelts to trade. That's why Lucassie and Tommy's group began crossing the peninsula to the Labrador coast.

One year, Lucassie and Tommy decided to spend spring in Navvaaq, a fjord on the Labrador coast they had visited before. Our family went also. My father, being the oldest of the brothers, felt he should go too. This was our first experience in that area, although his younger brothers knew it well. Navvaaq is near Kuururjuaq. It's very close to the Kuururjuaq river system, but not part of it. There is another watershed called Ramah Bay, which is to the south of Navvaaq. There are many places around there that used to be our favourite locations. There lie my kin. My younger brother, Lucassie Billy, is buried at Ramah. He may have caught some sickness from a dog. A sick dog probably licked his face or even his mouth. . . .

Once we were at Navvaaq the men got plenty of foxes. My uncles knew the fjord had plenty of seals. Even back then there were not many seals at Kangiqsualujjuaq. That spring, seals were especially abundant at Navvaaq. There were so many we didn't have enough bullets for them all.

Shortly after our arrival, I shot my first marine mammal. It was a young seal just learning to be on its own. That spring members of our party went every day to hunt the seals basking on the ice. We had an abundance of seal meat. Seal carcasses littered the shore. We were no longer eating much, but kept drying seal meat. We dried large quantities of meat. Some people were still preparing meat for caching inside sealskin bags, even though our supplies were clearly adequate. Obviously, no one was hungry. . . . My first seal was a small one, but it was the first large game I had ever caught. I was shy to be the centre of attention, because it seemed like a real big deal. I felt like I was important and yet I was embarrassed as we approached the village. There was food everywhere. The people were just leisurely preparing meat to dry. Many seal carcasses were abandoned to the dogs on the beach.

People were not hungry, but a feast to celebrate my first seal catch was organized. Everyone was invited and every edible part of my seal was devoured. The skin, small as it was, was even divided into four parts. People really enjoyed my first seal, although with the abundance of food, it would seem that not a single person would have any appetite left. Only a small piece of fat was left over. That was the beginning of our lengthy stay across the Quebec/Labrador Peninsula. We made occasional trips to Kangiqsualujjuaq to trade.[45]

## HBC Trade Policies, Closure of Port Burwell, and Inuit Movement to Hebron

The difficult times on the Ungava coast spilled over into Labrador. George Harp, a Moravian minister at Hebron during the 1930s, reported that some Inuit from Ungava Bay visited the community on three or four occasions during the winter of 1935 and "repeatedly asked to be allowed to live here."[46] However, they were denied permission "as they are Canadians."[47] Harp was

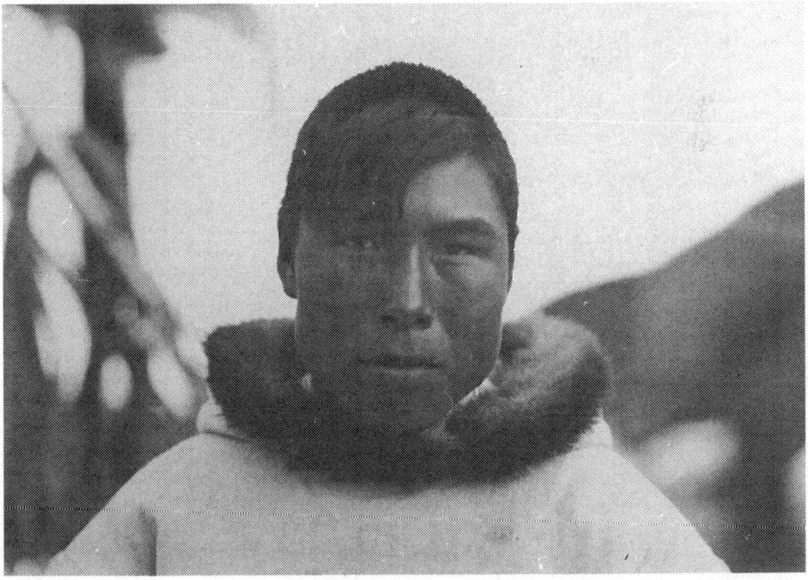

Killinek, 1934 (Peary-MacMillan Arctic Museum collection, Them Days Archive)

sympathetic to the Ungava Inuit, especially when they told him that they only saw their clergyman once a year or every few years.[48]

In 1938, after many difficult years, the HBC closed its establishment at Port Burwell; the RCMP detachment had been transferred four years earlier to Wakeham Bay (Kangiqsujuaq) and an officer made summer patrols in the area.[49] When the trading post closed, the HBC gave people a $10 advance when the HBC vessel arrived to dismantle the station, a sum intended to last until the men went to obtain their "fall debt" from Kangiqsualujjuaq in September.[50] This credit had to be repaid with fox pelts by April, when families would be given a spring advance that they had to compensate with sealskin boots before they could receive another fall account. Widows and destitute people were issued rations at ship time and were expected to obtain further provisions from Kangiqsualujjuaq.[51] This arrangement may have been convenient for the HBC, but it caused great hardship for Inuit remaining in the Killinek area. Their seal catch was reduced, as they could no longer obtain nets from the store, and they had no access to credit for provisions except by travelling to Kangiqsualujjuaq.[52] Families risked running out of food if they were unsuccessful in hunting game, as typically happened at times during the year, and the elderly people found it difficult to live so far from a store.

Many Inuit decided to move to Hebron or to Kangiqsualujjuaq. Boas Jararuse later recalled those days:

> In 1938, the white people left Killinek and for a long time there was no white men, those who worked at the stores. When they left, we found ourselves struggling to try to survive off the land. We were facing hunger and left alone without things that we needed. One of the most difficult times I have ever experienced was when we had to travel by dog team to pick up our supplies from Kangiqsualujjuaq. We were gone for one month. It was hard going because of deep snow; it was when my uncle died, and I was faced with terrible hardship.

> The Inuit families who were there at the time were very few, and the thought of leaving their homeland was so unbearable. We Inuit longed for our land. We did not want to leave it, but we were told that we had no choice in the matter if we wanted to find a better life elsewhere. We then moved to Hebron [in August 1944] where we began to find life much easier, and food was more available to us. . . . Hebron was a beautiful place when we first moved; it was a beautiful place to see.[53]

Noah Angnatuk also described his memories of the time:

> When the HBC left Killiniq, there wasn't any trading post there so we had to go to Kangiqsualujjuaq to trade. . . . The HBC left Killiniq because there weren't enough people there and therefore they couldn't afford to have their post there. They planned to leave for a long time and finally left. HBC expected us to be perfect and they wouldn't treat us fairly unless we satisfied their standards with stuff to sell. In the earlier days, they even contributed to support to the elderly and the poor but these days they don't have that service.[54]

Noah and his family eventually moved to Kangiqsualujjuaq.

The Hudson's Bay Company withdrew from northern Labrador a few years later. In 1942, the Company prematurely terminated its lease to operate the trade stores along the north coast, forcing the Commission of Government for Newfoundland to assume control of trade. The Commission established the Northern Labrador Trading Operation to manage the trading posts at Hebron, Nutâk, Nain, Davis Inlet, Hopedale, and Makkovik.[55]

Over the next decade, many Inuit from Ungava Bay moved eastward into Labrador. In the early 1940s, Lucas and his brother Peter Ukuatsiajuaq/Ukuatsiaq/Okuatsiajoak moved inland from Kangiqsualujjuaq, searching for better hunting areas. They gradually moved into Labrador territory, settling in the vicinity of Nachvak, as Tivi Etok described above.[56] The HBC agent at the George River post had refused them credit;

as they told the Hebron minister Frederick Grubb in the spring of 1943, "they had been unable to get supplies from George River as they had no fur to trade."[57] Lucas left all the food he could spare with Peter and took his family to Hebron, arriving there at Easter. Peter remained at Nachvak with his wife and five children, hoping to hunt seals or caribou. When he failed to find game, he decided to follow Lucas to Hebron.[58]

Given the circumstances, Peter's family would likely have starved at Nachvak had they stayed. As it was, they almost perished on their journey to Hebron. Grubb described their experience as follows:

> They ate first their dogs, then started out, having to eat the dogs' harness, then their own skin clothes and bedding. They were all emaciated, the one child (the youngest one) had died on the way from hunger and exposure. We gave him clothing for himself and his family and the Ranger gave him a stock of food on Government relief. One of our people who had known Peter in the past said: "We called him Petertannak (or Fat Peter) but he is not Fat Peter now! We hardly knew him, he is so thin!" Peter was here today having walked over from the little shack he had made for his family about five miles away, and I am glad to say that he is once more Fat Peter, and there is plenty of meat, thanks to the good sealing season.[59]

The two families, including 13 people, became members of the Moravian congregation, with their names entered in the Hebron Supplementary Catalogue.[60] Grubb noted that they had belonged to the Chimo Congregation of the Church of England, but they had lost contact with the church when they moved away from Kangiqsualujjuaq.[61] The Itulak families at Ikirasakituk, near Abloviak fiord, also found the HBC manager at George River "troublesome to deal with" and his behaviour motivated them to move to Hebron at the same time.[62]

The following year, several more Inuit appeared at Hebron. The families had lived mainly in the Killinek area after the Moravian station was closed; two groups, including 33 people, arrived in May and August 1944 via Kangiqsualujjuaq.[63] The sudden increase of almost 50 Inuit to the Hebron population in less than two years constituted its largest growth spurt since the movement of Killinek Inuit to the community in the mid-1920s. Harsh trading policies and a lack of wildlife forced the Ungava Inuit to resettle in Hebron in 1944, according to the Moravian minister Siegfried Hettasch: "Poverty is the chief cause which makes them migrate south to join up with our community. They could not get anything to trade and so often had to starve, and so finally they decided to move south and look for better living conditions."[64] Their desperation in moving to Hebron stemmed from the HBC's approach to trade and relief in the northeastern Ungava Bay region. The Company had been tasked with providing relief provisions to Indigenous families in Ungava by the federal government, but these supports were often grossly inadequate. Inuit throughout Ungava Bay had fiercely criticized the HBC approach to relief payments in the 1930s and early 1940s, and many held the Company responsible for Inuit starvation in the region.[65]

The large-scale movement of Inuit from Ungava Bay and Killinek to Hebron in 1944 was unique in its administrative implications. Officials viewed it as an issue of immigration, as the families had left Canadian territory for Labrador – an event that apparently had never occurred in the region. When the resettlement prompted a complaint, the Commission of Government, which administered Newfoundland between 1934 and 1949, launched an inquiry. Inspector Walter Rockwood, the Newfoundland Ranger tasked with investigating the situation, pointed to a political motive behind the complaint.[66] The relocation of Inuit would not have been questioned, Rockwood believed, if the HBC had a monopoly on all trade in the region. After the Company had withdrawn from its posts in Labrador in 1942, the Commission of Government had assumed control of trade. When an agency in Canada lodged a complaint about the immigration to the Commission of Government, Rockwood assumed that it must have come from one of three institutions having an interest in the Inuit population in Ungava: the Canadian government, the HBC, or the Anglican Church. As he commented, "one naturally suspects that if the trade at Hebron was still operated by the Hudson's Bay Company that nothing would have been said on that side at all."[67]

Rockwood interviewed Inuit, HBC post officials, and Moravian missionaries about the reasons behind the immigration. He noted in his report that northern Inuit found that having to visit Kangiqsualujjuaq to obtain supplies two or three times a year had made circumstances difficult for them. Mathilda Jararuse, a widow with three children, told him that she had nearly starved at Killinek and did not wish to return to the area because she feared she would die of hunger.[68] Other Inuit stated flatly that they would not return to the north and were determined to remain at Hebron. David Assivak, for example, who had arrived in August 1944 in a motorboat with 19 others, told Rockwood, "I don't want to go back and I'm not going back."[69]

Rockwood felt that people had been treated too leniently at Hebron by the store manager and by other officials in the community. Inuit expected to receive more assistance at Hebron than they would have

**Hebron school, 1944 (Hettasch family fonds, Labrador Inuit through Moravian Eyes collection)**

received at Kangiqsualujjuaq, as he explained: "This leniency seems to have coincided with, if reports from the Eskimos are true, a very firm policy at the George River post. Undoubtedly the stories spread and consequently the Burwell people decided to move to the 'Promised Land.'"[70] Rockwood was evidently told about the termination of credit to Lucas and Peter Ukuatsiajuaq, and about the low advances given to Inuit along the Ungava coast.

After completing his inquiry at Hebron, Rockwood received a message indicating that the secretary for natural resources in the Commission of Government did not want northern Inuit to remain at Hebron. He subsequently directed Ranger J. Ford, who was stationed in the community, to inform the people that they must return to their former hunting grounds and trading post, adding this advice:

> You will have to use your discretion re amount of pressure you apply but care should be taken to see that no Eskimo is asked the impossible, and no lives are endangered. If any refuse to return have them put such refusal in writing, with reason for refusal, and sign same.[71]

Rockwood further advised Ford to register the northern Inuit as "non-residents," but any woman who married a local inhabitant should be accorded resident status. This provision provided a means for some people to remain at Hebron, for as Rockwood remarks, "the question of their return to Canadian Territory will not arise."[72]

Ford's list of northern Inuit included 42 people but omitted the members of Lucas's and Peter's families, whose names he did not know; he also noted their surname as Oluak, but the Hebron minister initially recorded their family name as Inulu and later added the surname Okuatsiajoak. Table 9 summarizes the list of registered Inuit from both Ford's outline and information contained in the Hebron Supplementary Catalogue. A few more people arriving at Hebron from Killinek and Kangiqsualujjuaq in 1945–46 have been added to the list, making a total of 63 people settling in Hebron from 1943 to 1946.

Despite the official request that northern Inuit return to Ungava Bay, little was done to compel people to leave. Rockwood presumed that either the Newfoundland or Canadian government would have to arrange transportation by ship during the summer, if northern Inuit refused to return to Ungava Bay while ice conditions lasted in the winter of 1945.[73] However, he frankly admitted in his final report, "I would not on my own accord send them back but I agree that steps should be taken to prevent more from coming."[74] No action was taken to transport Inuit back to Ungava Bay, although two families consisting of 10 people were noted to have returned to Kangiqsualujjuaq in 1946 (Table 9).[75] The other families remained at Hebron and were integrated into the community, with several adults and young people ultimately marrying Labrador residents. No other people were reported to have emigrated from Kangiqsualujjuaq over the following years.[76]

## Inuit of the Killinek Region

Inuit who left the Killinek region during the 1930s and 1940s had occupied three distinct areas associated with specific family groups, according to detailed research on land use and occupancy patterns conducted by Randy Ames.[77] The families were based at Killinek, Ikirasakituk near Abloviak Fiord on the northeastern Ungava Bay coast, and Aulatsivik Island on the northern Labrador coast.[78] The residents of another encampment situated at Natsituk, immediately southwest of Killinek, harvested in the same area as the Killinek population and were considered part of that community.[79]

Killinek was composed of people who originated from both the Labrador and Ungava Bay coasts and had the largest number of inhabitants. Families lived in seasonal campsites extending south of the community along the two coastlines and utilized the entire area from the Button Islands to Kangalaksiorvik fiord on the Labrador coast, and to Keglo Bay on the Ungava Bay coast.[80] Their harvesting activities focused primarily along the northern Labrador coast because Killinek Island was a very poor hunting area in winter and the Labrador littoral was more productive for marine mammals, fish, birds, and other game than the Ungava coast.[81]

Inuit dwelling at Aulatsivik consisted of the descendants of families with the surnames Onalik, Semigak, and Kajuatsiak, who had a long heritage on the northern Labrador coast. Their core area of seasonal land use extended to the Button Islands in the north and to Kangalaksiorvik in the south, although they also ranged as far as Nachvak and Ramah.[82] They were joined by families from Killinek and Ikirasakituk, particularly in late spring and early summer, because Aulatsivik was the richest area for all kinds of game.[83]

In contrast, the Ungava Bay coast was the least populated area as it lacked the diversity and abundance of seals, fish, and birds found along the northern Labrador coast. Both Ikirasakituk and Natsituk were occupied during the fall and winter by people who originated in the vicinity of Kangiqsualujjuaq. John and Maggie Ittaluk (Itulak) and their sons Josiah, Nikodemus, and Lucas lived at Ikirasakituk from 1915 until the sons' families moved to Hebron in 1943 and 1945.[84] Peter and Mary Ulluak, their daughter Lizzie Ulluak (Okuatsiajoak), and their sons Bobby

**Dog team and people on ice, Hebron, 1950s (Hettasch family collection, Them Days Archive)**

Nacholak and Stanley Annanak lived at Natsituk in the 1920s.[85] Their core area of land use extended from Keglo Bay on the Ungava coast north to the Button Islands and encompassed an area southeast of McLelan Strait centring at Ekortisarsuk and Noodleook fiords, north of Aulatsivik, where the families hunted during the spring and summer.[86]

**TABLE 9. Names of Inuit by Household Groups Migrating to Hebron, 1943–1946.**

| **1943 (from Nachvak)** |
|---|
| *Lucas Inulu [Oluak; also Okuatialuk, Okuatsiajoak, Ukuatsiajuaq, Ukuatsiaq, Okkautsiak] b. 1894 in Kangiqsualujjuaq<br>wife: *Minnie Inulu Okuatialuk b. 1894 in Kangiqsualujjuaq<br>son: *Lucase Inulu Okuatiajoak b. 1917 in Kangiqsualujjuaq<br>wife: *Lizzie Maggie Okkautsiak (Ulluak) b. 1917 in Kangiqsualujjuaq<br>son: *Tommy John Inulu Okautsijoak b. 1925 in Kangiqsualujjuaq<br>dau: *Maggie Jenny Inulu b. 1929 in Kangiqsualujjuaq<br>dau: *Jessie Eva Inulu b. 1933 in Kangiqsualujjuaq |
| *Peter Inulu [Oluak; also Okkautsiak, Okuatsiajoak, Ukuatsiajuaq/Ukuatsiaq] b. 1905 in Kangiqsualujjuaq<br>wife: *Jenny Inulu b. 1919 in Kangiqsualujjuaq<br>dau: *Kitty Inulu b. 1927<br>son: *Charlie Inulu b. 1929 in Kangiqsualujjuaq<br>dau: *Susie Lydia Inulu b. 1931 in Kangiqsualujjuaq<br>dau: *Berta Eva Inulu b. 1935 in Kangiqsualujjuaq |
| **1944 (from Killinek in May)** |
| Jako Jararuse b. 1917 in Killinek |
| Elizabeth Jararuse (widow) b. 1917 in Killinek |
| Paulus Annatok b. 1940 in Killinek |
| *Lavinia Bertha Mary Asivak b. 1940 in Killinek |
| Nikodemus Itulak b. 1914 in Kangalaksiorvik fiord<br>wife: Minnie Itulak (Etok) b. 1919 in Kuujjuaq<br>dau: Maggie Mary Itulak b. 1941 in Ikirasakituk<br>dau: Sophia Louisa Itulak b. 1942 in Ikirasakituk |
| Lavinia Itulak (widow) (Akupivik) (Inugalloak) b. 1905 in Kangiqsualujjuaq<br>son: James Itulak b. 1929 in Kangiqsualujjuaq<br>dau: Annie Itulak b. 1934 in Ikirasakituk<br>son: Paulus Imatalak Itulak b. 1939 |
| **(from George River/Kangiqsualujjuaq in May)** |
| Mary Naggolak (widow) b. 1885 in Kangiqsualujjuaq |

**(from Killinek in August)**

*David Atsivak b. 1909 in Abloviak
wife: Lucy Atsivik b. 1912 in Killinek
son: Jimmy Job Atsivik b. 1941 in Killinek
son: William Annahatak (adopted) b. 1936 in Killinek

Johnny Naggolak (returned to Kangiqsualujjuaq in 1946) b. 1918 in Killinek
wife: *Sara Naggolak b. 1919 in Killinek
dau: *Minnie Naggolak b. 1939 in Killinek
son: *Jimmy Naggolak b. 1943 in Killinek

*Mark Annahatuk (returned to Kangiqsualujjuaq in 1946) b. 1916 in Killinek
wife: *Emily Annahatuk b. 1916 in Killinek
dau: Jenny Sara Annahatuk b. 1938 in Tunnisalik
sister: Dora Annahatuk (widow) b. 1911 in Abloviak
sister: Jenny Annahatuk b. 1903 in Abloviak
son: Jimmy (adopted) Annahatuk b. 1930 in Killinek

Emily Inugaluak (widow) b. 1915 in Killinek
dau: Agnes Inugaluak b. 1932 in Killinek

Mathilda Jararuse (Annartok) b. 1905 in Abloviak
son: Boas Jararuse b. 1929 in Killinek
dau: Naemi Jararuse b. 1936 in Killinek
dau: Basel Sara Jararuse b. 1938 in Killinek

**1945 (from Nachvak in February)**

Adam Okkautsiak/Okuatsiak/Okuatsiajoak/Ukuatsiajuaq/Ukuatsiaq (returned to Nachvak 1946) b. 1890
wife: Sara Okkautsiak b. 1895
son: David (Tivi Etok) Okkautsiak b. 1929
son: Lucas Okkautsiak b. 1934
son: William Okkautisak b. 1938
son: Joele
son: Moses
wife: Lara [Clara]

**(from Killinek)**

Harry Kallu

*James Josiah/Joshia Itulak b. 1908 in Kangiqsualujjuaq
wife: Lilli Itulak (Imak) (Anerpiak) b. 1920
son: Peter Jeremias Imak (adopted) b. 1934
son: Heinrich Itulak b. 1937
dau: Mary Rasa Itulak b. 1936
son: Lucas Itulak b. 1940 in Ikirasakituk

**1946 (from Killinek)**

Daniel Kajue b. 1921 in Abloviak
wife: Anni Kajue (Jararuse) b. 1925 in Killinek

**Total: 63**

* Denotes membership in the Church of England.

Sources: Hebron Supplementary Catalogue; Ames, 1986.

Each of the three groups occupied specific areas in the Killinek region. As Ames emphasizes, however, the groups did not comprise separate entities isolated from contact with each other. The families met frequently, lived close to each other for extended periods of time, and shared the same hunting grounds, particularly from spring to early fall when they were camped in the vicinity of Killinek or southeast of McLelan Strait on the northern Labrador coast. Although the groups remained apart from late fall until early spring, they also occasionally met in winter while hunting caribou and trapping foxes in the interior or hunting seals around Ikirasakituk. As well, some Inuit who left Killinek and moved to Hebron from 1923 to 1926, along with people from Aulatsivik who settled at Hebron in 1926 and 1933, continued to hunt along the coast as far north as the Button Islands and utilized the same harvesting areas as families who still resided in the Killinek region.[87]

For the families who remained in the Killinek region after the HBC post closed in 1938, the next decade was especially difficult. In 1942, the HBC moved about a dozen Inuit from Killinek to Southampton Island in northern Hudson Bay.[88] The relocation was part of an effort by the Company and the federal government to redistribute Inuit to areas of high game populations and addressed both the HBC's fur-trading interests and the Canadian government's concerns about welfare dependency and Inuit self-sufficiency. At the same time, Inuit from around Ungava Bay decided to move to Kuujjuaq after the American military began building an air base near the community in 1941.

**Killinek, 1934 (Peary-MacMillan Arctic Museum collection, Them Days Archive)**

Thousands of American servicemen arrived in the area, providing jobs and food for local people. According to some Inuit, including Dorothy Mesher (granddaughter of Labradorians Job Edmunds and Clara Lane), the air base saved many from starvation and provided an alternative livelihood to the trapping economy.[89] The US military closed the base in 1949–50.

The families remaining at Killinek relied on the abundant seal population in the area and the char fishery. They travelled to Kuujjuaq and Kangiqsualujjuaq, often only once a year to trade.[90] Tivi Etok describes his family's move to Killinek from Nachvak: "When I was older, we moved to Killiniq from Labrador. By the time we arrived, the Qallunaat had already left. Then the Inuit of Killiniq went to Kuujjuaq or Kangiqsualujjuaq to trade."[91] In 1950, the federal Department of Resources and Development organized an experimental cod fishery at Killinek to test its commercial viability, but Inuit there did not like eating the salt fish and were not overly enthusiastic about fishing for cod.[92] Approximately 20 Inuit remained at Killinek in 1955.[93]

The George River HBC post at Kangiqsualujjuaq closed in 1952 and became an outpost store.[94] About 150 Inuit lived in camps nearby in 1954,[95] as Tivi Etok describes:

> At the time we were scattered in many small camps. My family was at Kuururjuaq [Koroc River]. There were other camps including Tasikallak, Tuunulliq, Tuttutuuk, and Marqalik. Kangiqsualujjuaq had only two families, Willie Emudluk and Josephie Sammy Annanack.[96]

Tivi's father, Adam Ukuatsiajuk (Itok), ran the outpost store at Kangiqsualujjuaq until about 1960.[97]

For Inuit who had settled at Hebron, visits back to Killinek were rare. Families could satisfy their economic and subsistence needs closer to the community and had no practical reason or adequate equipment for travelling that far north. The limit of people's land-use activities extended primarily to Kangalaksiorvik fiord, just north of Komaktorvik, where people fished the abundant deep red char in the summer.[98] This area was also harvested extensively until fall for ranger seals, due to a bounty placed on them; periodically, hunters went farther north looking for ranger seals at the Avayalik and Home Islands, midway between Aulatsivik and Killinek.[99] Brothers Solomon Kajuatsiak and Sem Kajuatsiak, for example, would travel with their families by motorboat in early July from Hebron to Avayalik Island and Kangalaksiorvik fiord. There they would hunt ranger seals, jar seals, and young square-flipper seals, and their wives would clean the pelts – sometimes as many as 20 per day. They also fished for the large red char of Kangalaksiorvik fiord that could be sold at the Hebron store for double the price of pale char. When the char run ended in late summer, they returned to Hebron for the fall and winter.[100]

Another southward movement of families from Hebron occurred in the late 1940s, again involving people from Killinek. The shortage of firewood at Hebron and better cod-fishing grounds in the Okkak area

**Tent and dogs, 1934 (Peary-MacMillan Arctic Museum collection, Them Days Archive)**

attracted households to Okkak Bay, where they could trade at a small government store at Nutâk.[101] About half of the Hebron congregation resided in the Okkak area by 1951, and the Hebron minister was responsible for providing religious and emergency medical care to the entire Inuit population. Reaching all the widely dispersed households around both Hebron and Nutâk throughout the year was a difficult task for the missionary, as well as for other officials with an interest in the medical and social condition of the local inhabitants.[102] These difficulties in administering medical, educational, spiritual, and social services were soon to cause massive upheaval for northern Inuit.

CHAPTER ELEVEN

# Divergent Government Policy: Evictions from Nutâk and Hebron and Commercial Fishing at Killinek

## Nutâk and Hebron Evictions: Going against the Wind

By the 1950s, most Inuit in northern Labrador had joined the Hebron congregation, but they spent most of the year at their hunting and fishing places outside the community. The provincial government worked to support their resource-based economy by improving fishing facilities in Hebron and Nutâk in Okkak Bay.[1] However, the Moravian missionaries and the medical officials responsible for the region found it difficult to administer their services to such a dispersed population.

Soon after Newfoundland and Labrador joined Canada in 1949, the new province gained access to federal funding for services provided to Indigenous populations. The International Grenfell Association (IGA), which delivered medical care to northern Labrador under the new funding arrangement, was vocal in its calls for the centralization of northern Inuit. In a 1955 memo, the IGA's director of northern medical services, Dr. Anthony Paddon, dismissed the Inuit land-based way of life. He argued that inadequate housing at Hebron and a lack of firewood for fuel were the root causes of all health issues, and that northern Inuit should be moved south into a planned community in Okkak Bay:

> The old Eskimo way of living off of the land by hunting is irretrievably lost. There are many who urge a program to bring the

> Eskimo back to living by the harpoon. With the increasing scarcity of game and seals this would be impossible. The only future for the Eskimo lies in community life, better education, and gradual adaptation to Canadian life. Amalgamation of the Eskimos in the Nutak area would give rise to a strong community, with a reasonable standard of health, an adequate education system, facilities for entertainment of the people, and the resources of church, village government, good communications, reduced transportation costs and easier administration generally.[2]

The Moravian Mission had also been toying with the idea of a new community in the Okkak area since the 1940s but had been unable to accomplish it due to a lack of funds.[3] Given the broad support, provincial officials gave serious consideration to Dr. Paddon's suggestion.[4]

A few months later, the IGA superintendent, Dr. Charles Curtis, travelled to Nain. He was so appalled by his glimpse of northern Labrador that he wrote a strongly worded letter to provincial and federal officials, arguing that all Inuit north of Nain should be relocated south.[5] Instead of moving them to a new settlement in Okkak Bay, Curtis argued that the families should be moved into established communities. The Moravian superintendent, Rev. Peacock, disagreed with Curtis's condemnation of Inuit living conditions, but did agree that northern Inuit should be moved into settled communities:

> Our only hope as far as the Eskimos are concerned is to get them used to community life, for it seems certain that the process of "civilizing" is only hindered by dispersion and if the Eskimos are to become self-supporting citizens, they must have all the social amenities possible, and these amenities are not possible to folk living in bays and on islands often in squalid houses.[6]

The official provincial approach towards the Inuit "problem" crystallized at the Labrador Conference of February 1956. Representatives from the IGA, churches, and government congregated in St. John's to discuss the future. No northern Inuit leaders were invited, and they were not consulted. Instead, the non-Indigenous "experts" framed northern Inuit society in terms of their own interests and assumptions. In the view of these officials, the traditional harvesting economy was delaying the modernization of northern Inuit. They believed that Inuit should be settled in permanent communities, provided with education and medical services, and encouraged to adopt wage labour jobs.[7] Centralization would minimize the cost to the government, the Moravian Mission, and the International Grenfell Association in providing these social services. Participants pointed to Inuit adaptability and examples of Inuit relocation in Canada to further justify their strategy. "Efforts to move Eskimos to new surroundings and occupations in other parts of Canada have met with a reasonable degree of success," the Conference report reads.[8]

**(Back, l-r): Sophie Semigak and Dina Semigak; (middle, l-r): Amalia Jararuse and Katalina Tuglavina; (front): Tabea Nochasak, Hebron, 1950s (Hettasch family collection, Them Days Archive)**

In the summer of 1956, the provincial government told the families residing in Okkak Bay, comprising 158 people, to leave their dwellings and move south. Tom Uvloriak's family was one of them: "It was in the winter when we went to buy our grub from Nutâk. We were in Umiagajak at the time. My father was told by the store manager, Max Budgell – Sam Lyall was the interpreter – that we will have to move."[9] The families were given materials to construct new houses in other communities, financed through a $90,000 fund cost-shared by the provincial and federal governments.[10] Four families were sent to Makkovik, four others were sent to North West River, and the rest were sent to Nain."I don't know why they relocated us," Susie Onalik commented years later. "There was a lack of communications on the government's side. . . . No explanation whatsoever."[11]

After Nutâk was closed, government agents delayed the relocation of Hebron residents while they assessed how Nutâk Inuit assimilated to their new surroundings. But the eventual resettlement of Hebron was never really in doubt. In discussions about federal funding for Labrador Inuit, the Federal Treasury Board decided in 1956 not to give any further assistance "towards works at any point north of Nain."[12] The decision to starve the north of federal funding signalled the demise of any sustainable Inuit community in northern Labrador. Hebron was to be deprived of a future.

Despite the authorities' discussions and decisions about them, Inuit in Hebron expressed no interest in moving south; in fact, as the Hebron missionary reported in 1955, most moved north to Ramah and Nachvak for the summer.[13] When rumours about eviction reached them in 1956, the Hebron Elders (AngajokKauKatiget) and the chapel servants (Kivgait) convened a meeting.[14] They wrote a letter in Inuktitut to Dr. Rowe, the acting minister of public welfare:

> We people from Hebron have heard that Hebron is going to be closed down without giving us enough information about it. We would like to know if this is true or not so that we can be prepared for it.
>
> We are asking not to be removed from our community because we are used to our traditional ways of hunting and it is very excellent. Hunting seals, char, caribou and other animals is our livelihood and are plentiful. Because we feel that we would be poor when we can't make any money, if there are any ways of earning money if we are moved, perhaps we might not be making a wrong decision in moving.

> Also if we are asked to move, our houses would have to be replaced and then we would agree to move.
>
> We would be very thankful if we are not moved from our community, and we would appreciate it if you could consider our interests in not moving. And also we would be very thankful if someone could let us know what is going to happen to us in the future.[15]

When the letter reached provincial officials, it was accompanied by a translation that communicated a slightly different message. Provincial officials read Rev. Siegfried Hettasch's translation of the letter, which implied that the Hebron elders would agree to move if jobs and housing were promised. His translation read, "... until such time that we can be assured of having steady work with good wages for our livelihood; when such a good time comes it should not be too bad to move. Also if we are promised good houses in exchange, we would agree to move."[16] Reading this version, provincial officials may have felt assured that Hebron Inuit would comply with the relocation south if they were provided with jobs and houses.

One government official, however, recognized the Elders' reasons for staying in Hebron. Walter Rockwood, the director of the division of

**Agnes and child, Hebron, 1950s (Hettasch family collection, Them Days Archive)**

northern Labrador affairs, was a firm advocate of the northern land-based economy. He emphasized the Elders' perspective in their letter and pushed for a cautious approach: "They do not wish to leave their homes, hunting, and fishing grounds at this time for fear of suffering hardship. They say that when they can be assured of having steady work with good wages they will be prepared to move."[17] Closing Hebron would be "taking a leap in the dark," he argued. "I think the letter from Hebron means the same thing, when the time is ripe the Hebron People and many of the Nain folk will move of their own accord."[18] Rockwood argued that the rich resources of the Hebron area could support Inuit families in the meantime.

In his response to the Hebron Elders' letter, Dr. Rowe's deputy minister reassured them that "no overt action to compel the Hebron people to leave their homes is being contemplated. . . . You may rest assured that only when steady work is assured elsewhere will the People be expected to move."[19] He then promised the Elders that they would be given a year's notice of any such move.[20] But behind the scenes, officials were pushing for relocation. The IGA's Dr. Paddon and Moravian Superintendent Rev. Peacock applied in 1957 to the provincial resettlement program for the closure of Hebron. The community was "unfit for human habitation," argued Paddon, and to perpetuate their "[e]xistence [there was] pauperizing the people of Hebron, wasting money and resources."[21] Citing health problems and difficulties in obtaining wood for fuel, Peacock wrote, "The cost both to Mission and Government in maintaining this settlement is high. . . . To further education, improve health, and create better social conditions, it would be wise to close Hebron. Furthermore to close Hebron would be to save man-power and money."[22]

Official support for moving northern Inuit out of the north eventually overruled Walter Rockwood's reservations about the decision. In 1958, the provincial Minister of Public Welfare decided to notify the people of Hebron in early 1959 that the trading depot would close in August 1960, thus honouring the government's promise to give them a year's notice of eviction.[23] However, the Moravian Mission forced the government to accelerate its plans. Anxious to eliminate expenses, the

**(l-r): Andrea Webb and Doris Piercy, Laura Millie and Thomas Tuglavina, Jimmy Tuglavina and Boas Millie, Jimmie Andersen and August Andersen, Hebron, 1950s (Hettasch family collection, Them Days Archive)**

missionaries decided to remove their minister from Hebron in the summer of 1959. If the trading depot remained open after the minister had left, the depot manager would be solely responsible for any medical or social problems that might arise. Not wanting that burden, provincial officials quickly changed course, launching a poorly planned and chaotic eviction of families from the community.

Shortly after Easter 1959, officials from the Newfoundland government, the Moravian Mission, and the International Grenfell Association arrived in Hebron to announce the closure. The men signed the Hebron Visitors Book for April 10, 1959:

> W. Rockwood – "On the occasion of the Mission 'confirmation' of closing Hebron station"
>
> F.W. Peacock – "On the occasion of the Government decision to close Hebron"
>
> W.A. Paddon MD – "(Innocent by-stander)"
>
> Geoffrey Henderson – "Pilot of the get-away car EYW"

R.C. Shyre (RCMP) – "Pursuer of the above car"
Ian W. Mackie
F.C.P. Grubb – "How are the mighty fallen"

The officials gathered the people in the church and notified them that the depot would be closed. Boas Jararuse remembered the day:

> We were told that the meeting will be held in the church and nothing about the relocation beforehand. Not one person said "You are going to be relocated" until we were in the church. When it was said, no one said anything because to us the church is not the place for anything controversial. We were really shocked.[24]

"No one said anything because you're not supposed to say anything in the church, because they were religious," Sabina Nochasak later remarked. "If all the AngajokKauKatiget [Elders Council] were together at the meeting it would have been a lot better. . . . [The officials] said that we're moving to a place where there is lots of things, lots of seals everything, lots of animals and fish. That's what they said. That there were jobs available also."[25] Respecting the sanctity of the church, the people of Hebron felt unable to publicly question the eviction. No room for negotiation seemed possible.

Government officials scrambled to organize the move south. The depot manager packed up the store, only to be told by the Department of Public Welfare in June to reopen it, as the plans for building houses for the Hebronimiut in the south had stalled. A few weeks later, after some frantic coordination, the government once again reversed course and instructed the manager to close the depot for good. The IGA sent a nurse to Hebron in August after the minister left, but then instructed her to move to Makkovik in September.[26] Without a nurse or a store, Hebronimiut felt they had no choice but to leave. Jako Semigak remembered the confusion and upheaval of the exodus. "We didn't agree with them. We didn't want to move; there was nothing we could do. They said the *Trepassey* was on the way. Then we started to get ready."[27]

Hebronimiut left their community as exiles, carrying only their portable belongings. Some left in their own boats, while others travelled south on the mail boat. "My mother and stepfather were depressed, crying because they were leaving," recalled Sophie Lampe. "The brass band was playing on the wharf. They kept crying, Joshua Obed and my mother Maria, I felt that they both didn't want to leave their land. . . . When Hebron was barely showing I said, 'We've been on our land for a long time, why are we leaving our land?'"[28]

By October, all 247 people in the community had been moved south.[29] They were instructed that five families could move to Nain, 10 families to Hopedale, and 43 families to Makkovik. Makkovik was selected as the main destination because the population of Nain had substantially increased with the arrival of Inuit from Nutâk and Okkak Bay. However, about 150 Hebronimiut had to live in makeshift shelters at Hopedale for the first winter because new houses had not yet been constructed for them at Makkovik. John Jararuse's family moved to Nain, where they found no house to live in, either. "We lived in a tent when we first came here because we had no place to stay. So we stayed down

**People loading boats, Hebron, 1959 (Hettasch family collection, Them Days Archive)**

**Brass band plays as families leave Hebron, 1959 (Hettasch family collection, Them Days Archive)**

where the airstrip is now, in that area, for one summer. We had no place to stay so we stayed in a tent."[30] "I thought we would have a house because we were told we would; we are going to have a house when we move," recalled Sophie Lampe. "That was not true. They lied."[31] Poorly built cottages were not actually completed for several years; it took until 1962 for all 33 families to be moved to the "Hebron end" of Makkovik, a segregated and isolated subdivision.[32]

Relocation was a profoundly traumatic and degrading experience.[33] Instead of gaining a higher standard of living, Inuit families from Nutâk and Hebron found their self-sufficiency and independence radically undermined. Many had been separated from other family members, and close social bonds were broken. Makkovik residents spoke English, a foreign language to the relocatees, and Hopedale Inuit spoke a different dialect of Inuktitut. Northern Inuit were unfamiliar with places to hunt, fish, and trap near their new homes, and the best harvesting areas were already taken by the original residents of the southern communities. The supply of game was also less abundant than at Hebron, which was recognized for its superior char and seal resources. The promised jobs never materialized. Northern Inuit experienced hunger, racism, and poverty, and were forced to depend on social welfare allowances.[34] Children were taunted with derogatory names, and many learned to feel ashamed of their identity. Frustration, despair, and depression fuelled alcohol abuse, family breakdowns, and incidents of violence and criminal offences.[35] The profound trauma of eviction and the destruction of family ties led many exiled Avanimiut to drift from community to community as permanently displaced people. As Nicodemus Menzel said in 1973:

> To Hopedale, Makkovik, and Nain, people from Hebron, people from Nutâk, going against the wind. Some of them, even close relatives, were separated from one another by being placed in other villages. That is why it seems some of us are poor here. We are also hungry for seal meat, for caribou meat and trout. In the winter we are always hungry now when we always had these foods in Hebron. Now we are living like nothing, like a void.[36]

Within a decade, most of the evicted Avanimiut had shifted to other communities, especially to Nain.

For some, this was the second displacement they had to endure. Conrad Jararuse, for instance, had been forced to leave Killinek years before. His resilient attitude towards the evictions inspired others, as William Onalik relates:

> [Conrad Jararuse] was born in Killinek; that was his real hunting ground. He told me when we were leaving Hebron not to be looking back, that life does not belong up north. If we move south, I was to move on south. . . . What was said to me I will follow because he was an old man and I don't know what he went through when he moved from Killinek. [He said] that life does not move in the past; life belongs to our Saviour towards the south . . . I got to understand that I was raised by Conrad who was also moved from Killinek, from the land he loved so much. He was also told by his uncle not to be looking back.[37]

The option to look north, however, was being pursued by governments on the other side of the peninsula.

## Conflicting Federal and Provincial Approaches

While provincial authorities were relocating northern Inuit to more southerly Labrador communities, the federal Department of Northern Affairs was encouraging Ungava Inuit to move north to Killinek. Federal officials aimed to help Ungava Inuit become self-sufficient by exploiting the rich char and seal resources of the region, and they planned to develop a commercial fishery at Killinek and a co-operative store at Kangiqsualujjuaq.[38] The federal approach followed the strategy articulated at the 1952 Conference on Eskimo Affairs to "assist the natives to continue to follow their traditional way of life as hunters."[39] The declining fur trade and fluctuating wildlife populations had decimated Inuit livelihoods across the Arctic, and the Canadian government was anxious to reduce Inuit reliance on relief payments. By encouraging Inuit to maintain a land-based life, federal officials hoped that they could "keep the native 'native'" and avoid dependency on government services.[40] This approach often involved relocating Inuit from crowded communities to underpopulated areas of rich resources, with the assumption that Inuit could adapt to any environment.[41]

**Carrying firewood, Hebron, 1956 (Joan and Ross King photo, Them Days Archive)**

In 1953, in one of the best-known examples, the federal government moved 93 people from Inukjuak in northern Quebec to the High Arctic, ostensibly because they would be better able to support themselves on the abundant wildlife.[42] In 1957, the federal government also moved Ahiarmiut from their homeland in the Keewatin region at Ennadai Lake, where the Canadian military had built a radio station, to North Henik Lake, 125 miles away.[43] Like the other relocations, the intention was to move Inuit away from a sedentary life at posts or settlements, where they relied heavily on government relief payments, to a "wilderness" where they would have to support themselves. The move was the second relocation for the Ahiarmiut, who had endured several forced removals between 1950 and 1960. Although initially praised as successful operations, both the Inukjuak and the Ahiarmiut relocations resulted in famine and death and are now widely recognized as catastrophic examples of state social engineering.[44] Canada later admitted that asserting national sovereignty was its motive for the High Arctic relocation, and issued an official apology and compensation in 2001.[45] The federal government apologized and provided compensation for the Ahiarmiut relocation in 2019.[46]

Relocation was not a new concept in the Killinek region. The Hudson's Bay Company had relocated Inuit from Port Burwell/Killinek to Southampton Island in 1925 and again in 1942 to address official concerns about "thinning out the population of New Quebec by transfer to the Northwest Territories."[47] In the late 1950s, however, federal officials were increasingly sensitive to criticism about Inuit starvations caused by relocations, as well as the famine endured by Inuit at Garry Lake in the central Arctic in 1958.[48] But instead of reconsidering resettlement altogether, Ottawa decided to support the relocation decisions by using resource surveys to determine whether wildlife populations could sustain relocated Inuit. At Killinek in 1959, for instance, federal officials based their relocation and economic strategy on biological studies that indicated that the site had rich marine resources and could support a larger population.[49]

The federal approach towards the governance of Inuit affairs stood in sharp contrast to that of the Newfoundland government, despite the similarity of conditions in the Hebron and Ungava Bay regions. While both governments were concerned about reducing Inuit dependence on social assistance and improving their standard of living and health, Labrador relocation plans dismissed the value of the Inuit land-based way of life. Federal plans for establishing a commercial char fishery at Killinek and Kangiqsualujjuaq, on the other hand, aimed to establish new economic opportunities based on local resources.[50] Despite their differences, however, both governments relied on displacement as an essential element of their social engineering efforts and were confident in their right to make unilateral decisions about Inuit life.

Authorities did not inform Inuit in either region of the different government approaches towards shaping their future and did not offer them the option of moving elsewhere. However, this secretive approach was not universally supported. The year before Hebron was relocated, the resident missionary Siegfried Hettasch had suggested that people be given the choice to move where they wished:

> I am strongly convinced that not all the Hebron folks will move south [when Hebron is closed], and I feel that some would rather move North instead of South, at least if they were given the choice and the opportunity to do so. – Could the Government be approached on this matter, if they might be willing to let those who wish, go north, making the needed arrangement for them there, as well as transportation and let them be rehabilitated, say in Ungava Bay, Cape Chidley, or Frobisher, if acceptable there. – If this idea is acceptable, I would like to see the Government allow these people to choose, those who wish to go north let them, and the others south. To stay behind, eventually without a store, they will hardly be able to do, though some talk about this.
>
> And again to have the people go south against their wish (this does not mean all, but a good number, who wish not to move) would be very regrettable. So if they could choose between either north or south they would all be happy, and we all would feel happier too. I am sure that this would apply to only a few families, the bulk, I am sure would follow south.[51]

Despite Hettasch's suggestion, the Moravian Mission would have risked embarrassment if many of its Hebron congregation chose to leave its fold and move north. The provincial government would have been embarrassed as well, if Hebron Inuit had chosen to move out of its jurisdiction and settle instead at Killinek, which was now part of the Northwest Territories, or to Kangiqsualujjuaq in Quebec.[52]

Communication between the provincial and federal governments about their plans also seems to have been lacking. In June 1959, Newfoundland bureaucrats were notified of Canada's scheme for developing Killinek and Kangiqsualujjuaq, but by that point the Hebron relocation was already in motion. Provincial official Walter Rockwood expressed his frustration at the lack of coordination between the governments: "If there had been closer liaison [between the federal Department of Northern Affairs and the provincial Department of Public Welfare], we would have been aware of the Federal plans for George River and Port Burwell months ago."[53] As it was, the provincial government recognized that the federal plans to encourage northern settlement contradicted its own relocation scheme. "If the Federal Government's plans materialize," Rockwood argued in the summer of 1959, "it will be very difficult to proceed with the plan for closing Hebron in 1960."[54] Provincial officials did not widely share news about the federal scheme for Killinek; if information about the federal approach had been made public, the Inuit reaction may well have made the closure of Hebron more difficult.[55]

The federal government, likewise, did not share the news of its plans for Killinek and Kangiqsualujjuaq with Labrador Inuit. When federal officials initially sought more permanent residents for Killinek, the head of the program considered approaching Inuit on the Labrador coast who had originated in the Killinek area, but the notion was later rejected to avoid conflict with the Newfoundland policy of moving Inuit southward.[56] By keeping the information to themselves, both the federal and the provincial governments thus prevented Hebron Inuit from having the option to move farther north to Killinek instead of south to existing Labrador communities.

## Commercial Char Fisheries at Killinek and Kangiqsualujjuaq

The Canadian government's plans for Killinek took years to unfold. Despite having an abundance of seal and other wildlife, Killinek had a "bad reputation" in Ungava Bay.[57] It was isolated, had a vicious climate, and offered no wood for fuel and no trading store. These factors accounted for its small population; people faced many hardships in trying to remain independent and self-sufficient in the region. After the 1940s, few people continued to live in the area, and they travelled periodically to obtain supplies from Kangiqsualujjuaq or Kuujjuaq. The George River HBC store at Kangiqsualujjuaq was reduced to an outpost in 1952 and the Company contemplated closing even this facility in 1958 due to weak fur markets and insufficient business.[58] About 20 Inuit were reported to be living in the vicinity of Killinek in the early 1950s.[59]

In the fall of 1957, the Killinek families were almost forced to abandon the place after they became ill with influenza on a visit to Kuujjuaq. They lost their Peterhead boat in drifting ice during freeze-up and lacked food for the winter because they missed the fall seal hunt at Killinek.[60] The families were stranded for the winter at Kuujjuaq, during which time the leader of the group, Tommy Assevik, died, but they survived on relief assistance. Federal officials encouraged them to return to Killinek and provided a second-hand boat so they could travel back; they felt that the families would have a better living relying on country food if they returned.[61] Nevertheless, the group occasionally had difficulty obtaining sufficient food. In April 1959, the federal government had to airlift emergency supplies to them, as they were desperately short of provisions.[62] Five households, headed by Henry Annatok (Angnatuk), Noah Annatok (Angnatuk), Willy Annatok (Angnatuk), Matthew Assevik, and Mark Annahatukhis (Annahattak), and numbering 22 people lived at Killinek in 1959.[63]

In contrast to other communities in Ungava Bay, Killinek was perceived during the 1950s as having a surplus of resources and too few people to exploit them. Federal officials recognized that a trade store was needed in the area, not only to make conditions easier for the present inhabitants, but also to encourage Inuit living in other areas to begin harvesting game along the northeastern Ungava coast to improve their own standard of living.[64] In 1956, some Inuit from Kangiqsualujjuaq hunted around Killinek in the winter, but they expressed no interest in moving there; instead, they wanted to move to a new location about 150 km to the east on the Labrador coast, likely Nachvak fiord.[65] Their proposal was rejected partly because Inuit residing at Hebron were known not to be well-off and government officials believed that resources were more limited than Kangiqsualujjuaq Inuit expected. The region was also under Newfoundland jurisdiction, which was not likely to welcome or assume support for more inhabitants. Consequently, government authorities advised Inuit at Kangiqsualujjuaq to find more feasible options in their own territory.[66]

By 1958, federal officials recognized that the HBC was not interested in reopening a store at Killinek. Instead, they suggested that the government start a small store that eventually would operate as a co-operative managed by the community. Northern Affairs officials, especially Donald Snowden, were strong proponents of co-operatives in Indigenous communities and they encouraged Inuit at both Killinek and Kangiqsualujjuaq to develop co-ops to share resources within a regional economy: those at Killinek could provide seal meat and char to Inuit at Kangiqsualujjuaq, while those at Kangiqsualujjuaq could provide wood to the people of Killinek.[67]

Officials also felt that a local store at Killinek was an essential requirement for attracting more permanent residents and for encouraging them to disperse along the eastern Ungava Bay coast, as well as the Atlantic seaboard.[68] If people had access to proper supplies and equipment for exploiting resources in the area, government bureaucrats predicted that the population of Killinek could reach at least 30 families, or about 200 people, comparable to the peak size of the community when the Moravian Mission and HBC were present earlier in the century. The Newfoundland government was not expected to oppose a movement of Inuit into Labrador territory if they were administered by a federal agency at Killinek.[69]

Henry Annatuk, speaking at a 1963 conference on Arctic co-operatives in Iqaluit, described the beginning of the Killinek co-op:

> The people were thinking of leaving Killiniq for Labrador – it was difficult to get supplies and make a living. . . . Then came the idea of a co-operative through government officers – a change came over the community. . . . Now we are confident we can make a living by staying and working through the co-operatives.
>
> In the first year of the co-operative, a freezer was set up and the fish were caught and brought to the freezer. . . . That first year, the engine did not work properly and we did not do well. . . . A year later the freezer was working good and we got it full of char. We also did jigging of cod and got quite a lot of this fish, and we carried out hunting for seals after the cod fishing.
>
> Before we had a co-operative, we almost moved from Killiniq to be near a trading post. . . . We did not want to go to Kuujjuaq as we did not know the area. . . . We were going to go to the Labrador coast. . . . Now we do not think of this move anymore.[70]

In 1958, the federal government authorized the development of a commercial char fishery, and the following year a large freezer unit and a store were erected at Killinek; a second freezer was placed at Kangiqsualujjuaq.[71] Ten men from Kuujjuaq and Kuujjuarapik, along with six local residents, were employed to install the facilities at Killinek.[72] Fishing operations began successfully at Kangiqsualujjuaq in 1959 but faulty equipment led to a delay in the fishery at Killinek until 1960.[73]

The challenges were many. Even prior to its start, a northern officer warned that tidal conditions and winds made travel hazardous for small boats, and locations for char were too distant for a practical commercial fishery.[74] However, the main obstacle in developing a commercial fishery at Killinek was the shortage of labour, as there were only five adult men among the permanent inhabitants.[75] Federal officials identified two options for increasing the labour force: either get families from Kangiqsualujjuaq to fish in the area during the summer season or encourage families from western Ungava Bay to become permanent residents at Killinek. Inuit from Kangiqsualujjuaq were not expected to remain over the winter because they were accustomed to having firewood and living in a less rigorous situation. However, people from Kangirsuk, Quaqtaq, or Salluit were considered better prospects for increasing the resident population as they lived in a similar environment.[76]

As plans were made to begin char fishing operations at Killinek in the summer of 1960, officials worked to find a boat for travelling in rough water and more people to participate in the fishery.[77] A longliner, the M.V. *Joan Ryan*, was chartered to transport families from Killinek to a good fishing site located to the southeast, on the northern Labrador coast at the head of Ikkudliayuk fiord.[78] Arrangements were also made for several people from Kuujjuarapik, in western Ungava Bay, to spend the summer fishing in the area. Four frame houses were erected in the community to entice them to become permanent residents.[79]

Conditions at Killinek improved after the small co-op store opened and the commercial fishery commenced. As Tivi Etok remembers:

> After Kangiqsualujjuaq established a co-op, the people in Killiniq started a co-op of their own. They were determined to stay in Killiniq. With the establishment of the co-op we were able to sell our furs at Killiniq, even if we didn't get much for them. We were able to buy our staples. We were happy.[80]

As families could now buy food supplies if necessary while the hunters were away, men could travel greater distances away from the community on hunting and trapping ventures.[81] Four families from Kuujjuarapik, composed of 13 people, decided to remain in the community in the early 1960s because they had access to a store, housing, work in the fisheries project, and a government interested in promoting activity at Killinek.[82] Another 36 residents joined the community in 1961, but considerably more people were needed to harvest char for the commercial program.[83]

**Benjamin Jararuse, Hebron, 1956 (Joan and Ross King collection, Them Days Archive)**

The first summer of the fisheries program in 1960 saw a low char catch, likely due to a late start, shortage of small boats, and lack of experience on the part of the nine men involved in the operation.[84] An expanded program was planned for 1961, but the northern service officer responsible for Killinek, Max Budgell, stressed that more participants were essential because the current population was too small to handle all the work. He noted that the future of the community was balanced "on a tight wire" and would be determined within three to five years.[85] Two crucial factors were the success of the fishery and the success in attracting more permanent residents.[86] Another significant consideration was the advancing age of many of the people who had originally lived there. Unless new families arrived in a short period of time, the active hunters would not be able to pass on their hunting and fishing experience as they were becoming too old to continue going out on the land.[87]

In the fall of 1961, project officers arranged with federal officials based at Frobisher Bay [Iqaluit] to move people from that community and from Resolution Island who were interested in the fisheries project.[88]

Meetings were also held in April 1962 at Kangirsuk and Quaqtaq, in western Ungava Bay, to recruit families to participate in the Killinek fishery.[89] Officials at these meetings told people that the government "was anxious" to have people move to Killinek on a permanent basis. If they were not satisfied with the community, the department would make arrangements for them to return to their original homes.[90] Ten male household heads at Kangirsuk and five men at Quaqtaq agreed to move to Killinek, leading to plans for the construction of 20 new houses in the fall of 1962.[91] According to a newsletter at Kuujjuaq, the migrants had to provide their own transportation and food, supplemented by some welfare assistance, in order to reach Killinek.[92]

Although government agents made no official invitation to Inuit in Labrador, some family members did spread the news. In journalist Edith Iglauer's book about the Killinek and Kangiqsualujjuaq co-operatives, *Inuit Journey*, Noah Annatuk (Angnatuk) said in 1961 "that he had been talking to his relatives on the Labrador coast about coming to Burwell [Killinek] in the summer, and they were anxious to return."[93] Benjamin Jararuse's family, who were from the Killinek area originally, moved from Labrador to Killinek in the 1960s.[94]

## Decline and Closure of Killinek

Another 60 to 70 people settled in Killinek between 1965 and 1967, including several families from Kuujjuaq. By 1971, the population had grown to about 140 residents.[95] An academic study by David Riches described a robust economy:

> On Killiniq Island, the 150 Inuit of Port Burwell (27 families) enjoy flourishing seal, cod and char fisheries, eiderdown collection and handicraft industries based on local products. The consumer and producer co-op around which the community focuses (and to which all 84 adults belong) paid off its loans long ago, and by 1970, was renowned for its financial success, almost unequalled among Arctic settlements.[96]

By this point, the settlement was situated at Fox Harbour, about a mile away from the original site at Mission Cove. Mike Keelan, who lived with his wife Sophie Jararuse Keelan in Killinek in the 1970s, described the community:

> Because of the rugged terrain, the village was built on three different levels. The first lay alongside the shoreline, then about four hundred feet back and up on the next ridge was the second level, with a third section about a hundred feet back on another ridge.[97]

The settlement contained a nursing station, a co-op store and warehouse, a school, recreation centre, fish plant, church, gas station, and houses. A few people had government jobs or worked at the school or the co-op, but most men were full-time hunters.

> Most of the people lived off the land and received welfare assistance. The only time that almost everyone had paid work was when the fish plant was operating. But when it closed in the early seventies, the majority of people once again relied on government assistance.[98]

During a research study conducted in 1974 on Inuit land use and occupancy in the Northwest Territories, the fieldworker could not find anyone who had hunted in the Killinek area prior to 1925.[99] Inuit of Killinek hunted mainly seals, polar bears, caribou, and waterfowl, fished for char and cod, and collected berries and clams.[100] The core area for harvesting activities extended southward on the Labrador coast to Noodleook fiord, although caribou were occasionally hunted in more distant areas ranging to Hebron fiord.[101]

In the early 1970s, the economy at Killinek faltered when the value of pelts dropped. Rumours that some families wanted to leave Killinek and move to other communities in Ungava Bay led the government director of the Baffin Region, J.B.H. Gunn, to visit the community in early March 1971.[102] The administration of Killinek had been transferred from

Kuujjuaq to Iqaluit in 1970, and the government of the Northwest Territories had assumed jurisdiction over the community. In his assessment of why some people wanted to move, Gunn attributed most of the reasons to social factors. He reported that the "dominating factor in the migration lies with the older people, who want to return to their place of origin to see their relatives before they die."[103] He described social problems in the community as another reason people wanted to move. Gunn reported excessive consumption of "home brew," especially during winter, which contributed to acts of physical violence. Residents were afraid of being assaulted and complained about inadequate policing services provided by occasional patrols from Nain.[104]

Due to these circumstances, Gunn described the community as divided between 71 people intending to leave and 69 people determined to remain.[105] The departing families made two requests for assistance, asking first for supplies to travel to their destinations and second for help in getting employment at Deception Bay, where the new Raglan mine promised many job opportunities. Gunn agreed to provide them with food and gasoline, but he stated that the government would not arrange air transportation for them and would not commit to help with future employment.[106]

At a meeting with the community council, Gunn cautioned that a major exodus of the population would significantly affect the status of the community and services provided by the government, as the budget for services was based on the number of residents. The school, for example, might close if the population declined. According to Gunn's report on the meeting, the council was not disturbed by this warning and was confident that new residents would arrive and replace those who had left. Gunn also noted that people leaving the community would lack housing at other places, particularly at Kangiqsualujjuaq where many families intended to move.[107] Lack of accommodation may have led families to delay their departure because the population of the community remained at 121 residents in 1974, but then dropped to 77 people by 1975.[108]

Other interpretations of the situation at Killinek have identified this rapid decline of government services as the catalyst for the remaining people to leave. A 1978 Makivik Corporation report blamed the deterioration in government services for the departures between 1975 and 1978, after the James Bay Agreement was signed:

> The decline in services permeated every aspect of community life. Some of the problems simply caused inconveniences while others threatened the essential safety and well-being of the Inuit. No additions or improvements were made to community infrastructure; there was no new housing or renovations; economic assistance programs were severely reduced or terminated and there was no attempt to improve air services. . . . As services were reduced, jobs were lost, the economy declined, and there was a serious deterioration in morale and social climate.[109]

Continuing difficulties related to services and social relations at Killinek led the Community Council to pass a resolution on January 24, 1977, in favour of relocating to a different area and forming a new community in the vicinity of Bell Inlet (Taqpangajuk). During that year, three families comprising 38 people moved to Kangiqsualujjuaq, prompted mainly by inadequate medical care in Killinek. This further reduction in the population led the NWT government to close the nursing station in the fall of 1977.[110] This closure came as a surprise for many in the community, as Mike Keelan describes:

> The first inkling of something amiss was one evening in October of 1977. The nurse currently stationed there requested that everyone come down to the nursing station. Of course we were all puzzled and curious. . . . Family by family, the nurse dispensed medication . . . and other first aid supplies. . . . It seemed like every family was being issued a homemade first aid kit.
>
> After everyone received their allotment — which looked to be about a six-month supply — the nurse announced that the nursing station was closing permanently. We were utterly

> amazed, and then shocked into silence when she said that a helicopter was coming the next day and she was leaving.[111]

The announcement was a surprise for many in the community, but some residents did have prior knowledge of the planned closure. At a meeting held to discuss the decision at Iqaluit in September 1977, several residents from Killinek advised government officials that they also wished to leave the community. On hearing this statement, the officials assumed that all remaining residents had agreed to leave the community, but this view evidently reflected the wishes of only three families.[112] As residents stated afterwards, many were determined to stay, despite warnings from government officials that the school and even the power might be shut down in the coming months.

Mike Keelan describes a meeting in Killinek in January 1978 at which government officials offered to pay all costs if everyone was willing to move. The residents, however, would have to arrange their own housing in their new communities. "But most of us didn't want to move," Keelan wrote, "and [we] made that clear."[113] The government representatives then told the residents they could not guarantee that Killinek would have power after February.

> I personally felt that the government wouldn't dare shut power down in the middle of winter. But the big question was, how far would the government go to get the rest of us to move? With the nursing station already closed and the threat of closing the school and settlement office, it looked like they were determined to drive us out. After a somewhat sleepless night, we once again gathered at the recreation hall. Most of the remaining families had unwillingly decided to accept the move offer.[114]

Officials in Iqaluit discussed details of a move in February 1978, and the NWT government arranged to airlift the remaining 47 people from Killinek on February 8, 1978, to other communities in Ungava Bay.[115] News of the relocation reached the Killinek residents through a late-night phone call, informing them that a plane would arrive the next morning to take them away. The sudden move was a surprise to even the Killiniq Council, led by Norman Snowball, who were given no advance warning.[116] The last eight families were relocated to Kangiqsualujjuaq, Kuujjuaq, Quaqtaq, and Kangiqsujuaq.[117] As a Makivik Corporation report later described, they arrived "without housing, without income, and without many of their personal effects. Family groups were broken up and the people separated from their seasonal hunting territory."[118]

After the relocation, Killinek Inuit continued to push for establishing a new community, and they launched a lawsuit against the federal government. Minutes from a meeting held at Kuujjuaq in early March 1978 show Killinek representatives confirming that they did not want to return to the community due to lack of medical services and an airstrip. Zebedee Nungak, then the vice-president of the Northern Quebec Inuit Association, stated, "the people were unanimous in their wish to move to Bell Inlet, where they would probably be joined by northern Quebec Inuit."[119] Rights accorded to Killinek residents in the James Bay Agreement consequently led to discussions on government support for creating a new community. The Makivik Corporation ran an experimental fisheries project in the Killinek area between 1983 and 1986, and negotiated with the federal government about relocation to Taqpangajuk, a site 30 km southwest of Killinek.[120] Multiple feasibility studies examined the potential move, but the government made no firm plans.[121] In the summer of 1987, six families of former Killinek residents moved to Taqpangajuk, having been told by the Quebec government that it would establish a permanent community if they settled there.[122] After a year, when it became clear that the government would not fulfill its promise, the families left, and a permanent community was never created.[123] In 1987, the federal government settled the relocation lawsuit with the Makivik Corporation and provided $2 million in compensation.[124] People from Kangiqsualujjuaq continued to hunt in the vicinity during summer and fall.[125]

The coerced relocation of Inuit from Killinek in 1978 was the final chapter in a long history of Inuit settlement in the region. If the Department of Northern Affairs had not promoted the development of a char fishery and use of other natural resources at Killinek after 1959, the few families residing there would likely have abandoned the area and moved to other communities. The recruitment of additional Inuit to live in the new community mirrors the action of the HBC and Moravian Mission in prompting people to settle in the region to support their new trade posts. Families moved to Killinek from other communities after 1959 because of job opportunities through the char fishery, housing, and other services provided by the federal government. But just as economic hardship after the closure of the HBC store led most people to depart after 1944, social problems along with inadequate services were primary considerations in the exodus of families during the mid-1970s. In both situations, Killinek proved to be an adverse environment for permanent residence when economic and government services are withdrawn.

## The Northern Labrador Evictions: Aftermath

Since 1959, some Avanimiut living in Labrador communities have tried to return north, if only temporarily. Most Hebronimiut in Makkovik eventually moved north to Nain.[126] From Nain, northern Inuit could travel to Okkak Bay and north to fish for char during the summer and hunt for seals, caribou, and other game during the spring and fall seasons.[127] For those living in Hopedale and Makkovik, however, Okkak Bay and north was often too far to travel by dog team or trapboat. Nevertheless, some Inuit returned to Hebron, Saglek, and Nachvak each summer.[128] In an ironic contradiction of the relocation scheme, char fishing at their former fishing grounds in northern Labrador was often the northern families' only option for making an income.

In the 1960s and early 1970s, Inuit travelled as far north as Komaktorvik and Kangalaksiorvik fiords to fish for char, which they preserved in brine and shipped off on longliners at the end of the season. However, the fishery changed significantly in 1971, when a fish plant at Nain was built to process fresh frozen fish. To be marketable, char had to be

**Johannes Tuglavina, Makkovik, after 1959 (Hettasch family collection, Them Days Archive)**

transported quickly to the plant. Collector boats were too slow to reach the northern fishing areas, so fishers restricted their activities to the waters around Nain and Okkak Bay.[129] Pressure on the char population in that area then led to fishing quotas in the late 1970s; in 1993, a federal government program purchased commercial char and salmon licences from fish harvesters, significantly reducing participation in the commercial fisheries.[130] With fewer people able to make a living by fishing the northern waters, fewer Inuit could afford to travel north.

Tensions between the political organizations of Inuit in Labrador (represented by the Labrador Inuit Association) and Inuit in Quebec (represented by the Makivik Corporation) due to land claims negotiations also prevented Inuit from moving back to the northern tip of Labrador. Anthropologist Tony Williamson felt that these tensions caused unnecessary complications when he was interviewed years later:

> One thing made me particularly sad, because I saw it as a possible saviour. In Nain in 1984, I was chairing a fisheries conference in which was raised an invitation from Makivik Corporation to the

> Labrador people. They didn't say Hebron people but anybody in Labrador who was interested in joining them at Killinek in an arctic char fishery there. They'd applied for permission also to fish the fiords between Killinek and Kangalaksiorvik fiord, which was the area not being used any longer. Because of the whole land claims business, the lawyers argued and convinced the Labrador Inuit that they're being pressured and pushed from the north; and they want to take your resource and don't have anything to do with them. I think that was a tragedy, that point of view, because they were basically, the people who wanted to develop that operation at Killinek were closely related to the people who came from Aulatsivik and all around there. And there would have been a chance for them to live busy lives .... They wanted to put a fish plant in there. And also go off and get some deep-water fish [turbot].[131]

Despite losing this opportunity to reconnect with the north, some families did maintain close relationships with relatives in Ungava Bay and to the region. One family with roots in the far north went to live at Killinek in 1966, and other Hebronimiut and Nutâmiut have since moved

**Char fishing camp, Nachvak, 1957 (Hettasch family collection, Them Days Archive)**

to communities in northern Quebec. Benjamin Jararuse was one of the first. He had been born at Killinek and was evicted from Hebron in 1959. When he and his family arrived in Makkovik, they had to live in a tent:

> Our children suffered the most because they were always cold. There was no housing available, we who went to Makkovik, we had to wait for our housing. . . . What little belongings we had were always covered up with snow, as it was in the fall. We suffered living in tents, but our children were the ones who suffered the most.[132]

When it became clear that life in Makkovik was not as the missionaries had promised, Benjamin moved his family north to Killinek. A decade later, when Killinek was closed, the family was once again forced to move; they ended up in Kangiqsualujjuaq in Quebec.[133] By the year 2000, approximately 100 Hebron and Okkak Bay relocatees and their descendants had moved to Kangiqsualujjuaq.[134] As Lude Jararuse told the *kinatuinamot illengajuk* magazine in 1999, it was as close as he could get to being at his home in Hebron. Both he and Silima Onalik, who had

**Nick Ittulak, Johannes Semigak, and Benjamin Jararuse, Nachvak, 1960s (Hettasch family collection, Them Days Archive)**

also left Labrador in the 1980s for Kangiqsualujjuaq, cited the abundant resources, familiar landscape, and dry community as reasons for their move.[135]

For most Avanimiut, however, the connection with the north was almost completely lost. The successive closure of Ramah, Killinek, Hebron, and then Killinek again alienated Inuit from the homeland of their ancestors. The 1956 and 1959 evictions were the largest exercise in social engineering ever experienced in Labrador, uprooting 418 people in 104 families.[136] Inuit families lost connections with their land and with their relatives. Younger generations grew up not knowing their families' homeland or their family trees. This caused many children and grandchildren of the Avanimiut to suffer a feeling of disconnect from their Elders by not knowing the homeland that their Elders treasured so dearly. By growing up as descendants of relocation, many have suffered feelings of rootlessness and not feeling at home. Many also did not fully understand the hardship that relocation caused them and how it set them behind everyone else in their community. Social networks and established means of Inuit governance were shattered. Respected Elders and leaders suffered indignity, poverty, and helplessness, as Sophie Tuglavina describes in her family:

> When we were growing up [in Hebron], my father was an "angajukKauKatiget" (community Elder) and he was always gone late into the night, helping other people. After we were in Makkovik, our stove broke down and we could not afford to get it fixed. They gave us electric heat after a long while, but we lost that right away because it was too expensive. Then when my father was old and blind, I tried to seek help, but I didn't get anywhere with that . . . .[137]

"I would like to go back there if I had my own way of transportation," Boas Jararuse said in 1996. "But we don't have a boat or anything to go back with. Now I have nothing, and I feel that I have been deprived of my life."[138] Inuit had been dispossessed of their lands, their way of life, their community, and their well-being. This caused profound heartbreak that was felt through the generations and continues to manifest in descendants to this day.

Government authorities were eventually forced to recognize the Hebron and Nutâk evictions as failures of the state. Donald Snowden, one of the main federal architects of the economic development efforts and co-operative at Killinek in the late 1950s, chaired the Royal Commission on Labrador in 1974. He was especially interested in the northern relocations and interviewed many former Hebron and Nutâk residents. The Commission's final report called the relocations "ill-considered," and recognized that the post-Confederation federal funding for services for Indigenous people had prompted authorities to minimize expenses for their new burden of responsibility:

> The resettlement of Labrador Eskimos from Hebron and Nutak, no matter how well-intentioned, was designed to meet administrative convenience of Government and health agencies who were faced with difficult problems in supplying services to these communities. . . . Under the Federal-Provincial Agreement respecting Labrador Indians and Eskimos, Federal funding provided an opportunity, previously lacking, to bring social and other services to northern residents. In order to reduce expenditure, to facilitate provision of air and sea transportation systems, to amalgamate social, medical and educational services in three communities instead of seven, the Government agency, (then designated Division of Northern Labrador Affairs) and the International Grenfell Association decided to close the northern communities of Hebron and Nutak.[139]

The new federal funding arrangements prompted the evictions, the report argues, despite the fiscal support for Inuit in Labrador being well below the level of support for Inuit elsewhere in Canada.[140] Although Snowden criticizes this inequity, he makes no reference in the report to the concurrent federal efforts at Killinek to move Ungava Inuit north into the revitalized community of Killinek.

Two decades later, the Royal Commission on Aboriginal Peoples (RCAP) also examined Indigenous relocations across Canada, and Carol Brice-Bennett was contracted to write a report on Hebron. Her book, *Dispossessed: The Eviction of Inuit from Hebron, Labrador*, provides an overview of the lead-up, execution, and impacts of the forced move, and includes an extensive collection of historical written excerpts and quotes from people involved.[141] The final RCAP report, released in 1996, condemned the many attempts in Canadian history to resettle Indigenous peoples, calling the relocations "part of a broader process of dispossession and displacement, a process with lingering effects on the cultural, spiritual, social, economic and political aspects of people's lives."[142] The report also noted the sense of grievance and pain that Indigenous relocatees such as Hebronimiut continue to feel, and the need for governments to accept responsibility for their actions and to move towards reconciliation.[143]

Determined to overcome the devastation caused by the evictions, Avanimiut became prominent leaders in the Indigenous rights movement in Labrador, and they worked to re-establish a viable Inuit community in

**Conrad Jararuse's house, Tikkigatsukuluk, 1950s, with Selma Jararuse hanging seal skins and Onalik children (l-r): Augusta, Jako, David, Boas, and Amos (Hettasch family collection, Them Days archive)**

Hebron, 1976 (Hettasch family fonds, Labrador Inuit through Moravian Eyes collection)

the north. In the 1970s, the Labrador Inuit Association (LIA), representing Inuit and Kablunângajuit of northern Labrador, claimed Indigenous rights to traditional lands and resources used by Inuit in the Labrador Peninsula. From the beginning, proposals for a land claims settlement always included a provision to rebuild a community north of Nain in the ancestral homeland of the Avanimiut. Many northern Inuit felt this goal was essential in preserving the cultural heritage and future of Inuit society in Labrador. However, in 1996, under pressure from the federal and provincial governments, the LIA agreed to drop the proposal for a new community.[144] Instead, as part of the final Labrador Inuit Land Claim Agreement, the governments provided compensation for the people who had been evicted from Hebron and Okkak Bay/Nutâk, and the Newfoundland and Labrador premier issued an official apology at the land claims signing ceremony in 2005.[145]

The Labrador Inuit Land Claim Agreement created the Nunatsiavut Government and the Torngat Mountains National Park Reserve, which encompasses much of northern Labrador from Cape Chidley to Saglek. When the Nunavik Land Claims Agreement also came into force in 2008, the Torngat Mountains National Park (Tongait KakKasuangita SilakKijapvinga) was officially created.[146] In recognition of the cultural connection that Inuit in both Nunatsiavut and Nunavik have to the region, the management of the park is guided by an all-Inuit Co-operative Management Board, consisting of representatives from Nunatsiavut, Makivik Corporation, and Parks Canada, with an independent chairperson.[147] The

Board, the National Park, and the Nunatsiavut Government all provide some degree of Inuit governance, such as the management of wildlife interactions, hunting, tourism, and land use. The park and the National Historic Site of Hebron, located just outside the park and managed by the Nunatsiavut Government, also offer Inuit some opportunities for visiting, fishing, and hunting in the land of their ancestors through tourism infrastructure, employment, and cultural programs.

Despite the long history of Inuit eviction from northern Labrador, the Tongait KakKasuangita SilakKijapvinga/Torngat Mountains National Park now officially acknowledges the land as the ancestral homeland of northern Inuit and stands as a symbol of Inuit identity for all of Nunatsiavut and for Canada. Long recognized as a region rich in wildlife, its cultural richness was unfortunately only recognized after its people had been expelled. The park stands today as a gift from northern Inuit to the rest of Canada. The intricate human history of northern Labrador, as documented in this book, serves as a memorial of an Inuit society that has endured countless upheavals, transformations, and traumas in the

**Salome Jararuse Nochasak with Jako, Lukas, and Sem, Hebron 1959 (Tony Williamson Collection, Memorial University, courtesy of Sharon Taylor)**

name of British, Newfoundland, and Canadian colonialism, modernization, and assumed cultural superiority. But the descendants of the Avanimiut, now some of the strongest leaders in Inuit language and cultural movements in Nunatsiavut, continue to honour and celebrate the legacy of the land of their ancestors.[148]

APPENDIX 1

# Inuktitut Place Names and English Translations

| | |
|---|---|
| Abloviak / Abloriak / Ablorilik / Alluviaq | The step (in a journey across the Labrador peninsula) (Wheeler, 1953; Ames, 1986, p. 17) |
| Aiviktok | Place of walrus (Taylor, 1975, p. 270) |
| Akpatok Island (in Ungava Bay) | Place of many razor-billed auks (Wheeler, 1953) |
| Amittok | The narrow one (Wheeler, 1953); Narrow bay (Ames, 1986, p. 186) |
| Agvitok / Arvertok (Hopedale area) | Place of whales |
| Attanarsuk (Attanârsuk: Wheeler, 1953) (isthmus near Aulatsivik) | The nice little low narrow isthmus (Wheeler, 1953) |
| Aulatsivik | The place of dominating (referring to the height of land above the adjacent channel) (Wheeler, 1953); Place where you can control things from, place of movement (Ames, 1986, p. 186) |
| Aupaluk | The red place (?) (Taylor, 1975, p. 270) |
| Avayalik | Place of walrus (Ames, 1986) / Who looks cut in two (Vezinet, 1982, p. 140) |
| Ekortisarsuk fiord | Place of calm (Ames, 1986, p. 186) |
| Ikkerasak (campsite near Killinek) | The strait (Wheeler, 1953) |
| Ikkirasagaluk (McLelan Strait) | Big tickle with strong tides (Ames, 1986) |
| Ikkudliayuk fiord | Clam bay (Ames, 1986) |
| Ikirasakituk (near Abloviak fiord) | Place of the small tickle (Ames, 1986, p. 7) |

| | |
|---|---|
| Ikorliarsuk | Ikkordliarsuk: The nice little place where caribou swim across (Wheeler, 1953) |
| Iqaluit | Place of many fish |
| Ittibime | (Ittibli: something to do with an isthmus? Wheeler, 1953) |
| Kangalaksiorvik fiord | Place to get out of storms, good anchorage (Ames, 1986, p. 186) |
| Kangiqsualujjuaq / Kangertluluaksoak | The enormous bay (Wheeler, 1953) |
| Kakkeviak (cape in Ungava Bay) | The part between the nose and the mouth (Vezinet, 1982, p. 141) |
| Kikkertaujak (island west of Akpatok) | Peninsula |
| Killinek / Killiniq | The land nearest the ocean (Wheeler, 1953) / land's end / the edge of the land (Ames, 1986, p. 186) / drift ice (Vezinet, 1982, p. 138) |
| Koksoak River | Big river / The very big brook (Wheeler, 1953) |
| Komaktorvik fiord | The place of eating lice (Wheeler, 1953) (in periods of famine when people would eat their clothing and their lice: Vezinet, 1982, p. 143); The place with lots of sea lice (Ames, 1986, p. 186) |
| Kuujjuaq | Great river |
| Kangalaksiorvik fiord | The place to hunt for winter caribou skins (Wheeler, 1953); The place to get out of storms, good anchorage (Ames, 1986) |
| Kangidlusuak (Hebron) | The very big bay (Wheeler, 1953) (kangerdluk: bay) |
| Kangivak / Kangiva | (Derived from kange – on the landward side – Wheeler, 1953) |
| Kangerdluarsuk Bay (south of Aulatsivik) | The nice little bay (Wheeler, 1953); Little bay (Ames, 1986) |
| Kaumajat Mountains | Shining ones (from sunlight) (Brice-Bennett, 2015) |
| Kiglapait Mountains | Large rough edges (Brice-Bennett, 2015) |
| Koroc River / Koroksoak / Kuururjuaq | Korok: The steep-walled valley; Koroksoak: The very big steep-walled valley (Wheeler, 1953) |
| Marqalik | Maqalik: The place with mud (Wheeler, 1953) |
| Nachvak | The find (?) (Wheeler, 1953) / A place where something is sunk (Haven, 1773a) |
| Naksariktok (cove at mouth of Nachvak fiord) | The place having one or more big valleys with gentle slopes (Wheeler, 1953) |
| Napâttuk Bay | Forest / The tree (Wheeler, 1953) |

| | |
|---|---|
| Natsituk (campsite southwest of Killinek) | Place of seals (Ames, 1986, p. 186) |
| Noodleook fiord | The way to thread a needle (Ames, 1986, p. 186) |
| Nulattatok (Ramah Bay) | The place where there are many seal blow holes in the ice (Wheeler, 1953) |
| Nunainguk (Nain) | The image of no land (because the bay is so long and straight, no land can be seen from its mouth: Wheeler, 1953) |
| Nutâk | The new one (Wheeler, 1953) |
| Okkak | The tongue (Wheeler, 1953) |
| Operngevik / Opingivik | The place where Inuit spend the spring in tents (Wheeler, 1953); A spring place (Ames, 1986, p. 186) — applies to many places |
| Saglek Bay | The low land (name originally applied to Saglek [Rose] Island: Schledermann, 1971, p. 28; Wheeler, 1953, p. 74) |
| Silukpak (a good char area in Saglek Bay) | Silupâk: The big carcass of a sea animal (?) (Wheeler, 1953) |
| Taqpangajuk | The one that is increasingly broad towards one end (Wheeler, 1953) |
| Tallek Bay (near Nachvak) | The arm (Wheeler, 1953) |
| Tasiujak | The saltwater pond (Wheeler, 1953) |
| Tessiujaksuk | Tessiujârsuk: The nice little saltwater pond (Wheeler, 1953) |
| Tessiujaluk | The big salt water pond (Wheeler, 1953) |
| Torngait / Tongait / Tunngait | Spirits (Brice-Bennett, 2015) |
| Tuunulliq | Tunilik: The place having a back (Wheeler, 1953) |
| Tutsaets / Tutjuat / Tutjat | Button Islands: Stepping stone islands (Ames, 1986, p. 34) |
| Tuttutuuk | Tuktutoq: the place of many caribou (Wheeler, 1953) |
| Uivaksoak | The very big cape facing the open sea (Wheeler, 1953) |
| Ungavak | ungata: beyond it (?) (Wheeler, 1953) |

APPENDIX 2

# People Living in Aulatsivik in the 1920s

| Name | Other Information |
|---|---|
| Mal Onalik | Grandfather of William Onalik |
| Sekepa Onalik | Father of William Onalik |
| Agnes Onalik (Tuglavina) b. ca. 1888 | Mother of William Onalik (had 10 children) |
| William Onalik (Sekepa) | Born 1922 in Aulatsivik (lived in Hopedale after 1959) |
| | |
| Jerry Onalik | Brother of Agnes Jararuse |
| Carolyn Onalik | |
| Pauline Onalik | Born 1920, married David Jararuse of Killinek, mother of Henry Jararuse of Hopedale |
| Ningeochiak (pretty little lady) Onalik | Father of Mary Menzel |
| Mary Menzel | Born 1908 in Aulatsivik, married Nicodemus Menzel, later lived in Hopedale |
| Gustav Semigak | Brother of Henry Semigak |
| Henry Semigak | Brother of Gustav Semigak |
| | |
| Wilson Semigak | Born 1911 in Aulatsivik |
| Susie Semigak (Jararuse) | Born 1922 in Killinek |
| Amos Semigak | Father of Johannes Semigak |

| | |
|---|---|
| Johannes Semigak | Born in Hebron, grandson of Gustav Semigak and Wilson Semigak, later lived in Hopedale |
| Joshia Semigak | |
| Sabine Semigak | |
| Jako Kajuatsiak | Father |
| Emma Kajuatsiak | Mother, sister of William Onalik |
| Tommy Kajuatsiak | Born 1922 in Aulatsivik, later lived in Kangiqsualujjuaq |
| Paulus Jararuse | |
| William Jararuse | |
| Bobby Nacholak | Brother of Lizzie Okkuatisiak / Okuatsiajoak / Ulluak of Natsituk |

Source: Ames (1986).

# NOTES

## Abbreviations

| | |
|---|---|
| BC | Bethlehem, USA Collection, Moravian Archives |
| GRHBC | Journal of the HBC post at George River, HBC Archives |
| HBC | Hudson's Bay Company |
| HC | Herrnhut, Germany Collection, Moravian Archives |
| HCB | Hebron Church Book |
| HSC | Hebron Supplementary Catalogue |
| KCB | Killinek Church Book |
| NAC | National Archives of Canada, Ottawa |
| NHBC | Journal of the HBC post at Nachvak, HBC Archives |
| PA | *Periodical Accounts* of the Moravian Mission |
| PANL | Provincial Archives of Newfoundland and Labrador, St. John's |
| PBHBC | Journal of the HBC post at Port Burwell, HBC Archives |
| RCB | Ramah Church Book |
| SFG | Society for the Furtherance of the Gospel |

Complete bibliographic data to other sources cited in the Notes are in the following Bibliography.

## Preface

1. *Periodical Accounts* (PA) 21: xx.

## Introduction

1. Hiller, 1967.
2. Brice-Bennett, 2017.

3. Brice-Bennett, 2017; Evans, 2013.
4. Brice-Bennett, 2017.
5. Makivik, 1987a.
6. Makivik, 1987a.
7. Budgel and Staveley, 1987.
8. Canada, 1975.
9. Kleivan, 1966.
10. Rollmann, 2009a.
11. Rollmann, 2008.
12. Rollmann, 2008.
13. Brice-Bennett, 1981.
14. Andersen and Johns, 2005; Andersen, Kalleo, and Watts, 2007.
15. Kohlmeister and Kmoch, 1814.

## Chapter 1

1. Fitzhugh, 1972, 1980, 1994; Hood, 2008; Tuck, 1976; Kaplan, 1980.
2. Ramsden and Rankin, 2013; Fay, 2016.
3. Ramsden and Rankin, 2013.
4. Fitzhugh, 1994; Hood, 2008; Ramsden and Rankin, 2013; Kaplan, 1985; Woollett, 2007.
5. Fitzhugh, 2019: 54; Fitzhugh, 2009: 130; Mailhot, 1997: 7.
6. Kaplan, 1983: 63, 66.
7. Kaplan, 1983: 194–212.
8. Barkham, 1984.
9. Tuck, 1995.
10. Mitchell, 2013.
11. See Tuck, 1995: 54–57; Taylor, 1984: 509–11; Trudel, 1978.
12. See Brice-Bennett, 1981: 2.
13. Jordan and Kaplan, 1980: 41.
14. Brice-Bennett, 1981: 6.
15. Taylor, 1984: 511; Kaplan, 1980, 1985; Kaplan and Woollett, 2000.
16. Taylor, 1976: 1–2, 7; Kaplan, 1983.
17. Hiller, 2009.
18. See Hiller, 1971: 75; Mitchell, 2013.
19. Taylor, 2009.

20. Rollmann, 2009a.
21. Hiller, 1971: 75–76.
22. Hiller, 1967.
23. Hiller, 2009; Kennedy, 2015.
24. Rollmann, 2009b, 2007; Taylor, 1972.
25. See Hiller, 1977.
26. Stopp, 2009.
27. See Hiller, 1971, and Brice-Bennett, 1981, for more discussion about the Moravian influence on Inuit society.
28. Taylor, 1976: 3.
29. Hiller, 1971: 85, 92–95.
30. Loring, 1998.
31. Haven, 1773a: 64.
32. These reports provide incomparable information on the distribution of the Inuit population and on a trade network extending across and beyond the Labrador Peninsula. One document was a journal of the voyage and a second account described Inuit dwelling places north of Nachvak; both reports were originally written in German and subsequently translated into English. Demographic information contained in the English documents has been analyzed previously by Taylor (1974: 10–15; 1975). Copies of the journal voyage in English (Haven, 1773a) and of the account of Inuit dwelling places in German (Haven, 1773b) and in English (Haven 1773c) were examined for this summary.
33. Taylor, 1975: 269–70.
34. Haven, 1773b: 194.
35. Taylor, 1974: 13; Taylor, 1975: 272.
36. Haven, 1773b: 191.
37. Williams, 1963: xvii.
38. Haven, 1773b: 191–92.
39. Haven, 1773b: 202.
40. Haven, 1773b: 190–91.
41. Taylor, 1977: 53.
42. See Taylor, 1975: 276.
43. Haven, 1773a: 77–78; Kaplan, 1983: 66.
44. Haven, 1773a: 78.

45. In his report, Haven wrote, "The more Northern Eskimaux come often here and stay all winter to get Iron ware here in exchange for wood for Boats, Kajaks, and Tools, and return home. They bring no whalebone hither from the N. as whalebone was here in no Esteem" (Haven, 1773a: 92). As northern Inuit had few sources of wood at home, this may have been a misunderstanding on his part or a mistranslation of his original German account.
46. Haven, 1773a: 91–93.
47. Haven, 1773a: 75.
48. Haven, 1773b: 202–03.
49. Haven, 1773b: 192.
50. Haven, 1773b: 193.
51. Haven, 1773b: 202.
52. Haven, 1773b: 190–91.
53. Haven, 1773b: 192–93. "One speaks of the Algonquians rather than Naskapi, Cree, or Innu (Montagnais), who did not become distinguished as cultural groupings until they were ascribed ethnonyms by the Europeans" (Morantz, 2016: 17).
54. Haven, 1773b: 192–93.
55. Haven, 1773b: 192–93.
56. Taylor, 1975: 270.
57. Haven, 1773b: 203.
58. Haven, 1773b: 203.
59. Haven, 1773b: 203.
60. Barr, 1994: 236–37.
61. Barr, 1994: 241. This inference was supported by an analysis of the quantity of baleen traded annually in Hudson Strait by Inuit from 1737 to 1778, amounting to one average bowhead whale per year, which would have been hunted by people in the immediate vicinity (Barr, 1994: 242, 244).
62. Haven, 1773b: 203.
63. Haven, 1773a: 92.
64. Haven, 1773a: 91.
65. Haven, 1773a: 91–92.
66. Haven, 1773a: 92.
67. Haven, 1773a: 202.
68. The Moravian party consisted of five missionaries, including Jens Haven, who chose a small harbour called Okkak on the island of Kivallek, located

about 130 kilometres north of Nain, as the best location for a community. They continued travelling northward to Kangidlusuak, Saglek, and Nachvak, where they terminated their journey when they were unable to find a pilot to take them to Killinek (Hiller, 1967: 93). Details on this expedition have not been located. Two missionaries who participated in the 1774 expedition, Christian Lister and John Hill, repeated the journey from Nain to Nachvak in the summer of 1775 with instructions to gather more information about place names, Inuit settlements, and trade activities at Nachvak. One of their informants was an Inuit man named Tiguatsiak, who was born at Ungavak. Lister's report added a few new geographical details to Haven's 1773 account and indicated that changes had apparently occurred in the population distribution and in trade activities. Most significant were alterations in the population at Killinek and Kangivak, and direct trade exchanges by Ungava Inuit with European ships at Igloarsuk, which was described as an island where ships arrived on the south side to trade with Inuit (Lister, 1775: 013282).

69. Hiller, 1967: 94–95, 98–99.
70. Kaplan, 1983: 123–24.
71. See Hiller, 1967: 146–58; Brice-Bennett, 1981; Kaplan and Woollett, 2000.
72. PA 4: 79.
73. PA 4: 129, 292; Hiller, 1967: 141–42; Brice-Bennett, 1990: 233.
74. PA 2: 56, 327.
75. Okkak Diary, NAC M512/3:16.
76. Okkak Diary, NAC M512/3:19.
77. PA 3: 21.
78. In January 1806, for instance, Inuit travelling from Kangidlusuak [Hebron] informed the Okkak missionaries that many people at Nachvak had moved to Killinek, due to a shortage of food. In late April, three men arrived from Killinek stating that people in that community and at Nachvak were forced by hunger to eat some of their dogs; the men had made the long journey to purchase gunpowder and shot. In the autumn of 1809, famine forced 15 families from the north to move to Okkak. Although they professed an interest in converting to Christianity, several families returned to their former dwellings when they found that they would not be given plenty of food (PA 5: 60).
79. Okkak Diary, NAC 512/3:117–18r (emphasis added).
80. Taylor, 1975: 270, note 2.

81. Okkak Diary, NAC 512/3: 117–18.
82. See Brice-Bennett, 1981: 218–20.
83. See Brice-Bennett, 1981: 222–31.
84. PA 3: 245, 447.
85. Anonymous, 1833: 346.
86. Kohlmeister and Kmoch 1814: 5, 8; PA 3: 279.
87. The other Inuit members of the party were "Jonas, Jonathan's son, and his wife Agnes, about thirty years of age, both intelligent, clever Esquimaux; they had their five children with them; Sophia, twelve years old, Susanna, Jonathan, Thamar, and Sybilla, the youngest but half a year old. Paul, and his wife Mary, very agreeable, sensible people, about twenty years of age. Paul is Jonathan's cousin, and a man of a very warm temper. In activity and skill, he was next to Jonathan. David, and his mother Rachel, the first a hopeful young man of about twenty, and the latter a good-natured old woman, who had the care of our clothes and linen, and kept them clean and in good order. Besides these four families, we took with us a boy, Okkiksuk, an orphan, about sixteen, whom Jonathan had adopted, and who promised to reward the kindness of his guardian by his good behaviour. He was always ready to render us every service in his power. We were attended on the voyage by a skin-boat (or woman's boat) in which were Thukkekina and his wife, and their adopted child Mammak, a boy twelve years old. Their age is about forty" (Kohlmeister and Kmoch, 1814: 8–9).
88. Anonymous, 1833: 346.
89. Kohlmeister and Kmoch, 1814: 5.
90. Kohlmeister and Kmoch, 1814: 5.
91. Kohlmeister and Kmoch, 1814: 16, 18, 38.
92. Kohlmeister and Kmoch, 1814: 40–41.
93. Kohlmeister and Kmoch, 1814: 39–40.
94. Ames, 1986: 34.
95. Kohlmeister and Kmoch, 1814: 41.
96. Kohlmeister and Kmoch, 1814: 42.
97. Kohlmeister and Kmoch, 1814: 46–47.
98. Kohlmeister and Kmoch, 1814: 47.
99. Kohlmeister and Kmoch, 1814: 47.
100. Kohlmeister and Kmoch, 1814: 47.

101. Kohlmeister and Kmoch, 1814: 47.
102. Kohlmeister and Kmoch, 1814: 49. It is not clear from the last statement whether the islands were located to the "true" or geographical north, placing them in northern Hudson Strait, or to the "due" or compass north, situating them along the southern shore of the strait.
103. Taylor, 1969: 152–53, notes 39–40.
104. Kohlmeister and Kmoch, 1814: 57–59.
105. Kohlmeister and Kmoch, 1814: 70–72.
106. Kohlmeister and Kmoch, 1814: 72.
107. Kohlmeister and Kmoch, 1814: 57.
108. Kohlmeister and Kmoch, 1814: 57, 67.
109. Kohlmeister and Kmoch, 1814: 76.
110. Kohlmeister and Kmoch, 1814: 73, 77.
111. Kohlmeister and Kmoch, 1814: 78.
112. Kohlmeister and Kmoch, 1814: 37.
113. Kohlmeister and Kmoch, 1814: 44.
114. See Brice-Bennett, 1981: 250–51.

## Chapter 2

1. PA 6: 343.
2. PA 6: 344. Kohlmeister thought Igloarsuk might be Nottingham Island, which was situated at the western entrance of Hudson Strait. This was contrary to his belief in 1811 that it was Resolution Island when Uttakiyok indicated a location north-northeast beyond Cape Chidley. However, a more plausible explanation is that the place name referred to a location in the vicinity of the Upper and Middle Savage Islands off the southern coast of Baffin Island. Inuit living along the northeastern coast would have seen European ships that pursued whales annually since 1719 during the open water period in Davis Strait (Lubbock, 1937: 82). However, people residing along the southeastern coast would not have observed these vessels, or even ships passing through Hudson Strait, because they were inland hunting caribou in late summer and fall when vessels appeared in the region.
3. PA 6: 344.
4. PA 6: 344. This estimate must refer to the number of boats in 1814 because the 21 boats mentioned in 1813 would have held about 430 people.

5. PA 6: 344.
6. Williams, 1963: xxxvi–xxxvii, xxiv.
7. See Brice-Bennett, 1981: 217, 219, 257.
8. Packard, 1891: 3.
9. Williams, 1963: xxxvi–xxxvii.
10. Williams, 1963: xxxii–xxxix; Richling, 1985: 474–75.
11. Kaplan, 1983: 33, 363.
12. Kaplan, 1983: 178–84.
13. Brice-Bennett, 1981: 145–55.
14. Brice-Bennett, 1981: 65; Hiller, 1967: 209.
15. PA 7: 160.
16. PA 9: 58, 219, 377.
17. See Brice-Bennett, 1981: 185.
18. PA 10: 66.
19. PA 9: 219.
20. Brice-Bennett, 1981: 144, 194.
21. Brice-Bennett, 1981: 256-58.
22. Kohlmeister, 1814: 138. In suggesting the village had a large population, the missionaries assumed that all houses were occupied at the same time. However, certain dwellings may have been inhabited by families who did not always winter in the bay or some structures may have replaced older abandoned houses, resulting in fewer inhabitants at a given period. Based on the conventional estimate of 20 people per winter house, a maximum of about 260 to 280 Inuit may have occupied the settlement and about 60 Inuit could have resided in the three habitable houses.
23. Kohlmeister, 1814: 139.
24. See Brice-Bennett, 1981: 265–67, 259–60.
25. Kaplan, 1983: 136–37.
26. Kaplan, 1983: 278–79.
27. Kaplan, 1983: 279, 300, 306.
28. Kaplan, 1983: 306.
29. Korneski, 2016: 1–29.
30. Williams, 1963: lvi.
31. Cooke, 1969: 77.
32. Cooke, 1969: 77.

33. See Brice-Bennett, 1981: 302–05, 324–32.
34. Cooke, 1969: 109.
35. Korneski, 2016: 10.
36. Williams, 1963: 227.
37. Cooke, 1969: 79; Trudel, 1991: 102.
38. McLean in Wallace, 1932: 226.
39. Trudel, 1991: 109.
40. Fort Chimo Report on District, 1837–38: 14–14d, in Richling, 2000: 57, note 15.
41. Hebron Diary, Jan. 1836: 46, 431, in Richling, 2000: 66.
42. PA 14: 426.
43. PA 15: 409.
44. PA 16: 174.
45. PA 16: 98.
46. Cooke, 1969: 120–22.
47. Cooke, 1969: 131.
48. PA 13: 91.
49. See Brice-Bennett, 1981: 299, 309, 335.
50. Cooke, 1969: 185–87.
51. Trudel, 1991: 105.
52. Cooke and Holland, 1978: 171.
53. Korneski, 2016: 10–11.

## Chapter 3

1. PA 16: 528.
2. PA 17: 216.
3. PA 17: 415–16.
4. PA 17: 415. The meaning of the last statement is unclear as Inuit may have been referring to the number of inhabitants in the general region of either George River or Ungava Bay. At the time Hebron had 233 residents and about 150 Inuit were dispersed along the northern Labrador coast. References to the population around George River made in earlier and later reports consistently state that only a few families usually occupied the area. Inuit may have included in their neighbourhood the eastern shores of Ungava Bay, or possibly the coastal region extending west to the Koksoak River, as many Inuit from this area had customarily traded at

Hebron before the HBC established Fort Chimo at Kuujjuaq. This last explanation is the most likely interpretation of the comment.

5. PA 17: 216.
6. PA 17: 468.
7. PA 17: 315.
8. PA 18: 81.
9. PA 18: 81–82.
10. PA 18: 82.
11. PA 15: 317, 412.
12. PA 16: 178.
13. PA 17: 216.
14. PA 15: 380.
15. PA 16: 98.
16. PA 16: 174.
17. PA 18: 384.
18. PA 18: 289.
19. PA 18: 384.
20. PA 18: 385.
21. PA 23: 567; for more information on Renatus, see Rollmann, 2017.
22. PA 23: 567.
23. PA 19: 19–20.
24. PA 17: 218. The next largest community was at Killinek, which was said to be inhabited by 53 Inuit (PA 17: 216).
25. Kaplan, 1983: 129–30.
26. PA 16: 175.
27. Kohlmeister and Kmoch, 1814: 17–18.
28. PA 16: 175–76.
29. PA 17: 218.
30. See Brice-Bennett, 1981: 357–59, 362–63.
31. PA 17: 219.
32. PA 18: 384.
33. PA 20: 127.
34. PA 19: 17.
35. PA 19: 18.
36. PA 19: 131.

37. See Anonymous, 1835: 318.
38. PA 19: 131.
39. PA 19: 131.
40. PA 19: 131.
41. PA 19: 498.
42. PA 23: 300.
43. PA 23: 242.
44. PA 17: 217.
45. PA 23: 242.
46. PA 19: 225.
47. PA 19: 331.
48. PA 20: 128, 188.
49. PA 19: 497.
50. Hebron Diary, Jan. 1850: 47, 316, in Richling, 2000: 64.
51. PA 19: 431.
52. PA 19: 431.
53. Cooke and Holland, 1978: 35, 168.
54. SFG Minutes, Vol. 7: 136.
55. Marsh, 1964: 427.
56. SFG Minutes, Vols. 5–7: 79.
57. PA 20: 188–89.
58. PA 20: 399.
59. PA 21: 236.
60. PA 20: 398.
61. PA 21: 301.
62. PA 23: 497.
63. PA 22: 110.
64. PA 24: 471.
65. PA 24: 471.
66. PA 24: 471.
67. PA 24: 471.
68. PA 25: 321.
69. PA 25: 538.
70. PA 22: 325.
71. PA 23: 294, 568.

72. PA 24: 270.
73. Rollmann, 2017: 150.
74. PA 27: 62.
75. PA 24: 270–72.
76. PA 27: 63.
77. PA 27: 63.
78. PA 30: 154.
79. PA 33: 427.
80. PA 19: 131.
81. PA 23: 492–93.
82. PA 23: 492–93.
83. PA 23: 569.
84. PA 23: 569.
85. PA 24: 403, 543.
86. PA 24: 404.
87. PA 24: 543. A later account also blamed the conflict on the British sailors' sexual assault of Inuit women. See Heyes and Helgen, 2014: 250.
88. PA 24: 543.
89. PA 24: 543–44.
90. Payne, 1889: 223.
91. PA 24: 404.
92. PA 24: 544.
93. PA 24: 544.
94. PA 24: 544.
95. SFG Minutes, Vols. 8–10: unpaginated.

## Chapter 4

1. SFG Minutes, Vols. 8–10: unpaginated.
2. SFG Minutes, Vols. 8–10: unpaginated.
3. Brice-Bennett, 1981: 224.
4. Brice-Bennett, 1981: 451–81; Markham, 2021.
5. See Brice-Bennett, 1990: 244.
6. Markham, 2021: 94.
7. Brice-Bennett, 1990: 244–45.
8. Reichel, quoted in Rollmann, 2010: 22.

9. SFG Minutes, Vols. 8–10: unpaginated.
10. SFG Minutes, Vols. 8–10: unpaginated.
11. Markham, 2021: 96.
12. PA 27: 16.
13. SFG Minutes, Vols. 8–10: unpaginated.
14. Minutes, Brethren's Society for the Furtherance of the Gospel 8, 1868, in Richling, 2000: 68, note 19.
15. Cooke and Holland, 1978: 228, 232.
16. Cooke, 1964: 148.
17. Donald Smith to T. Fraser, Hudson's Bay House, London, 23 July 1863, HBCA, A.11/50, fo 61 (in Richling, 1985: 471).
18. Hastings, 1985: 92.
19. Morantz, 2016: 37.
20. Gosling, 1910; Morantz, 2016.
21. Morantz, 2016: 37.
22. Brice-Bennett, 1981: 472–73, 479–81.
23. PA 23: 241.
24. PA 24: 406.
25. PA 26: 100.
26. PA 26: 100.
27. PA 27: 67.
28. PA 26: 375; PA 27: 6.
29. PA 27: 67; Packard, 1891: 226.
30. D. Smith to W.G. Smith, London, 13 Aug. 1867, Boundary Dispute documents, p. 2825.
31. Korneski, 2016: 12–13.
32. PA 29: 69.
33. Kleivan, 1966.
34. See Hiller, 1977: 87.
35. PA 27: 233.
36. PA 27: 63–64.
37. PA 27: 64.
38. PA 27: 65.
39. Kaplan, 1983: 134–36.
40. PA 27: 65.

41. PA 27: 64–65.
42. PA 27: 3, 14.
43. PA 27: 3.
44. PA 27: 71.
45. PA 27: 14.
46. PA 27: 15–16.
47. PA 27: 17. The original German version of Weitz's report also stated that most of the Nachvak Inuit had traded at Hebron and that a similar number of Inuit lived at Nulattatok, a bay south of Nachvak, where the residents possessed five Kajait and a skin boat (Weitz, 1868: 434, 436, 456).
48. PA 27: 16.
49. PA 27: 15.
50. PA 27: 17.
51. PA 27: 4.
52. PA 27: 18.
53. PA 27: 19.
54. PA 27: 19.
55. PA 27: 19.
56. Weitz, 1868: 452.
57. PA 27: 20.
58. PA 27: 4.
59. Kaplan, 1983: 282–85.
60. PA 27: 20.
61. PA 27: 20.
62. PA 27: 17.
63. Weitz, 1868: 441.
64. PA 27: 4.
65. PA 27: 2.
66. SFG Minutes, Vols. 8–10: unpaginated.
67. Hebron Diary, 3 Jan. 1869: 48, 138, in Richling, 2000: 69–70.
68. PA 27: 225.
69. PA 27: 67.
70. PA 27: 277.
71. PA 27: 277, 433.
72. PA 27: 233.

73. PA 27: 489.
74. Kaplan, 1983: 184.
75. Rollmann, 2010: 21–22.
76. PA 26: 318; PA 31: 247.
77. Brice-Bennett, 1981: 355–56, 430–40; Rollmann, 2017.
78. Rollmann, 2010: 9.
79. Rollmann, 2010: 23.
80. Rollmann, 2010: 23.
81. PA 28: 390.
82. PA 26: 324; PA 27: 21.
83. "Report of the Eskimoes, Daniel and Gottlob, on their missionary journey to the extreme north of Labrador and Ungava Bay," PA 27: 20–24; see also Evans, 2013: 135.
84. PA 27: 20–21.
85. PA 27: 22.
86. PA 27: 22.
87. PA 27: 23.
88. Daniel, 1867: 395–420.
89. PA 27: 22–23.
90. PA 27: 23.
91. PA 27: 23.
92. Daniel, 1867: 412–13.
93. Daniel, 1867: 412–13.
94. PA 27: 23; Daniel, 1867: 412–13.
95. PA 27: 24.
96. PA 27: 3; 13–14.
97. PA 27: 19.
98. PA 27: 281.
99. PA 27: 281.
100. PA 27: 282.
101. PA 27: 234, 278.
102. PA 27: 419; 433.
103. PA 27: 489.
104. Rollmann, 2010: 23.
105. Rollmann, 2010: 25; PA 29: 65, 67.

106. Rollmann, 2010: 24.
107. PA 27: 234, 434.
108. PA 28: 111.
109. PA 28: 111.
110. During this time, the HBC agent had been left in charge of the Mission's property, including a stock of trade goods. While Nachvak Inuit had not touched the Mission's possessions, missionaries learned that Kajuasiak had broken into the house at one point to do some single-handed trading. Kajuasiak had arrived at Nachvak intending to trade. Finding the HBC employees away on a caribou hunt, he forced open the door and took some provisions. In payment for the goods, he left some seal pelts behind, and later reported his actions to the HBC agent and the missionaries. Missionaries noted that "he gave quite a correct account of what he had taken, and from the fact that he might have taken a great deal more than he did without leaving any payment at all, it is evident that he did not intend to do more than trade with himself" (PA 28: 121). In addition to revealing Kajuasiak's honesty, this incident demonstrates his acuity in dealing diplomatically with European agencies that often relied on punishments for theft.
111. PA 28: 121, 111, 119.
112. PA 28: 120.

## Chapter 5

1. References include the Moravian quarterly journal *Periodical Accounts* and a manuscript map prepared in 1898 by the Mission's trade inspector, Carl Linder, which identifies place names and the location of Inuit dwellings mentioned in reports by Daniel and Gottlob in 1867 (see Map 7). Another map credited to Weitz in 1868, and published by Packard (1891: 226), includes more details on place names and dwelling sites, and also traces winter Kamutik routes linking bays north of Hebron (see Map 8). Supplementing this information are the journals [called "outfit"] kept by the HBC agent at Nachvak, which contain cryptic daily comments on the personal names and places of origin of Inuit trading at the post, resources bartered, and local harvesting activities. However, the surviving HBC records are incomplete and journals exist for only the following early periods: September 1868–August 1869, June 1871–January 1872, and April 1873–March 1875; journals are

also available for January 1898–September 1906. Only one record, covering the period from March–October 1874, exists for the HBC post at Saglek but it did not contain any relevant information; the post was closed in 1876. References to the Nachvak journals are cited with the abbreviation NHBC; general comments include the year of the notation in the journal but significant details about people or events include the full date by day, month, and year (e.g., 26.11.1873 for 26 November 1873). The records of the Moravian mission station at Ramah are another important source of information on economic conditions, and particularly on demographic features of the Inuit population after 1871. The primary records include annual reports published in the *Periodical Accounts*, and the Ramah Church Book, which is a register of candidates for baptism, baptized adults and children, births, marriages, and deaths. When Inuit initially joined the congregation and became candidates for baptism, their traditional personal name, kinship relationship to other people, and often date and place of birth were entered in the Church Book. This unique demographic record thus provides vital details that enable family genealogies to be reconstructed for those living during the late nineteenth century; extracts from the Ramah Church Book will be cited with the abbreviation RCB. Additional demographic details were obtained from the Church Book of Killinek (KCB), a mission station opened in 1904, and from the Hebron Supplementary Catalogue (HSC), a register of Inuit moving to Hebron from other mission stations beginning in 1831. The Moravian Church Books are especially significant because they include the names of women and children, which are commonly omitted in historical records. Other Moravian reports and the HBC journals generally refer only to the male leader and other adults of a family group. On rare occasions when females are mentioned, their existence is noted solely in a descriptive manner as the wife or daughter of a particular male. Female Inuit who became candidates for baptism at a mission station were at least given individual identities by having their personal names and places of birth recorded in the Church Book. The Moravian method of spelling Inuit personal names and place names is used in the following discussion, as their renditions were more phonemic and consistent than the versions of names appearing in the HBC journals, which varied as new agents were sent to manage the post.

2. Alia, 2007: 28.
3. 2PA 3: 372.
4. Louisa Flowers, Nain (personal communication with Carol Brice-Bennett); Ben-Dor, 1966.
5. Rollmann, 2018: 146–47.
6. Rollmann, 2018: 155.
7. PA 25: 98; PA 27: 23.
8. RCB.
9. HSC.
10. RCB.
11. RCB.
12. NHBC.
13. RCB.
14. KCB.
15. RCB.
16. HSC.
17. PA 25: 497.
18. RCB.
19. PA 28: 122; RCB.
20. PA 28: 122.
21. PA 29: 203–04.
22. PA 29: 204.
23. PA 30: 103.
24. NHBC.
25. PA 30: 103.
26. PA 30: 105.
27. RCB.
28. Taylor, 1981: 39–43; Rivet, 2014. Carl Hagenbeck was a German exotic animal trader supplying zoos throughout Europe as well as to P.T. Barnum in the United States, and operated a zoo in Hamburg that displayed animals in a natural habitat. In the mid-1870s, he began doing the same with "exotic" human peoples, creating what came to be known as "human zoos." After displaying Sami people from northern Scandinavia, he then toured a small group of Labrador Inuit in 1880 to zoos in major cities throughout Europe. All eight Inuit, including Abraham Ulrikab, died of smallpox.

29. NHBC 29.12.1874.
30. NHBC 23.1.1874.
31. PA 31: 28.
32. Tuttle, 1885: 59.
33. Tuttle, 1885: 59–60.
34. Tuttle, 1885: 61.
35. Tuttle, 1885: 65. Tuttle was probably unaware that Inuit residing at Killinek bartered for imported goods at the HBC post in Nachvak as well as at the Moravian store in Ramah. Thus, Kajuasiak may have obtained his clothing from either of these places or indeed from Kuujjuaq.
36. PA 27: 23.
37. NHBC 19.8.1869.
38. PA 27: 23.
39. Weitz, 1868.
40. Grenfell, 1897: 111.
41. RCB.
42. 2PA 371–72, 416.
43. NHBC 30.6.1869.
44. NHBC 26.8.1871.
45. PA 29: 66.
46. PA 29: 66.
47. PA 29: 203.
48. 2PA 3: 372.
49. NHBC 22.10.1900.
50. NHBC 27.4.1873.
51. KCB.
52. PA 28: 185.
53. PA 31: 350.
54. NHBC 27.4.1873.
55. PA 32: 369; 2PA 6: 225.
56. NHBC 16.7.1871.
57. NHBC 10.1.1869.
58. RCB.
59. RCB.
60. NHBC 22.12.1871.

61. KCB.
62. 2PA 2: 544; 2PA 5: 168.
63. RCB.
64. NHBC 7.9.1878.
65. 2PA 4: 584.
66. 2PA 6: 225.
67. 2PA 3: 371.
68. 2PA 6: 225.
69. NHBC 29.12.1871.
70. NHBC.
71. PA 33: 425–26; RCB.
72. HSC.
73. RCB.
74. PA 32: 590.
75. PA 32: 370.
76. RCB.
77. NHBC 7.4.1873.
78. NHBC 14.3.1875.
79. NHBC 21.12.1868; 17.10.1871; 21.1.1874.
80. RCB.
81. HCB.
82. PA 29: 65.
83. PA 29: 68.
84. RCB.
85. RCB.
86. PA 30: 101, 104.
87. RCB.
88. HSC.
89. PA 29: 68.
90. NHBC 22.7.1869.
91. PA 29: 67; NHBC 19.4.1873.
92. NHBC 23.5.1873.
93. NHBC 13.4.1873.
94. PA 29: 431.
95. PA 29: 203.

96. RCB.
97. PA 28: 356.
98. RCB.
99. PA 29: 203.
100. RCB.
101. NHBC.
102. RCB.
103. NHBC.
104. PA 29: 66–67.
105. NHBC 2.8.1871.
106. NHBC 12.4.1873.
107. NHBC 25.4.1873; 11.7.1873.
108. NHBC 25.4.1873.
109. NHBC 7.12.1874.
110. PA 29: 68.
111. PA 29: 68.
112. PA 29: 66.
113. NHBC.
114. PA 31: 351.
115. PA 32: 589.
116. PA 32: 589.
117. Taylor, 1974: 74–75.
118. PA 30: 102.
119. PA 30: 103.
120. PA 28: 185.
121. PA 29: 431.
122. PA 30: 336.

## Chapter 6

1. Kaplan, 1983; Whitridge, 2012; Jurakic, 2007; Negrijn, 2011.
2. Kaplan, 1983; Weitz did not visit the Komaktorvik area during his survey, as it appears that the families associating with Kavanga had spent the previous winter in the Nulattatok area and subsequently moved to Komaktorvik.
3. NHBC 15.8.1871 passim; 25.4.1873; PA 29: 66.

4. Kaplan, 1983: 286–89.
5. PA 29: 67.
6. PA 29: 434.
7. NHBC 22.12.1871.
8. For example, NHBC 10-12.10.1873.
9. Brice-Bennett, personal observation.
10. NHBC 7.1.1874; 8.1.1875.
11. PA 28: 354–56.
12. PA 29: 65.
13. NHBC 22–26.4.1873; 12.5.1873; 5.6.1873; 11–16.6.1874.
14. Kaplan, 1983: 288.
15. NHBC 25.5.1874.
16. HNBC 27.6.1873; 5–15.7.1874.
17. PA 31: 349.
18. NHBC 7.10.1873; 22.5.1874.
19. NHBC 19.4.1874; 3.10.1874.
20. PA 31: 21.
21. Half an ell would be about six inches (Rivet, 2014: 44, note 41).
22. Jacobsen, 1894, in Rivet, 2014: 44–45.
23. See Brice-Bennett, 1990: 228–29, 245.
24. PA 29: 429.
25. PA 30: 335.
26. PA 31: 349.
27. PA 30: 336.
28. PA 31: 28.
29. PA 29: 434.
30. PA 29: 434–35.
31. See Brice-Bennett, 1981: 95–96; Taylor, 1974: 80, 91.
32. Taylor, 1974: 60, 69.
33. 2PA 3: 371–72.
34. Willway, 1897: 359.
35. 2PA 4: 416.
36. PA 28: 355.
37. PA 28: 355.
38. NHBC 6.3.1874.

39. NHBC 4.4.1873.
40. NHBC 14.3.1875.
41. George Ford (1857–1918), HBC Biographical Sheets, Hudson's Bay Company Archives, Winnipeg.
42. For instance, George Ford's half-brother, John Ford Jr., acted as HBC postmaster and then clerk at George River from 1884 to 1905. John Jr.'s son, Samuel Ford, worked for the HBC and Revillon Frères in Ungava between 1905 and 1950, and was married to Mary, daughter of Job and Clara Edmunds, another Labrador family of mixed ancestry with long ties to the HBC in Ungava (Morantz, 2016: 48, 78; John Ford Jr. and Samuel G. Ford, HBCA Biographical Sheets).
43. Harriet's father was Thomas Merrifield, and her mother was Elizabeth Lane (M33 G1 Fieldnotes, 1975–1978, Carol Brice-Bennett Collection, Labrador Institute Archives).
44. Henry and Solomon eventually worked for the HBC in Ungava Bay and northern Quebec (Morantz, 2016: 92–93), and Sarah Elizabeth (Anauta) is the author of *Land of Good Shadows: The Life Story of Anauta, an Eskimo Woman* (New York: The John Day Co., 1940).
45. Rivet, 2014.
46. See Rivet, 2014.
47. George Ford (1857–1918), HBC Biographical Sheets, Hudson's Bay Company Archives, Winnipeg.
48. Gordon, 1885: 203.
49. See Brice-Bennett, 1990: 237–38.
50. PA 30: 336.
51. PA 28: 182.
52. Cooke and Holland, 1978: 227.
53. NHBC 2.8.1871; 27.8.1871.
54. NHBC 6.6.1873.
55. NHBC 4.4.1873.
56. NHBC 1.2.1874.
57. Loring, 1998.
58. PA 31: 351; PA 32: 118.
59. PA 31: 351.
60. PA 32: 370–71.

61. Low in Morantz, 2016: 61.
62. Morantz, 2016: 138–39.
63. Morantz, 2016: 52.
64. PA 32: 118.
65. Laugrand and Oosten, 2010: 375–76.
66. Turner, 1979: 179–80.
67. Turner, 1979: 179–80.
68. Turner, 1979: 176.
69. Turner, 1979.
70. Turner, 1887: 104.
71. Turner, 1887: 104.
72. Turner, 1979: 177.
73. Turner, 1979: 176.
74. PA 33: 423.
75. Heyes and Helgen, 2014: 12.
76. Taylor, 1984: 520.
77. Taylor, 1975: 274.
78. Turner, 1979: 177.
79. Turner, 1979: 177; Turner, 1887: 101.
80. Payne, 1889: 229.
81. Turner, 1979: 177.
82. Payne, 1889: 221.
83. Payne, 1889: 221.
84. Payne, 1889: 217, 230.
85. Turner, 1979: 177.
86. Turner, 1979: 177.
87. Low, 1906: 66.
88. Turner, 1979: 179.
89. Turner, 1887: 100; 1979: 179.
90. PA 32: 370.
91. PA 33: 619.
92. PA 29: 69; 31: 28; 33: 426.
93. 2PA 1: 412.
94. 2PA 3: 37.
95. HSC.

96. 2PA 3: 37, 131.
97. 2PA 2: 440, 544.
98. 2PA 2: 544.
99. 2PA 3: 38.
100. NAC 511, reel 38:05746-7.
101. 2PA 3: 37–38.
102. 2PA 3: 175.
103. Martin, 1898: 010885 (emphasis in original).
104. PA 34: 477.
105. Turner, 1979: 177.
106. PA 34: 478.
107. Or possibly Ikauja's foster son, whose original personal name and subsequent surname were unusual.

## Chapter 7

1. 2PA 4: 250-51.
2. 2PA 4: 327.
3. 2PA 4: 331–33.
4. 2PA 4: 251.
5. LaTrobe, cited in Lewis, 1904: 160.
6. 2PA 4: 252.
7. 2PA 4: 254, 333–34.
8. 2PA 4: 252–53.
9. 2PA 4: 254.
10. 2PA 4: 254.
11. 2PA 4: 254.
12. 2PA 4: 334–35.
13. 2PA 4: 255.
14. 2PA 4: 251.
15. Pilot, 1899: 42–43.
16. Peck, 1922.
17. Harper, 1985: 143.
18. Dorais, 2010: 176.
19. Dorais, 2010: 176.
20. Harper, 1985: 143–46, 147–48.

21. Harper, 1985: 146.
22. Harper, 1985: 147–48.
23. Harper, 1985: 152.
24. Lewis, 1904: 69–71, 78.
25. Lewis, 1904: 81.
26. Harper, 1985: 147.
27. Lewis, 1904: 82.
28. Lewis, 1904: 130.
29. See Brice-Bennett, 1971: 198.
30. Lewis, 1904: 88–89, 115.
31. Low, 1906: 65.
32. Lewis, 1904: 77, 141.
33. Lewis, 1904: 139.
34. Lewis, 1904: 165, 192.
35. Lewis, 1904: 95.
36. Peck, 1922: 14.
37. Lewis, 1904: 87, 139.
38. Lewis, 1904: 149–50.
39. Lewis, 1904: 151–57.
40. Peck, 1922: 17; Lewis, 1904: 162.
41. Lewis, 1904: 194.
42. Lewis, 1904: 196.
43. Peck, 1922: 17.
44. Lewis, 1904: 202; Peck, 1922: 19–25.
45. Peck, 1922: 20; Lewis, 1904: 213.
46. Harper, 1981: 44.
47. Peck, 1922: 21; 2PA 6: 233.
48. Low, 1906: 65.
49. Cited in Lewis, 1904: 158–59.
50. Lewis, 1904: 158–59.
51. Lewis, 1904: 160–61.
52. Lewis, 1904: 160–61.
53. Lewis, 1904: 160.
54. Peck to LaTrobe, 1 Sept. 1900, HC.
55. Avataq Cultural Centre, 1988: 1, 4.

56. Low, 1906: 7; MacGregor, 1906: 17–18.
57. MacGregor, 1906: 17–18; see Hiller, 1995: 2.
58. Blandford to LaTrobe, 2 Oct. 1901, HC.
59. Blandford to LaTrobe, 2 Oct. 1901, HC.
60. 2PA 4: 417.
61. Canon W. Pilot to Bishop LaTrobe, St. John's, 19 Feb. 1901, HC; 2PA 4: 418.
62. Pilot to LaTrobe, 19 Feb. 1901, HC.
63. SFG Minutes, Vol. 10, 7 Mar. 1900.
64. SFG Minutes, Vo1.10, 3 July 1900.
65. 2PA 4: 419.
66. SFG Minutes, Blandford to LaTrobe, Vol. 10, 2 Oct. 1901, HC.
67. SFG Minutes, Vol. 10, 2 Oct. 1900.
68. SFG Minutes, Vol. 10, 2 Oct. 1900.
69. 2PA 4: 415.
70. Taylor, 1974: 76.
71. 2PA 4: 415.
72. 2PA 4: 416; MacGregor, 1906: 157.
73. 2PA 4: 416. During Stecker's visit, a search party was launched for several families who were reported to have travelled from Kangivak to Uivaksoak, a cape forming the northwest point of the east coast of Labrador. Stecker noted that the party's guide, a man named Kuttaktok, "had never before made the tour per sledge, but had only seen the islands whilst out reindeer [caribou] hunting" (2PA 4: 416). Despite seeing many old camping places, they did not find any trace of the people and assumed they had gone somewhere to the west.
74. 2PA 4: 417.
75. 2PA 4: 417.
76. 2PA 4: 584.
77. 2PA 4: 584.
78. 2PA 4: 585.
79. Annual Report from Rama, 1902, BC: 57868–69. However, according to the Nachvak HBC agent, Tuglavina had moved his camp to the north in February 1899 and occupied winter quarters there in January 1900 (NHBC).
80. Annual Report from Rama, 1902, BC: 57869–70.
81. Annual Report from Rama, 1902, BC: 57869.

82. See Laugrand and Oosten, 2010: 248.
83. Annual Report from Rama, 1902, BC: 57871.
84. Annual Report from Rama, 1902, BC: 57872.
85. Annual Report from Rama, 1902, BC: 57869.
86. Annual Report from Rama, 1902, BC: 57877.
87. 2PA 5: 169.
88. Annual Report from Rama, 1902, BC: 57877–78.
89. Annual Report from Rama, 1902, BC: 57877.
90. Annual Report from Rama, 1902, BC: 57877–78.
91. Annual Report from Rama, 1902, BC: 57878.
92. Annual Report from Rama, 1902, BC: 57878–79.
93. RCB; 2PA 7: 7.
94. Benjamin LaTrobe to Bishop Llewellyn Jones, 20 Feb. 1902, as cited in Rollmann, 2010: 36.
95. Annual Report from Rama, 1902, BC: 57877–78.
96. Letters to LaTrobe and to the Moravian Church and Mission Agency, 24 May 1902, HC.
97. Bishop Jones to LaTrobe, 25 May 1902, HC.
98. Draft letter to Jones, 21 June 1902, HC.
99. Jones to LaTrobe, 12 July 1902, HC.
100. LaTrobe to Jones, 5 Aug. 1902, HC.
101. Conference letter from Ramah, Aug. 1902, BC: 57695.
102. Conference letter from Ramah, Aug. 1902, BC: 57695.
103. Conference letter from Ramah, Aug. 1902, BC: 57696.
104. Kaplan, 1983: 144; Ames, 1986: 7.
105. Ames, 1986: 10.
106. Kaplan, 1983: 146.
107. Conference letter from Ramah, Aug. 1902, BC: 57741–42.
108. Letter from Eckhart and Merten to the Missions Direktion in Berthelsdorf, 25 July 1903, HC: 57741.
109. Kaplan, 1983: 139–41.
110. Bishop Jones to LaTrobe, 25 May 1902, HC; Martin, 1909, BC: 013574.
111. Martin, 1909, BC: 013574.
112. Martin, 1909, BC: 013573.
113. Martin, 1909, BC: 013573.

114. Martin, 1909, BC: 013573.

115. Indenture between Job Brothers and company and Unitas Fratrum of London, England, NAC 511, reel 12:015593.
116. General Missions Conference in Nain, 14 Apr. 1904, BC: 57229–300.
117. 2PA 6: 147.
118. Julius Lane had left Killinek to work for the Royal Canadian Mounted Police on the western side of Cape Fullerton, Hudson Bay, but his wife, Clara Lane, and his stepdaughter, Sophie, remained (Report from Kikkertaujak (Killinek): 1 Jan.–1 July 1905, BC: 58237–38; Station Corresp. from Killinek. Dec 1904, HC: R15Kb 171; Report from Kikkertaujak (Killinek): 24 Sept.–31 Dec. 1904, BC: 058229.
119. Report from Kikkertaujak (Killinek): 24 Sept.–31 Dec. 1904, BC: 058229.
120. General Missions Conference, 14 Apr. 1904, BC: 57229–300.
121. Station Corresp. from Killinek, Dec. 1904, HC: R15Kb 171.
122. Low, 1906: 6.
123. Low, 1906: 7.
124. MacGregor, 1906: 17.
125. MacGregor, 1906: 14, 17.
126. MacGregor, 1906: 17.
127. MacGregor, 1906: 17.
128. MacGregor, 1906: 15.
129. MacGregor, 1906: 18.
130. Gordon, 1884: 203.
131. Gordon, 1884: 203.
132. MacGregor, 1906: 18.
133. Bernier, 1909: 62.
134. 2PA 6: 242.
135. Samuel Hutton, 1909, 1912; Whitridge, 2008: 288–309.
136. Letter from W. Grenfell to SFG, 9 Mar. 1909, NAC 511, reel 12:015627.
137. 2PA 5: 617; 2PA 6: 226.
138. Marsh, 1964: 433.
139. 2PA 5: 617.
140. 2PA 7: 195.
141. 2PA 7: 195.

## Chapter 8

1. Letter from Brothers Gericke and Schmidt to the Missions Direktion in Berthelsdorf, 29 Aug. 1904, HC.57745.
2. Letter from Brothers Gericke and Schmidt to the Missions Direktion in Berthelsdorf, 29 Aug. 1904, HC.57745.
3. Journals kept by the HBC agent at Nachvak for the period from April 1898 to September 1904 include references to several people from Aulatsivik and Killinek who visited the post occasionally to trade.
4. About 35 people would have occupied the seven snow houses (illuvigait) reported there by Stecker in the winter of 1900 (2PA 4: 415), but the population gradually dropped as families moved to Killinek. Waldmann noted in the summer of 1902 that the largest family residing at Aulatsivik had already moved to Killinek (Waldmann, "Conference Letter from Rama: Aug 1902," Bethlehem Collection, 57695–96).
5. 2PA 7: 454.
6. 2PA 10: 267.
7. 2PA 10: 267; Station corresp., from Killinek, 20 Aug. 1908, HC: R15Kb 171. Sekepa may have been the son of Tuglavina and Pitsuratsuk because, at the time Tuglavina's family was living at Aulatsivik, Sekepa's mother was reported to have accompanied him on a trade visit to Nachvak (NHBC 11.05.1905). In addition, Tuglavina's third wife, Arnatuk, was reported to have been born at Aulatsivik in 1874 (HSC) and consequently she may have been Onalik's sister.
8. Between 1898 and 1906, the Nachvak HBC agent noted that Onalik and Sekepa had travelled from Eclipse Harbour to trade at the post (NHBC 2.12.1898; NHBC 9.11.1904; NHBC 14.08.1906).
9. One of Onalik's wives may have been a daughter of Kajuasiak because a grandson was given his name. As well, his daughter Koliligak later married a man named Ijaitok who was likely Kajuasiak's grandson, as he adopted that name for his surname when his family eventually was baptized (HCB).
10. Report from Killinek, 1 Jan.–1 July 1905, BC: 58236.
11. Report from Killinek, 1 Jan.–1 July 1905, BC: 58236.
12. Report from Killinek, 1 Jan.–1 July 1905, BC: 58236.
13. KCB. In 1901 and 1902, Onalik and a man named "Annashuk" travelled to trade at Nachvak "from their place" (NHBC 19.09.1902). In 1899, "Annashuk"

accompanied Ikkera, Semigak's son, to the post (NHBC 02.08.1899); previously an "Arnashuk," likely the same person, was reported to have travelled with Paniguniak, another of Semigak's sons, to Nachvak from Komaktorvik (NHBC 29.11.1898). The HBC agent also noted "Arnashuk" was the brother of a man named "Anga," who originated from the Killinek area (NHBC 08.03.1901). These references suggest that "Annashuk/Arnashuk [Arnasuk]" may not have been directly related to either Onalik or Semigak but had a kinship connection of some kind with them to account for his association with the two families.

14. KCB. Since Arnasuk's family was apparently residing in the same vicinity as Semigak's extended family, it seems likely that his wife Serkoak was Nangmartvarsuk's daughter and Arnasuk was the son-in-law mentioned by Waldmann in March 1901 to be living at Komaktorvik with Semigak's "old cast-off wife."
15. KCB.
16. KCB.
17. Kajoe was believed to have been born about 1860 (KCB), which establishes an approximate age for Avigiak, as he was probably a little older than his wife. Avigiak named one of his sons Onalik, indicating a close kinship tie. In addition, Avigiak's eldest son was named Kajuasiak, which suggests that his wife Kajoe may have been Kajuasiak's daughter. Once Avigiak's family settled at Killinek, his eldest daughter Annekordluk married a man named Kupa living in the area, who was apparently related to Kajuasiak. The marriage of the couple may have been the reason for the departure of Avigiak's family from Aulatsivik.
18. Koktok appears to have had a strong kinship relationship with Angutaunek. He named a son Angutaunek, who was born in November 1904 (KCB), soon after the elder Angutaunek's presumed death, which suggests that they were closely related. In addition, one of Koktok's brothers was named Kavanga and had been born in about 1889 (KCB), following the elder Kavanga's death, which further alludes to a close kinship bond with Kavanga's family group.
19. NHBC 07.05.1899; 04.06.1902; 09.01.1906.
20. Report from Killinek, 1 Jan.–1 July 1905, BC: 058236.
21. Killinek Station Report, July 1917–July 1918, HC: F.c.3.b.

22. KCB.
23. Koktok and his brothers appear to correspond with an observation made by Stecker, when he visited Killinek in 1900, that six adult brothers living there, of which four were married, were all sons of Kajuasiak (2PA 4: 416). However, other men are also identified as having lived in the area and one of them adopted the surname Kajuatsiak after he was baptized, which suggests a close kinship relationship with the renowned chief of the Killinek area. In addition, Koktok's only sister was named Pullanersoak (KCB), as was one daughter in a family described to be Kajuasiak's servants in 1884. Koktok's sister, born in about 1894, was likely named after this woman whose family was subordinate to Kajuasiak's household. If Koktok and his brothers were sons of Kajuasiak, rather than related to Kavanga's family group as has been presumed, the discrepancy may be due to different women —Kajuasiak's three wives — being the mothers of the two groups of sons. His wives would have been similar in age to Kavanga, and one of them could have been his sister, which would explain the close association of personal names with Kavanga's kinship group. Furthermore, one of Koktok's brothers, Anga, was also cited to be the brother of Arnasuk, who adopted the name Tobias Kairtok after his baptism. Thus, Arnasuk may have actually been a step-brother and the son of another of Kajuasiak's wives; the origin of the name Kairtok cannot be determined.
24. KCB. The only traditional Inuit personal name that can be broadly associated with this unusual surname is the rendition of a name recorded by the HBC agent at Nachvak from 1868–74 for a man called "Shipanesi/Sjevanca/Sjevanesi." He was active in the Nachvak and Komaktorvik areas and may have been related to Kavanga's extended family group.
25. KCB. Paksau had a wife and a son named Kajuasiak, who was born in 1901 and died in 1906; he may also have been the father of a boy named Ijaitok, who was born in 1898 and as well adopted the surname Kajuatsiak when he was eventually baptized at Hebron in 1933 (see Figure 10). By 1909, Paksau was a widower and three years later he married Tuglavina's daughter, Tigujak (KCB). Paksau had two younger brothers, one of whom, Serlek, was married to a woman named Lucy (or Louisa), with whom he had a daughter named Sara in July 1904. When Serlek and Lucy had marital troubles, she left with Sara for her previous home at Ablorilik [Abloviak] (Report from

Killinek, 1 Jan.–1 July 1905, BC: 058237–38; Station Corresp. from Killinek, 24 Mar, 1906, HC: R15Kb 171; KCB). Paksau's second brother was named Kupa; he was likely the man "Kuber" who Governor MacGregor was told claimed ownership of the Button Islands. Kupa's wife was Avigiak's daughter, Annekordluk, and their first child, a daughter born in July 1904, was named Kajuasiak, which further alludes to a close kinship relationship between Kupa and the senior Kajuasiak. Both Kupa and Serlek died in 1906, after which Annekordluk married one of Koktok's brothers, named Serlek, while Lucy became the second wife of Paujunge, another of Koktok's brothers (Station Report from Killinek, 1 July 1906, HC: R15Kb 171; KCB).

26. Koktok's wife Sapa and Kavanga's wife Paungak were sisters, and their mother Hanna came from George River; Paungak had been divorced from a man living on the Koksoak River (KCB). Serlek's wife Lucy apparently also had a previous husband named Aggaroalsiak and was related to a family living at Ablorilik [Abloviak] (KCB).
27. 2PA 4: 416.
28. 2PA 5: 621.
29. 2PA 5: 621.
30. RCB; 2PA 7: 7.
31. 2PA 5: 621.
32. RCB.
33. 2PA 3: 177; HCB. Her son Kippinguk remained in Nachvak and appears to have lived with Paksaut, Semigak's younger brother.
34. NHBC 4.10.1904; 15.10.1904.
35. NHBC 3.7.1905.
36. 2PA 6: 224–25.
37. Waldmann, the Moravian missionary at Killinek, referred to Paksaut's tempestuous relations with his third wife, Paniguniak, in his station reports from August 1905 to December 1907 (HC: R15Kb 171).
38. Paksaut appears to have left the Killinek area in 1908 and had two wives living with him when he was residing at Nachvak in 1909 (2PA 7: 451).
39. NHBC 16.10.1904.
40. At Killinek, Nangmartvarsuk's daughter Tigujak married a widower also named Paksau and they both became candidates for baptism in January 1912 (KCB).

41. When Paniguniak was baptized, she was described as the widow of Semigak's eldest son (2PA 9: 196), although another sibling named Kudjaijok was also described as his senior son.
42. KCB.
43. Report from Killinek, 1 Jan.–1 July 1905, BC: 58236.
44. Hutton, 1912: 40.
45. Hutton, 1912: 41.
46. Killinek Annual Report, HC: F.c.3.b.
47. KCB.
48. KCB; see Figure 6.
49. Report from Killinek, 1 Jan.–1 July 1905, BC: 58236. Paniguniak had intended to move from Komaktorvik to Nachvak before he died in the influenza epidemic (NHBC 16.11.1904; NHBC 15.09.1904).
50. Station Report from Killinek for 1912, 31 Dec. 1912, BC: 058097.
51. Killinek Annual Report: July 1917–July 1918, HC: Missions Direktion F.c.3.b.
52. HCB.
53. HCB.
54. HCB. A close blood relationship between the families of Kutaktuk and Tuglavina, and their husbands' assumed lineage, is shown in the repetition of personal names associated with Semigak and Tuglavina in different generations.
55. NHBC 10.10.1904.
56. 2PA 6: 219.
57. NHBC 15.03.1904.
58. 2PA 5: 616. "Attatotsoak" was frequently reported in HBC journals dating from 1898 to 1904 to have travelled from Komaktorvik to Nachvak accompanied by men associated with Semigak's family (NHBC).
59. 2PA 6: 504. Attataksoak had intended to take his elderly mother with him to Nain (2PA 5: 616) and he also had a wife, according to the Nachvak HBC agent (NHBC 9.01.1904). However, his wife may have been a victim of the epidemic because only Attataksoak's name was mentioned when his baptism was noted in January 1906 (2PA 6: 504). His mother's connection with Tuglavina's family is indicated by the fact that Tuglavina's third wife, Arnatuk, gave her third son the name Kedlik; since he was born in 1906 (KCB), he was likely named after Attataksoak's mother (see Figure 6).

60. 2PA 6: 225.
61. NHBC 13.07.1904.
62. 2PA 6: 225.
63. 2PA 6: 225; RCB; see Figure 5.
64. RCB.
65. HSC.
66. HSC.
67. NHBC 22.08.1905; 2PA 10: 267. In addition, all three men were usually reported in HBC journals dating from 1898 to 1906 to be travelling to or from Komaktorvik (NHBC).
68. HCB.
69. NHBC 22.06.1906.
70. NHBC 18.07.1901.
71. NHBC 18.07.1904.
72. NHBC 18.02.1905.
73. KCB; HSC.
74. NHBC 11.04.1906.
75. The HBC agent reported the three brothers' movements in the Nachvak and Komaktorvik areas from the fall of 1905 until September 1906 (NHBC 18.09.1905–1.09.1906).
76. NHBC 18.02.1905; 16.05.1906.
77. 2PA 7: 191.
78. 2PA 7: 454.
79. KCB; see Figure 7.
80. RCB.
81. KCB.
82. RCB.
83. KCB.
84. Annual Report from Killinek for 1912, BC: 058097; Station Report from Killinek, July 1917–July 1918, HC: Missions Direktion F.c.S.b.
85. 2PA 9: 196.
86. 2PA 9: 196; see Figure 7.
87. HSC.
88. 2PA 7: 451.
89. 2PA 7: 429.

90. HSC.
91. 2PA 7: 451.
92. HCB.
93. HCB.
94. HSC.
95. 2PA 9: 276.
96. HCB.
97. HCB.
98. The same circumstance was noted in the earlier review of HBC journals from 1868 to 1875.
99. NHBC 06.05.1902. Several months earlier he and "Kogjijook," likely a rendition of the name of Semigak's eldest son Kudjaijok, arrived at the HBC post in George River to trade seal oil (GRHBC 08.09.1901). Kudjaijok usually wintered in the Komaktorvik area while the activities of "Ettigaitook" were reported in HBC journals for the George River post from 1900 to 1907.
100. NHBC 03.05.1904. HBC journals for the George River post make references to "Old Man Emaduluk" from 1930 to 1935 (GRHBC).
101. NHBC 19–23.12.1903.
102. NHBC 19.07.1901.
103. 2PA 5: 373.
104. NEC 05.06.1903.
105. Nicodemus's Christian name would have been given to him by Mr. Guy, the HBC agent at George River, who baptized several Inuit in the area (KCB). A man called "Echluk/Ekalut," whose presence in Nachvak was briefly mentioned in 1902–03, appears to have accompanied Nicodemus or Ananak because his activities were subsequently described in the HBC journal for George River from 1908 to 1911.
106. In April 1900, Nicodemus and his wife stopped briefly in Nachvak on their way from Ramah to Cape Chidley (NHBC 25.04.1900), but the purpose of their journey was not stated.
107. GRHBC 15.10.1901; 7.11.1901.
108. GRHBC 20.05.1902.
109. NHBC 13.02.1903.
110. NHBC 21.01.1903.

111. NHBC 25.03.1903. The purpose of their journey may have been to hunt caribou in the interior since Nicodemus went to Hebron at the same time a year earlier for this reason (NHBC 07.03.1902).
112. Killinek Station Report, 1 July 1906, HC: R15Kb 171.
113. Ford noted in 1903 that Attataksoak had sold a white fox at Ramah, which had been caught in the company's traps (NHBC 05.05.1903). Attataksoak was probably prohibited from borrowing any more equipment, as occurred to Ikkera, who had caught char using company nets but brought a scanty amount of salted fish to the post because he had dried a quantity of it for his winter food supply (NHBC 22.08.1905).
114. NHBC 13.08.1901.
115. NHBC 30.08.1898.
116. NHBC 29.10.1905.
117. NHBC 16.11.1905.
118. NHBC 23.12.1898; 30.12.1898.
119. NHBC 13.05.1901.
120. NHBC 8.9.1906.
121. RSC.
122. 2PA 6: 6656; 7: 198.
123. 2PA 7: 5.
124. 2PA 7: 6.
125. 2PA 7 124.
126. 2PA 7: 6.
127. 2PA 7: 6.
128. Bonesteel, 2006.
129. 2PA 7: 12.
130. 2PA 7: 124.
131. 2PA 7: 124.
132. 2PA 7: 450.
133. 2PA 7: 429.
134. 2PA 5: 621.
135. 2PA 7: 429.
136. HCB.
137. Levi Nochasak, in *Them Days* 5, no. 4 (1977): 16.

## Chapter 9

1. Report from Killinek, 24 Sept.–31 Dec. 1904, BC: 058230.
2. Report from Killinek, 24 Sept.–31 Dec. 1904, BC: 058230.
3. Station Corresp. from Killinek, Aug. 1905, HC: R15Kb 171.
4. Report from Killinek, 1 Jan.–1 July 1905, BC: 58236.
5. Report from Killinek, 1 Jan.–1 July 1905, BC: 58233.
6. Report from Killinek, 1 Jan.–1 July 1905, BC: 58236–37.
7. Report from Killinek, 1 Jan.–1 July 1905, BC: 58236–37.
8. Station Corresp. from Killinek, Oct. 1906, HC: R15Kb 171; KCB.
9. Station Corresp. from Killinek, May 1906, HC: R1SKb 171.
10. Station Report from Killinek, July 1906, HC: R15Kb 171.
11. Annual Report from Killinek, July–31 Dec. 1906, BC: 058064.
12. Station Corresp. from Killinek, Oct. and Dec. 1906, HC: R15Kb 171.
13. Station Report from Killinek, July 1906, HC: R15Kb 171.
14. Annual Report from Killinek, 1 Jan.–1 July 1907, BC: 58069.
15. 2PA 7: 8–9; Killinek Station Report, 1 July–31 Dec. 1907, HC: R15Kb 171; BC: 058072–73.
16. 2PA 7: 8–9; Killinek Station Report, July–Dec. 1906, BC: 058064.
17. 2PA 7: 190.
18. 2PA 7: 191.
19. Killinek Station Report, 1 July–31 Dec. 1908, BC: 058077.
20. Killinek Station Report, 1 July–31 Dec. 1908, BC: 058077.
21. 2PA 8: 188.
22. Station Corresp. from Killinek, Dec. 1906, HC: R15Kb 171.
23. Station Corresp. from Killinek, May 1906, HC R15Kb 171.
24. KCB.
25. Annual Report from Killinek, 1 July–31 Dec. 1906, BC: 58065.
26. Annual Report from Killinek, 1 July–31 Dec. 1906, BC: 58065; Station Corresp. from Killinek, Mar. 1906, HC: R15Kb 171.
27. KCB.
28. See Station Corresp. from Killinek, July 1906, HC: R15Kb 171.
29. Station Corresp. from Killinek, Aug. 1905, HC: R15Kb 171.
30. KCB.
31. Report from Killinek, 1 Jan.–1 July 1905, BC: 58234.
32. 2PA 7: 8; Station Corresp. from Killinek, Mar. 1906, HC: R15Kb 171.

33. 2PA 6: 436; Killinek Annual Report, 1 July 1909–30 June 1910, HC: Missions Direktion F.c.3.b.
34. Bernier, 1909: 65.
35. Bernier, 1909: 65.
36. Bernier, 1909: 66.
37. Bernier, 1909: 65.
38. 2PA 8: 413.
39. 2PA 8: 413.
40. HCB.
41. Station Corresp. from Killinek, Aug. 1908, HC: R15Kb 171.
42. Killinek Annual Reports, 1 July 1909–30 June 1911, HC: Missions Direktion F.c.S.b.
43. Killinek Annual Reports, 1 July 1909–30 June 1911, HC: Missions Direktion F.c.S.b.
44. Station Corresp. from Killinek, May 1906, HC: R15Kb 171.
45. MacGregor, 1906: 15–16.
46. MacGregor, 1906: 59.
47. Station Corresp. from Killinek, May 1906, HC: R15Kb 171.
48. Station Corresp. from Killinek, July 1906, HC: R15Kb 171.
49. Station Corresp. from Killinek, July 1906, HC: R15Kb 171.
50. 2PA 10: 265.
51. Ames, 1986: 96.
52. Ames, 1986.
53. Killinek Annual Report, 1 July 1909–30 June 1910, HC: Missions Direktion F.c.3.b.
54. 2PA 9: 277.
55. Killinek Annual Report, 1 June 1912–20 Jan. 1913, HC: Missions Direktion F.c.S.b; Annual Report for 1912, Dec. 1912, BC: 58100.
56. Killinek Annual Report, 1 June 1912–30 Jan. 1913; 1 July 1914–30 June 1915, HC: Missions Direktion F.c.3.b.
57. Killinek Annual Report, 1 July 1913–30 June 1914, BC: 58116, 58123–24; KCB.
58. KCB; Killinek Annual Report, 1 July 1914–30 June 1915, HC: Missions Direktion F.c.3.b.
59. Killinek Annual Report, 1 July 1914–30 June 1915, HC: Missions Direktion F.c.3.b.

60. Killinek Annual Report, 1 July 1914–30 June 1915, HC: Missions Direktion F.c.3.b.
61. Killinek Annual Report, 1 July 1914–30 June 1915, HC: Missions Direktion F.c.3.b.
62. Annual Report from Killinek, 1 July 1913–30 June 1914, BC: 58124.
63. Annual Report from Killinek, 1 July 1913–30 June 1914, BC: 58124.
64. Killinek Annual Report, 1 June 1912–30 Jan. 1913, HC: Missions Direktion F.c.3.b; SFG Minutes, Vol. 12, 14 Jan. 1914.
65. SFG Minutes, Vol.12, 16 Jan. 1916.
66. Killinek Annual Report, 1 July–31 Dec. 1913, BC: 58113–14.
67. Killinek Annual Report, 1 July–31 Dec. 1913, BC: 58113–14.
68. 2PA 6: 90.
69. Killinek Annual Report, 1 July 1915–30 June 1916, HC: Missions Direktion F.c.S.b.
70. Killinek Annual Report, 1 July 1914–30 June 1915, HC: Missions Direktion F.c.3.b.
71. Killinek Annual Report, 1 July 1915–30 June 1916, HC: Missions Direction F.c.3.b.
72. 2PA 10: 360, 405–06.
73. Corresp. from Killinek, 28 Dec. 1911, BC: 58055–143; Killinek Annual Report, 1 July 1911–30 June 1912, HC: Missions Direktion F.c.3.b.
74. Leechman, 1950: 152.
75. Killinek Annual Report for 1912, BC: 58099.
76. Killinek Annual Report for 1912, BC: 58099.
77. Killinek Annual Report for 1912, BC: 58099.
78. Annual Report from Killinek, 1 July 1913–30 June 1914, BC: 58123–24.
79. Caldwell, in Morantz, 2016: 110.
80. Caldwell, in Morantz, 2016: 110.
81. Caldwell, in Morantz, 2016: 110; Selma Voisey Ford and Leonard Budgell interview, F513, Them Days Archive.
82. Ames, 1986: 53.
83. Sam Lyall 1977, F027 Sam and Bella Lyall interview, Them Days Archive.
84. Lyall, 2011: 28–31.
85. Conference Letter from Killinek to London, 1910, BC: 058045.
86. Killinek Annual Report for 1912, BC: 58099.

87. Morantz, 2016: 110.
88. Joseph Townley had replaced Karl Filschke, who had been deported to London with his family in 1916 on suspicion of being a German sympathizer in the war (Bassler, 2006: 157).
89. Killinek Annual Report, July 1917–July 1918, HC: Missions Direktion F.c.S.b.
90. Killinek Annual Report, July 1917–July 1918, HC: Missions Direktion F.c.S.b.
91. SFG Minutes, Vol. 12, 19 Jan. 1917.
92. Killinek Annual Report, July 1916–July 1917, HC: Missions Direktion F.c.3.b.
93. MacGregor, 1906: 15; Bernier, 1909: 62.
94. SFG Minutes, Vol. 12, 16 Nov. 1917.
95. SFG Minutes, Vol. 12, 16 Nov. 1917.
96. KCB.
97. Noah Angnatuk, in Avataq Cultural Centre, 1988: 20, 22.
98. SFG Minutes, Vol. 12, 16 Nov. 1917.
99. SFG Minutes, Vol. 12, 16 Nov. 1917; 2PA 10: 398.
100. 2PA 10: 396.
101. 2PA 10: 398
102. 2PA 10: 399.
103. Budgell, 2018.
104. Budgell, 2018.
105. Budgell, 2018.
106. 2PA 10: 351–52, 398.
107. 2PA 10: 398–99.
108. 2PA 10: 490; HSC.
109. HSC.
110. 2PA 10: 490–91; 11: 88.
111. 2PA 10: 490.
112. 2PA 11: 82, 322.
113. 2PA 11: 151–52, 216–17.
114. Conference letter from Killinek, 1921/2, BC: 58052.
115. Conference letter from Killinek, 1921/2, BC: 58052.
116. Conference letter from Killinek, 1921/2, BC: 58053.
117. 2PA 11: 330; KCB.
118. 2PA 11: 155.
119. Morantz, 2016: 145.

120. SFG Minutes, Vol. 12, 14 Oct. 1921, 15 Nov. 1921; Hiller, 1995: 7.
121. PBHBC 16.03.1921.
122. PBHBC 27.01.1921.
123. PBHBC 26.01.1921; 14.03.1921.
124. 2PA 11: 229.
125. Brice-Bennett, 1981; Evans, 2013; Whitridge, 2008.
126. Anonymous, 1833: 103.
127. Brice-Bennett, 1981; Whitridge, 2008; Cabak, 1991.
128. 2PA 7: 193–94; 8: 444; Hutton, 1909, 1912.
129. Conference letters from Killinek, 1910, BC. The mission stores reduced the mark-up on building materials to 25 per cent.
130. 2PA 11: 229.
131. 2PA 11: 229.
132. 2PA 11: 229.
133. 2PA 11: 229–30.
134. 2PA 11: 229.
135. 2PA 11: 332.
136. Conference letters from Killinek, Aug. 1923, BC.
137. Conference letters from Killinek, Aug. 1923, BC.
138. Conference letters from Killinek, Aug. 1923, BC.
139. Conference letters from Hebron, Feb. 1924, BC.
140. Conference letters from Hebron, Feb. 1924, BC; 2PA 11: 334.
141. PBHBC.
142. Interview by Boas and Mary Millie, 1975, in Brice-Bennett, 2017: 107.
143. Conference letters from Hebron, Oct. 1924, BC.
144. 2PA 12: 15.
145. HSC; see Table 8.
146. Noah Angnatuk in Avataq Cultural Centre, 1988: 22.
147. KCB.
148. 2PA 10: 490.
149. SFG Minutes, Vol. 12, 5 Apr. 1921.
150. Waldmann to Hennig, Hebron, 19 Oct. 1924, Conference letters from Killinek, BC: 58040–54.
151. 2PA 12: 159.
152. Hiller, 1977: 91.

153. 2PA 12: 159.
154. See Brice-Bennett, 1994.
155. Jacko Kajuatsiak, 1977, F296 interview, Them Days Archive.
156. Emma Kajuatsiak, 1977, *Them Days* 6, no. 2: 45.
157. William Onalik, 1977, F294 interview, Them Days Archive.
158. Klain and Levesque, 2019: 123–51.

## Chapter 10

1. 2PA 144: 80–81; Kleivan, 1966: 130.
2. 2PA 137: 330; Kleivan, 1966: 130–31.
3. 2PA 144: 80–81; Kleivan, 1966: 130.
4. Morantz, 2016: 135.
5. Morantz, 2016: 135. Revillon Frères sold its remaining interest to the HBC in 1936.
6. Morantz, 2016: 136; Killinek Annual Report, 1 July 1914–30 June 1915, HC: Missions Direktion F.c.3.b.
7. Morantz, 2016: 113.
8. Morantz, 2016: 136–37.
9. Morantz, 2016: 136–37.
10. 2PA 142: 87.
11. 2PA 146: 103; Kleivan, 1966: 130.
12. Kleivan, 1966: 130; 2PA 144: 86.
13. See Brice-Bennett, 1986: 10–11.
14. 2PA 136: 248.
15. 2PA 136: 249.
16. 2PA 138: 419.
17. 2PA 142: 90–91; HSC.
18. 2PA 137: 330.
19. Augusta Jararuse in Brice-Bennett, 2017: 31.
20. Clara Ford, in Brice-Bennett, 2017: 39.
21. 2PA 141: 259; 2PA 145: 101.
22. PBHBC 24.07.1932.
23. Sabina Nochasak, in Brice-Bennett, 2017: 32.
24. Dick Kairtok, in Brice-Bennett, 2017: 32.
25. Augusta Erving, in Brice-Bennett, 2017: 32.

26. PA 147 (1939): 121.
27. Brice-Bennett, 2017: 19.
28. Boas Jararuse, in Brice-Bennett, 2017: 33.
29. Sophie Lampe, in Brice-Bennett, 2017: 33.
30. Tivi Etok, the son of Adam Ukuatsiajuaq, describes how the family's name was changed: "My father was Aatami and my mother was Sarah. Actually Father's last name was Ukuatsiajuaq, Aatami Ukuatsiajuaq. All our family should really be called Ukuatsiajuaq, but our surname was changed to Ittuk. It made it difficult to keep our identity as a clan. Ittuk was not what we were called when I was growing up. Wherever we travelled we were known as the Ukuatsiajuaq family. Then the surname of my part of the family was changed to Ittuk. Now it seems that we are two clans, the Ukuatsiaq and the Etok, when in fact we are not" (Etok, 2008).
31. GRHBC 20.08.1931.
32. GRHBC 02.03.1933.
33. GRHBC 24.03.1934.
34. Morantz, 2016: 73.
35. GRHBC 24.03.1934.
36. GRHBC 21.05.1934.
37. Etok, 2008: 187.
38. GRHBC 21.05.1934.
39. PBHBC 10.07.1934.
40. GRHBC 21.05.1934.
41. GRHBC 21.05.1934.
42. GRHBC 21.05.1934.
43. GRHBC 21.05.1934.
44. GRHBC 27.02.1935.
45. Etok, 2008: 165–67, 170–71.
46. 2PA 144: 89.
47. 2PA 144: 89.
48. 2PA 144: 89.
49. Morantz, 2016: 115; Hiller, 1995: 9.
50. PBHBC 24.01.1939.
51. PBHBC 24.01.1939.
52. Ames, 1986: 137.

53. Boas Jararuse, M33 G2 Hebron Relocation interviews, Brice-Bennett Collection, Labrador Institute Archive.
54. Noah Angnatuk, in Avataq Cultural Centre, 1988: 24.
55. Jenness, 1965: 69.
56. 2PA 152: 46.
57. 2PA 152: 46.
58. 2PA 152: 46.
59. 2PA 152: 46.
60. HSC.
61. 2PA 152: 46.
62. Ames, 1986: 137.
63. 2PA 153: 52; HSC.
64. 2PA 153: 52.
65. Morantz, 2016: 146.
66. Rockwood memorandum to Chief Ranger, 4 Apr. 1945, PANL, GN 3/B, NLH1.
67. Rockwood memorandum to Chief Ranger, 4 Apr. 1945, PANL, GN 3/B, NLH1.
68. Rockwood memorandum to Chief Ranger, 4 Apr. 1945, PANL, GN 3/B, NLH1.
69. Rockwood memorandum to Chief Ranger, 4 Apr. 1945, PANL, GN 3/B, NLH1.
70. Rockwood memorandum to Chief Ranger, 4 Apr. 1945, PANL, GN 3/B, NLH1.
71. Letter from Rockwood to J. Ford, 3 Apr. 1945, PANL, GN 31,3/B, NLH1 (emphasis in original).
72. Letter from Rockwood to J. Ford, 3 Apr. 1945, PANL, GN 31,3/B, NLH1.
73. Letter from Rockwood to J. Ford, 3 Apr. 1945, PANL, GN 31,3/B, NLH1 (emphasis in original).
74. Rockwood memorandum to Chief Ranger, 4 Apr. 1945, PANL, GN 31,3/B, NLH1.
75. HSC.
76. HSC.
77. Ames, 1986.
78. Ames, 1986: 28.
79. Ames, 1986: 61, 69.
80. Ames, 1986: 63, 64, Figure 4-1, 69.
81. Ames, 1986: 70.
82. Ames, 1986: 67, 66, Figure 4-3.
83. Ames, 1986: 67, 66.

84. Ames, 1986: 67.
85. Ames, 1986: 67.
86. Ames, 1986: 65, Figure 4-2, 69, 106.
87. Ames, 1986: 62, 137.
88. Damas, 2004: 36. The Hudson's Bay Company had also relocated Inuit from Port Burwell to Southampton Island in 1925, a year after establishing a trading post at Coral Harbour (Marcus, 1995: 48).
89. Morantz, 2016: 147; Mesher, 1995.
90. Findlay, 1955: 95, 225.
91. Etok, 2008: 171.
92. Dunbar, 1952: 14.
93. Findlay, 1955: 225.
94. Arbess, 1966: 14.
95. Findlay, 1955: 186.
96. Etok, 2008: 194.
97. Morantz, 2016: 115.
98. Ames, 1986: 138–39, 143.
99. Ames, 1986: 143–44.
100. Ames, 1986: 146–49.
101. 2PA 159: 29; HSC.
102. 2PA 160: 38.

## Chapter 11

1. Brice-Bennett, 2017: 91.
2. Anthony Paddon, "Community Aspects of Health and Welfare in Northern Labrador," 27 Feb. 1955, memorandum sent to Dr. F.W. Rowe, 77.1.01.022 F.W. Rowe Collection, Centre for Newfoundland Studies Archive, Memorial University, p. 2.
3. Brice-Bennett, 2017: 21–22.
4. Dr. F. Rowe to Dr. H.L. Pottle [Minister of Public Welfare], 8 Mar. 1955, 77.1.01.022 F.W. Rowe Collection, Centre for Newfoundland Studies Archive, Memorial University.
5. Charles Curtis to Dr. Leonard Miller [Nfld. Deputy Minister of Health], 23 Aug. 1955, 077.1.01.022 F.W. Rowe Collection, Centre for Newfoundland Studies Archive, Memorial University.

6. Rev. Peacock to Walter Rockwood, 20 Sept. 1955, MG 908, Rockwood Collection, PANL.
7. See Brice-Bennett, 1994; Brice-Bennett, 2017: 22–72.
8. "Special Problems Affecting Eskimo Citizens," Labrador Conference, 13–16 Feb. 1956, Chairperson Dr. F.W. Rowe, St. John's: Government of Newfoundland, p. 19.
9. Tom Uvloriak, 1999, in Evans, 2012: 103.
10. As outlined in the 1954 Newfoundland–Canada funding agreement, the federal government agreed to pay two-thirds of expenses related to Inuit housing in northern Labrador (Brice-Bennett, 2017: 92–93).
11. Susie Onalik, 1999, in Evans, 2012: 103.
12. F. Cunningham, 1956, in Evans, 2012: 101.
13. Rev. Peacock to Walter Rockwood, 20 Sept. 1955, MG 908, Rockwood Collection, PANL.
14. Evans, 2012: 104.
15. Levi Nochasak, William Millie, Hebron Elders to Dr. F.W. Rowe, Acting Minister of Public Welfare, "Petition of the Hebron People to Government in St. John's," 9 Aug. 1956, translation by Rita Andersen, in Brice-Bennett, 2017: 98.
16. Levi Nochasak, William Millie, Hebron Elders to Dr. F.W. Rowe, Minister of Public Welfare, "Petition of the Hebron People to Government in St. John's," 9 Aug. 1956, translation by Siegfried Hettasch, in Brice-Bennett, 2017: 70.
17. Walter Rockwood, 1958, in Evans, 2012: 105.
18. Walter Rockwood, 1958, in Evans, 2012: 105.
19. R.L. Andrews, 1956, in Brice-Bennett, 2017: 73.
20. R.L. Andrews, 1956, in Evans, 2012: 105.
21. Paddon, 1957, in Evans, 2012: 106.
22. Peacock, 1957, in Evans, 2012: 106.
23. S.J. Hefferton, 1958, in Brice-Bennett, 2017: 78.
24. Boas Jararuse, in Brice-Bennett, 2017: 100.
25. Sabina Nochasak, in Brice-Bennett, 2017: 100, 101.
26. Brice-Bennett, 2017: 96.
27. Jako Semigak, in Brice-Bennett, 2017: 107.
28. Sophie Lampe, in Brice-Bennett, 2017: 104.
29. Brice-Bennett, 2000.
30. John Jararuse, in Brice-Bennett, 2017: 110.

31. Sophie Lampe, in Brice-Bennett, 2017: 110.
32. Brice-Bennett, 2017. An Elders council at Nain, consisting of elected representatives from the community, customarily regulated the social order and economic well-being of local inhabitants, and controlled residence by requiring people to apply for permission before moving to the community. This rule enabled the Elders to monitor the character of prospective residents and ensured compliance to their authority, as they also sanctioned and sometimes expelled unruly members (see Brice-Bennett, 1977: 165–66; Brody, 1977: 328). Although the relocation program ignored the established procedure for the entrance of new residents at Nain, several people from Nutâk and Hebron nevertheless sought the endorsement of the Elders after they were moved to the community and agreed to comply with their rules. A notebook kept by the council records the signatures of nine household heads from October 1958 to October 1965; the document is still in the possession of Nain Elders. Three of the households had Ungava Bay ancestry, with two families moving to Nain from Nutâk, including Peter and Agnes Imak, and Josiah and Lilly Itulak along with a single female relative named Basa [Pasha] Imak; the third family, consisting of Elizabeth Anatuk and her son Tommy, came from Kuujjuaq. Other families from Hebron whose signatures appear were Solomon and Sophia Kajuatsiak, William Millie, Ida Millie, Jako and Augusta Obed, Nicodemus Menzel, and Julius and Henrietta Basto. Their application for formal acceptance by the Elders indicates a respect for Inuit convention at Nain; other families may not have sought the Elders' approval because they had not voluntarily chosen to reside in the community.
33. For a full examination of the Hebron and Nutâk relocations, see Brice-Bennett, 2017; Evans, 2013.
34. Ben-Dor, 1966; Kennedy, 1985.
35. See Brice-Bennett, 1994: 104–05; OKalaKâtiget Society, 1987.
36. Menzel, in Brice-Bennett, 2017: 121.
37. Onalik, in Brice-Bennett, 2017: 116.
38. Morantz, 2016.
39. Marcus, 1995: 48.
40. Marcus, 1995: 48.
41. Tester and Kulchyski, 1994: 312.
42. Marcus, 1995.

43. Tester and Kulchyski, 1994: 220.
44. Marcus, 1995; Tester and Kulchyski, 1994.
45. Marcus, 1995: 50.
46. Government of Canada, Statement of Apology for the Relocation of the Ahiarmiut, 22 Jan. 2019, https://www.rcaanc-cirnac.gc.ca/eng/1548170252259/1548170273272
47. Damas, 2004: 36; Marcus, 1995: 48.
48. Tester and Kulchyski, 1994: 319.
49. Dunbar, 1952.
50. Dunbar, 1952: 7; Snowden, 1961: 384.
51. Siegfried Hettasch, letter addressed to Brethren, 9 Apr. 1958, in Brice-Bennett, 2017: 76.
52. Brice-Bennett, 2017: 95–96.
53. Memo to Deputy Minister of Public Welfare, Re: Hebron, 5 June 1959, Box 1, File 4, MG 908, Rockwood Collection, PANL.
54. Memo to Deputy Minister of Public Welfare, Re: Hebron, 5 June 1959, Box 1, File 4, MG 908, Rockwood Collection, PANL.
55. See Brice-Bennett, 2017: 56, 71.
56. D. Snowden, Memorandum for the Director, 4 Nov. 1959, NAC, RG 85, Vol. 383, file 251-8/314 part 2; D.F. Symington, Memorandum for the Chief, Industrial Division, 19 Jan. 1960, NAC, RG 85, Vol. 383, file 251-8/314 part 2.
57. Max Budgell, Memorandum for Administrator of the Arctic, 20 May 1961, NAC, RG 85, Vol. 1953, file A1000/315 part 1.
58. Budgell, Memorandum for Administrator of the Arctic, 20 May 1961: 7; R.A. Hodgkinson, Memorandum for the Chief, Arctic Division, 14 Aug. 1958, NAC, RG 85, Vol. 1353, file 1000/315 part 7.
59. Dunbar, 1952: 12.
60. RCMP Report, 15 May 1958, NAC, RG 85, Vol. 1353, file 1000/315 part 7.
61. RCMP Report, 15 May 1958.
62. Donald Snowden, Memorandum for the Director, 20 Apr. 1959, NAC, RG 85, Vol. 1449, file 1000/315 part 8.
63. R.A. Hodgkinson, Memorandum for C.M. Bolger, 23 Apr. 1959, NAC, RG 85, Vol. 1449, file 1000/315 part 8.
64. J.G. Walton, Memorandum to B.G. Sivertz, 15 Oct. 1956, NAC, RG 85, Vol. 1270, file 1000/315 part 6.

65. J.G. Walton memorandum to B.G. Sivertz, 4 Apr. 1956, NAC, RG 85, Vol. 1070, file 251-4 part 2.
66. Memorandum for Mr. Walton from B.G. Sivertz, 26 Apr. 1956, NAC, RG 85, Vol. 1070, file 251-4 part 2.
67. Morantz, 2016: 186–87; Bonnière, 1964. Donald Snowden later chaired the Royal Commission on Labrador in 1974, paying close attention to the impacts of the Labrador relocations (Royal Commission on Labrador, 1974).
68. R.A. Hodgkinson, Memorandum for the Chief, Arctic Division, 14 Aug. 1958, NAC, RG 85, Vol. 1353, file 1000/315 part 7.
69. Hodgkinson, Memorandum for the Chief, Arctic Division, 14 Aug. 1958; W.G. Kerr, Memorandum to Mr. Symington, 28 Aug. 1958, NAC, RG 85, Vol. 1353, file 1000/315 part 7.
70. Henry Annatuk, First Conference on Arctic Co-operatives, Frobisher Bay [Iqaluit], NWT, 12–18 Mar. 1963, in Avataq Cultural Centre, 1988: 28.
71. V.F. Valentine, Memorandum for the Advisory Committee on Northern Development, 9 Dec. 1959, NAC, RG 22, Vol. 969, file 99-2-269 part 1.
72. W.G. Kerr, Memorandum to Chief of the Industrial Division, 30 Sept. 1959, NAC, RG 85, Vol. 365, file 251-8/314 part 1.
73. Snowden, 1961: 383.
74. W.G. Kerr, Memorandum to Donald Snowden, 30 Sept. 1959, NAC, RG 85, Vol. 365, file 251-8/314 part 1.
75. R.A. Hodgkinson, Memorandum to C.M. Bolger, 3 Oct. 1959, NAC, RG 85, Vol. 365, file 251-8 part 1; D. Snowden, Memorandum for the Director, 4 Nov. 1959, NAC, RG 85, Vol. 383, file 251-8/314 part 2.
76. D.F. Symington, Memorandum for the Chief, Industrial Division, 19 Jan. 1960, NAC, RG 85, Vol. 383, file 251-8/314 part 2.
77. Symington, Memorandum for the Chief, Industrial Division, 19 Jan. 1960.
78. S.A.H. Dodds, Memorandum for Administrator of the Arctic, 9 Aug. 1960, NAC, RG 85, Vol. 1382, file 1012-13 part 5.
79. D. Snowden, Memorandum for the Director, 2 May 1960, NAC, RG 85, Vol. 383, file 251-8/314 part 2.
80. Etok, 2008, 171.
81. Snowden, Memorandum for the Director, 2 May 1960.
82. Max Budgell, Memorandum for Administrator of the Arctic, 20 May 1961, NAC, RG 85, Vol. 1953, file A1000/315 part 1.

83. Budgell, Memorandum for Administrator of the Arctic, 20 May 1961.
84. S.A.H. Dodds, telegram to Headquarters, 31 Aug. 1960, NAC, RG 85, Vol. 383, file 251-8/314 part 2.
85. Dodds, telegram to Headquarters, 31 Aug. 1960.
86. Dodds, telegram to Headquarters, 31 Aug. 1960.
87. D.F. Symington, Memorandum for the Chief, Industrial Division, 19 Jan. 1960, NAC, RG 85, Vol. 383, file 251-8/314 part 2.
88. Max Budgell, Report on resource development, 18 Dec. 1961, NAC, RG 05, Vol. 519, file 251-8/314 part 3.
89. J. Evans, Memorandum for Mr. Snowden, 26 Apr. 1962, NAC, RG 22, Vol. 969, file 99-2-269 part 1.
90. Evans, Memorandum for Mr. Snowden, 26 Apr. 1962.
91. Evans, Memorandum for Mr. Snowden, 26 Apr. 1962.
92. *Northern Star*, 28 Apr. 1962, NAC, RG 85, Vol. 1953, file A1000/315 part 2.
93. Iglauer, 1962 [2000]): 91.
94. Jararuse, 1999: 44.
95. Ames, 1986: 58; J.B.H. Gunn, Report to Commissioner S.M. Hodgson, 9 Feb. 1971, NAC, RG 22, Vol. 950, file 83-7-5 vol. 20.
96. Riches, 1971.
97. Keelan, 2019: 15.
98. Keelan, 2019: 18.
99. Ames, 1986: 159.
100. Val, 1976: 121–23.
101. Ames, 1986: 157.
102. J.B.H. Gunn, Report to Commissioner S.M. Hodgson, 9 Feb. 1971, NAC, RG 22, Vol. 950, file 83-7-5 vol. 20.
103. Gunn, Report to Commissioner Hodgson, 9 Feb. 1971.
104. Gunn, Report to Commissioner Hodgson, 9 Feb. 1971.
105. Gunn, Report to Commissioner Hodgson, 9 Feb. 1971.
106. Gunn, Report to Commissioner Hodgson, 9 Feb. 1971.
107. Gunn, Report to Commissioner Hodgson, 9 Feb. 1971.
108. Cited in Ames, 1986: 58.
109. Makivik, 1987b: 4.
110. Resolution passed by the Community Council of Port Burwell, 8 Mar. 1978, Fort Chimo: private collection.

111. Keelan, 2019: 49.
112. Resolution passed by the Community Council of Port Burwell, 8 Mar. 1978; Minutes of a meeting between the Working Group on Port Burwell and representatives of the Northern Quebec Inuit Association and former residents of Port Burwell, 7 June 1978: private collection.
113. Keelan, 2019: 51–52.
114. Keelan, 2019: 52.
115. Minutes of a meeting between the Working Group on Port Burwell and representatives of the Northern Quebec Inuit Association; Dawson, 1984: 46.
116. Dawson, 1984: 42.
117. Ames, 1986: 59.
118. Makivik, 1987b: 4.
119. Minutes of a meeting between the Working Group on Port Burwell and representatives of the Northern Quebec Inuit Association.
120. Avataq, 1988: 8–9.
121. Makivik, 1987b.
122. Keelan, 2019: 63.
123. Barret, 1994; Makivik, 1987b; Makivik, n.d.: 40.
124. Keelan, 2019: 125.
125. Ames, 1986: 59.
126. Brice-Bennett, 2017: 3.
127. Brice-Bennett, 2017: 145. After 1960, a few families originating from Okkak and Hebron decided to return to the Okkak area permanently, visiting Nain periodically to obtain supplies. The last family living year-round in the region finally moved to Nain in 1984.
128. One man, Sem Nochasak, made extensive use of the northern coast. He had been born in Ramah in 1954, grew up in Makkovik, and travelled north to hunt seals and fish char in the late 1960s. In 1979, while living in Nain, he travelled to Killinek and the Button Islands for three months to hunt seals (Ames, 1986: 154).
129. Brice-Bennett, 1977: 189–94; Brice-Bennett, 2017: 146–47.
130. Brice-Bennett, 2017: 147.
131. Tony Williamson, in Brice-Bennett, 2017: 195.
132. Benjamin Jararuse, in Jararuse, 1999: 44.
133. Pigott, 1999: 57.

134. Pigott, 1999: 56.
135. Pigott, 1999: 56.
136. Brice-Bennett, 2000: 13.
137. Sophie Tuglavina, in Brice-Bennett, 2000: 87.
138. Boas Jararuse, M33 G2, Hebron Relocation Interviews, Brice-Bennett Collection, Labrador Institute Archive.
139. Royal Commission on Labrador, 1974, Vol. 6: 1211–12.
140. Tanner, 1998: 248.
141. Brice-Bennett, 2017.
142. Department of Indian and Northern Affairs, 1996: 396.
143. Department of Indian and Northern Affairs, 1996: 480.
144. "Going Home," *kinatuinamot illengajuk* (Fall 1999): 50.
145. Government of Newfoundland and Labrador, press release, 22 Jan. 2005: https://www.releases.gov.nl.ca/releases/2005/exec/0122n03.htm
146. Lemelin et al., 2016.
147. Stopp, 2017.
148. Many leaders in Nunatsiavut are descendants of Avanimiut families, including past and present political leaders: Roxanne Barbour, John Jararuse, Johannes Lampe, Julius Merkuratsuk, Henoche Obed, Natan Obed, Susan Onalik, Andrea Webb; past and present leaders in preserving the Inuktitut language: Rita Andersen, Louisa Flowers, Bertha Holeiter, Selma Jararuse, Wilson Jararuse, William Kalleo, Josephine Kalleo, Simeonie Merkuratsuk, Gordon Obed, Amos Onalik, Gus Semigak, Silpa Suarak, Sarah Townley, Sophie Tuglavina, Katie Winters; and past and present leaders in maintaining and teaching traditional skills and knowledge: Joey Angnatok, Clara Ford, William Ikkusek, Simon Kohlmeister, Rutie Lampe, Boonie Merkuratsuk, Buddy Merkuratsuk, Eli Merkuratsuk, Jako Merkuratsuk Jr., Jako Merkuratsuk Sr., Maria Merkuratsuk, Minnie Merkuratsuk, Levi Nochasak, Noah Nochasak, Joshua Obed, Karrie Obed, Joas Onalik, Lena Onalik, Susie Onalik, Andrew Piercy, Regina Saimat, Sue Webb, Nellie Winters, and Jessie Wyatt. This is not an exclusive list – many other Avanimiut descendants are leaders in their communities.

# BIBLIOGRAPHY

## Unpublished Sources

Daniel. 1867. Daniel's Bericht von ihrer Reise nach Norden 1867 [Daniel's report of his journey to the north 1867]. Moravian Archives: Herrnhut Collection, R15Ka No. 217h.

Haven, Jens. 1773a. Extract of the Voyage of the Sloop George from Nain to reconnoitre the Northern part of the Labradore in the month of Aug. & Sept. 1773. Moravian Archives: Muswell Hill Collection, London. MF 513, Reel 5, pp. 64–99.

Haven, Jens. 1773b. Kurze Nachricht von denen nach Norden von Nagvak an, bis an die Hudsons-Straight liegenden Wohnplätzen der Eskimos, ihrer Lage u[nd] Nahrung. Moravian Archives: Herrnhut Collection, R.15.K.a.No.11, pp. 190–204.

Haven, Jens. 1773c. A brief account of the dwelling places of the Eskimaux to the north of Nagvack to Hudsons Straits, their situation and subsistence. Moravian Archives: Muswell Hill Collection, London. CNS, MF 513, Reel 5, pp. 101–10.

Kohlmeister, Benjamin. 1814. Kurze Anmerkungen von einer Besuchs-Reise auf einiger der von Okkak nördlich liegenden Wohnplätze der Eskimos mit Capt. Fraser in Begleitung der Brr. Kohlmeister u[nd] Stuermann vom 4. bis 18. Aug. 1814. [Brief Remarks about a Visitation Journey of Some Dwelling Places of the Inuit North of Okkak, with Capt. Fraser, in the Company of Brethren Kohlmeister and Stuermann from 4–18 Aug. 1814]. Moravian Archives: Herrnhut Collection, R15.Ka. No. 26, pp. 137–40.

Lister, Christian. 1775. Br. Listers Bericht von seiner Reise nach Norden vom 19t. Aug. bis 12t. Septbr. 1775. [Bro. Lister's Report of his Travel to the North, from 19 Aug. to 12 Sept. 1775]. Moravian Archives: Bethlehem Collection, fol. 013275-013284.

Martin, C.A. 1898. Bericht von der Labrador mission zur Synode 1899. [Report on the Labrador Mission for the 1899 Synod]. Moravian Archives: Bethlehem Collection, fol. 010866-010896.

Martin, C.A. 1909. Bericht über die Untersuchungsreise nach Killinek. [Report about the exploration journey to Killinek]. Moravian Archives: Bethlehem Collection, fol. 013572-5.

Society for the Furtherance of the Gospel (SFG). Minutes of meetings held by the Executive Committee. Moravian Archives: Muswell Hill Collection, London. Copies on microfilm at the Centre for Newfoundland Studies, Memorial University of Newfoundland, St. John's. 5 Reels.

Weitz, Samuel. 1868. Kurzes Tagebuch über die Reise nach Nachvak. [Brief journal of the journey to Nachvak]. Moravian Archives: Herrnhut Collection R15Ka No. 27h; also Bethlehem Collection, fol. 013521-56.

## Published Sources, Reports, and Articles

Alia, Valerie. 2007. *Names and Nunavut: Culture and Identity in the Inuit Homeland.* New York: Berghahn Books.

Ames, Randy. 1986. *Labrador Inuit Land and Resource Use and Occupancy in the Killinek Region.* Confidential report prepared for the Labrador Inuit Association.

Andersen, August, William Kalleo, and Beatrice Watts, eds. 2007. *Labradorimi Ulinnaisigutet: An Inuktitut–English Dictionary of Northern Labrador Dialect.* Nain, NL: Torngâsok Cultural Centre.

Andersen, Catharyn, and Alana Johns. 2005. "Labrador Inuttitut: Speaking into the Future." *Études/Inuit/Studies* 29, nos. 1–2: 187–205.

Anonymous. 1833. *The Moravians in Labrador.* Edinburgh: J. Ritchie.

Arbess, Saul. 1966. *Social Change and the Eskimo Co-operative at George River, Quebec.* Ottawa: Department of Northern Affairs and National Resources.

Ashe. E.D., RN. 1860. "The Late Eclipse. Journal of a Voyage from New York to Labrador." Paper read on 24 Oct. 1860. 16 pp.

Avataq Cultural Centre. 1988. *Killiniq: Glimpses of a Fading Past.* Inukjuak, Que.: Avataq Cultural Centre.

Barkham, Selma. 1984. "The Basque Whaling Establishments in Labrador 1536–1632: A Summary." *Arctic* 37, no. 4: 515–19.

Barr, William. 1994. "The Eighteenth-Century Trade between the Ships of the Hudson's Bay Company and the Hudson Strait Inuit." *Arctic* 47, no. 3: 236–46.

Barret, M. 1994. "Killiniq (Port Burwell): An Environmental Survey." Report submitted to Indian and Northern Affairs Canada for Makivik Corporation, Kuujjuaq, Quebec.

Bassler, Gerhard. 2006. *Vikings to U-Boats: The German Experience in Newfoundland and Labrador.* Montreal and Kingston: McGill-Queen's University Press.

Bell, Robert. 1885. "Observations on the Geology, Mineralogy, Zoology, and Botany of the Labrador Coast, Hudson's Strait and Bay." In *Sessional Papers of the Third Session of the Fifth Parliament of the Dominion of Canada*, 9-9C, Vol. XVIII, No. 6, Appendix A: 207–28.

Ben-Dor, Shmuel. 1966. *Makkovik: Eskimos and Settlers in a Labrador Community.* St. John's: ISER.

Bernier, Captain J.E. 1909. *Report on the Dominion Government Expedition to Arctic Islands and the Hudson Strait on board the C.G.S. Arctic, 1906–7.* Ottawa: King's Printer.

Bonnière, René. 1964. *The Annanacks* [film]. Ottawa: National Film Board.

Bonesteel, Sarah. 2006. *Canada's Relationship with Inuit: A History of Policy and Program Development.* Ottawa: Indian and Northern Affairs Canada.

Brice-Bennett, Carol. 1977. "Land Use in the Nain and Hopedale Regions." In *Our Footprints Are Everywhere*, edited by C. Brice-Bennett, 97–203. Nain, NL: Labrador Inuit Association.

Brice-Bennett, Carol. 1981. "Two Opinions: Inuit and Moravian Missionaries in Labrador, 1804–1860." MA thesis, Memorial University of Newfoundland.

Brice-Bennett, Carol. 1986. "Renewable Resource Use and Wage Employment in the Economy of Northern Labrador." Background report prepared for the Royal Commission on Employment and Unemployment. St. John's.

Brice-Bennett, Carol. 1990. "Missionaries as Traders: Moravians and the Inuit, 1771–1860." In *Merchant Credit and Labour Strategies in Historical Perspective*, edited by Rosemary Ommer, 223–46. Fredericton, NB: Acadiensis Press.

Brice-Bennett, Carol. 1994. "The Redistribution of the Northern Labrador Inuit Population: A Strategy for Integration and Formula for Conflict." *Zeitschrift für Kanada-Studien*, Nr. 2, Band 26: 95–106.

Brice-Bennett, Carol. 2000. *Reconciling with Memories: A Record of the Reunion at Hebron 40 years after Relocation.* Nain, NL: Torngâsok Cultural Centre.

Brice-Bennett, Carol. 2015. "Labrador Inuit History." Report written for Nunatsiavut Government Department of Education.

Brice-Bennett, Carol. 2017. *Dispossessed: The Eviction of Inuit from Hebron, Labrador.* Montreal: Isberg.

Brody, Hugh. 1977. "Permanence and Change among the Inuit and Settlers of Labrador." In *Our Footprints Are Everywhere*, edited by C. Brice-Bennett, 311–47. Nain, NL: Labrador Inuit Association.

Budgel, Richard, and Michael Staveley. 1987. *The Labrador Boundary*. Happy Valley-Goose Bay, Labrador: Memorial University of Newfoundland, Labrador Institute of Northern Studies.

Budgell, Anne. 2018. *We All Expected to Die: Spanish Influenza in Labrador, 1918–1919.* St. John's: ISER Books.

Cabak, Melanie Ann. 1991. "Inuit Women as Catalysts of Change: An Archaeological Study of 19th Century Northern Labrador." MA thesis, University of South Carolina.

Canada, Government of. 1975. The James Bay and Northern Quebec Agreement (JBNQA). Ottawa: Department of Indian Affairs and Northern Development.

Cooke, Alan. 1969. "The Ungava Venture of the Hudson's Bay Company, 1830–43." PhD diss., University of Cambridge.

Cooke, Alan, and Clive Holland. 1978. *The Exploration of Northern Canada, 500 to 1920: A Chronology.* Toronto: Arctic History Press.

Damas, David. 2004. *Arctic Migrants/Arctic Villagers: The Transformation of Inuit Settlement in the Central Arctic.* Montreal and Kingston: McGill-Queen's University Press.

Dawson, Bob. 1984. "The Expulsion of the Killiniq Inuit." *Taqralik* (Feb. 1984): 42–46.

Department of Indian and Northern Affairs. 1996. "Relocation of Aboriginal Communities." *Royal Commission on Aboriginal Peoples.* Volume I, Part Two, Chapter 11. Ottawa: Government of Canada.

Dorais, Louis-Jacques. 2010. *The Language of the Inuit: Syntax, Semantics, and Society in the Arctic.* Montreal and Kingston: McGill-Queen's University Press.

Dunbar, M.J. 1952. "The Ungava Bay Problem." *Arctic* 5, no. 1: 4–16.

Etok, Tivi. 2008. *The World of Tivi Etok.* Québec: Éditions MultiMondes.

Evans, Peter. 2012. "Abandoned and Ousted by the State: The Relocations from Nutâk and Hebron, 1956–1959." In *Settlement, Subsistence, and Change among the Labrador Inuit: The Nunatsiavummiut Experience*, edited by David Natcher, Lawrence Felt, and Andrea Procter, 85–120. Winnipeg: University of Manitoba Press.

Evans, Peter. 2013. "Transformations of Inuit Resistance and Identity in Northern Labrador, 1771–1959." PhD diss., University of Cambridge.

Fay, Amelia. 2016. "Understanding Inuit–European Contact along the Labrador Coast: A Case for Continuity." PhD diss., Memorial University of Newfoundland.

Findlay, Marjorie. 1955. "The Means of Improving the Economic Situation of the Ungava Bay Eskimos." PhD diss., McGill University.

Fitzhugh, William. 1972. *Environmental Archaeology and Cultural Systems in Hamilton Inlet, Labrador*. Smithsonian Contributions to Knowledge. Washington, DC: Government Printing Office.

Fitzhugh, William. 1980. "Preliminary Report on the Torngat Archaeological Project." *Arctic* 33, no. 3: 585–606.

Fitzhugh, William. 1994. "Staffe Island 1 and the Northern Labrador Dorset–Thule Succession." In *Threads of Arctic Prehistory: Papers in Honour of William E. Taylor*, edited by David Morrison and Jean-Luc Pilon, 239–68. Mercury Series, Paper 149. Ottawa: Canadian Museum of Civilization.

Fitzhugh, William. 2009. "Exploring Cultural Boundaries: The Less 'Invisible' Inuit of Southern Labrador and Quebec. In *On the Track of the Thule Culture from Bering Strait to East Greenland*, edited by Bjarne Grønnow, 129–48. Studies in Archaeology and History. Copenhagen: National Museum of Denmark.

Fitzhugh, William. 2019. "Paradise Gained, Lost, and Regained: Pulse Migration and the Inuit Archaeology of the Quebec Lower North Shore." *Arctic Anthropology* 56, no. 1: 52–76.

Fossett, Renée. 2003. "Mapping Inuktut: Inuit Views of the Real World." In *Reading Beyond Words: Contexts for Native History*, 2nd edition, edited by Jennifer Brown and Elizabeth Vibert, 74–94. Peterborough, ON: Broadview Press.

Gordon, Lt. Andrew R. 1885. "Report of the Hudson's Bay Expedition, under the Command of Lieut. A.R. Gordon, R.N., 1884." In *Sessional Papers of the Third Session of the Fifth Parliament of the Dominion of Canada*, 9-9C, Vol. XVIII, No. 6, Appendix No. 30: 189–207.

Gosling, William Gilbert. 1910. *Labrador: Its Discovery, Exploration, and Development*. London: A. Rivers.

Grenfell, Wilfred T. 1897. "How We Found Prince Pomiuk." *Toilers of the Deep* 136, no. 12: 111–13.

Harper, Kenn. 1981. "The Moravian Mission at Cumberland Sound." *The Beaver* (summer): 43–47.

Harper, Kenn. 1985. "The Early Development of Inuktitut Syllabic Orthography." *Études/Inuit/Studies* 9, no. 1: 141–62.

Hastings, Clifford. 1985. "Mercantilism and Laissez-Faire Capitalism in the Ungava Peninsula, 1670–1940: The Economic Geography of the Fur Trade." MA thesis, McGill University.

Heyes, Scott A., and Kristofer M. Helgen, eds. 2014. *Mammals of Ungava and Labrador: The 1882–1884 Fieldnotes of Lucien M. Turner together with Inuit and Innu Knowledge*. Washington, DC: Smithsonian Institution Press.

Hiller, James. 1967. "The Foundation and Early Years of the Moravian Mission in Labrador." MA thesis, Memorial University of Newfoundland.

Hiller, James. 1971. "Early Patrons of the Labrador Eskimos: The Moravian Mission in Labrador, 1764–1805." In *Patrons and Brokers in the East Arctic*, edited by R. Paine, 74–97. St. John's: Institute of Social and Economic Research, Memorial University of Newfoundland.

Hiller, James. 1977. "Moravian Land Holdings on the Labrador Coast: A Brief History." In *Our Footprints Are Everywhere*, edited by C. Brice-Bennett, 83–94. Nain, NL: Labrador Inuit Association.

Hiller, James. 1995. "Killinek and Port Burwell: An Outline." Report Prepared for the Labrador Inuit Association. Nain, NL.

Hiller, James. 2009. "Eighteenth-Century Labrador: The European Perspective." In *Moravian Beginnings in Labrador: Papers from a Symposium Held in Makkovik and Hopedale*, edited by Hans Rollmann, 37–52. St. John's: Newfoundland and Labrador Studies.

Hood, Bryan. 2008. *Towards an Archaeology of the Nain Region, Labrador*, edited by William Fitzhugh. Washington, DC: Arctic Studies Center, Smithsonian Institution.

Hutton, Samuel. 1909. *A Thesis on the Health and Diseases of the Eskimos: Being the Result of Observations Made during Five Years Residence among the Eskimos of Labrador, 1903–1908*. Derby: James Harwood.

Hutton, Samuel. 1912. *Among the Eskimos of Labrador: A Record of Five Years' Close Intercourse with the Eskimo Tribes of Labrador*. London: Seeley, Service & Co.

Iglauer, Edith. 1962 [2000]. *Inuit Journey: The Co-operative Adventure in Canada's North*. Madeira Park, BC: Harbour Publishing.

Jenness, Diamond. 1965. *Eskimo Administration: III. Labrador.* Montreal: Arctic Institute of North America.

Jordan, R.H., and S.A. Kaplan. 1980. "An Archaeological View of the Inuit/European Contact Period in Labrador." *Études/Inuit/Studies* 4, nos. 1–2: 35–45.

Jurakic, Irena. 2007. "Up North: European Ceramics and Tobacco Pipes at the Nineteenth-Century Contact Period Inuit Winter Village Site of Kongu (IgCv-7), Nachvak Fiord, Northern Labrador." MA thesis, Memorial University of Newfoundland.

Kaplan, Susan A. 1980. "Neo-Eskimo Occupations of the Northern Labrador Coast." *Arctic* 33, no. 3: 646–58.

Kaplan, Susan. 1983. "Economic and Social Change in Labrador Neo-Eskimo Culture." PhD diss., Bryn Mawr College.

Kaplan, Susan. 1985. "European Goods and Socio-economic Change in Early Labrador Inuit Society. In *Cultures in Contact*, edited by W. Fitzhugh, 45–69. Washington, DC: Smithsonian Press.

Kaplan, Susan A., and Jim M. Woollett. 2000. "Challenges and Choices: Exploring the Interplay of Climate, History, and Culture on Canada's Labrador Coast." *Arctic, Antarctic, and Alpine Research* 32, no. 3: 351–59.

Keelan, Mike. 2019. *Killiniq and Taqpangayuk: Places That Used to Be. A Personal Report on the Last Days of Two Inuit Villages.* Montreal: Avataq Cultural Centre.

Kennedy, John. 1985. *Holding the Line: Ethnic Boundaries in a Northern Labrador Community*. St. John's, ISER Books.

Kennedy, John. 2015. *Encounters: An Anthropological History of Southeastern Labrador*. Montreal and Kingston: McGill-Queen's University Press.

Klain, John, and Mario Levesque. 2019. "Revisiting the Labrador Boundary Decision to Include Indigenous Interpretations of the Region." *Journal of Canadian Studies* 53, no. 1: 123–51.

Kleivan, Helge. 1966. *The Eskimos of Northeast Labrador: A History of Eskimo–White Relations, 1771–1955*. Oslo: Norsk Polarinstututt, Skrifter nr. 139.

Kohlmeister, Benjamin, and George Kmoch. 1814. *Journal of a Voyage from Okkak, on the Coast of Labrador, to Ungava Bay, Westward of Cape Chudleigh*. London: W. McDowall.

Korneski, Kurt. 2016. "Planters, Eskimos, and Indians: Race and the Organization of Trade under the Hudson's Bay Company in Labrador, 1830–50." *Journal of Social History* 50, no. 2: 1–29.

Laugrand, Fréderic, and Jarich Oosten. 2010. *Inuit Shamanism and Christianity: Transitions and Transformations in the Twentieth Century.* Montreal and Kingston: McGill-Queen's University Press.

Leechman, Douglas. 1950. *Eskimo Summer.* London: Museum Press.

Lemelin, Harvey, Margaret Johnston, Dave Lough, Judith Rowell, Wayne Broomfield, Gary Baikie, and Kristie Sheppard. 2016. "Two Parks, One Vision – Collaborative Management Approaches to Transboundary Protected Areas in Northern Canada: Tongait KakKasuangita SilakKijapvinga." In *Indigenous Peoples' Governance of Land and Protected Territories in the Arctic*, edited by T.M. Herrmann and T. Martin. Switzerland: Springer.

Lewis, Rev. Arthur. 1904. *The Life and work of the Rev. E.J. Peck among the Eskimos.* London: Hodder & Stoughton.

Loring, Stephen. 1998. "The Archaeology of Eskimo Hütte (IkDb-2): Inuit Sovereignty in the Torngat." *Études/Inuit/Studies* 22, no. 2: 53–76.

Low, A.P. 1906. *Report on the Dominion Government Expedition to Hudson Bay and the Arctic Islands on Board the D.G.S. Neptune, 1903–1904.* Ottawa: Government Printing Bureau.

Lubbock, Basil. 1937. *The Arctic Whalers.* Glasgow: Brown, Son and Ferguson.

Lyall, Ernie. 2011. *An Arctic Man: Sixty-Five Years in Canada's North.* Halifax: Formac Publishing.

MacGregor, Sir William. 1906. "Report of an Official Visit to the Coast of Labrador by the Governor of Newfoundland, during the Month of August, 1905."

Mailhot, Josée. 1997. *The People of Sheshatshit: In the Lands of the Innu*, translated by Axel Harvey. St. John's: ISER Books.

Makivik Corporation. n.d. *The Inuit of Nunavik Statement of Claim to Labrador.* Montreal: Makivik Corporation.

Makivik Corporation. 1987a. "Land Use and Occupancy by the Inuit of Northern Quebec for the Coastal and Inland Areas of Labrador." Submitted to the Office of Comprehensive Claims, Department of Indian Affairs and Northern Development.

Makivik Corporation. 1987b. *Taqpangajuk Relocation: A Feasibility Study, Phase II.* Fort Chimo: Makivik.

Marcus, Alan. 1995. *Relocating Eden: The Image and Politics of Inuit Exile in the Canadian Arctic.* Hanover, NH: University Press of New England.

Markham, Nigel. 2021. "'Murmuring Against God': Inuit–Moravian Confrontations in Late Nineteenth-Century Labrador." *Newfoundland and Labrador Studies* 36, no. 1: 87–115.

Marsh, Rev. D.B. 1964. "History of the Anglican Church in Northern Quebec and Ungava." In *Le Nouveau Quebec: Contributions a l'étude de l'occupation humaine*, edited by J. Malaurie and J. Rousseau, 427–37. Paris: Mouton.

Mesher, Dorothy. 1995. *Kuujjuaq: Memories and Musings*, with Ray Woollam. Duncan, BC: Unica Publishing.

Mitchell, Greg. 2013. "The Inuit of Southern Labrador and Their Conflicts with Europeans, to 1767." In *Exploring Atlantic Transitions: Archaeologies of Transience and Permanence in New Found Lands*, edited by Peter Pope and Shannon Lewis-Simpson, 320–30. Woodbridge, UK: Boydell Press.

Morantz, Toby. 2016. *Relations on Ungava Bay: An Illustrated History of Inuit, Naskapi, and Eurocanadian Interaction, 1800–1970*. Montreal: Avataq Cultural Institute.

Negrijn, Megan. 2011. "Consumer Choice in Komaktorvik, Seven Islands Bay and Kongu, Nachvak Fjord." MA thesis, Memorial University of Newfoundland.

OKalaKâtiget Society. 1987. *The Relocation of Hebron* (film). Nain: OKalaKâtiget Society.

Packard, Alpheus Spring. 1891. *The Labrador Coast. A Journal of Two Summer Cruises to That Region*. New York: N.D.C. Hodges.

Payne, F.F. 1899. "Eskimos of Hudson's Strait at Cape Prince of Wales." In *Proceedings of the Canadian Institute*. Ser. 3, Vol. VI, 213–30.

Peck, E.J. 1922. *The Eskimo: Our Brethren of the Arctic*. Ottawa: The M.S.C.C.

*Periodical Accounts relating to the Missions of the Church of the United Brethren, established among the Heathen* [various titles], 1st century 1790–1889 [PA], 2nd century 1890–1960 [2PA]. London: Society for the Furtherance of the Gospel.

Pigott, Paul. 1999. "Labrador Nord Ouest." *kinatuinamot illengajuk* (Fall) 54–57.

Pilot, Rev. Canon W. 1899. *A Visit to Labrador*. London: Colonial and Continental Church Society.

Ramsden, Peter, and Lisa Rankin. 2013. "Thule Radiocarbon Chronology and Its Implications for Early Inuit–European Interaction in Labrador. In *Exploring Atlantic Transitions: Archaeologies of Transience and Permanence in New Found Lands*, edited by Peter E. Pope and Shannon Lewis-Simpson, 299–309. Woodbridge, UK: Boydell Press.

Reichel, Levin Theodor. 1863. "Labrador, Bemerkungen über Land and Leute [Labrador: Remarks on the Country and the People]." *Petermanns Geographische Mitteilungen* 10, no. 4: 121–27.

Riches, David. 1971. *Eskimos at the Farthest Reaches: A Critical Analysis in Ecology, Social Organization, and Social Change*. Belfast: Queen's University of Belfast.

Richling, Barnett. 1985. "Without Compromise: Hudson's Bay Company and Moravian Mission Trade Rivalry in Nineteenth Century Labrador." In *"Le Castor Fait Tout": Selected Papers of the Fifth North American Fur Trade Conference*, edited by Bruce Trigger, Toby Morantz, and Louise Dechêne, 456–84. Montreal: Lake St. Louis Historical Society.

Richling, Barnett. 2000. *Inuit Land Use and Occupation in the Québec–Labrador Peninsula*. Report for Makivik Corporation.

Rivet, France. 2014. *In the Footsteps of Abraham Ulrikab: The Events of 1880–1881*. Gatineau, Que.: Polar Horizons.

Rollmann, Hans. 2007. "The 1765 Map of Jens Haven: Linguistic, Toponymic, and Geographical Studies, with contributions by W. Gordon Handcock, Ludger Müller-Wille, and Douglas Wharram." Report for NunatuKavut Community Council.

Rollmann, Hans. 2008. "Moravian Education in Labrador: A Legacy of Literacy." In *Conference Proceedings: Post-Confederation Education Reform: From Rhetoric to Reality*, edited by Gerald Galway and David Dibbon, 227–36. St. John's: Memorial University of Newfoundland.

Rollmann, Hans. 2009a. "Johann Christian Erhardt and the First Moravian Exploration of Labrador in 1752." In *Moravian Beginnings in Labrador: Papers from a Symposium Held in Makkovik and Hopedale*, edited by Hans Rollmann, 53–68. St. John's: Newfoundland and Labrador Studies.

Rollmann, Hans. 2009b. "The Labrador Land Grants of 1769 and 1774." In *Moravian Beginnings in Labrador: Papers from a Symposium Held in Makkovik and Hopedale*, edited by Hans Rollmann, 104–31. St. John's: Newfoundland and Labrador Studies.

Rollmann, Hans. 2010. "Moravians in Central Labrador: The Indigenous Inuit Mission of Jacobus and Salome at Snooks Cove." *Journal of Moravian History* 9 (Fall): 6–40.

Rollmann, Hans. 2017. "'So that in this part you should not lag behind other missionary congregations . . .' The Introduction of National Helpers in the

Moravian Mission among the Labrador Inuit." *Journal of Moravian History* 17, no. 2: 138–59.

Rollmann, Hans. 2018. "The Adoption of Christian Names and Surnames in the Moravian Communities of Nunatsiavut, Labrador." *Journal of Moravian History* 18, no. 2: 145–58.

Royal Commission on Labrador. 1974. *Report of the Royal Commission on Labrador* (chaired by Donald Snowden).

Schledermann, Peter. 1971. "The Thule Tradition in Northern Labrador." MA thesis, Memorial University of Newfoundland.

Snowden, Donald. 1961. "Eskimo Commercial Fisheries." *Polar Record* 10, no. 67: 382–84.

Stopp, Marianne. 2009. "Eighteenth Century Labrador Inuit in England." *Arctic* 62, no. 1: 45–64.

Stopp, Marianne. 2017. "The Ramah Chert Quarries in Torngat Mountains National Park: A Place of National Historic Significance." In *Ramah Chert: A Lithic Odyssey*, edited by Jenneth Curtis and Pierre Desrosiers, 221–41. Inukjuak, Que.: Avataq Cultural Centre.

Tanner, A. 1998. "The Aboriginal Peoples of Newfoundland and Labrador and Confederation." *Newfoundland Studies* 14, no. 2: 238–52.

Tanner, Vaino. 1944. "Outlines of the Geography, Life and Customs of Newfoundland-Labrador." *Acta Geographica* (Helsinki) 8, no. 1.

Taylor, J. Garth. 1969. "William Turner's Journeys to the Caribou Country with Labrador Eskimos in 1780." *Ethnohistory* 16, no. 2: 141–64.

Taylor, J. Garth. 1970. "Structure of Early Contact Labrador Eskimo Social Units." In *Proceedings of the 38th International Congress of Americanists*. Stuttgart, München, 1968.

Taylor, J. Garth. 1972. "Eskimo Answers to an Eighteenth Century Questionnaire." *Ethnohistory* 19, no. 2: 135–45.

Taylor, J. Garth. 1974. *Labrador Eskimo Settlements of the Early Contact Period*. Publications in Ethnology, No. 9. Ottawa: National Museums of Canada.

Taylor, J. Garth. 1975. "Demography and Adaptations of Eighteenth-Century Eskimo Groups in Northern Labrador and Ungava." In *Prehistoric Marine Adaptations of the Circumpolar Zone*, edited by W. Fitzhugh, 269–78. The Hague: Mouton.

Taylor, J. Garth. 1976. "The Inuit Middleman in the Labrador Baleen Trade." Paper presented at 75th Annual Meeting of the American Anthropological Association (Nov.).

Taylor, J. Garth. 1977. "Traditional Land Use and Occupancy by the Labrador Inuit." In *Our Footprints Are Everywhere*, edited by C. Brice-Bennett, 49–58. Nain, NL: Labrador Inuit Association.

Taylor, J. Garth. 1981. "An Eskimo Abroad, 1880: His Diary and Death." *Canadian Geographic* 101, no. 5: 38–43.

Taylor, J. Garth. 1984. "Historical Ethnography of the Labrador Coast." In *Handbook of North American Indians*, vol. 5, 508–21. Washington, DC: Smithsonian Institution.

Taylor, J. Garth. 2009. "In the Wake of the Hope: Jens Haven's 1764 Reconnaissance Journey in Northern Newfoundland and Southern Labrador." In *Moravian Beginnings in Labrador: Papers from a Symposium Held in Makkovik and Hopedale*, edited by Hans Rollmann, 87–103. St. John's: Newfoundland and Labrador Studies.

Tester, Frank, and Peter Kulchyski. 1994. *Tammarniit (Mistakes): Inuit Relocation in the Eastern Arctic, 1939–63*. Vancouver: University of British Columbia Press.

Tompkins, Edward. 1995. "Things have not gone so well at Burwell: The Port Burwell Fisheries Projects c. 1950–1978." Report prepared for the Labrador Inuit Association, Nain, NL.

Trudel, François. 1978. "The Inuit of Southern Labrador and the Development of French Sedentary Fisheries (1700–1760)." In *Papers from the Fourth Annual Congress*, edited by R.J. Preston, 99–121. Ottawa: Mercury Series No. 40, Canadian Ethnology Service.

Trudel, François. 1991. "'Mais ils onts peu de besoins': Les Inuit de la baie d'Ungava et la traite à Fort Chimo (1830–1843)." *Anthropologie et Sociétés* 15, no. 1: 89–124.

Tuck, James A. 1976. *Newfoundland and Labrador Prehistory*. National Museum of Man (Canada), Archaeological Survey of Canada. Van Nostrand Reinhold.

Tuck, James A. 1995. "The Prehistory of Northern Labrador/Eastern Ungava." Report prepared for the Labrador Inuit Association, Nain, NL.

Turner, Lucien M. 1887. "On the Indians and Eskimos of the Ungava District, Labrador." *Proceedings and Transactions of the Royal Society of Canada*, Vol. V, Sect. II, pp. 99-119.

Turner, Lucien M. 1979. *Ethnology of the Ungava District, Hudson Bay Territory: Indians and Eskimos in the Quebec–Labrador Peninsula.* Reprint of a report originally published in 1894 by the Bureau of Ethnology, Smithsonian Institution, Washington. Quebec: Inuksiutiit Assoc./Presses Comeditex.

Tuttle, Charles R. 1885. *Our North Land: Being a Full Account of the Canadian North West and Hudson's Bay Route.* Toronto.

Val, Erik. 1976. "Inuit Land Use in the Port Burwell Area." In *Inuit Land Use and Occupancy Project, Volume One*, edited by Milton Freeman, 121–23. Ottawa: Indian and Northern Affairs.

Vezinet, Monique. 1982. *Occupation Humaine de l'Ungava: Perspective Ethnohistorique et Écologique.* Québec: Université Laval.

Wallace, W.S., ed. 1932. *John McLean's Notes of a Twenty-Five Year's Service in the Hudson's Bay Territory.* Vol. 19. Toronto: The Champlain Society.

Wheeler, E.P. 1953. *List of Labrador Eskimo Place Names.* Ottawa: National Museum of Canada, Bulletin No. 131.

Whitridge, Peter. 2008. "Reimagining the Iglu: Modernity and the Challenge of the Eighteenth-Century Labrador Inuit Winter House." *Archaeologies: Journal of the World Archaeological Congress* 4, no. 2: 288–309.

Whitridge, Peter. 2012. "Invented Places: Environmental Imaginaries and the Inuit Colonization of Labrador." In *Settlement, Subsistence, and Change among the Labrador Inuit: The Nunatsiavummiut Experience*, edited by David Natcher, Lawrence Felt, and Andrea Procter, 43–60. Winnipeg: University Manitoba Press.

Williams, Glyndwr. 1963. "Introduction." In *Northern Quebec and Labrador Journals and Correspondence, 1819–35*, edited by K.G. Davies and A.M. Johnson, xv–lxxix. London: Hudson's Bay Company Record Society, vol. 24.

Willway, Frederick W. 1897. "Our Present Season's Work in Labrador." *Toilers of the Deep* 144, no. 12: 358–61.

Wollett, James. 2007. "Labrador Inuit Subsistence in the Context of Environmental Change: An Initial Landscape History Perspective." *American Anthropologist* 109, no. 5: 69–84.

# INDEX

*(page numbers in italics indicate photos)*

# ABOUT THE AUTHORS

**Carol Brice-Bennett** (1949–2018) was an anthropologist who worked for decades with Inuit in northern Labrador. Originally from Montreal, she coordinated land-use research for the Labrador Inuit Association in the 1970s. Her edited volume, *Our Footprints Are Everywhere: Land Use and Occupancy in Labrador* (Labrador Inuit Association, 1977), formed the basis of the land claim agreement for Nunatsiavut. Among other posts, she served as the Director of the Labrador Institute from 1985 to 1996 and as the Director of Aboriginal Health Programs and Research with the Labrador Grenfell Health Authority before she retired in 2015. She is the author of several books, including *Dispossessed: The Eviction of Inuit from Hebron, Labrador* (Imaginaire|Nord, 2017). She earned an MA from Memorial University.

**Lena Onalik** is an Inuk and descendant of Avanimiut. She grew up in Makkovik with her grandparents, who were relocated there from Okkak Bay. She is an advocate for Inuit language and culture and works as the Archaeologist for the Nunatsiavut Government's Department of Language, Culture, and Tourism. She earned a BA in Archaeology from Memorial University. Lena is happiest when she is on the land and sea. She loves fishing and sharing experiences on the land with others, especially her family.

**Andrea Procter** is a historical anthropologist who focuses on settler colonialism and community-driven research. She has authored several books with Inuit partners, including *TautukKonik: A Portrait of Inuit Life in*

*Northern Labrador, 1969–1986* (Memorial University Press, 2022), and *A Long Journey: Residential Schools in Labrador and Newfoundland* (ISER Books, 2020), winner of the 2021 Atlantic Book Award for Scholarly Writing, the CLIO Prize (Atlantic), and the Newfoundland and Labrador Book Award for Non-Fiction. She earned a PhD from Memorial University and lives, hikes, and kayaks with her family in St. John's.

**Near Hebron (courtesy of Maria Merkuratsuk)**